# THE DURATION

2

...tion of the Dawn

...but a dream,
...s only a vision
...well-lived
...dream of happiness,
...a vision of hope.
...re, to this day!
...n of the dawn.
...nskrit.

...REETINGS FROM
...ASSETT-LOWKE
...RTHAMPTON.

A CHRISTMAS TIME GREETING

from Mr & Mrs Bassett-Lowke
New Ways · Northampton

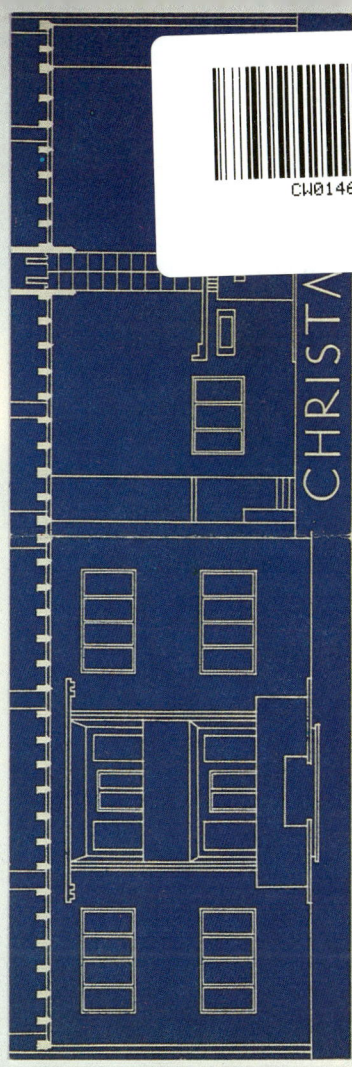

CHRISTMA...

THE
NUWAYS
BAROMETER

HANG OUT OF DOORS

WHEN TAIL DRY ...... FINE
WHEN TAIL WET ...... RAIN
WHEN TAIL MOVES ... WIND
WHEN TAIL WAGS ... STORM
WHEN TAIL INVISIBLE FOG
WHEN TAIL STIFF .. COLD

My good wishes for this
Festive Season are as sincere
and true as the Weather
Forecasts by this Modern
Weather Indicator.

from
W. J. BASSETT-LOWKE
NEW WAYS
NORTHAMPTON

WITH THE SEASONS
GREETINGS
FROM
W. J. BASSETT-LOWKE
NORTHAMPTON

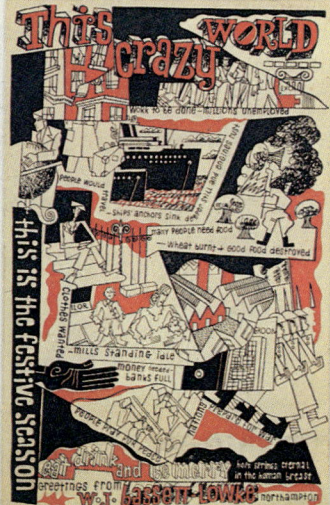

This is a crazy World

1953
CHRISTMAS AND NEW YEAR
GREETINGS FROM Mr & Mrs W. J. BASSETT-LOWKE

THOMAS E. JONES

344 DERBY STREET
BOLTON
BL3 6LF

344 DERBY STREET
BOLTON
BL3 6LF

# THE BASSETT-LOWKE STORY

The first London shop, 257 High Holborn, 1908.

# THE BASSETT LOWKE STORY

## by Roland Fuller

NC

New Cavendish Books

Dedicated to Henry Greenly
who did so much for Bassett-Lowke
and scale model railways

The publishers wish to thank all those at Bassett-Lowke,
Northampton, for their advice and co-operation, in particular Mrs.
Ann Ritchie. Our thanks to Mrs. Roland Fuller for making
available so much of her late husband's archive material. We are
particularly indebted to Ted Leech for making available the fruits
of many years research, in the form of the tables. Special thanks
are due to Mr. Robin Butterell who initiated this project and at all
times has been of great assistance. Thanks are also due to the many
people who came forward with documentation and anecdotes, in
particular Mr. Francis Parker for his forbearance in loaning much
unique material over the many years this book has been in
preparation

First edition published in Great Britain
by New Cavendish Books

Design and Artwork – John B. Cooper
Editor – Narisa Levy
Editorial direction – Allen Levy

Filmsetting and halftones by Wyvern Typesetting Ltd, Bristol
Printed and bound by Ebenezer Baylis, Worcester

New Cavendish Books is an imprint of
White Mouse Editions Ltd, 23 Craven Hill, London W 2
Distribution: ABP, North Way, Andover, Hampshire SP10 5PE
ISBN 0 904568 34 2

# Contents

# Preface

As a life long Bassett-Lowke enthusiast I felt most honoured when I was asked to write a preface for this book. My interest in Bassett-Lowke must have started when I was about seven, when, one day, my mother took me on a visit to London. It was during the Christmas holidays, and as a special treat, she had promised to take me to the Holborn Empire theatre in the afternoon to see 'Peter Pan'. An uncle joined us for lunch, after which he escorted us to the theatre. As we had arrived a little early my uncle suggested that I might like to have a look in the window of Bassett-Lowke's shop, which was just across the road, before going in. We did so – and I was completely enthralled by what I saw! There were beautiful models of locomotives, carriages and wagons in various gauges, and signals, signal boxes, stationary engines and ships, too. Young as I was, I was not too young to appreciate that these were *scale models*, and not mere toys. That must have been about 60 years ago, but my recollections of that day are still quite vivid. I was already under the Bassett-Lowke spell!

During my school days I would use some of my pocket money to buy Bassett-Lowke's model railway catalogues, and spend many happy hours studying them. I would often try to think up ways of raising enough money to buy a gauge 0 '112' tank, or perhaps just a wagon or two! When I was about 15 my uncle came to stay with us for a few days and gave me a tip of half-a-crown. With it I decided to buy a copy of Bassett-Lowke's *Model Railway Handbook*, and at the first opportunity visited 112 High Holborn and handed over my half-crown. Having bought the book, I asked whether I might have a look around the shop, and permission to do so was readily given. Again, I was completely enthralled by what I saw in this Aladdin's cave, which was full of all kinds of superb models. There was even a 7¼″ gauge L.M.S 'George the Fifth', complete with 'wide seat for driver' (to quote the description in the catalogue) in the tender, which I examined with great interest. I read *The Model Railway Handbook* from cover to cover. It was the eighth edition of a book which was to run to no less than fifteen editions. Even now, I do not think I could have spent that half-crown to better advantage, for that book (which I still have) was splendid value for money. It was beautifully produced on art paper, with hard covers, well written, well illustrated, and a mine of information on all aspects of model and miniature railways.

Soon after this – I think it must have been when my sixteenth birthday was approaching – my mother asked me what I would like for a present. I said that I would like to visit the Bassett-Lowke works in Northampton, and this was duly arranged. It was a most interesting and instructive experience, and I still look back on that day as one of the most enjoyable I have ever spent.

Some years later, when I had left college and was job hunting (jobs were almost as hard to get then as they are now), I heard that Bassett-Lowke's were in need of some temporary help in their London shop during the Christmas season. I immediately applied and was taken on – as I knew their *Model Railways* catalogue almost by heart and was familiar with many of their products, I may have had some advantages over the other applicants! It was a most rewarding experience, and I enjoyed every minute of my time at 112 High Holborn. While working there I met Mr. Bassett-Lowke who was always addressed as 'Mr. Whynne' by his employees. Although he was then about 60, he was as quick and alert as a man of half that age, and he always had a twinkle in his eye. After the war I met him again on a number of occasions and got to know him quite well. I had the greatest

admiration for him, for he was an amazing man, always full of enthusiasm, invariably courteous and helpful, and a terrific worker. He was much more than a manufacturer of fine models, for he was a man of many parts – author, lecturer, broadcaster, a keen businessman, an excellent organiser, an inveterate traveller, a skilled photographer (both still and cine) and a superb showman, who was always alive to the value of good publicity.

This book tells the story of this remarkable man, who, through his imaginative enterprise and sheer hard work, became something of a legend in his own lifetime. It also tells the story of the firm he founded, which, although not large, became world famous. It was a model firm in both senses of the work, and an excellent example of 'small is beautiful'. Few firms could have had a more intimate relationship with their customers than that enjoyed by Bassett-Lowke Ltd., which in many ways was probably unique. The book also describes and illustrates many of the vast range of models produced by Bassett-Lowke which have given so much pleasure to so many people, and which will undoubtedly continue to do so for many years to come. It is a fascinating story, which I am sure will delight all its readers.

Derek Brough

# The Bassett-Lowke Story

As the shop boy in 1917 it was natural that I should not be noticed by the 'Boss' when he came to the London shop – but the Great War was at its height and his visits were infrequent and irregular.

However, in late 1919 when there was a re-arrangement of the staff I was promoted to salesman and given the princely salary of £2.50 a week plus commission on sales of 2½ per cent. This meant that my average wage worked out at nearly £5 per week.

It was when I took this new position that I had my first conversation with Whynne. He was now coming to London at least once a week and his usual procedure was to come from Euston to the shop, arriving about 10.30 a.m. make some telephone calls, have a brief conversation with the manager and, if his timetable allowed, take him out to a Lyons tea shop for coffee. He would then go on his 'rounds' and rarely return to '112' before 6 o'clock. He would leave at 6.45 p.m. to catch the 7 o'clock train to Northampton.

He was a gregarious man – hating to be, or to do anything, alone. It happened one day that the manager and senior assistant were engaged and so he took me to have coffee with him. Strangely I did not feel nervous and he did nothing to cause me to be so. His conversation was bright – about the things we sold and the new models in preparation. He then took a serious note and told me to take care always to be courteous and helpful to customers. Nevertheless he knew what many 'society' people's attitude to shop staff was – and said then that I should never accept any treatment which was unreasonable and that, if he received a complaint he would first ask for my report and support me if he felt I had acted properly. That statement impressed me greatly and I always made sure to act in line with his suggestions. Strangely enough I found that those clients who did try to be overbearing dissolved when faced with a polite but unaffected assistant.

It was in 1919 that Whynne organised a trip to Ostend at Whitsun. I was still only the 'boy' earning an improved wage of 75/– but was told that if I could pay £4 I could be included in the party which comprised the London staff, the Northampton Office manager, W. J. Barnard, and Whynne's father, J. T. Lowke, who must at that time have been in his late 60s.

He was, like his son, tall and slim. He had a 'walrus' moustache which gave him a lugubrious look, while his canvas shoes, flannel suit, and panama hat gave him a curiously Edwardian gay-dog appearance. He was amazingly active and very chatty.

The trip was carefully planned – we left Victoria Station on the 2 o'clock boat train for Dover, got aboard the Cross Channel packet leaving for Ostend at 4 p.m. It was a bumpy crossing but Whynne was in his element. On the journey to Dover he walked the train – as was his habit – and as usual found someone he knew. Likewise on the ship he walked restlessly around looking for a familiar face. He had a most remarkable memory for places and names and would usually confound his aquaintance by his being greeted by name and reminded in detail of their last meeting, which may have been years earlier. If he couldn't find anyone he had met before he would make friendly conversation with someone – and how surprisingly often it was that the person would be someone of significance to be added to his 'mailing list' as he termed it.

I saw little of Whynne that weekend because he was busy trying to renew pre-war contacts and left the party to its own devices – having been given good detailed advice on where to go and what to see. However, three years later he organised a Whitsun week-end in Paris for the London staff only and on this occasion he stayed with us all the time.

This trip was a model of keen planning to see and do most for the least cost – and in this Whynne excelled all. It was then I could see what manner of man he was. In the first place he was abstemious in all things. He ate light meals but was careful to choose good ones. He drank very little and smoked hardly at all. He expressed dislike – almost disdain – for those who felt unable to limit their eating and drinking. A podgy person was total anathema to him. He liked wine and beer but would in no circumstances take spirits, which he called 'fire-water'.

Smoking an occasional cigarette and very occasional cigar seemed to be a primitive exercise – and all through his life he handled his 'smokes' like a schoolboy trying for the first time.

In conversation he could be most interesting, because even when still a quite young man he had a wealth of experience, and despite the fact of having had a brief formal education he made himself knowledgeable by conversing with experienced people and much reading – not of 'classic' writings but of technical, business and travel books. He studied Baedeker's *Guide Books* avidly and never journeyed on the Continent without one.

One element of conversation he totally disliked was the 'sexy' joke – and I have known him to walk out from a male function once the talk turned in this direction. It was not that he was a purist – for I had glimpses over the years of attachments to several ladies, but his activities in this field were limited and very controlled.

Although a lively conversationalist, a petulant side to his nature was revealed when anyone argued against his opinion. It was quite extraordinary really because he seemed such a reasonable person – but he just could not accept a contra opinion to his own. In some cases I have known him to search and research until he could find support for his view and he would often present his antagonist with his evidence months after the event. He never forgot – and rarely forgave.

His petulance was probably the reason why he loved to play one person against another. In this activity he found a childish pleasure in watching the discomfiture of people concerned. It was so contrary to his own capability that this practice was a source of wonder to me. Usually there was little general effect in what he did but eventually a really unhappy event arose when he broke the confidence of an old friend and valued business colleague – Henry Greenly. The resulting legal proceedings broke Henry. Afterwards Whynne was very subdued and it is doubtful if he ever was able to put that event behind him.

As with many successful men, his persistence in following up any matter of importance was prodigious. He would prod and probe, badger people by direct contact or by mail until he had secured the position. All this would be done in the nicest way – but it continued always right to the end. People were spurred into responding if only to stop the constant pressure.

All his working life, up until a few weeks before his death, he made an early start at the office and was generally the last to leave at about 6.30 p.m. It is no wonder, therefore, that his output was considerable. His great interest was in all kinds of publicity – preparing catalogues and pamphlets, writing articles for any publication that asked for,

or could be persuaded to print them. He was constantly being invited to give talks to organisations and schools – and was quite happy to make the most difficult journeys to fulfil engagements. This service started as early as 1906, when he had built up a programme of slides from his own photographs. These he would take complete with a cumbersome and heavy 'Lantern' and screen. In the early days William Rowe, the first Bassett-Lowke employee, then a young, strong man would go with him to handle the equipment and help run the slides through as Whynne gave his talk. William often talked later about some of the tough journeys made in wintry conditions – but Whynne had never been and never was deterred by weather conditions.

He had a great dislike of the motor car and travelled in them only when it was essential. He never possessed one. He loved travel by train and ship and became almost an authority on their facilities and features. It was a proud boast that despite working to very close schedules he had never missed a train. In Northampton and in any town visited he used public transport, only taking taxis when laden with heavy items – he was quite prepared to carry anything needed. Even when 'New Ways' was being built and pieces of decorative glass were available only from Hetleys in Soho Square he brought many parcels by bus to 112 High Holborn and on to Euston.

Partly this attitude to travel may have been due to his feeling of capability, but also there was a strong element of 'penny wise' living. I would not say he was a mean man but he was in no way generous and I cannot remember him making more than a trivial gift to anyone. At Christmas, for example, the London manager would be given 50 cigarettes while the members of staff received 20 each. When I went to Northampton to live I saw the Christmas gift list being worked out and realised that with such a large number of items to be considered the total cost could have been enormous. Nevertheless, I tried to imagine the reaction of a top business man or Government official on receiving similarly modest gifts. Curiously enough, most people I had contact with seemed to appreciate their gifts – due, I am sure, to Whynne's earnestness and sincerity.

He was an extremely healthy man – and boasted that he had only spent one day in bed when he was told he had pneumonia. On one occasion he severely sprained his ankle – but insisted on getting about immediately. He really had no sympathy with sick people – often expressing the view that their condition was the result of their own style of living.

He took his public work in Northampton very seriously – and apart from his success in having the Council build a fine modern public baths he pursued his work in various committees most diligently. Despite his strong socialist views he got on well with Councillors of all parties and was greatly respected. It was a pity that he chose not to go on to be Mayor – but he declared that, as he would have to sit on the Bench, he could not pass judgement on his fellow creatures. It must be assumed, however, that he would have found the Mayoral round time consuming and he would not have enjoyed the feasting in which every Mayor is expected to partake.

With the strange exception of Henry Greenly, he remained a faithful friend to many. Percival Marshall, whom he first met in 1899 was in regular contact until his death – as was Stefan Bing from their first meeting in 1900. He was faithful also to the many organisations of which he was a member – even of Freemasonry, in which he could generate no real interest.

His attitude towards the London staff was always cheerful and friendly and rarely critical. I found this to be in strange contrast to his relationship with all staff in Northampton. I first experienced this when transferring to Head Office in 1945 and was astonished to find that he was critical and often suspicious – with the result that staff in turn were inclined to be reticent and even cunning. There probably had been a good reason why this state of affairs existed – but it was uncomfortable and certainly counter-productive. For those 'working on the bench' it was impossible to feel at ease when he was around because of his critical attitude – but, then, of course, this did have the effect of maintaining good standards of workmanship.

## The Bassett & Lowke Connection

In the 1850s, Northampton, in common with many other industrial towns and their surrounding agricultural areas, was employing steam power at an ever increasing rate. Factories installed stationary engines and boilers, while farmers brought into use portable engines for theshing and other special operations, and traction engines for haulage and heavy ploughing.

As a consequence there was a requirement for the services of people qualified to repair and maintain them. This work was usually beyond the capability of the average blacksmith since it required particular understanding of the technicalities of boilers and engines, even though, at that time, they were mostly of simple design. Small businesses with the necessary knowledge and equipment were being established wherever such

need arose, and in Northampton a small but very competent company was founded at 18 Kingswell Street by Abraham Bassett in 1859. Abraham was not tall but his stocky, powerful frame would have leant him to the part of 'village blacksmith' of poetic fame. In addition, he was knowledgeable and efficient. His small works was equipped with everything necessary for making parts for engines and machinery, and also for boiler making which was a speciality. The works building was situated in the extensive yard at the rear of No. 18, a three floor house with a shop, in the window of which was displayed a range of tools, engineering fittings and parts for sale.

Abraham lived in the house with his wife, who bore him three sons. Unhappily, his wife died while still young and so a housekeeper was engaged. Her name was Mrs. Tom Lowke, a young widow with one small son, Joseph Tom who went with her to live in at 18 Kingswell Street. After a suitable passage of time Abraham Bassett married the widow Lowke. There were no children of that marriage and as the three sons of his first wife showed no interest in following their father's trade (it is believed, in fact, that they emigrated to Australia) it fell to Joseph Tom's lot to join his step-father. This combination was quite successful and the business continued to flourish for many years.

In 1876 Joseph Tom married Eliza Goodman and they set up home at No. 13 Kingswell Street – conveniently near the family business. The following year, on December 27, the first of two sons was born, and christened Wenman Joseph. Years later the second son was born, but because of difference of temperament and age they had little in common and were to lead separate lives.

Wenman grew up to be a most lively and active young man with many interests. He liked swimming and was a keen cyclist. Photography was a favourite pastime and his keen pursuit of still and (later) cine photography remained with him all his life. Other subjects came later – model making, architecture and politics and these were to have a profound influence on his life.

Joseph Tom was a practising engineer and hoped that his sons would join him in the business, changing the name to J. T. Lowke & Sons. He did not consider that a protracted education would benefit his sons in the career they were expected to follow and so Wenman's spell at Kingswell Street College and All Saints Commercial school ended when he was 13 years old.

He started working for his father but found that activity very unattractive and ultimately persuaded his father to let him become an architect. No doubt he had visions of a career designing fine buildings, for even at that early age he was profoundly interested in the subject. A local architect engaged him but the reality of the profession quickly became apparent. He saw that the opportunities for planning large and interesting projects were not likely to come to a small provincial office, and after about a year and a half he returned to work for his father.

He pursued his hobbies with great intensity and was fortunate in finding a fellow enthusiast in the person of Harry Foldar Robert Franklin, a young bookkeeper who came to work for J. T. Lowke & Sons. Their friendship continued throughout their lives and they became partners in the business which was to become world renowned. Father encouraged the two young men in their pastimes – even to the extent of having part of the attic of the office building (as No. 18 had become) converted to a photographic dark room. Strangely, this facility was to be one more link in the chain of events leading to future fame.

Wenman and Harry continued to share their hobbies, and inspired by the interest and enthusiasm of George Blake, a traveller for a tool and engineers sundriesman in Birmingham, they took up model engineering. In pursuit of this they were considerably aided by the facilities of the family business. This consisted of making patterns for castings to be made at the local foundry, the supply of materials and, of course, the use of tools and machinery. George Blake was extremely helpful in obtaining the smaller size materials, tools and screws.

The two young men made small engines and boilers, for which they needed special steam fittings. These they found to be available almost on their doorstep from a Mr. Claret at the neighbouring village of Moulton.

Wenman's eagerness and enthusiasm and thirst for knowledge led him to see that while there was quite a number of would-be amateur model makers, the sources of supply of materials, castings and parts were scattered and difficult to find. Also, apart from Steven's Model Dockyard in London, Clyde Model Dockyard in Glasgow and a few other businesses, there was no co-ordinated supply of essential items for the amateur. To supply this

WOOLMONGER STREET

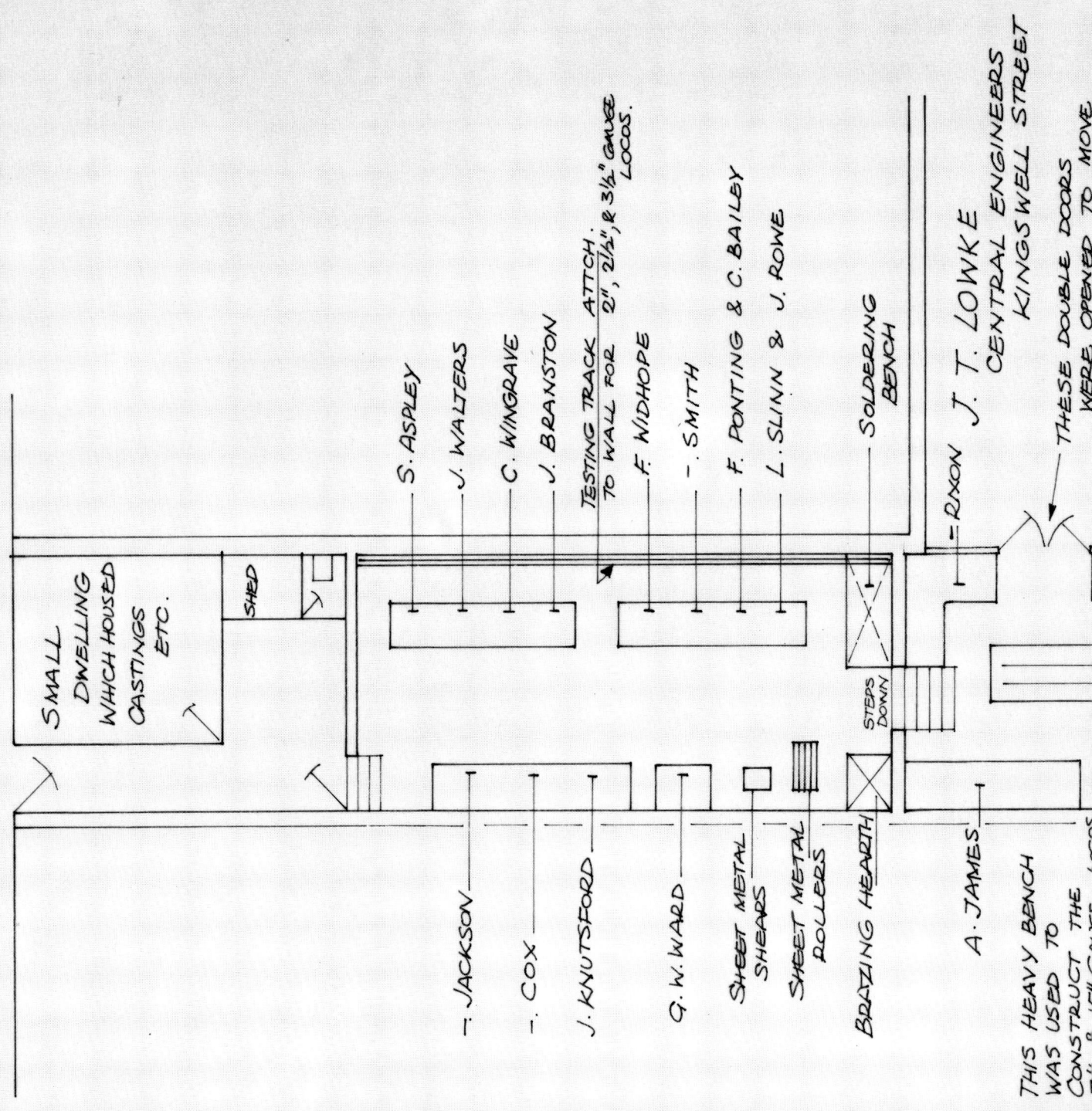

SMALL DWELLING WHICH HOUSED CASTINGS ETC.

SHED

S. ASPLEY

J. WALTERS

C. WINGRAVE

J. BRANSTON

TESTING TRACK ATTCH. TO WALL FOR 2", 2½", & 3½" GAUGE LOCOS.

F. WIDHOPE

- SMITH

F. PONTING & C. BAILEY

L. SLINN & J. ROWE

SOLDERING BENCH

- RIXON

J. T. LOWKE
CENTRAL ENGINEERS
KINGSWELL STREET

THESE DOUBLE DOORS WERE OPENED TO MOVE

STEPS DOWN

- JACKSON

- COX

J. KNUTSFORD

G. W. WARD

SHEET METAL SHEARS

SHEET METAL ROLLERS

BRAZING HEARTH

A. JAMES

THIS HEAVY BENCH WAS USED TO CONSTRUCT THE

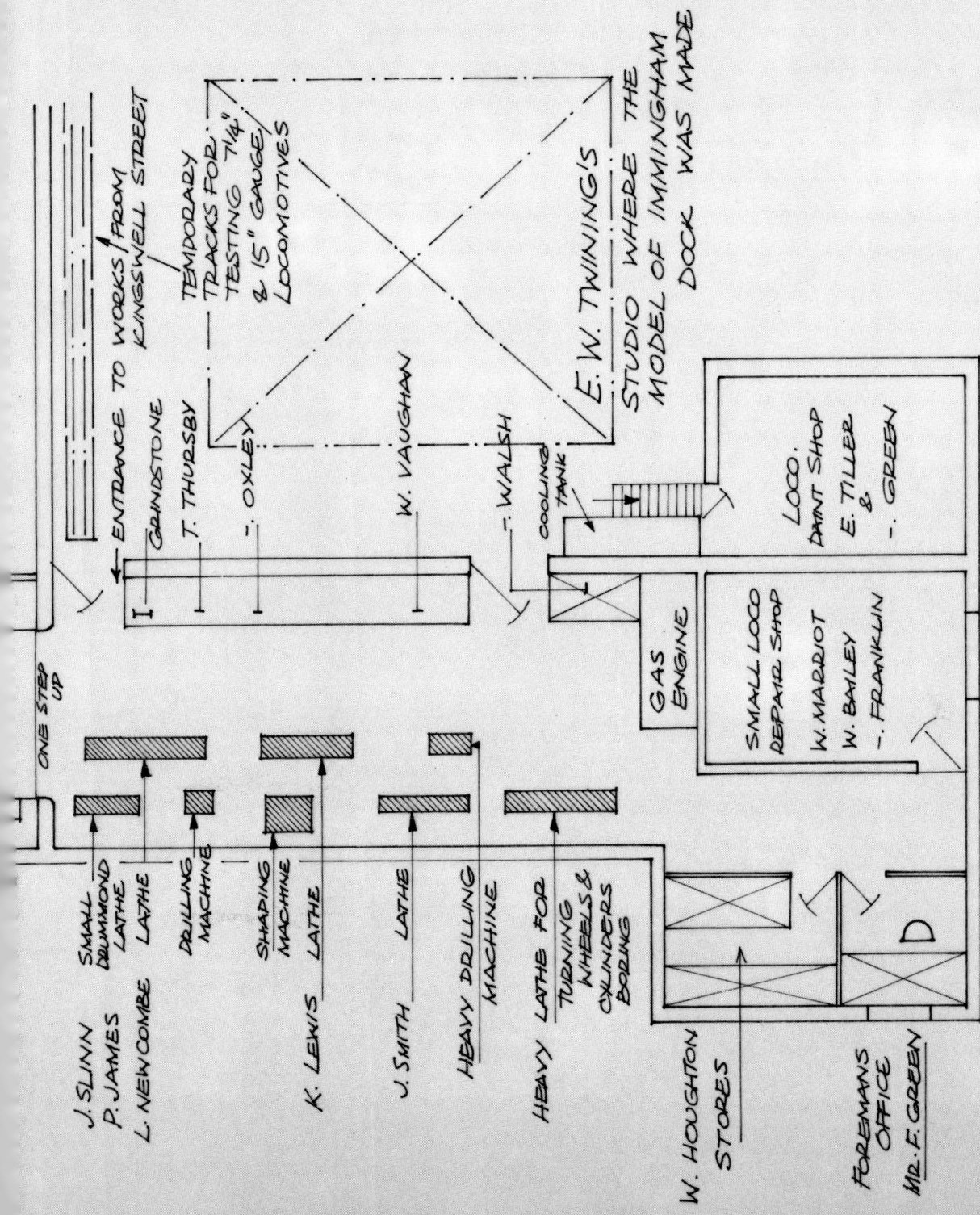

Sketch of W.J. Bassett-Lowke Ltd. Works in 1910-15 showing layout and names of personnel

J. SLINN
P. JAMES
L. NEWCOMBE — SMALL DRUMMOND LATHE — LATHE

DRILLING MACHINE

K. LEWIS — SHAPING MACHINE — LATHE

J. SMITH — LATHE

HEAVY DRILLING MACHINE

HEAVY LATHE FOR TURNING WHEELS & CYLINDERS BORING

W. HOUGHTON STORES

FOREMANS OFFICE
MR. F. GREEN

ONE STEP UP

ENTRANCE TO WORKS FROM KINGSWELL STREET

GRINDSTONE

J. THURSBY

– OXLEY

TEMPORARY TRACKS FOR TESTING 7¼" & 15" GAUGE LOCOMOTIVES

W. VAUGHAN

– WALSH

COOLING TANK

I

GAS ENGINE

E.W. TWINING'S STUDIO WHERE THE MODEL OF IMMINGHAM DOCK WAS MADE

SMALL LOCO REPAIR SHOP
W. MARRIOT
W. BAILEY
– FRANKLIN

LOCO. PAINT SHOP
E. TILLER &
– GREEN

D

Gerald Ward

need he and Harry decided to market castings which they had made from their own patterns, small sizes of metal tubing, rod and sheet suitable for model work and also small screws, rivets and tools obtained for them by George Blake.

Mr. Bassett co-operated by allowing them to use one of the larger rooms at No. 18 and also part of the shop window to display their wares. The results were moderately good and the amount of trade certainly encouraged them to carry on. However, Wenman's father felt that their small enterprise had little future, and, realising that Wenman would not be joining his company he persuaded him to take a two year student electrical engineering apprenticeship with Crompton Parkinson of Chelmsford, the very progressive firm of electrical engineers and contractors. The experience was valuable and during that time, he was engaged with teams working on the site at Hunslet Goods Yard and the York Corporation Electricity Works.

Nevertheless, Wenman's heart still lay with his nascent model business, which, in his absence was carried on by Harry Franklin. They kept in touch regularly, using duplicate books, so each had a record of all that was written. At times the correspondence was acrimonious, but mostly purposeful, and revealed the sharpness and perception of Wenman's mind. A constant preoccupation was how to enlarge the business, and in 1898 occurred two events which were to be of great importance.

In January of that year a new magazine appeared – the *Model Engineer and Amateur Electrician* – further described as 'a journal of mechanics and electricity for amateurs and students'. Wenman realised that this was the specialised publication that would enable him to reach a far greater number of potential customers. He took an early opportunity to visit the publishing office and there met the founder and editor, Percival Marshall. There appears to have been an immediate appreciation of each other's character and enthusiasm, which led to a friendship that continued until Percival Marshall's death.

Money to launch an advertising campaign came later in the year through a fortuitous photographic scoop. On September 2, at Wellingborough station, a luggage barrow fell in the path of an incoming train. The accident was not dangerous, but spectacular. Wenman was quickly on the scene and his resulting pictures produced

enough money to advertise regularly and bring out a catalogue, essential in a mail order business.

## The First Catalogues

Unfortunately, no copies of the first Bassett-Lowke catalogue have come to light. It was also the first time that the hyphenated name was used in order to distinguish the now developing business from the family firm of J. T. Lowke & Sons. The printers were Lea & Co., a medium-sized printing house in Gold Street (later in Broad Street)

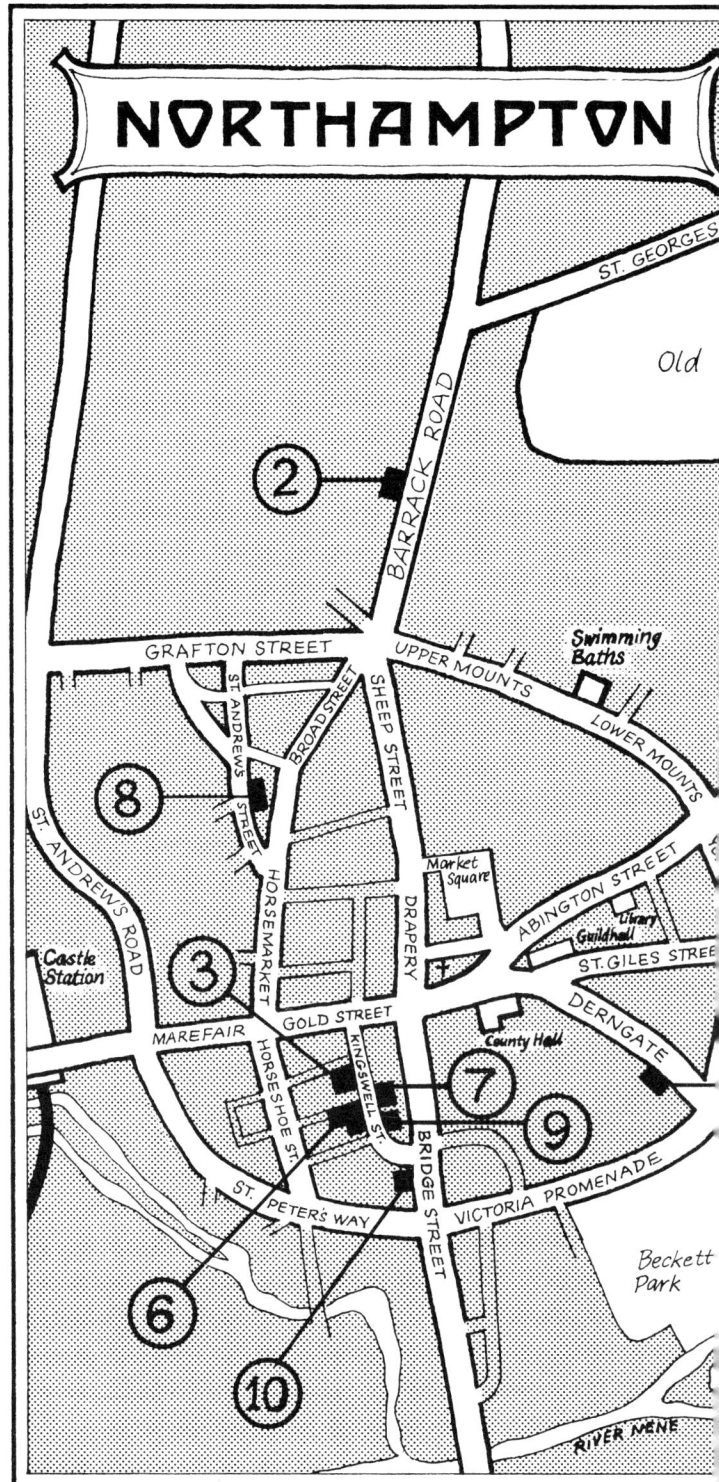

Northampton, which continued to do much printing for Bassett-Lowke until they closed down in 1965.

It was necessary to keep the cost of the catalogue to a minimum, although Wenman was adamant that it should be well illustrated. The perfect compromise was to have spaces left on the pages for photographic prints to be pasted in. The two young partners took photographs of their models, processed the negatives and pasted the pictures into the catalogue. A mammoth task indeed – but the photographs impressed customers and brought an immediate and profitable response.

The pattern was set for all future catalogues, and as much illustration as possible was the rule, although on occasion in later catalogues photographs of prototypes would be used as illustrations for the actual models. However, those models were nonetheless of good quality and style and there was no attempt to sell inferior products through false illustration.

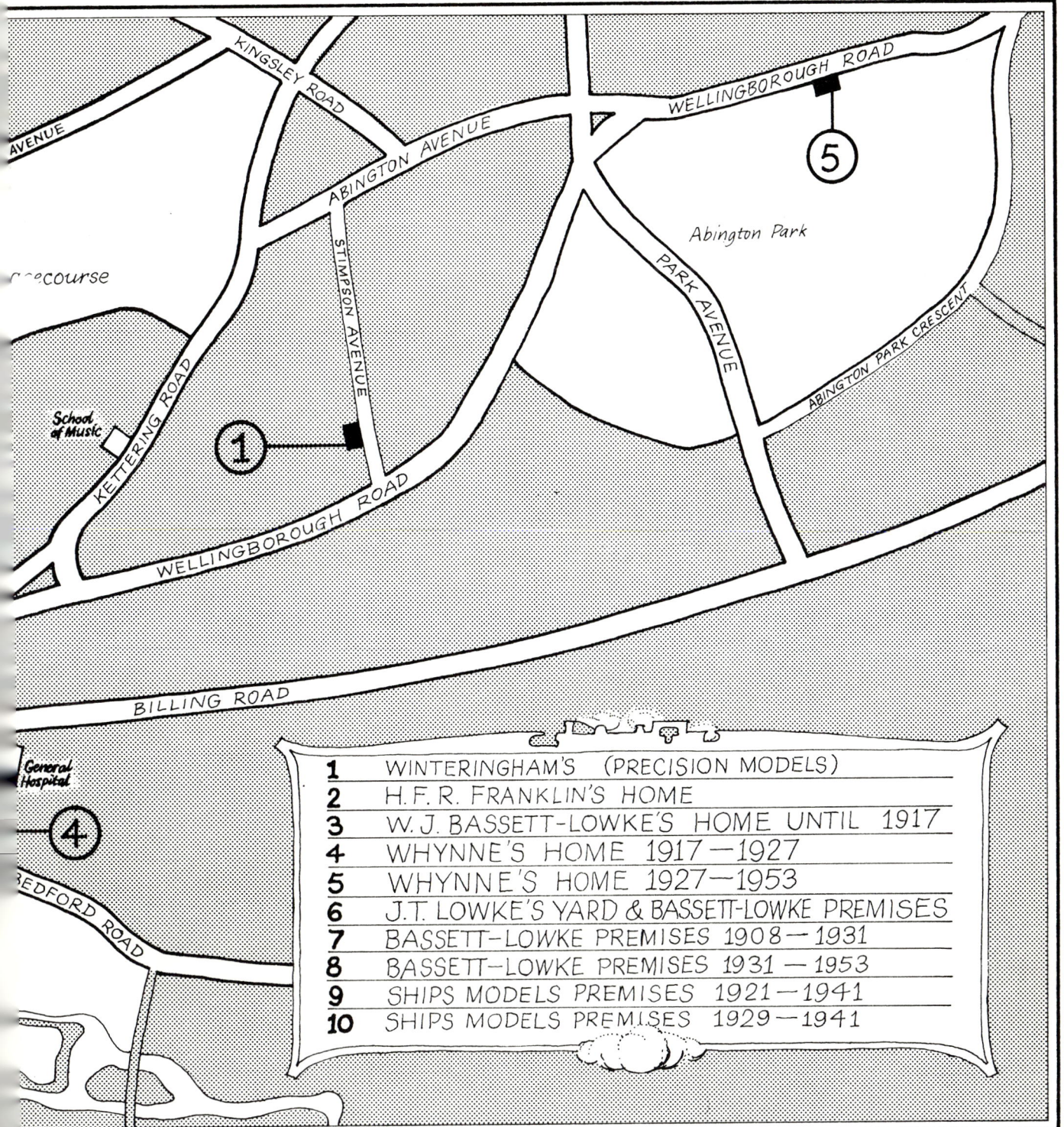

| 1 | WINTERINGHAM'S (PRECISION MODELS) |
| 2 | H. F. R. FRANKLIN'S HOME |
| 3 | W. J. BASSETT-LOWKE'S HOME UNTIL 1917 |
| 4 | WHYNNE'S HOME 1917 – 1927 |
| 5 | WHYNNE'S HOME 1927 – 1953 |
| 6 | J. T. LOWKE'S YARD & BASSETT-LOWKE PREMISES |
| 7 | BASSETT-LOWKE PREMISES 1908 – 1931 |
| 8 | BASSETT-LOWKE PREMISES 1931 – 1953 |
| 9 | SHIPS MODELS PREMISES 1921 – 1941 |
| 10 | SHIPS MODELS PREMISES 1929 – 1941 |

It is possible that Wenman's contact with George Carette, who had a very excellent factory in Nuremberg and made many products for Bassett-Lowke, influenced him to produce a catalogue in French as early as 1904. No attempt was made to issue a catalogue in any other language, but a larger model railway catalogue in French was produced in 1906.

Wenman realised early on that the range of models he offered catered for quite different interests and therefore, decided to make up the catalogues in sections. Up to the First World War there were variations in style and composition and in 1909–1910 five different catalogues appeared – model railways, stationary engines, ships, flying machines and electrical equipment.

The contents of these early catalogues show Wenman constantly testing the market, but after 1918 the range of goods became more consistent and were generally concentrated in three lists – Section 'A' for model railways, 'S' for ships and 'B' for steam stationary engines and fittings, castings and materials for the amateur model maker. There were occasional variations – for example, the railways list 'A' and stationary engine list 'B' were formed into an 'Everything for Models' edition.

From the beginning a charge was made for all standard catalogues – a necessary safeguard because there would have been an enormous response to offers of a free list. Nevertheless there was a regular output of leaflets and folders for distribution by post and from exhibition stands. Unfortunately, copies have not been kept of all these leaflets.

Construction booklets for the set of castings and finished parts added to the range of publications. These, with the catalogues and the *Model Railway Handbook* made a total of eight publications, prompting Wenman to produce a *Catalogue of Catalogues* which was offered for one penny!

One of the most interesting features about the Bassett-Lowke catalogues were the cover designs. They were the creation of various artists and draughtsmen. In many cases Wenman suggested the theme – but there was generally a boldness of subject and vigour of design that had great appeal and is now looked back upon almost as an art form. Wenman was greatly influenced in his cover designs by his interest in new trends in art encouraged by his friend Mackintosh. (See page 67.)

Early catalogue covers were drawn by Henry Greenly, Kenneth Cullen, George Winteringham and C. J. Allen and later, E. W. Twining was involved – his last being that for the gauge 0 catalogue of 1950.

For the later catalogues cover designs were concocted rather more than created – being put together by the printer's own illustrators.

## Percival Marshall and the *Model Engineer*

Wenman, having made close contact with Percival Marshall and placed regular orders for advertisements continually bombarded the editor with information and illustrations of any new or novel item. Naturally much of this could not be used, but there were frequent editorial references to Bassett-Lowke products which supplemented the advertising quite substantially. Models were sent to the publishing office for examination and tests. Published reports in the *Model Engineer* (which were mostly approving and sometimes quite flattering) gave a profound boost to sales. Quotations from such reports were used extensively in future catalogues and other literature. At this time the range of goods offered was limited to steam engines and boilers made in the J. T. Lowke workshops, castings and materials for making them, a selection of steam fittings by Claret and sundry materials, screws and tools.

Through his relationship with Percival Marshall, Bassett-Lowke was put in contact with specialist model makers, agents and importers. One of the latter was Louis Rees of Eisenman & Co. who represented several continental manufacturers. He showed Bassett-Lowke a number of excellent German made steam toys and advised him to visit the next Paris fair where he would see a remarkable range of products. Accordingly, in 1900 Wenman (by now known as Whynne to his friends) encouraged three of them to join him for that purpose. One of the party was Frank Jones, part of the shoe making firm, Crockett & Jones. It was Jones' daughter, Florence, who was to become Whynne's wife in 1917.

In Paris, Whynne was amazed by the ingenuity of design and high standards of several German or German-based companies. Two firms in particular attracted him – Bing Bros. and George Carette & Cie, both of Nuremberg (although there were also several early collaborations with Märklin). Later, a close personal relationship was to develop with both companies which lasted until Carette closed in 1917 and Bing was taken over in 1934.

One feature of these models which particularly impressed Bassett-Lowke was the piston valve double-action cylinders. These were made to a standard of precision which had not been achieved in Britain. The finely finished and fitted parts ensured great efficiency, with a power-to-steam consumption ratio that was remarkable. Arrangements were made to import an interesting range of engines and accessories. To Whynne's keen eye it was clear that some locomotives could, with only minor alterations, be accepted as representing English types.

The first model made to Bassett-Lowke requirements was the 'Black Prince', 1902. Produced originally as a continental style locomotive, it was eminently suitable for small modifications that would give it an acceptable appearance. Although it was not the first Bing engine to be imported, it was the forerunner of a series of models to be tailored to Bassett-Lowke specifications.

## Henry Greenly

It was at this time that Bassett-Lowke met Henry Greenly, an enthusiastic model railway man who had the background of good technical training and experience with the Metropolitan Railway. In addition he was a very skilled draughtsman whose considerable series of locomotives and railway drawings, created during his long career, are still regarded as outstanding. His association with Whynne was to continue for many years. Greenly brought to his work an extraordinary feeling of reality and it was this technique which was so successful in the re-vamping of continental design and in the development of new models to be produced by Bing and Carette for Bassett-Lowke.

The continental steam models were all low pressure designs – the working boiler pressure being about 15 lbs psi (no doubt having been adopted by the German designers as a convenient 'one atmosphere'). It was a safe pressure for the boilers which were made up from thin gauge sheet brass, rolled and seamed with all joints soft soldered.

However, for the real steam enthusiast, who demanded much more powerful performances than the low pressure models could give, engineer hand-built locomotives with working pressures of at least 60 lb psi were required. The first model

made by Bassett-Lowke in Northampton in 1905 was a Lancashire and Yorkshire railway 4–4–0 tender engine in 2½″ gauge. It was constructed largely from brass and iron castings, steel plate and for the boiler, heavy gauge seamless copper tube. The boiler itself, and all pipe connections, were brazed or silver soldered to withstand the high temperatures and pressures with a wide margin of safety.

Low pressure steam locomotives had what were termed 'pot' boilers, i.e. they were plain cylindrical drums beneath which was the methylated spirits burner, the flames of which played directly onto the underside of the boiler shell. The system was simple and cheap to manufacture but had the disadvantage of flames exposed to the elements, and, except on still warm days, such models could not be run successfully out-of-doors.

The high pressure locomotive could be used in all weather conditions having a type of boiler devised by Mr. Fred Smithies, who was in business at St. Albans with George Snooks. The Smithies principle was for the actual boiler to be small enough in diameter to fit inside an outer shell of scale size. Water circulating tubes were brazed into the underside of the inner boiler to increase the heating surface and to stimulate the flow of water from one end to the other.

The flames of the burner and hot gasses surrounded the inner boiler, flowed along its length to the smoke box and out through the chimney. The efficiency of the design and the high working pressure resulted in many years production of a wide range of types of locomotives in sizes from gauge 0 (1¼″) to gauge 3 (2½″).

There were critics who suggested that only coal-fired boilers were truly 'scale', but those who could afford such expensive 'toys' were not usually prepared to master the technique of working coal-fired boilers. The Smithies system ensured consistent performance and a reasonable length of unattended running time.

The two firing systems served two classes of customer, and with the growing interest in model railways there was a tremendous surge in the introduction of new models.

By the end of 1901 business was substantial and the range of goods offered was very wide – as a study of the 1902–1903 edition of the catalogue demonstrates.

In 1903 a quite remarkable British produced locomotive was introduced – a 3¼″ gauge steam

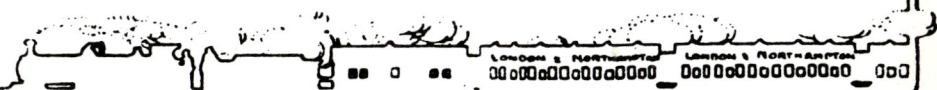

'Midland Compound'. The outstanding features were that virtually every part – main frames, footplating, cab sides, roof, and spectacle plate, tender body sides and ends, tender frames in addition to all the customary items – were supplied as castings in iron, brass or aluminium, so that very little additional metal material was needed to complete. It was a simple design, with two cylinders having slip eccentrics for reversing. The boiler was a water tube type (Smithies) fired by methylated spirits.

Although the use of so many castings reduced the amount of fabrication work to an absolute minimum, in those low-priced days it could still only be sold for £28.

The secret of their success was that all the castings were produced by the very efficient little foundry in the J. T. Lowke engineering works. Metal patterns were made for every part so that with careful and expert foundry work, the castings could be fitted with very little cleaning up and machining.

The first model was demonstrated to Percival Marshall, who was so impressed by its appearance, performance and price that he wrote a very laudatory article published in the *Model Engineer*, on September 10, 1903. This proved to be a very effective launching, and the model remained a standard product until 1913.

However, the principle of using castings for locomotive and tender body parts was discontinued when J. T. Lowke closed his foundry. Naturally, much better surface finishes were possible when those parts were fabricated from sheet metal. Nevertheless the Midland loco can be said to have been a remarkable experiment – in line with the progressive thinking and practice of Bassett-Lowke and Henry Greenly.

## Expansion

In the early years, production still took place in the J. T. Lowke workshops. H. F. R. Franklin was in partnership with Whynne but still was bookkeeper to J. T. Lowke. The confusion of work and finance can well be imagined and quite naturally that state of affairs could not continue. At the end of the yard at the rear of the J. T. Lowke workshops was a well founded building of suitable size which J. T. Lowke made available to his son. This was fitted out as a workshop with a comprehensive range of machine tools, a small forge and workbenches. A very capable employee of J. T. Lowke was

transferred to the new 'model shop' – Fred Green, who, as works foreman, was responsible for maintaining high standards of workmanship over a number of years in the building of an extensive variety of model locomotives, stationary engines and ancillary items.

J. T. Lowke no longer lived in the house at No. 18, preferring to make his home at No. 13, a little further up Kingswell Street. The upstairs rooms at No. 18 were given over to Whynne for use as offices and stores. A storekeeper was needed and William Henry Rowe, the 14 year old son of the Chief Fire Officer at Northampton was engaged. The arrangement was intended to be temporary as William's ambition was to follow in his father's footsteps as soon as he was old enough. In the event, however, the work held his interest and he remained with the Company until he finally retired at the age of 68.

The company being firmly and separately established with a substantial financial basis, Whynne literally stormed into action much to the trepidation of his timid partner. He extended the field of advertising – including the glossy boys' magazine *The Chieftain* and the then, widely popular *Strand Magazine*.

Production in Northampton was increased and suppliers, such as E. Cornish with his high class range of standard steam engine parts and J. Claret with his fine and comprehensive array of efficient steam fittings, were almost unable to keep up with the sales demand.

Regular consignments of Bing and Carette products were constantly arriving. The Post Office and the Railways Parcels depots in Northampton were very busy with Bassett-Lowke consignments in and out. As an early mail order business it was highly successful.

The range of work in Northampton was widened by the production of stationary steam engines and boilers in a variety of types and sizes. Whynne gained publicity by photographing heaps of several dozen horizontal engines, for example, and persuading editors to publish the pictures with a suitable caption mentioning Bassett-Lowke. The mixture of solid engineer-made Northampton products and low-priced continental imports provided a fascinating array for the customer and was splendid stuff for obtaining editorial reference (supported by illustrations produced by Whynne) in various periodicals.

During this time the friendship between

Bassett-Lowke and Henry Greenly grew stronger. Each admired the other for their great abilities – Whynne was the impatient and persistent entrepreneur while Greenly was the quick thinking man of practical ideas who could undertake any new project with almost impetuous fervour. They spent many hours together, each meeting being interspersed with lengthy correspondence.

Much of their effort was in attempts to standardise the scales and gauges of model railways. It was common sense for different manufacturers to produce model railway accessories that could be used together – and it was good for business. To secure acceptance of a set of standards was an uphill task, but Bassett-Lowke and Greenly had, by now, attained such status and authority that their proposals were accepted.

Naturally Bassett-Lowke attracted to itself several capable and enthusiastic personalities who, during the first 15 years, contributed much to the Company's authority and status as first class model makers.

An early recruit was James Mackenzie, a stocky figure, who was trained as an engineer in Scotland and had come down to work at Donald Curries Engineering Works, Blackwall in East London. He was an enthusiastic model maker, having built several small gauge steam locomotives. This ideal combination of professional training and private interest was exactly the expertise required to organise the work in a fast expanding factory. He was appointed Works Manager in 1904 and during the ensuing thirty years was to be responsible for the successful completion of many special projects.

## George Winteringham and the introduction of a Scale Model Permanent Way

Track for model railways, despite the great improvements in locomotives and rolling stock, remained rather primitive in both appearance and construction. For the majority 'tin plate track' was supplied. This comprised a hollow section rail and sleepers pressed from thin sheets of tin plate. It was supplied in relatively short lengths, about 12", and these joined together by steel pegs fixed in one end of each rail. Points were available and eventually there was a varied range of pieces – different radius curves, 'make-up' short lengths of straight and curved, and an ingenious variety of junctions and crossings. The user could, therefore, devise and then disassemble the most elaborate layouts.

For the more serious model railway-man this kind of track was unrealistic and many tried to devise a more acceptable appearance by attaching strips of metal to wood sleepers. Amongst the experimenters was George Winteringham, a skilled engineer and draughtsman. He incurred the expense of having made a miniature section of 'bull head' rail (the section then in general use on railways in Britain) in brass, and himself designed a machine in which to cast, in white metal, the wood, key chair also in general use. Having had to have much more rail 'drawn' than he could use, he decided to advertise for sale the new model permanent way. Whynne saw the announcement in the *Model Engineer* and was so impressed with the quality of the samples he obtained that he arranged to take regular supplies. This first track was to a scale of ¾" to the foot, suitable for models of about 3" gauge, but later on a smaller scale was produced. This remained the generally accepted standard for all small gauges until the newly formed Model Engineering Trades Association adopted a refined section in 1945. The introduction of a scale model permanent way not only improved the standards of model railways for the amateur, but was also the basis for making authentic layouts for training systems supplied to Railway Companies in the British Isles and overseas.

In addition to simple tin plate track and the scale permanent way, 'Lowko' track was introduced as an intermediate quality track. It comprised a hollow folded sheet metal section (slightly smaller than the customary tin plate rail) with a folded sheet metal chair secured to wood sleepers. The rail and chairs were offered in brass or tin plate and there was a special chair to secure the same rail section as a raised conductor rail for electric traction. As both rail and chairs were produced by press tools the cost was substantially lower than that of the solid brass rail and die cast chair used for the scale permanent way. 'Lowko' track, thereby offered a good looking, semi-portable track at very favourable prices.

In 1912, yet another form of track ('Simpull' (track) was devised by W. H. Hull, who had an excellent shop in Birmingham. Mr. Hull was very keen on model railways and, apart from creating a successful department in his store, arranged for the production in Germany of several locomotives and items of rolling stock. Amongst these was a

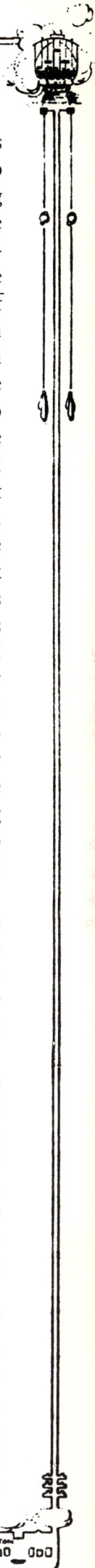

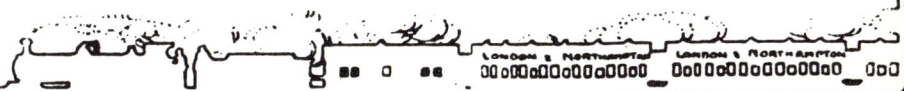

Birmingham Corporation coke truck and a private owner's wagon, bearing the name W. H. Hull & Sons and the Birmingham address. This latter copied the Bassett-Lowke private owner's wagon also made by Carette.

The track he devised consisted of a tin plate rail section of which the bottom was formed as an inverted V so that it could be slid into a suitably slotted wood sleeper. The straight and curved pieces were the same length as standard tin plate and they were joined together by spikes in the same way.

Black wood sleepers improved the appearance of 'Simpull' track and also, being a heavier wood, the track lay well. Thus by 1914 four kinds of track were available – Winteringham's Permanent Way in 'large' and 'small' scale for use on all gauges from 0 (1¼″) to 3½″, 'Lowko' track for gauges 0 and 1 (1¾″), 'Simpull' track for gauge 0 and imported 'tin plate' track.

After the war, 'Simpull' track gradually faded from the scene and 'Lowko' track, although persisting for a longer time was eclipsed by the introduction of simplified and standardised ready-laid permanent way in 18″ lengths. Tin plate continued to be the basic low priced track, but in order to provide for the larger gauge 0 locomotives introduced in the late 1920s, a large radius curved version, named appropriately 'Sixfut', based on a 16 piece six feet diameter circle, was introduced and remained on the market until the Second World War.

After 1945 when general production was resumed, all but Permanent Way were abandoned. However, no attempt was made to make the comprehensive range of Permanent Way units offered before 1939 with its various radius curves, 'make-up' short lengths of straight and curved, and assortment of types of points, crossings and double junctions. Nevertheless, the assortment available – two different radius curves to make double road layouts, various points and crossovers continued to provide a good track system until Bassett-Lowke gauge 0 production faded out.

Whynne greatly admired Winteringham's skill, keenness and ability and eventually persuaded him to come to Northampton to take overall charge of the model factory. Whynne was not interested in the day-to-day problems of manufacture and, therefore, arranged for this part of the company to become a separate business in 1908 under the title 'Winteringham Ltd.', with

George Winteringham as Managing Director and James Mackenzie as Works Manager. It was, in effect a 'limpet organisation' since all production was supplied to Bassett-Lowke. Indeed, Whynne disliked engaging any model maker directly and over the years there were several 'satellite' businesses whose sole outlet was Bassett-Lowke.

The production of boiler fittings by Claret of Moulton and of engine parts by Cornish was secured on the basis of total franchise. Thus, the combination of Winteringham production, supplies by 'out workers', some manufacturing by part of J. T. Lowke's facilities and the almost bewildering variety of items from the Continent enabled Bassett-Lowke to present a very exciting range.

## Passenger Carrying Railways

Despite the successful expansion of his business, Bassett-Lowke dreamed of another aspect of model making – miniature railways. Not far away, at Blakesley Hall, near Towcester, he had seen the system created in 1902 by Mr. C. W. Bartholomew. He had also visited Eaton Hall, Cheshire, where the Duke of Westminster had installed a 15″ gauge railway to provide a link between the house and Balderton Station on the G.W.R.

Already for some years, the Cagney Brothers in America had been building miniature railway locomotives and, in fact, it was from them that Mr. Bartholomew had obtained the first locomotive for his Blakesley Hall railway. One common feature in all these models was their non-scale proportions. In discussing the matter with Henry Greenly, Bassett-Lowke became convinced that a model built to scale proportions could give a satisfactory and profitable performance.

Greenly had designed an 0–4–4 tank locomotive in 10¼″ gauge for a partnership at Bricket Wood near St. Albans, Snooks and Smithies (the latter of water tube boiler fame). Whynne decided this would be an ideal model to test the public response to a miniature passenger carrying railway.

Accordingly, in 1904 together with R. Procter Mitchell (whose family was closely associated with the Regent Street Polytechnic) and other businessmen, he formed a company entitled 'Miniature Railways of Great Britain Ltd.', the secretary being Charles H. Battle who was later such a prominent figure in the fortunes of the Northampton General Hospital.

The first activity was to purchase the 0–4–4 tank, named 'Nipper', and to operate it on a section of line laid in a field adjoining Abington Park, Northampton. The railway opened on Easter Monday, April 20, 1905 and aroused enormous interest – the takings being sufficient to convince Whynne and his partners that a large model capable of hauling a bigger pay load and running on a site at a popular seaside resort would show a handsome return.

Blackpool was the obvious choice, and the Corporation was naturally always on the look out for novelties. There was no problem in obtaining a concession, and the new Company burst into frantic activity. 15″ gauge (nominally one quarter full size) was felt to be the practical gauge. Henry Greenly was commissioned to survey the site, design the track layout, a locomotive, rolling stock and lineside buildings – all in time for Whitsun and the start of the 1905 season.

The layout was roughly oval comprising 1,300′ of track and with one station, built by the firm of Trenery in Northampton to designs provided by Greenly. The platform was nicely paved and was given an adjoining booking hall and entrance. A train of 4-wheel passenger cars seating 8 persons each provided for a pay-load of 32 adults or older children with an unspecified number of small youngsters seated on parents' laps.

Speed was of the essence in the design and construction of the locomotive. Greenly was an admirer of the 4–4–2 'Atlantic' type that had been recently built for use on the North Eastern Railway. He considered the design to be ideal for miniature railway use because the boiler firebox could be much wider than a 4–4–0 or 4–6–0 would allow. He therefore recommended this wheelbase to Whynne and it was agreed to proceed. Time was short and Greenly was constantly travelling to Northampton as each section of drawings was completed in order that he could watch the progress of the work. It was a credit to James Mackenzie as Works Manager and Fred Green as Foreman, that the locomotive was completed in eight weeks.

It was necessary to carry out steam trials and the most suitable location was at Eaton Hall. The Duke of Westminster gave permission and in June, 1905, the model, named appropriately 'Little Giant' was placed on the rails at the Balderton Station end of the line to commence a rigorous series of runs. Speeds of up to 22 miles per hour with a load of 2½ tons were demonstrated in the presence of Henry Lea, M.I.C.E. and Allan G.

Robins M.I.Mech.E. who pronounced themselves as reasonably impressed. At once, the locomotive was sent to Blackpool to commence its duties.

As a public attraction on the South Shore it was a great success, but problems were caused by the fine sands and sea breezes. The bearings of the locomotive and rolling stock suffered badly and required constant servicing. Various methods were tried to protect them but were not entirely successful. Although the project did not lose money, it was not a total success and the company pulled out at the end of the 1910 season, transferring to Halifax, where experience was to show that although there were fewer crowds, maintenance costs were comparatively light. The running of 15″ gauge railways on suitable sites could be deemed a worthwhile proposition.

During succeeding years, until 1914, systems were operated in various towns in England and also in France, Belgium, Switzerland, Hungary and Norway. The big exhibitions, which were such regular features in the North European countries, were natural sites with throngs of visitors seeking novel forms of entertainment. It should be remembered that at that time real railways were at the height of their fame.

Unfortunately no record was kept of the number of 15″ gauge engines built, and because it was the practice to re-name and re-number models that were transferred from one site to another, attempts at research are often baffling. (The known history of the 'Little Giant' class locomotive and the improved 'Sans Pareil' version is given in the appendix.)

## Small Gauge Railways

Apart from the passenger carrying railways, the pre-1914–1918 war period also saw considerable progress in the development and improvement of the smaller gauge items. Following the first efforts by Bing and Carette to 'anglicise' some of their products to Bassett-Lowke requirements, they agreed to produce completely British outline models provided that certain basic standard parts, such as cylinders, could be incorporated. To this end Whynne and Greenly drew up a series of designs of locomotives and rolling stock which really established the Bassett-Lowke marque.

Not all the improvements were made in one step – the 'Black Prince' steam locomotive being a prime example. The first version was little different

from the standard Bing product, having only slight alterations, such as the chimney shape and the finishing in the livery and style of the prototype it represented.

In the early years of the company the general public was still uncritical and so, to introduce variety and cater for regional preferences, a model such as the 'Black Prince' of the L.N.W.R. would also be offered in L.S.W.R., M.R., and G.E.R. colours with only slight modifications to the models.

The reputation of Bassett-Lowke spread very quickly, and because of its acknowledged skills and ability Railway Companies approached the company to supply training models. The first contract was in 1904 for a small track section and signals for demonstrating correct train procedures. This was for the G.W.R. Within the next five years other and larger, more complex systems were made for the L.N.W.R. and the East Coast joint stock lines comprising the G.N., G.E. and G.C. Railways.

For the larger projects Mr. George Winteringham was brought in as consultant and designer.

## New Premises

The business had expanded so rapidly that the spaces occupied in the house and the yard were inadequate. There was now no room for extension and Bassett-Lowke had to seek other premises. In 1908 suitable factory accommodation in St. Andrews Street was found for the newly formed satellite company, Winteringham Ltd, and in 1910 an excellent warehouse became available almost opposite at No. 11. Apart from the production of larger engineering jobs such as the big locomotives, all production was concentrated in the Winteringham factory – the house adjoining the works providing ample office space.

Winteringham's move to St. Andrews Street enabled the enlargement of the machining and erecting shop in Kingswell Street, the building being extended to 50′ by 30′. It was well equipped with capacity for machining from very small items to such larger parts as those required for 15″ gauge locomotives. So efficient was the foreman, Fred Green, that he was put in charge, making it possible for James Mackenzie to transfer to Winteringham's with the purpose of taking charge of the day-to-day productive work. This left George Winteringham free to do the creative work of designing stock models as well as industrial and commercial projects.

George Winteringham was a true 'scale model' man. He considered 2″ as the ideal size for accommodating electric motors as well as retaining maximum detail. It was this size which was recommended for the signalling instruction models, and was also used in a portable exhibition layout (under the control of George and Herbert Sell) which toured the country between 1908–1912. Bert Sell later became manager of the London shop from 1945 to 1958.

No doubt, as a result of his early experience with Crompton Parkinson, Bassett-Lowke was keen to develop the use of electricity in models and to improve on the relatively under-powered continental motors. Together, he and George Winteringham designed a new cylindrical motor fitting inside the boiler shells and in sizes to fit all the small gauges up to 3½″. Its sturdy design and durability made it particularly suitable for exhibition use. In addition, a polarised magnetic reversing device gave the motor the benefit of maximum power from the wire-wound 'field' and the convenience of remote control reversing. First produced in 1907 the 'Lowko' remained the top class motor until in later years the quality of small permanent magnets was greatly improved.

The enlarged machinery and erecting shop continued to be fully occupied, even during the Great War when it supplied many parts required by the services by sub-contracts, but by 1921 it was clear that the market for large gauge model railways was gone, production was phased out and the machinery transferred to Winteringham's.

However, in 1912 the position was that Winteringham Ltd. supplied Bassett-Lowke with all quantity production standard catalogue items and made, in addition, models to special order – ships, industrial subjects and all classes of exhibition or museum models, also training layouts as supplied to railway companies.

E. W. Twining took all orders for architectural models and, by reason of his artistic sensitivity, any projects that called for particular aesthetic appreciation. The workshop conducted by Fred Green made all small boilers and steam stationary engines, steam locomotives from gauge 0 to 15″ gauge, passenger carrying vehicles and all other work of an engineering nature.

This production set-up combined with a flow of advanced German imports, added up to Bassett-Lowke's being a sound business of great promise.

## The First Retail Shop & Edward Hobbs

Whynne had formed many friendships amongst the business men of Northampton, one of whom was to be a tremendous supporter. This was Jack Sears, the dynamic and successful owner of the 'True Form Shoe Co.' He encouraged Whynne in all his enterprises and persuaded him to establish Bassett-Lowke & Co., into a Limited Liability Company, with himself as a shareholder and first Chairman in 1909.

Sears' greatest impact on the Company's status was, however, in urging Whynne to open a retail branch shop in London. He promised that if such a venture proved unsuccessful after a year's trading he would take over the lease to establish one more branch for his own business.

At that time the Strand was the flourishing shopping street in the West End – but rents were high. It happened however, that at the turn of the century there had been a clearance of the notorious Aldwych area, leading to excellent re-development and the building of Kingsway as a fine, broad thoroughfare with large commercial buildings, two churches and the handsome, but unsuccessful, Stoll Theatre. Kingsway itself was not a shopping street but its creation led to the improvement of High Holborn as a high class shopping area.

No. 257 was a shop available only on a short lease (in fact, the Pearl Assurance Co. were buying up premises in this area as leases fell out to enable them to build their fine Head Office). This situation was ideal as the rent was low and the lease long enough for Bassett-Lowke to evaluate the possibilities. Although small, the venture was an immediate success, attracting many famous people, including on two occasions the two princes – Edward and Albert, later Edward VIII and George VI. The shop opened in October 1908 and the first manager was Edward Walter Hobbs.

Edward Hobbs was born in 1885. At the age of 12 he was apprenticed to Frank Smith at the British Automatic Machine Company in Battersea. Through his apprenticeship, Hobbs had an extremely good training in manufacture, as well as coming into contact with other like companies and importers. Among the latter was Widman, a toy importer, who later introduced Hobbs to Bassett-Lowke.

During his training Hobbs had been for a period with the naval architect, Linton Hope, and indeed boats were a particular interest of the new manager. He built models and wrote articles for the *Model Engineer*, as well as producing two handbooks. In addition Hobbs was the leading figure in the creation of the Model Yacht Club Association which resulted from a gathering of several Model Yacht Club officers to be at the 'Bun Shop', a tea shop in High Holborn a few doors from No. 112 (the second and more famous London shop). Hobbs was also to give his attention to the design of power craft and produced a series of designs which appeared in the 1910 catalogue.

Undoubtedly his interest in ships and his active personality, attracted Whynne, who encouraged Hobbs in every way, and he was undoubtedly responsible for the success of the London shop both in its over-the-counter trade and the mail order business.

Edward Hobbs lived to a vigorous old age and in 1977 was still active in a small precision engineering business. Strangely coincidental – that business was located in Watford in a building where Butcher & Co. had made model locomotives until about 1916, when Bassett-Lowke took over the stock.

## The Model Railway Handbook

W. J. Bassett-Lowke was always a prolific writer, contributing articles to magazines, producing pamphlets and, of course, all the descriptive matter for the early catalogues. His experience in dealing with customers' correspondence and enquiries in the early years convinced him that a book on model railways would be popular and promote business.

In 1906 the first edition of the *Model Railway Handbook* was published priced 6d. It was very informative with articles on different aspects of model railways and real railway practice. It purported to be written by W. J. Bassett-Lowke, but from the style of writing in some chapters, it is evident that such capable contributors as George Winteringham and James Mackenzie were also involved. Certainly, C. J. Allen supplied considerable technical matter. The book was so successful that improved and enlarged editions were produced at intervals until 1953.

The first four editions were stapled and had thin covers, but subsequently all were bound with hard covers. The fifth edition was also substantially enlarged from the 96 pages of the fourth to 142, with additions in subject matter and illustrations.

Cover designs of the first four were by Cecil J.

Allen, but for the fifth to the eighth a new cover by Kenneth H. Cullen, was used, and in these a style of lettering for Bassett-Lowke was firmly established. For still later covers E. W. Twining was the artist.

It is strange that Bassett-Lowke was so sparing in his acknowledgements of contributors, for without doubt, he was entirely dependent upon them. Henry Greenly was aggrieved by this – thus Whynne thanked him and James Mackenzie in the fourth *Model Railway Handbook*, although there was no mention of the valuable articles by George Winteringham on permanent way (later revised by Mackenzie).

New editions did not appear regularly – there was, in fact a long spell of ten years between the eighth and ninth editions. For the latter, published in 1940, Cecil J. Allen did a very thorough job of revision and up-dating. From then on the subject matter remained much the same, there being a minor re-write for the fourteenth edition in 1948.

The sales of the handbook fell away after this as it had become redundant. With extensive coverage of the subject by the monthly model railway magazines, in addition to the publication of numerous handbooks on various aspects of the hobby – mostly influenced by the trend towards 00 gauge, there was almost a glut of information. The Bassett-Lowke handbook died – but it had been a pioneer in the field and for forty years had provided interest and inspiration for newcomers to the hobby.

## Models, Railways and Locomotives

Despite the success of the handbook, Bassett-Lowke felt that a regular periodical would have greater impact and publicity value. Henry Greenly had a similar ambition, although in his case he particularly wished to disseminate his ideas on locomotive building. The two men got together and the first edition of *Model Railways and Locomotives* price 3d, appeared on the bookstalls in January 1909, the publishing office being given as 257 High Holborn – the Bassett-Lowke London shop.

Probably because neither Whynne nor Greenly had direct experience of using small gauge model railways, the publication did not generate wide interest. They did not tackle the problems which confronted the model railway user in those early days of the hobby. This is not to say that the magazine lacked interesting matter – indeed there

were numerous informative and well-illustrated features – although perhaps more suitable for the *Model Engineer*. The main contributors were Whynne, Greenly, Winteringham, Mackenzie and Cecil J. Allen. Other articles were published under pen names, but, in most cases these were written by the same authors. Such articles as an erudite report on train performance would only be of minor interest to somebody trying to tackle the more basic problems of building a model railway. Much space would be given to the drawings and description of how to make a buffer stop, but little guidance was given on the question of how to make an average-sized, reliable track layout.

Sales of the magazine were disappointingly small – perhaps because of this lack of down-to-earth information. Greenly considered that the title appealed to too narrow a field of interest and perhaps with a secret wish to create a second and better *Model Engineer*, suggested the name should be changed by inserting an S and a comma, to read *Models, Railways and Locomotives*. Articles on other kinds of models, on aircraft and even wireless telegraphy were included in due course. But the truth of the matter was that both editors were too busy to give the magazine enough attention and several editions had the appearance of being hastily put together.

Despite these limitations publication continued until May 1919 when the magazine was merged with *Everyday Science*. During the years of production it is noticeable that whereas at first there were articles by Whynne and 'Lowko' (his pen name) and each edition carried extensive notes on Bassett-Lowke models and activities, there was a gradual falling-away and it seemed almost as though Whynne had opted out.

## The Second London Shop
## 112 High Holborn

Business at 257 High Holborn was very good and encouraged the company to seek other premises since the lease at 257 was short. It happened that the Adder Co., were vacating their showroom and basement at 112. The premises were much larger and part of a building constructed only about 10 years earlier. They were ideal in many ways and so a lease was signed. Elegant showcases, counters and office and store furniture were installed for the opening in January, 1910. E. W. Hobbs continued as Manager. As a result of his interest in model boats he designed a series of sailing yachts, which he had made by Carl Petersen, a first-class Danish craftsman with a workshop in Camden Town. Power craft were also designed, these at first being made in Northampton. Within a year Hobbs persuaded the Company to set up a workshop in Eagle Street, at the rear of the shop, where amongst other special items, a range of racing boats, warship and other models were made. This was of course, in addition to the model ship production in the Northampton works which now had space for further expansion.

## Architectural Model Work and E. W. Twining

The range of work undertaken by the company to special order extended very considerably once space allowed, but an order from Blackpool Corporation was to lead to an association with a remarkable man and a new direction for the company.

The corporation had for many years been publicity conscious and, deciding to have a London 'Tourist Office' in High Holborn (50 yards from 112), felt that a splendid window display attraction would be a model of central Blackpool, showing such features as the Big Wheel and the Tower. Bassett-Lowke was chosen to execute this large and very detailed model. A very skilled architectural model-maker, S. Auden, was engaged for the work, but less than half way through he decided to emigrate to the U.S.A.

Luckily, a few years earlier Bassett-Lowke had been introduced by Percival Marshall to E. W. Twining, who was in business in Hanwell making and selling model aeroplanes and parts, this being a time of intense interest in the very new adventure of powered flight. Bassett-Lowke had taken regular supplies of Twining products and included them with other imported items in a special aeronautic catalogue in 1910.

Twining's business was unfortunately not prospering and he accepted Bassett-Lowke's suggestion that he should take over architectural model work. Twining was in many ways like Winteringham in his great technical ability and artistic sense. He had the unusual quality of being a fine mechanical draughtsman as well as an artist. He was responsible for a number of illustrations and drawings for the Bassett-Lowke catalogue as well as his work for *Models, Railways and Locomotives*. He was also well known for his interest in stained glass windows and architecture

generally, having done some model-making in connection with the latter.

The completion of the Blackpool project was followed by an order for a large and detailed model of the new Immingham Docks, which was successfully completed in time for it to be on the site when George V formally opened the docks, and thus enabled his Majesty to appreciate the vast extent of the development.

Twining was encouraged to establish a permanent drawing-room in a small, specially and suitably converted studio at the end of the yard at the rear of J. T. Lowke's workshop. Once again, however, it was not to form part of Bassett-Lowke Ltd., but was to be an independent company trading as Twining Models Ltd. with Bassett-Lowke Ltd. as the sole concessionaires. Until 1940, when he went to join the Bristol Aeroplane Company, Twining was responsible for the production of a considerable number of high quality models of many and varied subjects, including some large scale steam locomotives which are now much regarded for their workmanship and authenticity. Twining Models Ltd. continued under the direction of Mr. E. H. Clifton until closure in 1965.

## Exhibition Models

The first decade and a half of this century was an era of great national and international exhibitions. Every year spectacular shows were mounted at White City or Earls Court, and big continental cities boasted similar displays. Bigger and better exhibitions became a matter of national pride. In Britain, every town of substance had an Exhibition Hall and the sum total of events in any one year was considerable.

Thus, exhibitions were an important activity for Bassett-Lowke Ltd., either as exhibitors or providers of exhibits to customer-exhibitors. Whynne was always keen for publicity and during the whole period until 1939 staged impressive displays at The Model Engineer Exhibitions (first in 1905), the British Industries Fair, the Shipping and Engineering Exhibitions, as well as at some continental and many smaller provincial shows and those organised by model clubs. In the 1909 'Model Engineer Exhibition', for example, the Bassett-Lowke stand occupied the whole of one side of the Horticultural Hall, with a multiple gauge track connecting two units situated at either end.

For the Canadian Pacific Railways an extensive 2½″ gauge layout was installed in their magnificent stand at the Vienna exhibition in 1909. In 1913, a model passenger carrying railway was installed at the Childrens Welfare Exhibition at Olympia organised by *The Daily News*. It was a relatively simple 7¼″ gauge layout, oval in shape to give continuous running, set amongst attractive background scenery. A station platform and booking office completed the railway which carried a very considerable number of passengers during the period at the Exhibition – including the wife of Winston Churchill and the great man himself.

The locomotive was an L.N.W.R. 'George the Fifth' developed from the 'Precursor' model introduced three years earlier, the first of which was supplied to Mr. Guy Mitchell of Tatley, near Sheffield. The 'George the Fifth' remained a popular model. Altogether over one hundred were made in the years until 1936, and very many sets of castings supplied to amateur builders. The passenger vehicles used at Olympia were a very simple four-wheeled type of two seater which must have been quite uncomfortably low for adult passengers and probably embarrassing for the ladies in those prim days.

## Ships Models Develop Apace

Concurrent with the expansion in all fields of model railway equipment, there was considerable development in the production of model ships. In addition to the centre of interest created by the manager, E. W. Hobbs at the London shop, there was a developing department in the Winteringham works for the production of miniature ships, from simple working models to the fine, highly detailed models that continue to be a dominant feature in the Bassett-Lowke story to the present day.

A very fine model of the Battle Cruiser *Queen Mary*, with twin screws powered by reciprocating steam engines, was made for Lord Howard de Walden in 1914. An unusually large order for ten models of the S.S. *France* was completed for the Compagnie Generale Transatlantique. The intense pre-war competition for the Blue Riband of the Atlantic was to lead indirectly to commissions from the various lines promoting their ships, including models of the famous *Mauretania* and the ill-fated *Titanic*.

## Waterline Models

Interesting small scale products were the 'Waterline Models' made in wood of warships and passenger liners. Once again, the department producing these models was independent of Bassett-Lowke Ltd., started when Hobbs first joined the company as London Manager in 1908. The two partners who developed the company were Denton and Checker. The former was a Northampton man, the latter a Czech who came to Britain in 1911.

The most popular size for these ships was to a scale of 100 ft to 1 inch, or 1/1200 scale, and they were much in demand as souvenirs by serving navy men and the travelling public. Being hand-made they were relatively expensive and so a series of models to a smaller scale suitable to die-casting in white metal was put on the market in boxed sets. These were packed in display boxes carrying the name and details of the ships, and ranged from a small flotilla of T.B.D.'s and leader, to a complete set of all the ships at The Spithead Review of 1911, mounted in a polished wood box. This included all types of warships, submarines and small auxiliary vessels such as mine-sweepers and supply ships, also a hospital ship, the Royal Yacht and the Admiralty Yacht. Altogether a most impressive collection.

It was, however, the hand-made series that interested ship lovers, and over the years until 1939, when production for retail sale was discontinued, models of every new ship of importance were produced and avidly collected by enthusiasts. It was also this class of model that interested the Admiralty as they realised that their three-dimensional depiction was much more useful for recognition training than the customary silhouette drawing. From 1911 on there were regular contracts from the Admiralty, and, in the Second World War, also from the R.A.F. During both World Wars, of course, enormous quantities were produced for personnel training. The fact that they were hand-made enabled any reconstruction of the prototype to be rapidly reproduced.

Of all the ship model work before the First World War the greatest and most dramatic was the series built for a special display at the Imperial Services Exhibition in 1913 at Earls Court. In all, nine ships, H.M.S. *Thunderer*, *Colossus*, *Neptune*, *King George*, and *New Zealand* with smaller models of cruisers and destroyers, comprised the fleet. The larger ships averaged 20 feet long and carried a crew of two who, lying prone in the hull, navigated their vessels and operated the search-lights and guns. In the smaller ships a one man crew did these duties.

At Earls Court, before a large auditorium, was a specially constructed lake at each end of which was a channel leading to the equivalent of the 'wings' in a theatre. At the back of the lake was modelled a sea port town which bore some resemblance to Portsmouth with Portsdown in the rear. The programme started with several dummy ships (supported by men in swimming costumes), approaching from the left, lining up and bombarding the port. After a short delay, and to the sound of suitable music, the Home Fleet sailed in, firing powerfully at the enemy which, each in turn, burst into explosive flames and sunk slowly while drifting left into the wings. The Home Fleet shone its search-lights, ran up lines of flags and manoeuvred triumphantly around, finally departing to the right in a cloud of smoke to the applause of the audience. The pyrotechnics of the display, with the generous flashing and noise were provided by Messrs. Brock, of firework fame, but the successful designing of the ships was totally due to E. W. Hobbs who had a frantic period in which he made the drawings and superintended the construction of the ships while still in control of the London shop. The whole project had to be completed in eight weeks – in itself a tribute to everyone involved.

## The Widening Stock Range

It is impossible to list in this narrative all the developments in Bassett-Lowke's range during these years. As many models as are traceable are listed in the appendix. In the period 1909–1910 the catalogue ran to 476 pages covering the whole field of model railways, stationary and traction engines, fittings and castings and parts for amateur model makers, ship models and machinery, fittings and parts for building them, passenger carrying railways from 15″ down to 7¼″ gauge, aeroplanes and parts for making them, tools and materials, electric motors, generating plants and associated items.

As a forward-looking man, Whynne was naturally impressed with the development of the aeroplane. The complete models and sets of parts produced by E. W. Twining plus those manufactured in France enabled him to get together a comprehensive range sufficient to justify using a special catalogue. Alas, although the public were greatly stirred by this new form of travel – as exemplified by the many popular songs at that time – they were not attracted to flying or building model aircraft. The catalogue was not repeated as a separate entity, although sections of other catalogues showed a small selection of aeronautical items.

## Orders from Overseas and Continued Expansion

The reputation of the Company seems to have very quickly spread overseas for it was in 1904 that the Sultan of Turkey ordered a complete 2″ gauge model railway for his Palace in Constantinople. In the same year the Duke of Zaragoza in Spain ordered a Signalling Instruction Table. Strangely there exists no record or photographs of the 15″ gauge railway, comprising a 'Little Giant' class locomotive, several passenger cars and a considerable quantity of track and points supplied to the King of Siam at Bangkok in 1910. Nor of the electric model table railway supplied to the Maharaja of Gooch Behar in 1911.

An early piece of exhibition model locomotive building was a Chinese State Railway 2–8–8–2 for the American Locomotive Company, to be displayed at the Panama Exhibition in 1913 before being presented to the Chinese Government. It was built to a scale of ¾″ to the foot and was mounted on the track base so that all the wheels could revolve, being driven by an electric motor. It was extremely impressive both in size and detail, mirrors being laid under the track at an angle enabling spectators to see the intricacy of the inside motion.

In less than a dozen years the business had been developed to such an extent that there seemed to be no field of model work that had not been exploited. The range of standard retail goods was broad enough to satisfy most public interests while the facilities developed for special work were such that any industrial or commercial requirement could be encompassed. Now a limited liability Company, providing employment for nearly 300 people, and with a London Branch that was fast becoming a centre of interest for visitors from overseas as well as for people from all parts of the British Isles, it was indeed a tribute to the Founder and Managing Director, W. J. Bassett-Lowke.

## London Shop Developments

With the removal of the London Branch to No. 112 High Holborn, the manager E. W. Hobbs was encouraged to attract as much attention as he could to that shop – and it is curious to note that in the model ship catalogue of 1910, 112 High Holborn was given as the only full address followed by the note 'Head Office and Works, Northampton'. The shop was indeed a hive of activity, with its staff of five salesmen (two of whom would be away at exhibitions in various parts of the country for several weeks in the year demonstrating the model railways referred to earlier), two packers and store keepers and two juniors in addition to two young lady typists/clerks. Shop hours were 8.30 to 7.30 p.m., with half-day closing on Saturdays.

In addition to supplies of Northampton and German made goods, Hobbs organised several manufacturers of specialised items. C. Petersen of Camden Town made the excellent range of model yachts designed by Hobbs and ranging in size from 18″ to 60″ in length. One series was a replica of the *Shamrock* – Thomas Lipton's famous contender. J. Pike of Clapham Junction produced steam traction engines, both single and twin cylinder, which although coarse in detail were to such a high standard of workmanship and efficiency in operation that they remained unsurpassed for twenty years. Alfred Campbell of Wandsworth had a quite remarkable faculty for making stationary and locomotive engines and boilers to a high degree of efficiency and quality of work. There were others who supplied their specialities to add to a wide range of quality goods.

Thus the London shop, like the Northampton Head Office, drew to itself a number of highly skilled 'satellite-workers' whose entire output was absorbed by Bassett-Lowke. Although it could be argued, of course, that these products were not really Bassett-Lowke models, the independence of their makers gave them a sense of entrepreneurial pride, encouraged them to maintain standards and to make improvements in their products when possible in order to hold their only customer.

The London shop became a magnet that attracted people from the provinces and overseas, so well known that few taxi drivers and hotel hall porters were unaware of its location. To attempt to list the names of famous visitors from those early days on to the day of closing would be tedious reading here, but the appendix includes a considerable number of them.

## Business Connections

Whynne had always been a frequent visitor to London, in pursuit of business, publicity and his private interests. Now there was a London Office his visits became regular and frequent – twice a week at least. This made an excellent jumping off point for his many activities and a convenient meeting place for business contacts and friends.

One such man whom he met during those early London years was to remain connected for very many years. Frank Derry was the proprietor of a successful and expanding mail order business – Ambrose Wilson Ltd. From his direct experience he was able to give much valuable advice on mail order procedure and on advertising. Whynne listened, marked and learned – much to the advantage of the business. Both men admired each other's business acumen. Later Frank's son Cyril took an immense pride in his acquaintance with Whynne. He developed a tremendous interest in the products of the Northampton factory, and, being a keen traveller and cine-photographer, was able to share these interests with Whynne. Some years later he was to become a strongly supportive Chairman of Bassett-Lowke Ltd. at a most difficult time in the between-the-wars years.

Whynne's exciting personality drew many people to him and friendships made lasted throughout the lifetime of those involved. Stefan Bing, of the famous German Company, whom Whynne first met at the Paris Exhibition in 1900 was an outstanding example. His son Franz was later to state that it was simply business courtesy and not friendship that kept the two men in touch, but continuous correspondence and visits to each other's homes for more than thirty years must surely have been more than business expediency. Why else, too, would Stefan have kept and then sold all the war-blocked stock to Bassett-Lowke at the agreed 1914 prices in 1919 if they had not been close friends? George Carette, whose company in Nuremburg supplied a fine range of lithographed tin plate rolling-stock made to Bassett-Lowke specifications, remained a personal friend, as did his son, Theophile, who lived in Paris after the closure of his father's business.

## Promotional Models

In the pre-First World War years there was intense competition between the railway companies. An important part of every General Manager's duties was to create the maximum of favourable publicity. The Caledonian Railway was particularly ambitious in this and engaged the publicity conscious Guy Calthorp for just such a purpose. At that time a powerful new locomotive was put into service – a 4–6–0 Express engine of very handsome proportions. Calthorp considered that a model of this and of the magnificent 6-wheel bogie carriages then in service on the '2 o'clock Scotchman' would have great publicity value if they could be distributed in large numbers. Whynne negotiated with him and finally secured a quite remarkable order for 30,000 of each. The locomotive, the famous 'Cardean' No. 903 was made to a scale of ¼" to the foot – the scale to which gauge 0 (1¼") models were then designed. It was fitted with a clockwork motor and the wheels were flanged, so that it could stand and run on straight track, but the construction was rigid with the bogie fixed so that it could not run on any curved model railway track. The 17" long model was beautiful and the lithographed tin plate body reproduced the handsome blue livery of the original, but although it could run on a smooth floor and haul the 18" long coach its 'play' value was limited. Despite the fantastic low price of two shillings and sixpence (12½p) for the locomotive, and one shilling and sixpence (7½p) for the coach, sales were disappointingly slow even though they were on display in every C.R. bookstall. The models were made by Carette of Nuremburg who was accustomed to competitive manufacture, but it is truly amazing how they could have been made for such a low price which must have included a profit for Bassett-Lowke even if the Railway Company was prepared to forego theirs. Shortly after the project was launched Guy Calthorp resigned from his post (August 1910) and the question must remain as to whether this ambitious and costly publicity scheme was the cause. The locomotive was available for sale in December 1908 and the coach followed a year later. The details of the contract were dealt with by Mr. A. Fulton of the General Superintendent's Office.

## Agencies are Established

With such an extraordinary range of products to offer, much attention was given to establishing agencies, both in the British Isles and on the Continent. Good and lasting arrangements were made with Salanson of Bristol and W. H. Hull & Sons of Birmingham, while Bond's of Euston Road took selected items over a period of years

until A. W. Bond died and the personal relationship was broken. There is no other record of agencies in this country, although a number of shops did occasional business. It has to be remembered that although the prices shown in early catalogues appear now to be almost trivial, in those days they were high and beyond the reach of most people.

Efforts were made to establish retail agencies in most of the countries of North Europe, but possibly for the same reason, met with little success. In an Electrical Catalogue issued in 1908/1909 an agency was listed in Holland at 13, Gedempte Burowal, The Hague, but no mention is made of it anywhere else. A lasting arrangement was made with Mr. E. P. Malaret who had a fine toyshop in the Rue de Rivoli, Paris, called 'Au Paradis des Enfants'. This connection lasted until the 1920s, although interrupted from August 1914 until December 1918 because Mr. Malaret was called up for war service.*

The extent of Bassett-Lowke publicity was really very substantial. Apart from Press advertising in the *Model Engineer* regularly and less frequently in magazines such as *The Captain*, *The Strand* and the *Boys Own Paper*, insertions would appear sporadically in newspapers or journals usually in conjunction with editorial support. Whenever displays were made at Exhibitions, leaflets and pamphlets on free issue would be offered in addition to the usual attractive catalogues which were always sold – usually for 6 pence (2½p).

All the advertising, plus the numerous exhibitions, not to mention the operations of 'Miniature Railways of Great Britain' installing and running 15" gauge railways, meant that the name of Bassett-Lowke became a household word. Indeed, many would claim to have had a Bassett-Lowke model in much the same way that they would drop the names of Rolls Royce, Harrods or Fortnum & Mason.

## The Great War 1914–18

In retrospect it is amazing how little people were prepared for war in the summer of 1914. In the August issue of *Models, Railways and Locomotives* there is no hint of the approach of war and the Editorial comment in the September issue opens with the words 'many of our readers have, no doubt, gone to the war' – and goes on to trust they will shortly return to normal duties. Further it said 'the shock of the crisis has affected the journalistic

*Ed. Note:   The Paris shop was in fact called 'Le Paradis des Enfants' but became more popularly known as Au Paradis de Enfants.
The Bassett-Lowe agency in Paris c. 1930–1950 was taken on by M. Filleaud at Rue de la Boetie.
Mr Hoppler ran a Bassett-Lowke agency in Switzerland from the early 1920's until the 1950's trading at 48 Bahnhofstrasse, Zurich.

world – but as soon as things settle themselves we hope to resume the ordinary number of pages'.

It was the practice to place an annual order with both Bing and Carette for goods to be delivered in the early autumn in time for the winter and, especially, the Christmas trade. The first effect of the war was that Bing was unable to despatch before the frontiers closed and so that winter there was an immediate shortage of their products for Bassett-Lowke. Carette had despatched in good time – but since their consignment was mostly of passenger and goods rolling stock there was an imbalance in the Bassett-Lowke stocks.

Because of the alleged German atrocities in the early days of the war, there was a tremendous public revulsion towards German made goods, and there was much talk about them being replaced by British manufacturers. Indeed, Whynne made it known through the editorial page of *Models, Railways and Locomotives* that he intended to replace all continental goods with those made in Northampton. This was not to come about immediately, however, because trade rapidly deteriorated both in mail order business and in the London shop.

As the days of the war lengthened it came to be accepted that it was going to be a long conflict. Many thousands of young men responded to a 'call to the colours', while others felt that they should be concerned with more serious matters than hobbies – the demand for models of all kinds shrank. War casualties were enormous in number and very many men suffered the loss of limbs. In 1915, the London shop manager, E. W. Hobbs, was invited to join a group of specialists in designing false limbs and so he was replaced by John Wills who had been active in the establishment and running of 15″ gauge railways at Rhyl, and later at Fairbourne and elsewhere. The first part of the Great War was one of great disturbance and enforced change for the Company. It was, for a while a case of just 'ticking over' to wait and see what would happen. The war itself quite quickly introduced an element that was outside the experience of the War Command and baffled military experts – trench warfare. Static warfare along hundreds of miles of front line required long periods of bombardment to pin the enemy down and so the need for supplies of guns and projectiles outstripped the capacity of the armaments industry as then established.

The principle of individual manufacturers supplying only complete arms or armament items had to be abandoned and standard component production spread amongst as many firms as possible in order to maximise supplies. All parts, therefore, had to be completely interchangeable irrespective of who made them – and this meant that check-gauges were needed to ensure that all component parts were finished within the range of very narrow minimum and maximum limits.

This was a system of manufacture hitherto practised to a very limited extent so that existing facilities were very few indeed. The central need for putting the new style production into being was the 'master' gauge. These were for checking the 'check gauges' used in the factories to ensure that all parts produced were within the correct tolerances. Not many firms had the necessary expertise or equipment for working to these very fine limits – but Winteringham's were so blessed, and for the duration of the war this was their main activity. Great credit was due to James Mackenzie who designed the lapping machines which speeded up the finishing of screw gauges in particular. The screw thread measuring wires he first produced during the Great War continued to be supplied until Winteringham's (by then known as Precision Models) closed down.

The Bassett-Lowke machine and erecting shop was engaged right through the war and E. W. Twining's studio was occupied in the making of training aids for the services. A small section of the Winteringham factory was employed continuously in the production of Waterline ships models, required in much larger quantities by the enormously expanded naval establishment. Altogether therefore, all personnel were fully engaged in a way that, while not extravagantly profitable to Bassett-Lowke, maintained the group of manufacturing units during the years 1915 to 1919.

Whynne was a pacifist, and would assist anyone, if he possibly could, to remain in civilian life. Perhaps his conscience bothered him as to whether he should have profited from the manufacture of some elements of warfare but, in fact, no excess profits accrued and nobody could suggest that Whynne was a war profiteer.

Several of his German friends and business contacts were in London at the outbreak of the war and they were all interned at Peel on the Isle of Man. Whynne secured a permit and regularly visited them until the time of their release. One internee's story was particularly poignant. A German manufacturer's representative in London, named Oppenheim was interned only a few days after marrying a young English girl, Miss Willmott, who had been secretary to the company's London manager, Hobbs. Although business was not sufficient to require her services, Whynne employed her right through the war until she could rejoin her husband at the end of 1918. They quite soon went to Germany, suffered during the years of depression in that country and then, being a jew, Oppenheim was sent to a concentration camp, where he died.

## Ravenglass and Eskdale Railway 1914–25

Although Whynne had always been interested in the operation of 15″ gauge railways at seaside resorts and exhibitions, he had for a long time wanted to establish a real, permanent miniature railway running all the year round. He and Procter Mitchell eventually heard of the Ravenglass and Eskdale Railway which in 1913, having been built in 1873 mainly for carrying iron ore and granite from the quarries to the rail head, had become derelict through the decline of quarrying.

Whynne, Mitchell and Henry Greenly surveyed the site and it was decided that 'Narrow Gauge Railways' (successor Company to Miniature Railways of Great Britain) should take it over, relay the track to 15″ gauge and institute a regular service for local residents and industry but more especially for the tourist trade.

It was the end of 1914 and already conditions were such that it was not feasible to build a locomotive specially for the Railway. However, in 1912, Capt. Howey had constructed a 15″ gauge track at his Staughton Manor Estate and for this had ordered from Bassett-Lowke the largest practical type of locomotive, a 4–6–2 'Pacific'. The model was designed by Greenly, and was put into service in 1913. However, Howey was only able to enjoy it for a relatively short time, being called up in the summer of 1914 and soon after landing in France was taken prisoner of war. Whynne wrote to him in Germany and made an offer which was accepted. 'Colossus' and a 'Sans Pareil' class 'Little Giant' were the first scale model passenger locos to run on the R & E Railway. The history of the railway is well recorded in a booklet issued by the Company now running it.

In all it was a most interesting adventure, but there was no hope of generating sufficient traffic to make it consistently prosperous and in 1925 Narrow Gauge Railways relinquished their holdings to Sir Aubrey Brocklebank who had supported the railway and was to use it for 30 years in connection with his quarrying company. This fortunate arrangement resulted in the railway being maintained until the beginning of the railway preservation era and the advent of Mr. David Robinson and the R & E Railway Preservation Society.

## Post-War Developments

The return to peace-time conditions at the end of 1918 presented Bassett-Lowke with a very different trading situation. Fortunately for the company the large consignment which Bing had been unable to despatch in 1914 was now sent on. Moreover Bing's were glad to start supplying again and canvassed for business.

Unfortunately little real thought had been given as to the future of the model railway market. Moreover the almost frantic buying of people released from the constrictions of war (Christmas trade in 1919 actually started in September) led to every kind and size of railway item being snapped up. This concealed the fact that, although there was a growing interest in model railways and therefore a good prospect for future trade, enthusiasts were more demanding with regard to realism, at the same time having less space to devote to the hobby. Thus smaller gauge railways were the real need. This trend had been partly perceived and catered for in the last three years before the war, but it did not influence post-war thinking as it should have done. In consequence, model railway goods were ordered from Bing in gauges 0, 1, and 2 with the result that substantial stocks of the two larger sizes built up and created financial embarrassment. Many items remained unsold for nearly twenty years.

The other main German supplier, G. Carette, had a rather unhappy ending. The proprietor was of French origin and in the early months of the war gave as much assistance as possible to his countrymen in difficulty with the authorities. This eventually put him in such a precarious and perhaps dangerous situation that he returned to France via Switzerland leaving the business in the capable hands of his partner, Paul Josephthal. However, conditions were so difficult that when in 1917 Josephthal was called up for service, the

business was closed down. Immediately after the war Josephthal and Whynne made contact and it was arranged that the press tools used for making Bassett-Lowke goods should go to Northampton, the purchase being partly funded by the transfer of some Bassett-Lowke shares to G. Carette. In this way, some of the items hitherto made in Nuremburg could now be made in Northampton.

However, the bulk of the small gauge items were still made by Bing. It was quite legitimate to trade with Germany but for several years after the Armistice there was bitter anti-German feeling and resistance to buying German products. There was public pressure for imported goods to be marked with the country of origin and a regulation was passed for this to be done. However, a number of influential businessmen, Whynne included, persuaded the Board of Trade that it was burdensome for traders to have to unpack every imported item in order to stamp it with the country of origin. A compromise was agreed whereby the mark need only be put on the box in which an individual article was packed. The result was that, as far as Bassett-Lowke was concerned, the German goods were sold away from their boxes or else the mark was removed from the box.

Apart from the anti-German feeling there was a growing demand for more realistic goods to be made in Northampton, generating more work and leading to a modernisation of facilities at Winteringham's.

It was also realised that the prospects for 15″ gauge railways were poor. The motor car was in the post-war period adopted by younger members of wealthy families as their foremost hobby. Driving a car gave greater thrills and more freedom than driving a steam locomotive. It became clear that the estate miniature railway was a thing of the past.

It was necessary, therefore to re-arrange the Northampton production set-up. The machine and erecting shop at Kingswell Street became quite uneconomic and it was decided to close this down. Two of the employees, Braunston and Walters who had considerable experience at building steam models decided to set up in business to supply Bassett-Lowke with model locomotives in all sizes up to 10¼″ gauge and any other steam models that might be required. Whynne agreed to take all their output – and this arrangement continued until the outbreak of the Second World War.

Winteringham's problem was more difficult to resolve. Hitherto, the entire production had been for Bassett-Lowke, but it was obvious that this restriction could not be satisfactorily continued. George Winteringham was an idealist who wanted only to make high quality model railways preferably in Gauge 2. Mackenzie was a pragmatist who considered that quantity production in the lower price range of all kinds of toys and models would provide a valuable and more secure trade range. He wanted to discontinue all specialist work such as exhibition ship models and take on only those jobs which could be done in a strictly engineering situation.

Ultimately it was agreed that Winteringham's would continue to make all Bassett-Lowke model railway goods, a range of small model boats and other items which could be produced in quantity. Also they would continue to make models to special order if they were of a kind which would be suitable within the revised work scheme. For their part Winteringham's wanted a free hand to produce any such goods which they felt could be successfully sold to the trade in general – direct and not through Bassett-Lowke. Exhibition model work, production of ships' fittings, hulls and other parts were to be phased out. The Winteringham toy range was to be marketed under a label W̵N which, to some suspicious minds constituted a copy of a label used for a time by Bing of Nuremburg, W̵ representing Bing – Werke.

## Ships Models, Ltd.

The problem for Bassett-Lowke in the new scheme of things was that there would be no provision for making high-class ship models, although Whynne felt these would be much in demand given the amount of ship building needed to replace the many fine ships lost during the war. Strangely enough it was not Whynne who solved this problem, but his partner Harry Franklin, who had been almost a silent partner during the company's 20 years.

In 1921 Harry decided he would set up a little independent business, which was called 'Ships Models', to make all such models and any other products entirely for Bassett-Lowke. He advertised for a ship model maker in the Sunderland area where there were several small model firms supplying the local yards. He attracted a very skilled man, George Shaw, to come to Northampton and take charge of the work. George was a competent and very quick metal worker but was

weak on woodwork. Harry engaged two or three men who had been in Winteringham's model ship department, including Percy Claydon who was similarly skilled in woodwork. This made an ideal set up because both men were keen and anxious to succeed.

A workshop was set up in Kingswell Street only a few yards down the road and on the same side as the Bassett-Lowke offices and warehouse. One of the earliest orders was for the Blue Star Line where, perhaps only coincidentally, a cousin of Whynne's was in an executive position. The quality of work was impressive, however, and the styling of the glass cases was more imaginative than was the case with Sunderland productions. Orders quickly followed from the White Star Line, the Royal Mail Steam Packet Co., Cunard Line and others, so that the steady stream of work got the new Company under way.

The new set up seemed to solve most of Bassett-Lowke's problems. They had now no direct responsibility for any manufacturing, and yet there were various separate organisations on hand all anxious to supply and maintain the high standards of quality for which Bassett-Lowke had become renowned.

Nevertheless, there remained a certain problem in connection with Winteringham's. Whereas Bing and Carette in pre-war days were quite prepared to accept orders for short 'trial' quantities, Winteringham's needed to have long runs if prices were to be kept at a reasonable level. Another new factor was that in 1920 Meccano Ltd. launched Hornby Trains making the field much more competitive than hitherto.

## Edinburgh and Manchester Shops

Bearing in mind the new situation, it seemed necessary to establish as many good retail outlets as possible. The connection with Hull in Birmingham, Salanson in Bristol, Bond of Euston Road and others continued. Mr. Malaret was back in business in Paris, and it is interesting to see that an announcement in the booklet reprint of *Model Engineer* articles entitled *The War Work of Bassett-Lowke Ltd.* listed the Company's addresses as London, Paris and Northampton! However, it was still difficult to sell goods in the higher price range to toy shops and toy departments of the big stores (model shops were not then in existence generally). A decision was made to open branch shops in the larger towns and cities.

It took some time to take the first step, but in 1922 it became known to Bassett-Lowke that Mr. Young, whose premises at No. 5 Frederick Street Edinburgh carried the title 'The Model Workshop' and who had regularly taken small supplies of Bassett-Lowke goods, was 'financially embarrassed'. He welcomed the approach from Bassett-Lowke and an arrangement was made that he should manage the new Bassett-Lowke Edinburgh Branch. An experienced Bassett-Lowke employee, James Walker, was sent up to be his assistant. 'Hookey' Walker had the dubious reputation of being the most widely employed member of the Bassett-Lowke staff, having been first engaged in London to work at Exhibitions, then in the London shop, transferred to the Northampton works for the duration of the Great War, seconded to the stores when peace returned, sent to the Edinburgh Branch and finally to the Manchester Branch when it was opened – only to depart, rather quickly, under a shadow.

At first the Edinburgh branch trading was good and it was considered that the premises were too small to provide for the anticipated future trading. Accordingly when, in 1924, a large shop at No. 1 Frederick Street became available the move was made. Unfortunately there was a strange and unaccountable fall in business, which resulted in 1930 in the Company withdrawing from Edinburgh and selling back the business as a going concern to Mr. Young.

The optimism generated by the early years of trading in Scotland meanwhile prompted the company to consider opening a branch in the industrial North West – either Liverpool or Manchester. In the event, suitable small premises were taken at 28, Corporation Street Manchester. The position of Manager was advertised and eventually Mr. Cecil B. Cox was engaged. He had no experience of models having gone to West Africa in his youth to be storekeeper for an English Trading Company.

The whole set-up of the new branch was rather extraordinary. To assist the Manager and to advise him about models generally 'Hookey' Walker was transferred from Edinburgh. Mr. Cox had not been well briefed at Head Office – except that he had been strongly exhorted by Mr. Franklin to 'make it pay'. After little more than a year Cox decided that, for reasons best not disclosed, Walker must go. He also came to the conclusion that the shop could never be run profitably if it offered only

Bassett-Lowke goods, for he considered that they were too expensive for the shrewd and careful Lancastrians. He demanded that he should do his own local buying and carry stocks that would have a quick turnover. Under threat of a closedown in the event of failure, he was allowed a free hand – with the result that bought-in items comprised nearly three quarters of the stock. Results were financially satisfactory and the shop never ran at a loss – even during the Second World War. However, the Manchester branch was never really a Bassett-Lowke shop in the sense that London was. There were no further plans for opening branch shops.

## New Winteringham Products

The Winteringham factory had to develop a range of products for general toy-trade. In steam, it produced a vertical steam engine and boiler more or less in line with German practice, except that the main parts were left in bright brass finish and therefore lacked the superior look which the commonly used oxydised finish gave the German products.

The first Gauge 0 steam locomotive was a truly horrible 'mongrel' which retailed for 10/6d (52½p). It had a single oscillating cylinder in the cab driving through gearing to the rear axle. It ran forward only. It was, altogether, little better than the '10/6d Dribbler' which Whynne had so scathingly criticised twenty years earlier.

The next attempt was remarkable in that it was the stepping stone towards the production of the very popular 'Mogul'. It was an 0–4–0 type with a 4-wheel tender whose appearance had more in common with a contractor's locomotive than a main-line runner. It was made partly from items produced with the Carette tools, but the new Northampton tools and jigs produced, amongst other parts, the double action piston valve cylinders which were the key items for all the later steam models. In every way, the cylinders were a copy of the German product – although in later batches the use of stainless steel for the piston rod and piston valve improved the performance considerably.

In 1925, came the most significant new production item – the 'Mogul'. It was not a case of simply producing one new locomotive. Although each railway group – L.M.S., L.N.E.R., G.W.R. and S.R. – had Mogul types they differed in style. Bassett-Lowke decided to produce one of each. To keep the cost of tool-making down to a minimum the four types were designed in such a way that the maximum interchange of components could be achieved. Nevertheless a considerable number of jigs, tools and moulds were needed in order that each of the four groups would be identifiable.

The Mogul project was very comprehensive, for it was further decided to make the four types in steam, clockwork and electric. For the latter two, entirely new mechanisms were introduced – and these also were of a standard of excellence greater even than any hitherto obtained from the Continent. The new series of twelve models was put on sale in the autumn of 1925, and in the 'A' (Model Railway) list published in November of that year was included a page of reproductions of three coloured photographs showing the L.N.E.R., the L.M.S. and the G.W.R. versions. These well-made, handsome models were priced at £5.5s.0d. each (£5.25) and were excellent value for money. The L.M.S. and L.N.E.R. versions were also produced in Gauge 1.

In that post-war period several manufacturers attempted to produce toys to replace German products, but the only steam locomotive made that could claim any degree of success was that made by Bowman. This was a gauge 0 4–4–0 tender type. In size it was rather over-scale but its general appearance as a British locomotive was very creditable. The remarkable thing about it was that it should have been designed without thought, apparently, for utilising many of the commercial tracks then on the market. This, and the fact that it could only run in a forward direction limited its popularity, but it was well and strongly made and quite well finished. Put on the market at less than £2 it was strong competition.

Although Bassett-Lowke sold a Bing 4–4–0 steam locomotive of much better proportions and with reversing motion, Bowman declared proudly that their engine was British-made – an emotive statement at that time. Bassett-Lowke decided that something should be done to take on this competition and so the 4–4–0 'Enterprise' came about. Although not to the extent of the Bowman, it was heavily proportioned, but of a more attractive style and somewhat better finish. That it could run for 40 minutes on one boiler filling in addition to being reversible made it wonderful value at £2.10s.0d. (£2.50) – and, of course, it would run on any standard track. Later a 4–6–0

version, the 'Super Enterprise' was produced to sell at £3.7s.6d. (£3.37½).

## Wembley Exhibition

1924 and 1925 were the years of the great Wembley Exhibition. There was an enormous volume of work in creating the wonderfully varied and striking Bassett-Lowke exhibits staged in pavilions of multitudinous styles. There seems to be no record of the total number of models used, but Whynne, who had visited, or been directly involved in, every big exhibition in Northern Europe since 1901 declared that nowhere else had so many models been used.

Bassett-Lowke benefitted very considerably, of course. The name and reputation of the Company was now so well known that enquiries for models poured in. The Ships Models department was engaged in making for the White Star Line, the *Majestic*, *Olympic*, and *Ceramic*, and for the Royal Mail Steam Packet Co., the *Ohio*, *Almanzora*, *Arcadia*, *Orca* and *Orduna*, amongst others. The C.P.R. Co. had a very large pavilion in which, on elevated shelving around the inside walls, a 2½″ gauge track was laid. Two trains, of the latest designs were run continuously during the long hours of each day. For the Whisky Distillers Association a large model was built to illustrate the series of processes involved in the production of this spirit. Architectural models included those of the town and harbour of Durban, South Africa, The Cardiff Docks of the G.W.R., The Hayes Works of the Gramophone Co., Horniman & Co.'s Tea Plantation, the works of The Salt Union Ltd. at Winsford, The Chloride Electrical Co. at Clifton and The Boots Pure Drug Co. at Nottingham.

All those and many other small individual models kept the various work sections in Northampton extremely busy.

Also in 1924 the magnificent Queen Mary's Dolls House (now housed at Windsor Castle) was completed. For this Bassett-Lowke and Twining made a number of items to the orders of such manufacturers as Rolls Royce, The Daimler and Austin Motor Cos. and some 33 other makers of household equipment and furnishing. Bassett-Lowke's own contribution was a model of a model railway set out on the floor of the nursery. On the oval track stood a locomotive and passenger coaches. There was a station – a replica of one of Bassett-Lowke's standard types – and some small

accessories. The Dolls House contained a wonderful collection of pieces of work by artists and craftsmen depicting all that was excellent in the world of the 1920s – and Bassett-Lowke could take pride in the thought that many items were made by their craftsmen.

For various reasons it was decided to hold the Wembley Exhibition again in 1925. In the main the composition remained the same, but one new feature in particular that involved Bassett-Lowke was 'Treasure Island'. Along the shore of the artificial lake surrounding the Island was laid a continuous track of 9½″ gauge. Although other models were put into service during the long season in which 150,000 passengers were carried, the principal locomotive was a Bassett-Lowke Atlantic type which was painted in Canadian Pacific livery and named 'Peter Pan'. In May, King George V and Queen Mary visited Wembley and there is a splendid photograph of them sitting on one of the passenger cars sharing the journey with a little girl who must, indeed, have thought herself to be in fairyland. This locomotive is still in existence and preserved in private hands.

## 'L.B.S.C.'

In 1924 a curious competition was staged at the Model Engineer Exhibition. It was the culmination of years of argument between Henry Greenly and 'L.B.S.C.' (the pen name of a regular contributor to the *Model Engineer* – L. Lawrence). Bassett-Lowke had always agreed with Greenly that for small gauge steam locomotives the best fuel was methylated spirit either for firing 'pot' boilers used on continental built locomotives, or for the Smithies-type used for Northampton-made high pressure locomotives. Greenly was also convinced that, given a large enough boiler to supply the steam and sufficient weight on the driving wheels, a spirit-fired model would give as much power as any other system.

'L.B.S.C.' argued that a miniature locomotive type boiler, fired by coal, was fast-steaming and could supply as much power as was needed to give maximum performance, as well as being more realistic. When letters to the Editor by Greenly and 'L.B.S.C.' were first published in the *Model Engineer* Percival Marshall thought that they were thought-provoking and interesting, as they gave many well-considered arguments and attracted correspondence from readers. However, when Greenly and 'L.B.S.C.' started to abuse each other, he thought it was time to call a halt and suggested that each should prove his case by a public demonstration at the next Model Engineer Exhibition. Each competitor was free to use any 2½″ gauge engine of his choice.

In the event, this freedom of choice resulted in a very indecisive contest, for the results in effect enabled both to claim that their model gave the most convincing performance. Greenly designed a handsome, massive 2–8–0 locomotive with three cylinders. It was made as heavy as possible to give the greatest adhesion. It departed from the usual Bassett-Lowke practice in that the driving axles were sprung.

There were two trials – the first being a time test. How anyone could make a comparison between the running time of coal and methylated spirit is difficult to see. The second test was load-hauling. The Bassett-Lowke locomotive, proudly named 'Challenger', hauled 476 lb equal to 2575 scale tons. 'L.B.S.C's' little Atlantic 4–4–2 engine hauled a lesser but still quite massive load. It should be noted that it had been made several years earlier and was not in any way special, having been regularly used all its life. In fact, its performance was *proportionally* better. Nevertheless, the recorded performance enabled Whynne and Greenly to claim a splendid victory – even though the arguments did not cease.

If only the talents of L.B.S.C., Greenly and Bassett-Lowke could have been combined, surely they would have produced a series of models that would have been unassailable for appearance and performance.

## Winteringham's New 'M.D.'

The situation at Winteringham's in the early 1920s was very unsatisfactory. James Mackenzie had re-organised production and, in addition to the Bassett-Lowke range, concentrated on making items for sale to the 'Trade' – toy goods, cinematographs and even radio receivers. However, it was not a success story. It may have been that Mackenzie, who was an engineer and had had great success during the years when the larger, engineer-built steam locomotives were made, had no heart for toy-making. Whatever the reason, after twenty years of great service he left the company and was replaced by a young man who, although responsible for producing the best standard commercial range of gauge 0 locomotives, now collectors items, remains practically

unknown – Robert Bindon Blood.

Bindon was proud to claim he was a descendant of the infamous Captain Blood of Crown Jewels fame and he did have a faint aura of the swashbuckler about him. However, he was well educated and trained in production engineering. He was also a most enthusiastic model railway man. He was in his mid-twenties when he took over Winteringham's management.

The first Northampton-made steam locomotive with double acting cylinders had been made under Mackenzie. The 'Mogul' was Bindon's first and most successful undertaking. In the ensuing 14 years he was responsible for the design and production of a series excellent gauge 0 models, starting with the 'Royal Scot' in 1929 and the 'Flying Scotsman'. These two productions were outstanding because, although the bodies were made from printed lithographed tin plate sheets (the pressed out parts assembled by being clipped together), the dummy cylinders and valve gear were true to scale in a degree never hitherto achieved. The retail prices were £3.15s. (£3.75) (clockwork) and £4.4s. (£4.20) (electric). Although the same clockwork motor was used as in the 'Mogul', a new and cheaper 'Junior Permag' mechanism was produced in order to keep the cost of the electric model down.

To launch the 'Royal Scot' a most remarkable stand was designed for the 1929 Model Engineer Exhibition. It consisted of a full-size replica of the front end of the prototype – comprising the smoke-box, front footplating, the forward portion of the cylinders and front wheels of the bogie – constructed from wood dummies and metal parts, such as the coupling, buffers, wheels, cyclinder front covers and the chimney.

The whole was mounted against a large backboard and stood on a short length of borrowed track. Supporting literature and posters on the backboard completed an impressive exhibit. Most visitors were amazed to see, from their ground level view point, how massive the steam locomotives of the day were. The gauge 0 model standing on the front footplate was able to demonstrate, by direct comparison, how accurate and realistic it was.

Bassett-Lowke had established cordial relations with Loftus Allen, the publicity officer for the L.M.S. and no doubt there was co-operation from the railway company in loaning the large metal parts for the replica. Furthermore, in pursuit of

publicity for both the L.M.S. and Bassett-Lowke, Loftus Allen arranged for a 'Royal Scot' to stop at Northampton (Castle) Station in order that the driver could be presented with one of the new gauge 0 models.

Of the two great rival locomotives, 'Royal Scot' and 'Flying Scotsman', the gauge 0 model of the former was more popular and sold many more than the latter but the reverse was the case with the 2½″ gauge steam versions.

## The B.D.V. Order

In 1926, negotiations were opened by Godfrey Phillips, the manufacturers of B.D.V. cigarettes, for the purchase of a large quantity of clockwork locomotives for distribution under their Coupon Scheme. By coincidence the quantity envisaged was the same as those taken by the Caledonian Railway Co. in 1910 – 30,000. The final deal struck was a very tough one – the model was to be a new design of the 4–4–0 tender type at a price to B.D.V. of a few pence over 10/– each.

The project tested Bindon's capabilities to the full. If one examines one of the locomotives it seems incredible that it could have been made for the price and include even a very moderate profit. A complete set of press tools had to be made, as well as designs for the lithography of the tin plate sheets. The clockwork mechanism followed the pattern of the German type and was the first Northampton-made unit.

The order had been placed on the assumption that the quantity would cover demand for at least a year. In fact the cigarette company found that their advance publicity created such a tremendous reaction that by Christmas it was obvious that the total requirement would exceed the quantity ordered, and a supplementary contract was placed. However, the whole enterprise was not financially beneficial for Bassett-Lowke Ltd. The price was very tight and even the utmost economy in handling did not produce a profit. The model carried the name 'Duke of York (His Royal Highness was a popular figure) and it became the first of a series. Later versions, with slight amendments to the body work, were entitled 'Princess Elizabeth' and, in 1950, 'Prince Charles'. In 1932 another such contract was completed for Kensitas with a similar quantity of the 'Princess Elizabeth' version.

## 00 Gauge

In spite of the comprehensive approach of Whynne and Greenly to model railways, they were slow to perceive the possibilities of the smaller gauge indoor layouts. It had not been until 1911 that a really positive programme of development for gauge 0 was begun. Prior to that time the emphasis was on the larger gauges reinforced by George Winteringham's particular leaning towards gauge 2.

However, early in this century, amateurs had already made quite small gauge locomotives approximately half gauge 0 size. There were as yet no standards and each individual effort was in effect an experiment. As the years passed more people became interested and Whynne pondered the possibilities of commercial production. It was not until after the 1914–1918 War that the opportunity arose. Bing's were back in business and were, by then, a very big manufacturing company producing toys, sewing machines, typewriters and kitchen ware. They were reasonably interested when Whynne proposed to place an order for a 00 gauge train, track and accessories. Greenly designed everything in conjunction with Bing's production team.

The result was that, in 1922, the first commercially made 00 range was put on the market. To look at the components now is to see them as crude and badly proportioned, but considering that they were made without previous experience in the days before plastics and miniature electronics they were quite marvellous. As developed over the following three years the range comprised nearly thirty different items, with clockwork and electric locomotives, passenger and goods vehicles, track and points, stations, crossing gates, buffer stops, telegraph poles and signals, and all at prices, even at that time, which were ridiculously cheap. Eleven boxed train sets were offered, commencing at 5/– (25p) and going up to 37/6 (£1.87½p). Unfortunately Bassett-Lowke's 00 did not succeed in holding the market. Perhaps if they had aimed for a true-to-scale system of better quality, it would have found wider acceptance and, indeed, have established Bassett-Lowke as the pioneers and leaders in the 00 market which is now the most popular size world wide. Nevertheless, the introduction by Bassett-Lowke of this Bing-made model railway stimulated interest and encouraged other English makers to develop their products.

## The B.L. Chairmen

Prior to the registration as a Limited Liability Company in 1909, Whynne had been on close friendly terms with Jack Sears, the founder of the True Form Boot Co. who supported him and gave much good advice – as, for example, in the opening of a London shop. His death in 1916 was a great personal sorrow for Whynne.

It is a curious fact that members of the footwear trade had much influence in his life. As a young man he was friendly with Frank Jones of the Crockett & Jones Co. – it was he and his partner James Crockett who accompanied him to Paris in 1900. Later, Whynne married Frank Jones' daughter, Florence. After Jack Sears' death, Edward Lewis, another footwear principal became Chairman of Bassett-Lowke Ltd. and continued in that office until 1927. At that point the pattern changed. For some years G. P. Keen had been a notable model railway enthusiast. He was wealthy and was able to embark on building a most comprehensive gauge 0 system, employing a model-maker full time. However, his project was so ambitious that he required to have much work done commercially. It was in this that he felt dissatisfied with supplies and services then available. He considered that the best solution would be to take a financial interest in a model-making company so that he could persuade it to make the things that he felt were needed by many fellow model railway men.

After one or two attempts which failed to provide the service he wanted he turned attention to Bassett-Lowke Ltd. and in 1927 became Chairman of both Bassett-Lowke and Winteringham Ltd. It was not a happy or lasting arrangement. There was a continual clash of ideas – Whynne and others looking at all problems in the light of their commercial experience while Keen acted mostly in furtherance of his amateur interest.

Nevertheless the period was not completely fruitless – it was he who was responsible for the introduction of Bindon Blood to Bassett-Lowke and his persuasion that brought into being the more true-to-scale aspects of the gauge 0 models subsequently produced. However, many of the things he introduced as Chairman were petty and irrelevant and the situation was generally unsatisfactory.

Frank Derry's son, Cyril, had become attached to Whynne, whom he greatly admired. When the situation was explained to him, he undertook to oust the troublesome Chairman and replace him, which he did in 1930. Cyril was not content, however, simply to be a figurehead and was determined to seek out and cure other problems in the little group of companies comprising Bassett-Lowke.

When Bassett-Lowke first started it had enjoyed the benefit of uncharged-for services and supplies from J. T. Lowke. When H. F. R. Franklin set up his Ships Model operation it received similar support from Bassett-Lowke and now, upon careful independent scrutiny, the inter-company accounts were found to be in a very dubious state – to the disadvantage of Bassett-Lowke. As a result the Ships Model operation was separated entirely, with its own accounting and buying arrangements, although it was still to supply its entire output to Bassett-Lowke. It was registered as a Limited Liability Company and from then onward all was well. The new Ships Models Ltd. incorporated several small departments such as the boiler fittings shop (to make those items previously supplied by Claret of Moulton) and the repair shops to service customers' Bassett-Lowke models.

## A Märklin Interlude

In the early 1930s there was a period of trading with Märklin of Germany. Whynne always had an affinity with the Germans – he much admired their business methods and, generally speaking, the quality and good value of their work.

At that time owing to the rise of the Nazis in Germany it became increasingly difficult to trade with Bing, who was Jewish, and it was thought that Märklin might be able to supply locomotives to Bassett-Lowke specification in the same way that Bing had for so many years. Several of their English style locomotives in gauge 1¾″ had been marketed in a small way by Bassett-Lowke and Märklin indicated they would be interested in producing some gauge 0 designs.

An interesting feature of Märklin production was the electric mechanism. This had a wire-wound field motor which incorporated a small rectifying unit, enabling it to be reversed by a polarity change-over switch in the same way as a permanent magnet motor. The advantage was that it was much more powerful than the permanent magnet motors of that time. A disadvantage was that the working voltage was 20 A.C. as compared with the 6 to 8 volt D.C. systems then in use in this

country. However, Märklin supplied a very neat controller-rectifier unit for use with a transformer to provide for operation from A.C. house mains. The English-made rectifiers at that time were still very expensive and so the German system had the benefit of being highly competitive.

Whynne decided to go ahead and from Greenly designs Märklin produced several locomotives – the S.R. 'Schools' class, the G.W.R. 'King George the Fifth', an L.M.S. 4–6–0 and a 2–6–4 tank. The bodywork was very well made and the finishing excellent. However, the Märklin motor design was such that it was necessary to use smaller than scale diameter wheels. The result was that the models had a 'high-waisted look' and this completely spoiled their appearance. Many were brought in as bodies and then fitted with Bassett-Lowke units.

At Winteringham's the challenge was solved by improving the permanent magnet motor and introducing a series of hand-assembled and finished models that set the highest standard for commercially produced locomotives. In addition the patent rights on rectifiers were running out and the era of the lower priced rectifier-controller began.

The period of co-operation with Märklin was, therefore, interesting but short lived.

## Changes of Address

In 1931, Winteringham Ltd. moved from the St. Andrews Street premises to a more modern building in Stimpson Avenue providing additional working space and better general conditions for production work. Bassett-Lowke moved from Kingswell Street to St. Andrews Street since the two buildings formerly occupied by Winteringham's gave good office and stores accommodation.

Twining Models considered they needed more space than the 'studio' in the Kingswell Street yard and they also removed to premises in Pike Lane. During the years up to 1939 a number of very beautiful models, including locomotives, were made by Twining – some to the order of Bassett-Lowke, others direct to customers, since Twining continued to be as independent as possible.

In the various rearrangements at Bassett-Lowke in the 1930s, Waterline Models continued to be independently produced under Denton and Checker, but after the Second World War when they were too old to carry out such detailed work, this speciality was discontinued.

## Garden Railway Locomotives

The Bassett-Lowke Company as established in the early 1930s continued without any major developments. The larger gauge passenger carrying 15″ gauge railway was an uneconomic proposition and the largest steam locomotive was the 9½″ gauge 2″ scale model of the G.N.R. (L.N.E.R.) 4–4–2 'Atlantic' which was first introduced in 1910. It was a very practical model and good value for money at about £450. Models were supplied to Sir Edward Nicholls for his estate at Littleton Park and the Maharajahs of Jodhpur and Patiala, and others. The 7¼″ gauge L.N.W.R. (L.M.S.) 'George the Fifth' was a useful model of which about fifteen were built between the wars but it was not really powerful enough for efficient passenger carrying. Price £250.

In 1933 an American client, Norvin Rynek of Pennsylvania, ordered a 7¼″ gauge model of the 'Royal Scot' – inspired by having seen the famous original when it toured the United States.

The opportunity to introduce a new model in the Bassett-Lowke range was welcome and Henry Greenly was asked to prepare drawings. A curious situation arose – Whynne, having promised quick delivery, pressured Braunson & Walters to get the work in hand. Greenly supplied drawings sheet by sheet as they were done, but Braunston & Walters were in advance of them once the main details were in their hands. In consequence, Greenly found it unnecessary to provide a complete set. The drawings remained incomplete until twenty years later, Greenly's daughter and her husband, Ernest Steel, made many additional drawings to finish the sets.

The first model was both handsome and efficient – a second was completed and shown in the London shop window. Drawings and castings were offered for sale – and from the 300–400 sets sold in the years to 1965 there must have been a number of amateur built models made.

After the Second World War no more were built by Bassett-Lowke. There were two orders – one for a customer in Venezuela – but the first of these was built for Bassett-Lowke by a small engineering company at Thame, the second by David Curwen who had followed Bassett-Lowke's practice of building passenger carrying railways and operating them at popular resorts. The pre-war models sold for £500 each.

Very few 1″ scale 4¹³⁄₁₆″ gauge models were made, the most notable being the G.W.R. 4–6–2 'Great Bear' for Sir Berkeley Sheffield in 1925. Most of the models built in this size were for publicity purposes or for museums since the scale proportion was so readily understood by the public.

3½″ gauge (¾″ scale) and 3¼″ gauge (¹¹⁄₁₆″ scale) models were more popular because they were suited for running in the average garden, although they were not really capable of serious passenger carrying service. It is curious that Bassett-Lowke persisted in building locomotives to ¹¹⁄₁₆th scale for 3¼″ gauge for quite a long time after it had been generally ousted by ¾″ scale. A popular type, of which about thirty were made, was the L.N.E.R. 'Flying Scotsman'. With few exceptions all the models produced were spirit fired with Smithies type boilers.

It was in 2½″ gauge (½″ scale) that the greatest numbers of high pressure steam locomotives were built in the interwar period. Again, with few exceptions, they were spirit fired with Smithies boilers. Except for a chubby 0–6–0 tank which sold at £18.18s.0d. (£18.90) undoubtedly the most popular engine was the 'Flying Scotsman' at £72.10s.0d. (£72.50) – this despite the fact that it was made with a parallel instead of tapered boiler and was thus not a good model. Among the series of types offered the next most appealing was the L.M.S. 'Royal Scot'. More than one hundred and twenty 'Flying Scotsman' and about eighty 'Royal Scots' were sold with other types being made in much lesser numbers.

Although gauge 2″ was perpetuated through Bing's production of a 4–6–0 tender locomotive in steam and a 4–6–2 tank (clockwork and electric) in L.N.W.R. and G.C.R. style, the size was virtually discontinued. Existing gauge 2 customers were provided for by widening the wheel spacing of suitable gauge 1 locomotives and rolling stock.

It is interesting to consider whether, if the production of gauge 1 models had been abandoned and concentration applied to gauge 0 and the development of gauge 00, the fortunes of Bassett-Lowke would have been better. However, perhaps because of the influence of such enthusiastic users such as Victor Harrison, of the famous stamp printing company, who built an extensive outdoor system, production of the larger gauges continued with several excellent locomotives by Bing. Sales were slow and getting slower every year mainly because so many people simply had not sufficient space for an indoor gauge 1 layout.

An attempt to stimulate sales by encouraging the building of layouts in the garden brought about a series of interesting 'mongrels'. Excepting in still, warm conditions the ordinary low-pressure steam locomotives, as made by Bing were not suitable for outdoor use. The first attempt was made with a gauge 1, G.W.R. 'Titley Court' 4–6–0 tender locomotive by Bing. The low pressure boiler was replaced by a 'Smithies type' (a water tube boiler about ⅝″ in diameter less than a dummy outer casing). The cylinder lubricator was taken from inside the smokebox and a large displacement type mounted on the running board alongside the boiler. A four burner wick-type spirit lamp replaced the original vapourising lamp and this was fed from the tender, which had two compartments, one for methylated spirit and one for water. A hand force pump in the tender enabled the boiler to be topped up as required.

As against the 15 lbs pressure of the Bing boiler the Smithies worked at 45–60 lbs, giving much greater power. The conversion was successful and over several years some sixty to seventy suitable locomotives were rebuilt – usually to order. Apart from giving a successful performance the advantage was that the total cost of a converted model was only about half that of an orthodox high pressure production.

Despite these and other promotional efforts, gauge 1 became less and less popular leaving gauge 0 to take the field. In this latter gauge, Bassett-Lowke could nevertheless claim that their series of locomotives and rolling-stock produced from 1930 until the outbreak of war in 1939 offered the best quality and style at remarkably low prices. Other individual model makers produced finer scale models, but those made by Winteringham for Bassett-Lowke were unequalled for appearance, performance and price. It should not be forgotten, however, that Frank Hornby's Meccano company was a worthy competitor from the 1920s onwards.

Thus compared with the pre-First World War years, the activities of the Company from 1919 onward were relatively more restricted and less dynamic. No locomotives larger than 9½″ gauge were built until 1938 when the 10¼″ gauge 'Royal Scot' was made for the Marquis of Downshire, and there were no passenger carrying railway projects other than that for the 1925 Wembley Exhibition. There is no record of the number of 9½″ gauge Atlantics

made, or of the 7¼" gauge 'George the Fifth' which was followed by the 'Royal Scot' in the same gauge, but it can be reasonably estimated that between the wars, no more than 14 Atlantics, 15 'George the Fifth's and 8 Royal Scot's were made, with prices at £450, £250 and £500 respectively, plus the cost of installing track.

There is little doubt however that Bassett-Lowke's reputation for making model railways brought them a contract that was not for a model. The promoters of the Irish Hospitals Sweepstake were very concerned that the public should be assured of the strict impartiality and fairness of the draw, which was carried out in public.

In 1931 it was decided to have a track of about 7¼" gauge in the form of a figure of 8, with points operated in such a way that the several four-wheel vehicles carrying drums of tickets would, when being pushed round by their decorative Colleen attendants, arrive at the position where a ticket was to be drawn in random and unpredictable order.

When tried out some derailments occurred because it was not allowed to fasten the track down. The promoters had insisted that they could install with their own labour, but, in the event, two men made a hurried trip to Dublin the day before the draw and worked overnight to counter the 'springiness' of the track which caused the trouble. All was well on the day, but it was not as effective as hoped and other methods were used in succeeding years.

## Ships Models Developments

The Ships Models company, formed in the early 1920s, was anxious to produce the widest range of models. Winteringham continued to make some small power boats in steam, clockwork and electric drive from 18" to 24" long and a 39" long steam powered T.B.D. They were, however, simple, even crude, being designed for sale generally through the toy trade. Harry Franklin considered that a better quality range would be more suited for Bassett-Lowke trade. He accordingly engaged E. W. Hobbs, the former London Manager, who was then a 'freelance', to design six ship models all to the standard length of 60 cm. Each was to be individually boxed in a portable wood case, and it was hoped that their style and detail would attract many customers who were looking for better quality.

The decision to make all six types the same length was unfortunate. Although wide-beamed boats such as the Tug and the Lifeboat were successful, the models of big ships – the Cross Channel Packet and the Exploration ship – were so narrow at the 60 cm length that they rolled badly. It was a pity because they were beautiful little models, being finished with the same quality fittings as exhibition models. There was a revision of sizes and, with the addition of two more types, they remained in production until 1939. Other models were made to a standard length of one metre (Hobbs was very keen to use metric sizes). The most popular were a T.B.D., and various liners of the period – the *Doric* (White Star) the *Arandora Star* (Blue Star), the *Mauretania* (Cunard) and *Asturius* (R.M.S.P.). All these were supplied in polished wood carrying cases, but another metre length model, designed by P. F. Claydon, was packed only in a stout cardboard box. This was *Streamlinia* a stylish looking but plain Cabin Cruiser powered by steam. It was a most popular product and very good value at nine guineas (£9.45). In all between four and five hundred were sold.

Ships Models gathered under its wings the boiler fittings unit created by Claret of Moulton and the repairs shop. These were well-equipped metal working shops different from the metal shop in which the ship fittings were made and also capable of heavier work. Apart from the boiler fittings numerous steam items were produced – engines and boilers, blowlamps, complete stationary steam plants, and traction engines.

Altogether Ships Models was well able to undertake almost any kind of work, and with Shaw and Claydon both being quick and very accurate craftsmen the pace of production was rapid – enabling some quite extraordinary feats to be undertaken. An example of this occurred in 1930.

In that year the Canadian Pacific put into service the new and magnificent luxury liner *Empress of Britain*. As part of the general publicity it was decided, very late in the day, to have a 'float' in the Lord Mayor's Show carrying a large model of that ship.

From the time the order was finally placed there were just three weeks in which to construct the 21′ long Waterline model. It was not intended that it should be a finely detailed exhibition style replica. Nevertheless, in order to portray the prototype satisfactorily a very considerable number of deck and superstructure fittings, porthole rings, anchors, lifeboats and davits were necessary. The hull was constructed with plywood secured to hardwood frames. Smaller superstructures were carved in solid wood while larger units were made, like the hull, in plywood secured to hardwood 'skeletons'.

In order to complete in time it was a case of 'all hands to the pumps' but even so considerable overtime hours were worked. In the second week, to ensure that progress was well forward, five men engaged on the assembly were paid for forty hours overtime – and that was in addition to the standard week of 48 hours. When finished, the model was mounted on a colourfully decorated lorry and attracted considerable attention.

## Model Cabins

By the end of the 1920s many shipping companies found that they had a surplus of passenger capacity on their usual runs. Several turned their attention to the holiday trade and 'cruising' became very popular. Amazingly, shipping companies found that the majority of possible customers were under the impression that life on board was still in the 'hammock and mess deck' era. It was difficult to persuade by description and so, for their main booking offices they commissioned Bassett-Lowke models of ships' cabins in ⅓ or ¼ full size. These splendid reproductions showed furniture and furnishings which equalled that of a good class hotel and did much to increase the popularity of this exciting vacation which took thousands of people to ports in the Baltic and the Mediterranian.

Principal customers were the Royal Mail Steam Package Co., and the Blue Star Line, but when the *Queen Mary* was built for the Cunard Company, much use was made of models showing the various facilities (swimming pools, restaurants etc.) in addition to actual cabins. Canadian Pacific had also used this form of publicity when *Empress of Britain* went into service.

## The Advent of the 'Wireless'

The inter-war years were difficult for commerce generally but a setback of surprising significance to Bassett-Lowke was the advent of the 'wireless'. When the B.B.C. first commenced broadcasting the effect was not considerable because most listening was from crystal sets through headphones enabling only one member of the family to 'listen in'. However, developments were rapid and very

soon valve sets with loud speakers became generally available at moderate prices. This was the beginning of family entertainment.

It is difficult for anyone not of that generation to understand how restricted were the opportunities for entertainment before radio. Apart from home-produced music the sources were limited to the bands playing in the park and the music and concert halls, with other special events occasionally organised. Theatres, like the music halls could only be experienced infrequently because of the cost. Suddenly the world of music and varied entertainment was available to all the family at the annual cost of only a few shillings for the licence.

Equally suddenly there was a withdrawal from all kinds of activities in and out of home. Model railways and model making, like so many spare time pursuits, lost vast numbers of followers – and trade was severely affected. It was nearly two years before the novelty began to fade and business picked up – the impact on Bassett-Lowke as well as many firms was considerable.

The 1929 crash and all its ramifications led to belt-tightening at Bassett-Lowke as elsewhere and all employees were told that wages would be reduced by 10 per cent. This situation did not change until 1933–1934 when trade improved, no doubt as a result of the rearming programme being stepped up, stimulating business generally. The improvement continued until the fateful September of 1939.

## The London Shop between The Wars

After Hobbs left the shop in 1915, he was succeeded briefly by John Wills. Wills was unhappy there and F. T. Underwood who succeeded him was demoted in 1919. The new manager was H. C. Foreman. He had been in the accounts department at the Ministry of Supply and had on many occasions been helpful to Bassett-Lowke Ltd. by servicing their accounts for early settlement. He knew nothing about and was not really interested in models, and therefore had to rely on the staff having knowledge and enthusiasm.

Herbert Sell had volunteered for army service in 1915 and was injured and invalided out of the army at the end of 1916, when he returned to the London shop. His brother, George, had been transferred to Northampton in 1915 to work on gauge-making in the Winteringham factory. He came back to London in 1919 to work under the

new manager. Underwood decided to leave and in 1920 the shop boy, Roland Fuller who had joined in 1917, was promoted to a salesman. The total staff thus comprised the Manager, three salesmen and a newly engaged packer and storekeeper.

The inter-war years saw the London shop suffering various vicissitudes. There were periods of intense activity and, of course, every Christmas period brought several frantic weeks trading. At all times, however, there was a flow of interesting visitors who were not necessarily customers but wished to visit the famous shop. The atmosphere seemed to persuade most of them to become quite expansive about themselves and their various interests. There were many famous people and colourful personalities such as the Indian Rajahs and members of the Siamese royal family, as well as many seemingly ordinary looking people who in fact had the most extraordinary backgrounds to their lives or pursued remarkable hobbies.

There was not, in those years, the same intense activity that had been before the war. The only change in the shop interior was that a 20 ft long waterline model of the battleship *King George the Fifth* was supported high over the far counter. This made a tremendous impression on visitors. The shop window remained a great attraction with a section of gauge 2″ model railway covering the floor area, three tiers of plate-glass shelves carrying a comprehensive display of all kinds of Bassett-Lowke specialities and behind all this a quarter full-size Gantry Signal with illuminated spectacles. In the foreground was a stencilled shade for the 'foot lights' which showed the wording 'Model Railway Specialists', while in front it carried glazed panels, painted by E. W. Twining, showing an L.N.W.R. train along the entire length.

The window was framed by an artistic pelmet. At night when lit up the window display was most striking and, even before a time switch was fitted in 1927 to keep the lighting on until late evening, it was only rarely that no-one was seen peering in the window. It was not until 1930 that a new shop front was fitted. It was much plainer, and it was difficult to display the many items of the Bassett-Lowke range. The large signal was demoted to the back of the shop and the battleship removed. Outside the shop a one-sixth full size bracket signal was fitted – with the branch arm set to direct pedestrians into the shop.

Apart from the removal of the battleship the interior of the shop was only very little changed.

However, it was felt that the sale of Bassett-Lowke items alone would not attract sufficient business to justify the continuance of a London shop and so the basement, which since the war had been used for storage and packing of goods, was re-arranged so that the area at the foot of the stairs could be used for the display of bought-in goods. A nice selection of toys and some games gave a brave display, but despite some publicity and a free illustrated price list, the venture was unsuccessful. It had to be accepted that people came to Bassett-Lowke to see their specialities and were not likely to be attracted by goods that could be brought from any good toy shop.

However, the new sales area was not wasted, for in 1935 the new Trix Twin trains arrived from Germany – and it made an ideal separate showroom for this remarkable new production.

## Trix Twin

As in the case of the 1922 Bing 00 gauge railways, Whynne was the inspiration. Although the famous Bing company was having severe trading difficulties and had discontinued production for Bassett-Lowke, Whynne kept in contact with Stefan Bing, his son Franz and their partners Oppenheimer & Erlanger in a new venture trading under the name Trix. This new company's first product was an ingenious variation of the Meccano construction toy, consisting of perforated metal strips with many more holes giving greater adaptability in use. The most ingenious factor was, however, that the several basic sets could all be sold at 6d (2½p) thus making it a strong candidate for selling in the extensive chain of Woolworth stores which, at that time sold goods only within the maximum price of 6d. (Woolworths were proud to be known as the 'three-penny and six-penny stores').

The Trix company was, nevertheless, seeking other ideas and Whynne urged them to consider producing a 00 gauge railway system. Who originated the clever principle of two train control is not known – but unfortunately the opportunity to make a true scale system was lost. It was not surprising that the Germans should wish to continue the use of coarse, heavy flanged wheels to ensure trouble-free running on even rough track. It was not appreciated, however, that as the 00 railway was small enough to be used on a table top, almost perfect conditions could be created to enable the successful use of finer scale wheels and track.

When the first hand made samples were made, they were brought to London by S. Kahn (a Bing Company man who transferred to the new company) with a view to seeking opinions from the Bassett-Lowke staff.

It was agreed that, despite the rolling stock being modelled on Continental lines, it would sell well. Nevertheless, suggestions were made that the wheels and track should be refined in line with the proportions then in use by 00 gauge makers, both private and professional. Kahn would not accept the criticism, being quite convinced that the tried and tested heavy wheels were best. How different it all might have been. However, the voices of the critics were drowned under the waves of success – for when imported on a sole concession basis by Bassett-Lowke in 1935 Trix created a sensation and sales were enormous.

S. Kahn and Franz Bing were Jewish and life in Germany was very unpleasant for them. Bassett-Lowke, with his many contacts, was able to arrange for them to come and live in England. They set up business in the Clerkenwell Road and were able, through some intricate arrangements, to first import and then produce in Northampton an anglicised version of Trix with an L.M.S. 4–4–0 tender locomotive and 'Pacific' types in L.M.S. and L.N.E.R. both of which suffered from having to accommodate the some-what heavily proportioned mechanism.

Nevertheless, the unique control systems and quick layout assembly on a largish table led to considerable business. The association of the name Bassett-Lowke with Trix made a further impact. The result, as far as the Bassett-Lowke London shop was concerned, was a massive increase in turnover which, added to the business engendered by the first class series of gauge 0 models produced in the 1930s, established a profitable period that lasted until 1939.

## Management Re-organisation

Captain J. B. Lockhart was a model railway enthusiast and a familiar figure to the London shop staff as a regular customer. In 1936 he retired from the Royal Navy after a distinguished career, mostly in submarines. He wanted to follow some business interest and pursue his hobby – so it seemed an ideal arrangement to be involved in Bassett-Lowke Ltd.

Whynne was then approaching his sixtieth birthday and H. F. R. Franklin was planning to retire to his cottage at Radwell. It therefore seemed a good idea for Lockhart, on buying a block of shares, to join the Company as a Director-cum-General Manager, with a view to relieving Whynne of much direct involvement in the running of the business and possibly succeeding him as Managing Director in due course.

Lockhart bought a house at Duston just outside Northampton, where he was able to have a very comprehensive gauge 1 outdoor track layout installed.

The arrangement was a great success. Lockhart assumed control and was soon impressing everyone with his firm fairness and his grasp of the problems of the model trade. It seemed as if the Company was established for a settled future but fate decreed otherwise. The crisis of 1938 resulted in reservists being called back into the services. Lockhart was directed to a submarine depot in Scotland where he remained until, early in 1940, he suffered a fatal heart attack. Bassett-Lowke were back to where they were. H. F. R. Franklin had retired and so P. F. Claydon was appointed to be Director in charge of Ships Models, Whynne deciding he would have to continue his duties as Managing Director.

## 10¼″ Gauge 'Royal Scot'

It was in 1937 that the Marquis of Downshire first visited the London shop to discuss the matter of installing a passenger carrying railway in the grounds of his stately home at Easthampstead Park, near Bracknell, Berkshire. The Marquis's father had had a system on his estate in Ireland and now his son wished to emulate him. The 'Royal Scot' was favoured and 10¼″ gauge considered the most suitable size.

The site for the railway was not ideal as the ground undulated sharply and it would have been costly to dig cuttings and raise embankments for a continuous oval length of track. The layout finally comprised a single road track following an agreed level, with a return loop at one end. At the 'home' end points provided a facility for the engine to run round the train, whilst a well built brick engine house was sited at the track end. In this a winch raised a length of track on which the locomotive could be brought to an easy height for servicing. There was also a well equipped workshop bench.

Henry Greenly was commissioned to design the locomotive which was, in the main, a simple enlargement of the 7¼″ gauge model introduced

## TRADE DISCOUNTS APPLYING TO CATALOGUE SECTION "A" MODEL RAILWAYS ISSUED NOVEMBER 1937.

----------------------------------------------------

| Page | Description of goods. | Discount. |
|------|----------------------|-----------|
| 10 | G. OO Twin Trains. | 25% |
| 11-18 | G. O Locomotives. | 25% |
| 20-31 | G. O Locomotives. | 25% |
| 32-36 | G. 1 Locomotives. | 25% |
| 51-65 | G. O Rolling Stock. | 25% |
| 69-81 | Track Gauge O and Gauge 1 | 25% |
| 82-87 | Signals. | 25% |
| 89 | Signal Cabins and lever frames. | 25% |
| 91-92 | Stations and Buildings. | 25% |
| 99-104 | Water Towers, over-bridges and station accessories. | 25% |
| 105 | Buffer Stops. | 25% |
| 106-108 | Station accessories, lamps etc. | 25% |
| 109 | Batteries. | 25% |
| 112 | Controllers. | 25% |
| 113-115 | Locomotive mechanisms. Clockwork and electric. | 25% |
| 117 | Carriage and Wagon wheels. | 25% |
| 118 | Bogies. | 25% |
| 119-126 | Loco parts. | 25% |
| 127-128 | Coach and Wagon parts. | 25% |
| 129 | Loco parts and fittings. | 25% |
| 130-133 | Drawings. | 25% |
| 134 | Paint and oil. | 25% |
| | | |
| 19 | Gauge O locomotives. | 20% |
| 37-38 | Gauge 1 Locomotives. | 20% |
| 88 | Locking frame parts. | 20% |
| 90 | Colour light signals. | 20% |
| 93-98 | Stations and Buildings. | 20% |
| 110-111 | Transformers and rectifiers. | 20% |
| 116 | Point Operators. | 20% |
| 137-138 | Hand-books. | 20% |
| | | |
| 39 | Super-detail locomotives. | 15% |
| 66-67 | Super-quality carriages. | 15% |
| | | |
| 41-43 | Steam locomotives high pressure | 10% |
| 47-50 | Garden railway locomotives. | 10% |
| 135 | Repairs. | 10% |

The discounts quoted above are usually maintained but the right to alter them without notice is reserved.

BASSETT-LOWKE LTD., Northampton.

in 1933. Braunston & Walters built the locomotive, although the boiler was made by a specialist, Goodhand of Gravesend, Kent, who had supplied Bassett-Lowke with all the larger steel and copper boilers required from about 1923 when J. T. Lowke discontinued that work.

When completed the 'Royal Scot' was taken for steam trials to the 10¼″ gauge railway owned by Harry Franklin at Radwell in Bedfordshire. Adjustments to the water feed arrangements and the brake gear were shown to be necessary, but, with these made, a very excellent performance was given when the maiden run was carried out at Easthampstead Park in 1938.

The vehicles supplied were two passenger cars and one mineral truck which was to be used for carrying ballast when track servicing was required. The Marquis had ideas for extending his railway and having more comfortable rolling stock, but the Second World War stopped such plans. Eventually the estate was sold for building development and the railway was dismantled.

## Winteringham's, Ships Models and Exhibitions in the 1930s

Although Winteringham's and Ships Models were entirely separate companies there were many occasions when they co-operated in the production of special projects. The reason for this was mainly because Winteringham's had closed the woodwork section and were less capable than in the past of carrying out work 'on site', such as Exhibition installations.

One excellent example of this co-operation was the Travelling Post Office model made for the General Post Office and first exhibited at Radiolympia in 1934. It was a gauge 1 track layout, 120 feet long arranged for continuous running with 12 foot diameter loops at each end. One loop was mostly concealed in a tunnel. At the centre of the track was a double road station of modern design. At two positions 'ground gears' were installed for the picking up and dropping of mail bags.

There were two seven-vehicle trains which included the mail vans fitted with delivery apparatus for the dropping and picking-up actions. The two locomotives were the L.M.S. 'Royal Scot' and 'Black Watch' fitted with heavy duty 12 volt motors.

Such an extensive layout gave ample scope for scenic work and the inclusion of railway lineside

detail. The scale of the system was 10 mm to the foot. Winteringham's, with their expertise, made the trains, track and lineside equipment together with electric control apparatus. Ships Models made the substructure and all scenic work. They were also responsible for installing on site at Olympia and later at other sites in various parts of the country.

It speaks well for the design and workmanship that the trains ran an actual distance of 125 miles, and attracted considerable public interest.

In the years following the Wembley Exhibitions, a considerable number of special scale models were built, many of which were for display in Exhibitions here and overseas, but it was not until the British Empire Exhibition in Glasgow in 1938 and the New York World's Fair of 1939 that really outstanding contracts came to hand.

For Glasgow the four Railway Groups decided to combine their display in one large pavilion, the main feature to be a gauge 0, 4-track model railway on which the famous trains of all the groups were to run. The full length replicas of the 'Cornish Riviera Express', the 'Southern Belle', the 'Royal Scot' and the 'Flying Scotsman', with other named trains made a very impressive and popular display, which was created by Bindon Blood.

Another exhibition model came about as the result of a meeting in Dusseldorf between Whynne and P. F. Claydon and representatives of the British Mining Federation. The purpose of meeting there was to see a large model of a coal mine, because the Federation wanted an even larger and more impressive one to be made for their Glasgow pavilion. In answer to the question 'could it be done in time' the answer was 'yes', and much toil, sweat and overtime was devoted to the work. The ¼″ scale animated model depicted all forms of surface and underground work then practiced in this country.

Strangely, Whynne showed little interest in those two massive displays with the result that very few photographs were taken. In contrast many were taken of the models which were to comprise the points of interest in a large mural display created for the Cunard White Star Co.'s exhibit at the New York World's Fair. The central feature was a half section model at ¼″ scale of the *Queen Elizabeth* which was mounted on a huge panel and framed by detailed reproductions to the same scale of the ship's public rooms and of earlier ships of the Cunard and White Star Companies that had

made record Transatlantic crossings. The model attracted considerable publicity in New York, but it was largely wasted because the *Queen Elizabeth* did not go into ordinary service until after years of troop-carrying and other war time duties.

It was after the war when the *Queen Elizabeth* came to Southampton for its first overhaul and refit that Bassett-Lowke's were commissioned to make a model of the total machinery – for which purpose the ship had to have extensive examination – and a large number of photographs were taken by Whynne's brother, Harold, who was then a professional photographer.

## Other Realignments

In 1938, H. F. R. Franklin retired to live in Radwell, Bedfordshire where he had bought a house some years before and installed a 10¼" gauge railway. There was a re-arrangement of the shareholding and Bassett-Lowke now had Ships Models as a wholly-owned subsidiary. The trading name was eventually changed to Bassett-Lowke (S.M.) Ltd.

Winteringham Ltd. also began to change at that time. Trix Ltd. were anxious to secure control of the manufacturing facilities for production of Trix Trains and so share-holdings were re-arranged and Winteringham's was re-named Precision Models Ltd. There was a strong connection between Kahn and Franz Bing (on the Trix side) and Whynne and also a feeling of gratitude for the great help Whynne had been in their transfer to England. It was promised that production of Bassett-Lowke goods would continue to be given priority – but, as will be seen later, the promise was to Whynne personally and after his death conditions changed.

## The Greenly Episode

The long standing friendship between Whynne and Henry Greenly ended abruptly and unhappily in 1939. Despite his generally good humoured nature, Greenly was obsessed with the thought that his drawings and designs were being reproduced without his authority. It is something that happens to those who are prolific in their work and there is no doubt that he suffered more than most. However, it was unfortunate that he made an accusation in writing, which was almost un-doubtedly true, against one who would take the matter seriously.

Bassett-Lowke and Greenly came to know F. J.

Camm at the time when *Models, Railways and Locomotives* ceased to be a separate publication and was merged with *Everyday Science*, a magazine produced by George Newnes Ltd., for whom Camm edited various periodicals including *Practical Mechanics*. Bassett-Lowke became very friendly with Camm and in later years contributed a monthly article – 'The World of Models', under the pen name 'Motilus'.

Greenly was concerned at this time that his drawings were being published without due regard to his copyright, and the last straw was when Camm produced a pamphlet for Bassett-Lowke giving working drawings, photographs and a description of a 2½" gauge L.N.E.R. Pacific which was clearly a copy of Greenly's own drawings even down to the smallest details and dimensions of such items as the cylinders. The inescapable conclusion was that his work had been pirated. Greenly wrote to Bassett-Lowke expressing his concern and having got the matter off his chest, would have probably thought no more of it.

Regrettably, Bassett-Lowke, one of whose least desirable characteristics was to play off people against one another, showed the letter to Camm probably only for this reason. Camm, a quick tempered man, took the letter seriously, and in due course sued Greenly for libel. Bassett-Lowke did little to stand by his old friend, offering the rather feeble excuse that Camm had snatched the letter from him and refused to return it. Greenly prepared to defend the action but withdrew at the last minute when advised by his solicitors that his chances of success were less than 50/50. As a result Camm was awarded damages of £500, plus costs, and due to Greenly's financial position at the time he had no option but to go bankrupt.

He was much hurt by the event and at 63 his health, previously excellent, suffered considerably. Most regrettable was Bassett-Lowke's failure, as Greenly's long standing friend and business colleague, not to be totally loyal to the man who had created so many excellent projects for him.

Over twenty years later the last 7¼" gauge locomotive built by Bassett-Lowke Ltd., 'Winston Churchill', was constructed from drawings especially produced by Elenora and Ernest Steel, Greenly's daughter and son-in-law, and it is a tribute to them that this commission was carried out without any feeling of bitterness.

# The Second World War

The twenty one years of peace had seen varying fortunes for the company. It seemed by the late 30s that many problems had been solved and that the future was settled. However, 1939 brought about sudden and complete change. Almost immediately Winteringham's became totally occupied with sub-contracting work for Government contractors, so that production for Bassett-Lowke ceased. At the same time Trix was phased out.

Substantially increased contracts for Waterline models had been placed with Bassett-Lowke in the crisis period of 1938 and it was necessary to combine the Denton-Checker Waterline model unit with Ships Models to cope with the increased orders. During the whole period of the war there was a substantial output of models – mostly of a scale of 100 feet to the inch, but for special purposes other scales were used.

The enlarged Ships Models Ltd. very quickly became totally involved in work for the services, mainly the Admiralty. In the October of 1939 there was an urgent Admiralty request for a competent model-maker to be sent to Bath, taking handtools and other equipment, and to remain there to work on an unspecified project (code named White Rabbit). The craftsman was Joseph Nutsford who, on arrival, was sworn to secrecy and put to work on an idea developed from suggestions by Winston Churchill. Nutsford came on alternate weekends but would not tell anyone what he was making. He was away for nearly four months and then returned to his normal position in Northampton. It was not until towards the end of the war that he divulged the secret. He had been engaged to build a working model of a mechanical trench digger. Churchill was of the opinion, based on the experience of the First World War, that many lives were lost when trenches had to be dug in forward positions. The trench digger, which in model form demonstrated it could work well and very fast, was not put into full scale production because all too soon it became clear that this war was to be mobile and that the tank had turned trenches into death traps.

A somewhat remarkable decision was made to divert some production away from pure 'war work' when Coventry was so savagely bombed on November 14, 1940. Britain was in a low state of morale, and Churchill saw that people needed lifting with positive hope and action for the future. Fortunately the Coventry City architect had for some time considered a plan for the re-development of the City Centre. As a matter of urgency he was instructed to complete his plans and Bassett-Lowke ordered to give absolute priority to the making of two main models – one at a scale of 24 ft to the inch of the entire project and another, to a larger scale of the shopping precinct.

When completed, they were displayed in Coventry and received much publicity throughout Britain, doing much to support the Churchillian theme that although the days ahead would be long and rough, there would rise, like Phoenix, a new and better Britain from the ashes of war.

Ships Models which had previously only occupied premises in Kingswell Street had added to its working space by moving part of its activities to a workshop in a 'jitty' lower down the road, and was finally removed to premises at the rear of the Bassett-Lowke Offices and Stores in St. Andrews Street. For the first time, therefore, in 1941 the complete Bassett-Lowke and Ships Models operation was located on one site, leading to greater efficiency all round. Although the premises were old and not entirely suitable they served a good purpose until the final move in 1953 back to Kingswell Street.

Ships Models facilities were not suited for quantity production but with first class craftsmen in both wood and metal work, they were able to produce items which required top quality workmanship, such as the Observation mirrors and the mobile targets required for the Gunnery Training School.

Once the Germans controlled Western Europe they were able to evolve a system of attack on warships that was effective and disastrous in terms of ship loss to the British Navy. Broadly, the method of attack was first for submarines to launch a torpedo strike and then make a hasty retreat. This in itself should not have been difficult to overcome, as by flooding suitable compartments the ship could have been brought back to 'trim', and although lower in the water would still have been manoeuvrable.

In practice, however, it was evident that training in damage control had been inadequate and ships' officers often failed to select the right compartments, thus making the unstable ship a sitting target for the follow-up attack by dive bombers.

The R.N. Damage Control School decided that models would provide the necessary demon-

stration of the right or wrong procedure of flooding. Bassett-Lowke were required as a matter of urgency to produce a model warship, made in brass and with all compartments sealed off. Each section had its own flooding valve, so that by flooding one compartment the effect of torpedo damage could be demonstrated.

The model would 'list' and be shown to be sluggish in movement and manoeuvrability. Correct practice in flooding corresponding compartments brought the model back to 'trim' and, although lower in the water it was controllable enough to take evasive action if further attacked. Obviously the model had to be made so that all the buoyancy factors of the prototype were correctly reproduced. This called for very exacting work in construction as every part had to be kept strictly within limits of weight and space.

In use the first model showed positively that practical demonstration was much more impressive than 'blackboard' instruction. Other models, representing different types of warship were ordered, and contracts continued to be placed with Bassett-Lowke until the 1960s.

No sooner had the Germans forced the British retreat from Europe then plans for the Allied invasion of the Continent were started. It was recognised early on that, if a landing was successful the enemy in retreat would endeavour to hinder the advance by destroying bridges and blowing up roads and railways. An urgent requirement, therefore, was for a portable, easy-to-erect form of bridging to get the tanks, trains and other transport quickly over rivers, streams and shell or mine craters. An early design was the Inglis Bridge and, a little later, the Railway Bridge. To prove their efficiency it was decided that a model of each should be made. When demonstrated both bridges were acknowledged to be first class, but it became evident that their manufacture would require the facilities of first-class engineering firms and their assembly first-class trained crews.

Further consideration of the problems resulted in another design – the famous Bailey Bridge. Apart from being easily assembled in multiples so that it could be made suitable for supporting railways, the individual components were such that they could be manufactured in even the least well-equipped workshops. Furthermore the simplicity of assembly required that personnel needed much shorter periods of training. Overall it meant that production of Bailey Bridges could be spread widely and training personnel in assembly could be completed in less time.

As in the case of the Ingles and Railway bridges, a pilot model was made to prove the design. It was then decided to have a large number of models made by Bassett-Lowke so that training centres could be set up in Britain and overseas. The models were sent out as sets of parts in strong wooden transit cases – in essence rather like huge Meccano sets. There were basic sets, supplementary and pontoon sets so that every permutation of bridge assembly could be practised. The special bonus was that such training could be done in army huts protected both from the weather and prying eyes. Many hundreds of sets were supplied during the war and after, when it was possible to supply Baileys for civilian uses.

A curiosity arising from the order that Bassett-Lowke was issued with a licence to build Bailey Bridges – and as it did not specify that it was for models only the Company apparently had the right to build in full size.

There was, of course, intense concentration by Combined Operations Command on the ways and means of effecting the invasion of Europe. It was obvious that the greatest hazard would be to get sufficient personnel and equipment landed in order to overcome resistance during the first few days; the Germans having demonstrated how competent they were in overcoming coastal attacks. They would certainly have massive defence systems at all docks and harbours, and their expertise in mobility could bring substantial forces to any point selected by the Allies.

The answer to this problem was Mulberry Harbour – a wonderful system by which harbour units could be floated into position and sunk in the shallow coastal waters to form a huge sea wall surrounding a massive pier-head designed to facilitate the speed of loading and unloading of ships to the maximum. Again it was decided to have a Bassett-Lowke model made to illustrate the facilities. Further models were made in order that landing operations could be formulated and, in model form, practised. For this purpose models to the same scale of all sorts of British and American war equipment were made to ensure that everything could flow off the pier head without hitch.

At Arromanche, on the Normandy coast, a museum exhibits a number of Bassett-Lowke models, in particular the Mulberry Harbour, demonstrating the overpowering effectiveness of the Allied landing on that strip of the Normandy mounted.

Bassett-Lowke was justifiably proud of its war record and of having been entrusted with much work of a confidential nature, although these results were only achieved by much dedication and years of unbroken overtime working.

Aerial warfare, which was such a dramatic feature under British skies from June 1940, revealed the urgent need for a system of assessing the effectiveness of gun fire from the fixed guns in the wings of fighter aircraft. Camera Assessors were produced which assessed, from the films taken in the wing mounted S.45 cameras, the quality of marksmanship. They proved to be a valuable aid to the fighter pilots. Not models, of course, but instruments that required the skills of model makers to make.

The Ministry of Aircraft Production also contracted Bassett-Lowke to produce 'Mirrors-Observation'. These were used in conjunction with special optical equipment to enable a 'spotter' to calculate with some degree of accuracy the height and speed of aircraft.

Early in the War, German E-Boats became a considerable menace to shipping in coastal waters. They were small, high speed craft carrying powerful weapons and were ideal for 'hit and run' warfare. Being very manoeuvrable, they proved to be very difficult targets.

An equal menace was the dive bombing attacks on shipping by Stuka aircraft. These aircraft were designed to intimidate those being attacked – for which purpose, in addition to the normal loud noise of a fast diving plane, high pitched sirens were fitted and were started up when an attack was started.

The Admiralty gunnery establishment, H.M.S. *Excellent*, created special training centres for the purpose of making gun crews familiar with these particular problems and giving practice in combating them.

Metal models of E craft were mounted on motorised bogies running on model railway tracks laid in a tortuous course simulating the evading movements of an E boat when being chased. The trainee gunners were handling full size guns, but the ammunition fired was $1/8''$ diameter steel balls. It was remarkable how quickly gunners were able to anticipate the movements of their targets and score successful hits.

In the same building a cable way was mounted from a high corner downwards in direct line to the anti-aircraft gun. The procedure was for a model Stuka to start down the cable way simulating a dive bombing run and at the same time powerful loud speakers blasted out the terrible noise of an actual incident.

Again, the anti-aircraft gun only 'fired' small steel balls but in the generally dim light a beam directed along the line of fire showed up the path of the steel balls so that the crew could see how good or bad was their aim. The importance of this training was to familiarise the crew with the noise and menace of the attack to such an extent that they became able to concentrate enirely on defensive firing.

All the models and ancillary equipment for both training systems were designed and supplied by Bassett-Lowke.

## The Shops During the War

The effect of the war on the London and Manchester shops was considerable. As stocks were sold out no further supplies could be sent from Northampton. The Manchester Manager was quickly in action and organised several 'home workers' to supply him. He also began trading in second hand models and developed a repair service which gradually satisfied a considerable local demand. Mr. Cox, with two young assistants, kept very busy right through the war and the shop was only slightly damaged in the air raids.

The London shop was sadly affected because its trade derived almost entirely from people looking for Bassett-Lowke specialities and Trix. The staff was small, George Sell having left the Company in 1937. There was the Manager, H. C. Foreman, H. M. Sell, R. H. Fuller and a shop boy. At the end of 1939 Fuller was instructed to establish a workshop in the basement and to engage two young men to train them in the making of Waterline ship models. From this there was a gradually increasing output until the flow of new war equipment from the U.S.A. required that models had to be made to be distributed to Service units throughout the country in order to familiarise everyone with the novel and strange types of tanks and transport. On frequent occasions special items were made and delivered to Combined Operations Command.

Although the Northampton premises suffered no war damage and the Manchester shop was only

slightly damaged on several occasions, the London branch suffered considerably from bomb blast on many occasions. In September 1940 the shop front was blown in completely and much of the interior glass and stock was ruined. No attempt was made to replace the plate glass window but a plaster board front with a small glass window served well for a year. It was flexible and thus 'took' the shock waves. The small window was blown in several times but was easily replaced.

In 1941, when air attacks were less frequent and damaging, a rather amusing ply-wood front with three glass windows was fitted. It was painted in black and yellow (Whynne's favourite combination that became known as the company's 'racing colours') and was decorated with silhouette drawings of trains, ships and other modelling subjects. This window was also flexible and having three windows gave more room to display the sparse selection of models. The glass was only 'blasted' twice.

In 1943 came a glimmer of hope for an end to the war, and the dour application to the war effort was interrupted to give thought to the post-war prospects. Every month a meeting was held in Northampton to which representatives from the London and Manchester branches were brought in. There was much debate about the probable future trends and possibilities which helped considerably in the framing of a policy.

At that time also the first meetings of the Model Engineering Trades Association (M.E.T.A.) were held with the idea of encouraging co-operation between member companies and the adoption of certain standard dimensions for model railways. All looked promising for a more organised future in the world of models.

For Bassett-Lowke however, there was another matter for consideration – that of personnel. In Manchester it was not considered that an early re-arrangement was necessary, but in London the manager, H. C. Foreman, was well into his sixties and it was decided that as soon as the war was over H. M. Sell should replace him.

The position in Northampton was more difficult. Whynne was 66 and although he had no intention of retiring it was clear that he was approaching the time when he might be less capable of dealing with all sides of the business. He was, and remained, well and active almost to the end but in the last two years up to 1953 his memory failed him and it was an unhappy sight to see the

man who had such a brilliant mind become almost childlike.

Resulting from discussions at the end of 1943, when it was felt that there was no-one in Northampton elegible for such promotion, R. H. Fuller of the London Branch was invited to transfer to Northampton, when peace returned, to be General Manager and ultimately Joint Managing Director with P. F. Claydon. In 1945 he closed the workshop at the London Branch and commuted each week to Northampton until 1947 when a suitable property became available and he moved home to become a resident in the town.

The building at 112, High Holborn, of which the London Branch shop formed part had been purchased by the Borough Bill Posting Co. and as they were not requiring a shop premises they offered the second part of the double front to Bassett-Lowke. It was not ideal because without substantial work being done there was no way that there could be direct access from one shop to the other. However, Whynne was keen to have an imposing Branch and took the premises on a lease.

The intention was to use it as a display devoted mainly to Trix Trains, with a working display. As set up it was indeed most imposing. The opening ceremony on December 11, 1946 was attended by several Press representatives in addition to Percival Marshall, Editor of the *Model Engineer,* an old friend of Whynne, J. M. Maskelyne, Editor of the *Model Railway News* and C. J. Allen, author and expert on railways who had been a contributor to Bassett-Lowke publications for over 40 years. However, the difficulty of operating the second shop at a time of staff shortage became such a burden that the lease was not renewed.

There were two occasions when the company had pleasurable contact with the British Prime Ministers of 1945. In 1947 Whynne, who had not met Winston Churchill since 1913 when he opened the Children's Welfare Exhibition and his wife was a passenger on the Bassett-Lowke railway, thought that as a token of respect he would present to him a set of Waterline models of Allied Landing Craft, as used for the Invasion of Europe. They were to a scale of 25 ft to the inch and ranged in type from the small personnel assault craft to the large Tank Carriers, 21 in all. Winston Churchill was most appreciative and in return sent a box of his special cigars as a token of thanks. One of these still remains as a prized relic.

# THE SHAPE OF THINGS TO COME.

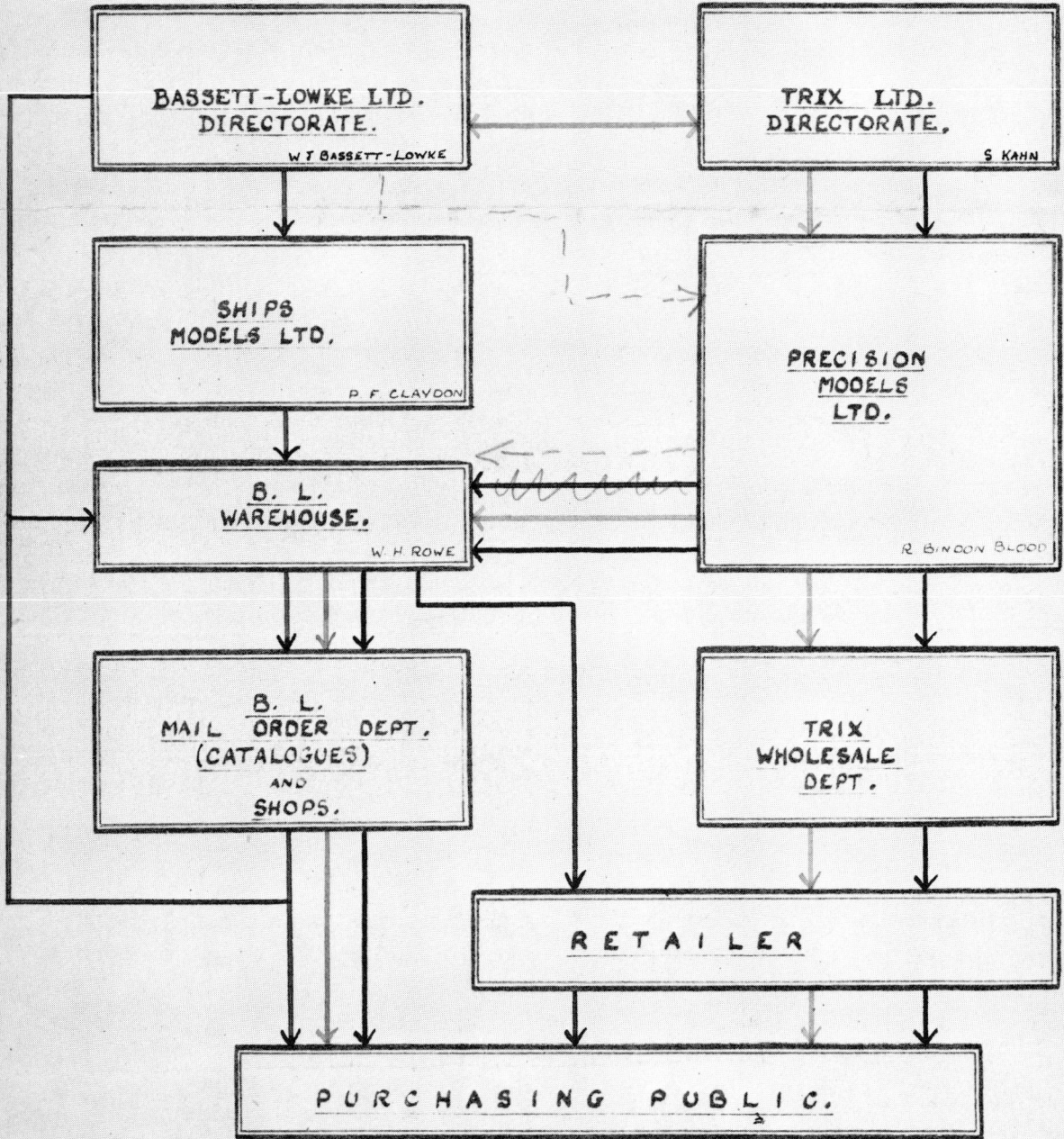

**BASSETT-LOWKE LTD. DIRECTORATE.** — W.T BASSETT-LOWKE

**TRIX LTD. DIRECTORATE.** — S KAHN

**SHIPS MODELS LTD.** — P. F. CLAYDON

**PRECISION MODELS LTD.**

**B. L. WAREHOUSE.** — W. H. ROWE

R. BINDON BLOOD

**B. L. MAIL ORDER DEPT. (CATALOGUES) AND SHOPS.**

**TRIX WHOLESALE DEPT.**

**RETAILER**

**PURCHASING PUBLIC.**

— Popular "O" Model Railways
— Super "O" Model Railways and other hand-made scale models, ships exhibition fittings and parts.
— Trix "OO" Model Railways

C. DERRY.
1945.

Later in the year, in the run-up to the General Election, Mr. C. R. Attlee and his wife were touring the country and, in the course of proceeding North, spent some time in Northampton. They visited Bassett-Lowke and although their time allowance was only brief they were so interested in all they saw and were told of the company's war time activities that they stayed for more than two hours.

The transfer from war to peace conditions was gradual, but conditions for returning to normal were most difficult. Scarcity of all raw materials restricted manufacturing severely and the frequent power cuts added to the problems. The bitter winter of 1946/1947 brought about almost total collapse – and there grew up a feeling that we had won the war but looked like losing the peace. Shortages of foodstuffs as well as other commodities required the continuance of rationing – which did not help morale.

## Post-War Work and Problems
An interesting series of models was made in the first years of peace. The Council of Industrial Design in conjunction with the Gas Council decided to illustrate various plans for houses and kitchens – an expression of the general feeling that a brave new world was to dawn. The models of kitchens were usually to a scale of 3 inches to the foot and the houses to a smaller scale.

The kitchens were very completely detailed with pots and pans to give an accurate impression of size. Houses were made to open out showing interior layouts, some being furnished or partly so to give the viewer a sense of size and space.

The models were displayed at the Ideal Homes Exhibition and other exhibitions in various towns and made a great impression on local authorities and general public alike. An early programme on the B.B.C., when television started up again, was entitled 'Models in Modern Planning' and these and other models were shown. Broadcasting was then from Alexandra Palace, to which Whynne went with several employees. Every programme was then 'live' and so it was necessary to rehearse very carefully.

This particular programme was timed for 9 o'clock and it was requested that everyone and the models should be on the spot at 3 o'clock. There were earnest discussions with the producers and other B.B.C. staff and 'trial runs', only broken by brief intervals for cups of tea taken wherever one

might be. At that time the equipment required powerful lighting which had to be placed near the subjects. The heavy cameras had restricted movement and while each section lasted everyone had to stand as still as possible.

The programme was declared to be successful and interesting but to the 'performers' the heat was almost unbearable – and it was agonising to see the necessarily thin material of which the models were made twist and warp under the intense heat. The performers, although bothered by the experience, soon recovered in the cool night air on route to Northampton, but the models required extensive treatment to bring them back to normal.

Whynne was an experienced broadcaster, having given talks on models on several occasions before the war on sound radio. When in 1947 Richard Dimbleby did a series of programmes from cities and towns in various parts of the country, he made a recording from the Bassett-Lowke premises, then in St. Andrews Street. This was Whynne's last broadcast, then aged 70, but being an habitué he made a lucid and interesting 'chat' feature.

## Ships Models Post-war
In the case of Ships Models the post-war scene was very different. Bailey Bridges, which played such an important part in the war were in great demand as 'first aid' bridging in much of the war-torn world. The makers, who were licensed by the Government to sell them for non-military purposes, found it expedient to offer model sets as part of their 'package deals'. Quite substantial orders came to Bassett-Lowke in consequence.

So successful was the Bailey Bridge in the war that the Government agreed to the development of a stronger version, called the Heavy Girder Bridge. It was for this that contracts for a large number of training model sets were placed with Bassett-Lowke – and this alone kept Ships Models extremely busy for nearly two years from 1951.

In 1948 the Cunard-White Star Co., ordered a model of the *Queen Elizabeth* as a companion to the ¼" scale model of the *Queen Mary* which was on display in their New York Offices.

This huge model, over 21 ft long and weighing 3½ tons complete in its glass case posed a problem because, although it could be made in the St. Andrews Street works it could not have been carried out owing to the rather restricted and tortuous access to the street. Fortunately there was

Below: Northampton Baths.
Bottom and right: Charts inspired and built by W. J.
Bassett-Lowke.

a disused Chapel in near-by King Street where all the component parts made in the works could be assembled.

For the hull a huge log of first grade West African Obechi was required and the timber importers, Mallinsons, had their agent select and ship a suitable one to their processing works where it was skilfully kiln dried and cut into planks before delivery to St. Andrews Street.

The process of building the larger ship model hulls involved cutting the planks to approximately the outside and exactly the inside shapes and then gluing and screwing them together. It is an arduous method, but ensured that the body would not develop a 'shake' or split as it might do if carved from the solid.

The complete model and glass case were packed in an enormous wood case bearing the proud announcement that it was a 'Bassett-Lowke model', and shipped to New York – on board *Queen Elizabeth*, of course.

A smaller model of this famous ship, at 3/16″ to the foot scale was made for the Clydebank builders, John Brown & Co. who added it to their model room, in which Bassett-Lowke felt very considerable pride, as it contained a number of their productions.

In the course of making this smaller *Queen Elizabeth*, the Prime Minister of Northern Ireland, Sir Basil Brooke with Sir Robert Grandsen and other members of his entourage visited Bassett-Lowke and very greatly admired the quality of workmanship. Mr. Bassett-Lowke took the opportunity to present a small 100 ft to the inch Waterline model of the ship in a neat glass case to Sir Basil.

## 50th Anniversary

1949 saw the 50th Anniversary of the founding of the company, and to mark the occasion, a booklet was produced which, strangely enough, was inaccurate in some details. It was written by a professional, George Holland, but Whynne insisted that he alone was to provide data and illustrations, and would not allow anyone to see the printer's proof. However, the errors have only minor importance and do not affect the real story.

The main 50th Anniversary celebration was a dinner at the Savoy Hotel in London at which Lord Brabazon was principal speaker. As will be seen from the details given in the Appendix many personalities came to pay tribute to the man, who,

by his untiring enthusiasm and artistic sensitivity established a reputation, both personal and for the company, accepted world-wide as representing a standard of quality and excellence of workmanship in model making.

## The Busy Years

With the gradual easing on the control of raw material supplies, it became possible to increase production substantially. Consequently, with a population still feeling desperately deprived, there was almost an immediate sale for goods as they became available. This was good for Bassett-Lowke. In addition, with the massive ship building programme in hand to replace war losses there was a boom in orders for ship models. This meant that the production capacity of Ships Models was devoted to special order work and, apart from a small amount of steam machinery and boiler fittings and the services of the Repair Department, nothing could be made for retail sale. It was fortunate that Precision Models were able to improve their output of Bassett-Lowke goods for a few years.

1951 was the year of the Festival of Britain – promoted by the Government to show the world that despite the ravages of war, Britain could display a very substantial scientific and industrial competence. It was a great pity that the political party in opposition did not co-operate, and secured the support of the Press in denigrating it in advance. Added to this the weather in the summer of that year was appalling and thus cut down the attendance.

All this did not affect the two years preparation work, and here, Ships Models became heavily engaged. Apart from some orthodox ship models for ship-builders' and owners' exhibits, there were some striking displays planned by the Exhibition design staff. In the shipping section was a 50′ long half-section model of a cargo ship showing the disposition of crew, machinery and cargo spaces. On the edge of an ornamental lake, poised as though ready for launching were quarter full-size models of stern ends of a passenger ship, a stern loading Whaler and a cargo ship. At the forward end the interior was revealed showing fully detailed layouts at the various deck levels. These massive models, the largest units ever made by Bassett-Lowke, made a striking and informative exhibit. The shells of the hulls were, in fact, too big to be made in the Bassett-Lowke buildings, and so these were constructed on the premises of A. Glenn & Son, a Northampton building company.

Generally speaking model-making is a straight forward practice of producing a replica, usually in miniature, of a massive prototype. It may be modified or simplified according to the client's needs – the one basic unchanging requirement is that the workmanship be of good quality and the reproduction true to the original.

However, there are occasions when the need is for the model to depict its purpose in life. If it is necessary to demonstrate active processes the customary type of static model will not serve the purpose. From time to time, Bassett-Lowke have been approached to give suggestions as to how such a model could be made, and contracts arising from such enquiries have led to some most interesting productions.

In the 1950s the Union Castle Company were having new offices built in Bond Street, concurrently with the construction of their luxury liner *Windsor Castle*. They wanted to devote a large window space to the new ship but felt that the usual static glass case model would not be sufficiently 'lively'. Bassett-Lowke were called upon for ideas and the result was a ⁵⁄₁₆″ to the foot Waterline scale model mounted on an animated sea. Portions of the hull and superstructure were cut away to reveal the fully modelled interiors – the Restaurant, the Captain's Day Room, various classes of cabins, the Nursery, the Laundry, the Children's Playroom, etc. All of these were fully furnished and human figures, passenger and crew, were included to depict the many activities on board. The model attracted considerable attention from passers-by. It remained in service for the lifetime of *Windsor Castle*, it being necessary, however, to change the dress of the passengers three times to keep in line with fashion.

In 1924, the Whisky Distillers Association had commissioned for display at the Wembley Exhibition a one-sixth full-size model of a (then) typical modern Distillery.

Then in the 1950s the first Distillery built this century was completed for the Distillers Company. It was a matter of some pride that the architect responsible for the design of the building had created an industrial structure which blended well with its highland setting. Two models were commissioned from Bassett-Lowke. One was an orthodox architectural model which faithfully reproduced the handsome stone building set in the sloping terrain. The only departure from strict truth was that a spread of scots pines were brought nearer than their true scale distance to act as a natural 'back drop' to the distillery.

The second model was required to depict, with some animation, the processes of whisky distillation. It was designed by Bassett-Lowke and consisted of buildings and the immediate grounds only to a much larger scale. Every piece of equipment was fully modelled, showing all stages of production from the intake of barley, through the stills to the locked containers in the Customs room and on to the cooperage.

To depict the flow through all these stages a continuous chain of bubbles was pumped through transparent tubing which connected all the units in their proper sequence. The front and rear walls of the main building were raised and lowered at regular intervals so that viewers had first a sight of the building and then of the interior.

These highly successful models were sent to the United States where they were on public display for a very long period. One feature that was given much publicity was the 'burn' from which it was stated that all the water used in the production of whisky was drawn from at Tormore. In the model this little stream was kept running continuously by a concealed pumping system.

By 1953, production was no longer restricted and customer demand was good. Precision Models were fulfilling their promise to Whynne that supplies of Bassett-Lowke items would be maintained and so, despite the shortage of model ship and boat items because of the total dedication of Ships Models to special orders, there was a sufficient supply of speciality goods to attract customers.

In September of that year Whynne died. What a sad approach to the end it was for him. For more than two years senile decay developed. At first it seemed like a simple failure of memory to be expected in an elderly person but soon he became almost childlike in his simplicity. During this time he depended entirely on the staff to support him in embarrassing occasions and was helped particularly by his secretary, Miss Molly Hardy, who loyally stayed with him until the end. All his life he had fought against the idea of being in bed so that fate at least was kind in so far that he was only confined for a few days.

Many obituaries were printed in technical and popular journals and newspapers, and there were

very many expressions of regret at the passing of a man who had established a marque of excellence in the field of model-making, apart from his outstanding record of sponsoring and advancing projects in domestic architecture and contemporary designing, plus active work in local politics and Repertory Theatre in Northampton.

For the company there was very little impact, since Whynne had been less and less effective in the last years of his life. Thus there was no change in activity, and the two people who had really been in total charge for a long time, Roland Fuller and Percy Claydon were nominated as Joint Managing Directors.

## Return to Kingswell Street

The position with Ships Models continued unchanged. There was still a considerable demand for ship and industrial models, but greatly improved facilities for production came about as a result of the move from St. Andrews Street back to Kingswell Street – in fact, to the site where the firm had been founded 54 years earlier.

The opportunity for this change arose from the termination of a 50 year ground lease which J. T. Lowke had granted to Bell & Co. (a manufacturer of grates and stoves and other ironware) in 1901. This was for land adjoining the house, No. 18 (which had been Abraham Bassett's home) on which stood some thatch-roofed stone cottages. The site was cleared and a four floor warehouse erected. In 1951 Whynne foreclosed the lease and took possession of the building. It was his private property but he agreed to give a 99 year lease to the company for the warehouse and the house and buildings at the rear.

A local architect, Harold Frost, was engaged and plans drawn up for development. The warehouse was to be used for the Ships Models works. Extra windows were put in, central heating installed and a new building constructed at the rear to be the erecting and paint shop. Considerable alterations were made in the house which became the offices, with a showroom and shop with window on the ground floor. At the rear a small extension provided an inner showroom in which a demonstration gauge 0 model railway was laid. Beyond this and parallel to the paint shop, a stores building of similar size was erected. The total cost was £15,000 which in the 1950s was a considerable sum, but it was a good investment since it provided such good working spaces for both the Ships

Models and Bassett-Lowke operations.

The work took nearly 18 months to complete but the buildings were finally occupied in September 1953, unhappily coinciding with Whynne's final illness. He did not set foot in the new premises, which was very sad, as he would undoubtedly have experienced great pleasure in seeing his various companies settled back on the site of their origins and in such greatly improved conditions.

## Industrial Models

A most interesting aspect of the model-makers life is the research which goes into each project. He must seek as much information about the construction and purpose of the prototype as possible in order to impart to the model the utmost character and authenticity.

The description 'Industrial Models' was usually applied to any model made to special order, for a company, museum or private client. It is not possible to list all here, but some are of special interest.

Bassett-Lowke made for Babcock & Willcox models of a number of their boilers, from the small portable to the huge High Head types required for Electricity Generating Stations. So complex were the latter, with actually miles of tubing assembled in complicated patterns that only a 3-dimensioned depiction could satisfactorily display the technical aspects of the design.

Hydro-electric programmes were being carried out in many parts of the world and several most impressive models were made for Companies such as Bovis, G.E.C., and B.T.H. They were of turbo-generators – massive installations in which the water turbine rotor with the generator armature of the prototypes weighed many tons and were suspended on single bearings. The speed of the rotor was controlled by a ring of vanes which could be adjusted to vary the rate of water flow. In the model the problem was that the support structure was required to be cut away in section to reveal detail of design, thus careful designing was needed in order to avoid any weakness of construction, as well as concealing the motor drive which revolved the rotor and operated the vanes.

Two quite interesting models of hydro-electric installations were supplied to customers in very contrasting countries – to Venezuela in the tropics and to Iceland in the arctic belt. Although different in many details they served the same purpose. In each case a large vertical panel depicted a section of hillside upon which a reservoir was modelled on the upper level and the generating station at a middle level. From the reservoir down to the generators, and on to the river at the bottom, the water pipe line was represented by a transparent tubing in which 'flow-lighting' was fitted. When the starter switch was pressed a recorded talk began to describe the construction of the installation and then, when it began to detail the operation of the generating system the 'flow-light lit' up to indicate the flow of water down through the generator turbine. The latter started to revolve and the flow of current along the power lines was stimulated by another form of 'flow-lighting'. In both cases the models were stationed in the main hall of the generating company's premises in order that interested visitors could hear and see the story of these modern wonders of engineering.

For the Kariba Dam Hydro Electric scheme, Bovis were the main contractors and justifiably proud of this enormous and difficult project. To illustrate the complexity of the system a contract was given to Bassett-Lowke to make a model of the dam, cut away at different depths of section to show the layout of the Turbo Generators and associated control equipment embedded in the massive concrete wall. One of the turbo generator motors was to revolve. The whole model was illuminated with concealed lighting and mounted in a glass-fronted wood display case, the timber of which had to match exactly the panelled walls of the Board Room in the Strand offices. It can be understood with what pride the Directors would have 'switched on' to show visitors the features of that enormous African project.

Messrs. Richards, Thomas & Baldwin instal-led a massive new plant for the continuous production of tinned steel plate – used by the canning industry. This was to replace the existing method in which individual sheets of steel were cleaned and tin-plated. It was a very complicated machine, with an electronic scanner to detect any blemishes in the plating and to have the faulty cut sheet rejected at the end of the processing. Despite this technical feature, however, a viewing point on top of the machine was manned by an experienced sorter who could also eject any faulty pieces. The Bassett-Lowke model which was static and mounted in a glass showcase, reproduced every detail of the prototypes, including the chair for the human sorter!

One contract lead to another. Thus Bowater placed an order for a model of their new and most advanced paper making machine, followed about two years later, by Reed's contract for a model of a very advanced plant for producing 'board' (thin card) used largely for food packaging. The models were similar in size approximately 12 ft long and most impressive in the extent of detail and the manner in which the processes were depicted. Messrs. Reed presented their model to the Science Museum, London, and it was a matter of pride for Bassett-Lowke that it was one more model of their make to add to several earlier works.

In the early 1920s Bassett-Lowke were com-missioned to make a model of a Dessau Retort, which was an important development in gas making. It was specified that the model should demonstrate the through-movement of materials as in the prototype. The attempt proved to be a salutary lesson for Bassett-Lowke as it showed that any attempt to manipulate granular materials in a working model results in fine particles invading all the working parts, especially the bearings, with dire consequences. The model had to be a static exhibition piece, made to the remarkable scale of two inches to the metre.

King George V did not enjoy good health and it happened that he was recovering from a bad spell at the time he had agreed to lay the foundation stone of Worcester College. In order that he could fulfil the engagement without endangering his condition a model electrically driven crane sus-pending a replica of the foundation stone was taken to Buckingham Palace. The G.P.O. connected it through their cable lines to the actual crane on site. The starting switch for the model simul-taneously activated the crane at Worcester. By cable the King was able to lay the stone and declare that it was 'well and truly laid', thus fulfilling a Royal engagement.

In the First World War Bassett-Lowke pro-duced a full sized replica of the Vickers Maxim Machine Gun. It could not fire bullets, but in every other function it duplicated the real thing. Designed for Service training purposes it was in official service for only a short time because the real thing soon became available in massive quantities. Bassett-Lowke, however, were permit-ted to offer it for sale to unofficial training units. Not many were sold.

For the famous Siebe Gorman company a ⅜″ to the foot scale model Travelling Gantry was made. It had to carry out all the functions of the prototype – Lifting, Lowering, Traversing and Travelling. At this time there would be no problem in making such a model with an enormous range of miniature electric motors and small transmission parts being readily available, but in the 1920s all such parts had to be made. That the model gave demonstration for many hundreds of hours is as much a tribute to the motor designers as to the model makers.

The General Post Office have used Bassett-Lowke models on two occasions to publicise their lesser known activities. For the 1924 Wembley Exhibition they ordered a 1″ to the foot scale model of a section of their underground railway for transporting mail between Central and West End sorting offices.

A much larger display at the 1934 Radiolympia (later used at exhibitions throughout the country), was a 10 mm to the foot scale model Travelling Post Office. It comprised a double road 1¾″ gauge track with return loops at both ends, 120 feet long overall, providing continuous running for two mail trains. These were hauled respectively by the L.M.S. locomotives 'Royal Scot' and 'Black Watch'. There were two sets of ground apparatus at which the coaches dropped and picked up pouches in passing. At Radiolympia the trains ran 125 actual miles without requiring service.

Working model railways are always a great public attraction and the newly formed London Passenger Transport Board used this medium to demonstrate the safety systems in use on the Underground. On a base 20 feet long by 10 feet a 1¼″ gauge oval form track ran through an underground station (modelled in section) upwards to a surface section with a station typical of the new and characteristic L.P.T.B. architecture. The whole of the centre part of the display carried an urban scene of dwellings and commercial premises. Two trains were put in service without an operator in control. They stopped and started automatically at stations, and if one overtook another it was stopped at signals and restarted when the line ahead was clear. The model was exhibited at Charing Cross Underground Station for several months in 1934 and attracted considerable public interest.

As mentioned elsewhere, Bassett-Lowke commissions were world-wide. In 1911 the Baro-Kano Railway was being built to cross the northern provinces of Nigeria. The Crown Agents of the Colonies appreciated that neither the Emir of Katsena or the Emir of Zara, through whose territories the line was to run, had ever seen a locomotive. They ordered from Bassett-Lowke two working steam models of the 4–8–0 locomotives being built for presentation to them in appreciation of their co-operation in developing the system in the areas they controlled.

The Science Museum does, when practicable and funds permit, order models from outside suppliers (although they have a very efficient workshop for making and repairing exhibits). The electrical industry had funded the cost of adding an Electricity Hall and providing exhibits. Bassett-Lowke enjoyed the satisfaction of supplying three large models showing different systems of generation which have a prominent position in this exciting display of the development of electrical technology.

Bassett-Lowke have supplied a number of museums in this country and abroad and over a period of fifteen years the Smithsonian Institution of Washington ordered a ½″ scale model of one of America's most handsome locomotives, the 4–6–4 of the Atlantic Coast Line, in addition to several ship models. Of the latter there was one for which Bassett-Lowke were able to provide an unusual service. It was the famous Confederate ship *Alabama*. Drawings of the hull and superstructure had survived but there was no record or drawings of the masts and rigging and as the practice of masting and rigging varied from shipyard to shipyard there existed no real standard practice at the time of building. Bassett-Lowke engaged Harold A. Underhill, an expert on the subject arising from a lifetime of study and research, to draw up what he considered would be the most likely set. The Institution accepted the recommendation and the model was rigged accordingly.

The Bombay Museum wished to have a model of H.M.S. *Cornwall*, which had a long connection with Bombay during much of the nineteenth century. The ship had returned to this country and it happened that the British Admiralty had stored a number of the main timbers when it was broken up. Bombay museum wished for the model to be made from those. In due course the Admiralty delivered a big load of timbers to the Bassett-Lowke works – an astonishing amount, it seemed, when the hull was only a little over 3 ft in length. However, when work was started the wisdom of the Admiralty was revealed, for it seemed as though the spare time activities of Jack Tar had been to drive nails and all kinds of spikes into the timbers. Out of more than 60 ft of timbers supplied it proved difficult to find a suitably clean, unspoilt length!

An unusual model display made for Plymouth City comprised a reproduction of the land area with Sutton Harbour from the Hoe as it appeared in 1620. It stood in a 7 ft × 11 ft fibreglass shallow tank which held 2,000 gallons of water. An underwater drive system propelled models of part of Drake's fleet, the 'Mayflower' and the 'Golden Hind' in a series of movements depicting their historic journeyings. An electronic system controlled a programme with lighting and a commentary. Set against a canvas back scene the 300 models of buildings, many with individual interior lighting, including the famous Guildhall, the Island House, the Castle, and the Parish Church, made a striking setting from which loud speakers gave the commentary written by Crispin Gill, author and historian. The model was on public display at Derry's Cross for the whole season of the celebration of the most dramatic period of Plymouth's history.

## The Problem Years

A feature of the Northampton routine was the staff meeting held each Tuesday, at which Directors and Managers met to discuss business trends and problems. The meetings were inaugurated in 1938 and continued until 1966. At first they were held in the morning at 11 a.m. followed by lunch at a 'restaurant or pub', always at a modest price. After Whynne's demise the programme was reversed – the meetings followed the lunch. There was much useful exchange of information and airing of problems. Bindon Blood, as Managing Director of Precision Models, attended to give and take information about production for Bassett-Lowke.

After the Second World War the conflict of interest between Trix and Precision Models became more and more of a problem. As far as Bindon Blood was concerned it was a 'pull devil – pull baker' situation. His personal interest was in the Bassett-Lowke work but his employers now were Trix. His divided loyalties led to a difficult situation for himself, and the solace he sought in drinking only served to break his health and he died a relatively young and very unhappy man.

Trix Trains had established a strong position in 1939 and there was, obviously, a flourishing market for it. There was, equally obviously, a demand for Bassett-Lowke products. Kahn and Bing had a problem – loyalty to their own company by getting production of Trix Trains flowing as quickly as possible on the one hand and honouring their promise to Whynne to keep Bassett-Lowke supplied on the other. The matter was complicated by the difficulty in obtaining materials. At that time applications for allocation had to be made, and decisions rested on the assumed importance of the goods to be made in relation to national needs. Toys came low in the list of priorities – models somewhat higher. Bassett-Lowke having such an excellent reputation and war time record were given sympathetic consideration. These allocations were only for industrial and commercial model work, so it was Ships Models which obtained good supplies.

Precision Models tried to be fair and the small output possible was divided between Bassett-Lowke and Trix, with Trix confirming in 1945 that they would make no changes in their system in order 'to be fair to their old customers' (Kahn's own words). What a tragic decision that was, because it tied them to outdated methods of operation. The ability to control two trains on one track was a novelty that faded in importance by comparison with the more true-to-scale appearance of Hornby 00 gauge. The basis of Trix thinking was that model railways should be designed to be assembled, used and then packed away for which their product was excellent, but 00 gauge was suitable for fixing permanently on a portable table top, changing the whole concept of the hobby. The effect on Trix was gradual, but with Lines Bros marketing a 00 system which was operated in the same way as Hornby 00 (albeit 2 rail) their sales fell away, and eventually Precision Models went ino liquidation and was taken up first by Dufay Ltd., a camera manufacturing Company, and later transferred to Courtaulds who made a brave decision to transform the whole Trix system to that in general use, namely 2-rail 12 volt D.C. Unfortunately further change of ownership ended the Trix operation in Britain.

The downfall of Precision Models was, of course, a great blow to Bassett-Lowke because all production of standard range gauge 0 models ceased, except for the steam 'Mogul' for which a very substantial quantity of parts had been produced shortly before the close-down. At Ships Models the parts were assembled and finished, enabling supplies to continue until 1968.

Fortunately at the time of Precision Models failure considerable stocks of gauge 0 locomotives – 'Prince Charles', 'B.R. Compounds', 0–6–0 tanks and complete electric mechanisms had been built up due to the fall away in trade. Television finished off for most hobby trades what radio had begun thirty years earlier – it seemed as though everyone spent all their spare time looking at this novel and exciting form of entertainment, and this state of affairs lasted for several years.

In the model railway world the tremendous competition between the manufacturers of Hornby and Triang 00 railways resulted in an extraordinarily wide range of low-priced models being offered. To compete with these, even smaller gauges were introduced. Gauge 0 nearly died.

However, the novelty of T.V. gradually wore away and hobbies became popular once again. The little sub-contracting firm, Wildman & Brauson, which had taken on the making of Permanent Way Track, signals and other accessories when Precision Models decided to discontinue that particular range of goods, were able to supply sufficient quantities for Bassett-Lowke to offer a reasonably complete gauge 0 range.

In addition, arrangements were made to take the entire output of a freelance model-maker, Victor W. Hunt, who stated he had been trained by the man who is justly acclaimed as the finest builder of gauge 0 locomotives in the world, Stanley Beeson. Hunt's standard was not as good as his tutor's, but, incorporating Bassett-Lowke mechanisms and other parts, he produced a range of models which were excellent 'middle-of-the-road' items in style and detail. With the combination of these various supplies the Bassett-Lowke gauge 0 scene was maintained until the closing down of retail trade at the end of 1964.

In the London shop, the Manager reached retiring age in 1958. The new manager endeavoured to create a different image for the shop but the results were disappointing. In Northampton an effort was made to enter the changed world. Stocks of a wide range of model items were carried and a comprehensive pocket size catalogue published in 1962 in connection with an unusually wide advertising programme. Here again it was a failure because, in the main, the goods offered were widely available. Two years later, at the end of 1964, the retail business of Bassett-Lowke was

closed down and the two shops were sold to Beatties.

Although it was an unhappy event and it marked the end of sixty-five years trading, the company was really returning to the speciality field by concentrating on making high quality models to order for commerce, for industry, for museums and for private individuals. This had, of course, been the sole activity of Ships Models, except for a small section devoted to the making of steam locomotives, traction and stationary engines and steam fittings, and the repair department.

In the years approaching the retail close-down considerable re-arrangements were necessary. Mr. Franklin's son, who had been active in the business all his working life, had a breakdown in health and resigned. William Rowe, the first employee, now in years well past normal retiring age, reluctantly took his pension. Other employees, not transferable to the new set-up, were phased out, leaving only the minimum number required for the administration of the slimmed down company.

When Cyril Derry died in 1964 a retired Northampton Bank Manager, H. Talbot Butler, succeeded him as Chairman. He was a personal friend of Mrs. Bassett-Lowke and it was natural that he should make every effort to secure her equity. He was, however, without experience of the business and its peculiarities. Also he was rather old and therefore had neither the motivation nor the expertise in that field to do other than consider a holding position and await the turn of events.

P. F. Claydon reached the age of 65 in 1964 and retired as Joint Managing Director being succeeded by 'promotion from within' of A. L. Cox, a skilled craftsman who had been appointed Works Manager three years earlier.

The useful position of earlier years, when the retail business often 'cushioned' any falling away by Ships Models business and vice-versa, was now over, and the impact of the rise or fall in orders was immediate. The fact that the company had been undercapitalised for many years did not help. The capital structure of Bassett-Lowke was for an issue of 20,000 ordinary shares of £1 in 1908 and of 1,000 5% Preference Shares at £1 each in 1930. The firm had generated a substantial reserve position but the fall away over the years eroded it and so, with recourse only to the bank the position became, to say the least, delicate and difficult. As usually happens, the urgent need to obtain orders meant that prices quoted were kept as low as possible, with narrow margins that did not allow for loss bearing contracts. Altogether it was a period that defied all efforts to improve. Consequently, when, in 1966 the son of Chairman Cyril Derry, Richard, and his friend, Barrie Riley, made an offer to buy the shares there was a ready acceptance by Whynne's widow and members of the family who, in total, owned the majority of them.

Thus the company reached a point of change when the Bassett-Lowke and Franklin families ceased to have a connection and the policy running of the business would be in a new style entirely.

It was a curious coincidence that at the time of the take over a 7¼″ gauge locomotive was being made. It was to the order of Mr. Timothy Eaton, of the massive Canadian Timothy Eaton Company. When Timothy was a young man, in the 1920s he was sent to the Company's London Office for about two years for experience. He was keen on models and visited the Bassett-Lowke London shop quite frequently during that time. He did not buy anything but loved to see and admire the locomotives then displayed.

Suddenly in 1962 an enquiry came to Bassett-Lowke through the Timothy Eaton London Office for a gauge 0 electrically driven model of the Southern Railway locomotive 'Winston Churchill' together with the full train of vehicles comprising the Funeral Train used to convey Sir Winston's body from Waterloo Station. Apparently that order was satisfactorily carried out because it was followed by an enquiry for a 7¼″ gauge steam model of the locomotive. This, too, was successfully completed just at the time of the change in proprietorship and a photograph of the two young men riding on the locomotive appeared in the *Financial Times* together with a statement of the aspirations for the future of Bassett-Lowke.

Thus one simple photograph showed the link between the original company and the new proprietorship with different ideas as to future development. For 67 years the business had been active in almost every aspect of models and model-making – growing from a small local enterprise to a world renowned company in the short space of ten years. Henceforth it seemed that the reputation it had for high quality special order model-making would carry it into the future.

There was one spell of traditional Bassett-Lowke model production which was, in fact, a farewell gesture. In 1966 there still remained in stock a small quantity of machined parts for the gauge 0 steam 'Mogul' locomotive – which had been a standard product since 1925. The parts were assembled in small batches until the final order was assembled for Bassett-Lowke Railways. They were the last low-pressures standard locomotives by Bassett-Lowke and it is almost certain that never again will they be made in that form.

## The New Standard Bearers
by Allen Levy

While Richard Derry, son of a former Bassett-Lowke chairman, may have had some knowledge of the business he had bought into, Barry Riley, his colleague in this transaction, had little knowledge or feel for the uniqueness of Bassett-Lowke. As may be observed later from Dudley Dimmock's fascinating account of the end of Bassett-Lowke's effective connection with the retail model railway trade, the period after the 'takeover' was yet another watershed in the life of this extraordinary business.

The new directors were faced with the problem of how to use what they suspected to be a valuable name without becoming involved in a significant new investment in the model business. Indeed, it was Barry Riley's aim to take Bassett-Lowke away from its traditional fields and make it part of an industrial holding group with an emphasis on light engineering of all kinds. An electro-plating business was acquired in Wales, one of whose main products was supplying plated refrigerator handles.

Bassett-Lowke was fortunate in that Roland Fuller was still on the scene to advise on the continuing industrial model building business with its in-built repeat orders and the continuous refurbishment programme of Bassett-Lowke's earlier work in all fields, particularly ships.

Ironically, it was the model railway side of the business that gave the new management considerable problems. They wished to play down this connection as they saw little prospect of re-entering the field save in supplying their wealthier customers with one-off railway items. The company still supplied parts for a relatively simple ¾″ scale traction engine, loosely based on a Burrell type.

During 1968, they were looking for outlets for

both the finished engine and the kit of parts. The London agency for this business was offered to Ivan Scott, who ran a fascinating vintage model shop in Cadogan Street, named 'Steam Age'. The writer was a regular customer of the shop and was often invited for 'early evening refreshment' at Ivan Scott's 'La Rascass' club below the shop (now like its owner, sadly no more). One evening Ivan Scott remarked to the writer that he had been offered the London agency for Bassett-Lowke traction engines, and I, in one of my more expansive moments proffered the suggestion that 'Steam Age' i.e. Ivan Scott should attempt to take over the virtually defunct model railway business of Bassett-Lowke. Ivan Scott immediately suggested that I should join him in this venture and whether it was the euphoria induced by the excellent malt whisky, or pure bravado, I agreed. I had prior to that evening no plans to become involved in such a venture, but even in the cold light of the following morning, it seemed like an irresistible challenge, and I have never been one to regard life as a series of wholly predetermined acts.

Several meetings in London and Northampton were arranged and around June 1968 a deal was struck. In return for Bassett-Lowke Ltd consenting to the formation of a company to be known as Bassett-Lowke Railways Ltd, the latter company agreed to procure as much work as possible for the Northampton factory and the factory was to have first option on any new model railway projects initiated by Bassett-Lowke Railways Ltd. 'Steam Age' remained in the sole proprietorship of Ivan Scott. The bluff had been called and if nothing else had come out of this arrangement, it at least ensured that all the Bassett-Lowke archive material was saved. It was Barry Riley's intention to 'clear-out' the archive room to make way for a new secretary. However, when the importance of this material was indicated, the order was rescinded (without which this book could not have been published). Part of the archive had already been given to Bassett-Lowke Railways Ltd under the agreement.

Before dealing with the trading relationships that developed between Northampton and London, it is worth reflecting on the Northampton factory as it existed in 1968. Apart from the archive material there were many tantalising reminders of earlier days. Piles of spares in corners of the train assembly room revealed old mechanisms and chassis of half-completed locomotives, unclaimed

customer repair equipment and all the bric-a-brac of some 70 years of model train production. Although some of these were cannibalised for current repair work, it virtually all disappeared in a mysterious deal concluded by Barry Riley, despite assurances that it would be offered to Bassett-Lowke's new associates.

A considerable amount of repair and restoration work flowed between Cadogan Street and Northampton. Each job was carefully logged by Roland Fuller and for a brief time the train shop in Kingswell Street was revitalised and long-serving employees greeted some of the jobs like long lost friends!

Obviously the main interest behind any revival of the Bassett-Lowke name in the model railway market would rest with new production. What could be produced? After some negotiation and examination of existing tooling, Bassett-Lowke Railways agreed to reintroduce the ubiquitous gauge 0 live steam Mogul as it went out of production in its Stanier form. Over 100 of these new Moguls were manufactured using the original tooling and were 100 per cent Northampton made. They were available in L.M.S. red or British Railways black and were offered in a distinctive Bassett-Lowke Railways box. Including purchase tax they sold for £105. They were way ahead of anything else in the semi-scale market at that time and also marked the real rebirth of batch-produced live steam locomotives in the post-war period. It was as if a barrier had been broken – the £100 Mogul, it having previously been listed at under £50.

At this time, I had embarked on the preparation of a new Bassett-Lowke catalogue, an experience I promised myself I would not repeat. Five years later, true to form, I founded the publishing company New Cavendish Books, but thankfully that is another story – perhaps not quite another story as it has at least enabled this story to be told in such an expansive form. The catalogue was not only a current catalogue but also included a resume of Bassett-Lowke's previous listings. In so doing it formed the first comprehensive vintage model train catalogue every published and spawned many similar works all of which have added to the enjoyment of vintage train collecting.

Whereas the Bassett-Lowke Railways enterprise presented a great challenge, it also brought enormous problems. I was aware of the responsibility of the name with all its connotations. It

Two views of the final batch of Bassett-Lowke Railways 'Moguls' under construction at Northampton during 1969.

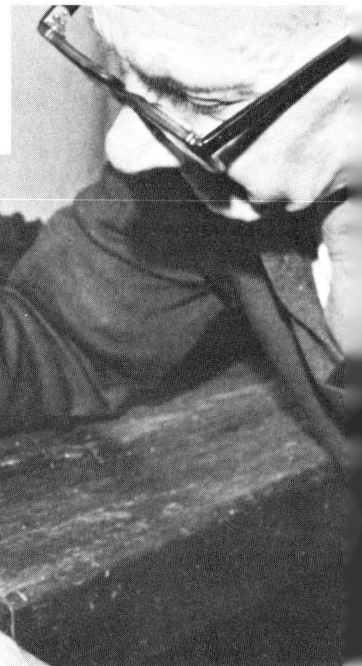

## 0-6-0 TANK ENGINE
## GAUGE '0' 2/0S

We are particularly pleased to announce the introduction of this model which will constitute a completely new live steam production and fill the large gap in gauge '0' railway systems left by the dis-continuance of the famous 112 0-4-0 tank engine. The prototype chosen is one of the more attractive outside cylinder 0-6-0 tank engines originally built by Messrs. Hudswell Clark and Company in 1909 for the Burry Port and Gwen Draeth Valley Railway, later absorbed into the GWR. The unusual safety valve was designed to carry the steam clear of the large cab front windows. The model is modified in proportion to include the proved basic elements, used in the successful series of Bassett-Lowke gauge '0' low-pressure steam locomotives; that is, the two Enterprise models and the Mogul.

## SPECIFICATION

**Length overall** 8¼".
**Wheelbase** 40 mm x 40 mm.
**Diameter of wheels** 1¼".
**Cylinders** Double acting piston valve.
**Reversing** Slip-eccentric.
**Boiler** Brass, fired by solid fuel.
**Fittings include** Safety valve, regulator, whistle and cylinder lubricator.
**Main frames and bodywork** Tinned steel plate.
**Wheels** Turned cast iron on steel axles.
**Buffers** Round head, sprung.
**Couplings** 3-link chain.

A device for stopping this locomotive by remote control is being prepared and will be available as an extra shortly after the locomotive is introduced.

An extract from the Bassett-Lowke Railways catalogue issued in 1968 announces the new Northampton-made tank engine, which in the event only reached the prototype stage.

Allen Levy and Harry Amies in January 1969 at the Model
Engineer Exhibition at Seymour Hall. The new gauge 1
live-steam 'Stirling Single' and 'Wainwright D' are illustrated.

A general view of the Steam Age and Bassett-Lowke Railways
stand at Seymour Hall. Mr. Laidlaw-Dixon can be seen
talking to Allen Levy in the centre of the stand.

Bing for Bassett-Lowke's 1902 South Coast 'Flyer' alongside
the 1968 offering of the 'Wainwright D'.

needed and indeed the catalogue proposed a steady and defined programme of new items. I was absolutely opposed to any idea that Bassett-Lowke Railways should hold itself out to be the original company – it was not. Apart from some temporary confusion in Cadogan Street advertising referring to 'our former production', the latter address became synonymous with 'Steam Age', and for all practical purposes Bassett-Lowke Railways Ltd as a company ceased to exist. Steam Age is now relocated in much expanded premises in Abingdon Road and continues to fulfil a unique role in offering a wide range of mechanical antiquities in the central London area.

Returning to the catalogue – the only one ever issued by the new company – it offered an exciting range of new items. Some superb continental production by Fulgurex and Darstead was included in much the same way as Bassett-Lowke had done in the past with other continental manufacturers. More daring and probably premature in commercial terms, were a range of relatively expensive gauge 1 locomotives in steam and electric. This range was inspired by two Swiss model engineers, Messrs Muhlethaler and Giannini who built a gauge 1 'Stirling' single in live steam and offered to batch produce these exclusively for Bassett-Lowke Railways. The first series of electric engines were duly delivered, but endless problems made further production impossible. Sadly Muhlethaler and Giannini were not a latter-day Bingwerke. Geoffrey Swift who was at that time well known as a superb model tram maker was commissioned to build coaches for these engines. The prototype 'Stirling Single' together with its coaches is now exhibited at the London Toy and Model Museum and some idea of the standards that were being aimed at in a relatively restricted price range (£400 for the set) can be appreciated from this exhibit. I do not know what happened to the original steam prototype but again it was a significant model in that it was a precursor of later more successful efforts to revive gauge 1 steam as a viable semi-mass produced item. It was Aster in Japan, albeit a decade later, who were to achieve this production breakthrough and several of these locomotives were made in batches significantly larger than those supplied by Bing for Bassett-Lowke earlier in the century. A prototype for the successor to Bing's SECR 'Wainwright D' for Bassett-Lowke Railways was made by French, Hefford and Littledale in

Brighton (mysteriously the tender for this locomotive was stolen). A live steam butane-fired Pannier tank was in preparation by Tony Hobson, a former gauge 2 enthusiast, but interminable production delays prevented this item becoming a reality for the new company.

Apart from restoration work and the reborn Mogul, both London and Northampton desperately wanted a Northampton-produced model train. This more than anything else would give the new company a stamp of authority and enable a true rebirth of the noble Bassett-Lowke legacy. An 0-6-0 tank locomotive based on the Burry Port type was conceived by Roland Fuller, and indeed a factory prototype was produced. This certainly marked the last serious effort by Bassett-Lowke in Northampton to come up with a model locomotive that could be made in considerable numbers. In the event the costings did not work under 2000 units. As I had put up virtually all the capital for the Bassett-Lowke Railways venture, Ivan Scott offering the use of the Cadogan Street premises as his contribution, I simply could not shoulder a new project of this magnitude. All these projects were presented at the Model Engineer Exhibition at Seymour Hall in the winter of 1968/9.

In 1969, Bassett-Lowke Railways were approached to take part in the legendary and disastrous tour of the United States by 'The Flying Scotsman' with its travelling exhibition of British goods. The hospitality bar franchised to one of the major brewery companies in the old Bournemouth Belle observation car proved to be the outstanding financial success of the trip as did an eager salesman selling Lea & Perrins Worcester Sauce!

Shortly after returning from the United States, Marcel Darphin, a long standing friend of mine and producer of extremely fine model railway equipment, agreed to take over my shares in Bassett-Lowke Railways. Despite exploring many possibilities the idea of a new reborn Bassett-Lowke marque withered although the name was occasionally attached to scratch built locomotives commissioned by Steam Age and several excellent rebuilds by Victor Reader who was associated with the company for some time and was a superb model builder in his own right.

There had been changes at Northampton too. Richard Derry's wife, Ann, had taken over from her husband after their separation, and Barry Riley disappeared to devote his energies to businesses more suited to his whizzkid ideas. Roland Fuller, like some ancient mariner, soldiered on still advising on this training railway for Egypt or that renovation of a locomotive or ship for an old customer. Ann Derry (later to become Ann Ritchie and be joined in the business by Ruben Ritchie her new husband) redefined the company's objectives. They lay in those areas where the traditions and skills of the existing workforce could be best applied. Thus ships and industrial models became and still remain, the main component of the business. A reasonably successful line under the Derry/Riley stewardship was the cannon, available as either a kit of parts or made up model and this still remains a small but interesting sideline of the company's production.

W. J. Bassett-Lowke would surely have applauded the company's recent work for GEC in the form of models of space satellites. It would be a great pity if the name Bassett-Lowke ever became a severed head, as have some of its former rivals in the Golden Era of model railways, being sold from one group to another without the tradition, history, or indefinable flavour that originally made it unique being transmitted with the name.

# W. J. Bassett-Lowke as Architectural Patron
by Narisa Levy

W. J. Bassett-Lowke did not confine his abundant enthusiasm and ability to model railways in particular or even model-making in general. Throughout his life, he still found time to be actively involved in numerous other pursuits. He was a socialist and local politician; he loved photography, both still and cine; he took part in amateur dramatics; he was a great traveller; he played a prominent part in the local life of Northampton. However, one of his more unusual preoccupations (for that time) was his interest in and support of modern architecture.

In 1926, his house at Northampton by Peter Behrens (1868–1940), one of the founding fathers of modern architecture, was completed and christened 'New Ways'. It was hailed both then and subsequently as 'the first modern house' in Britain, and, indeed, its stark white silhouette and unusual interiors must have mystified and even appalled some local inhabitants. The fact that the actual construction was traditional with brick load bearing walls was not realized and was immaterial. To the public at large, 'New Ways' symbolized everything that was modern with a capital 'M', and in the architectural press the house was also given prominent coverage in articles which appeared in *Ideal Home* and *The Architectural Journal* in 1926.

However, 'New Ways' was not W. J. Bassett-Lowke's first excursion in modern architecture. Some ten years earlier, he had contacted another famous architect, C. R. Mackintosh, and commissioned him to carry out alterations to a modest terraced house the end result of which was in many ways even more revolutionary than the Behrens house. This small, but significant conversion was to be Bassett-Lowke's first marital home at Derngate, Northamptonshire. Here, client and architect have transformed a traditional terraced house into an exciting experiment in the nascent International Style.

## 78 Derngate Northampton 1916–1920
Whynne had bought the small, nineteenth-century terraced house from his parents in 1914 in preparation for his marriage to Miss Jones in 1917. Quite when he decided to transform and extend the building is not known, nor when he decided to employ the Scottish architect, Charles Rennie Mackintosh, hitherto famous for his so-called 'art nouveau' work in Glasgow and the neighbouring district. It is possible that mutual friends (maybe the Newberrys) suggested Mackintosh and Bassett-Lowke made a trip to Glasgow to visit him in late 1915 only to find that the former had already left for London.

Bassett-Lowke was not an uninformed outsider in his approach to architecture. He was an early and active member of the Design and Industries Association, and as such was well aware of more progressive approaches to design. He was also widely travelled on the Continent, organising the DIA annual tour, and through his German friends and business associates such as Stefan Bing had made contact with members of the Deutscher Werkbund before 1914. Finally, his knowledge and appreciation of fine machinery must have encouraged a desire for correspondingly clean, functional lines in his house. It is clear from correspondence that Bassett-Lowke wished to be, and was, closely involved in the project and the commission is an interesting example of the interaction that can occur between architect and client. It is probable that it was Bassett-Lowke who drew Mackintosh's attention to the use of a new type of plastic, Erinoid, and Bassett-Lowke also

Entrance facade of 78 Derngate,
with Mrs. Bassett-Lowke in the doorway.

The balcony of the main bedroom
at 78 Derngate also showing the
adjoining terraced house.

The hall/lounge at
78 Derngate showing the room
before it was revised by
Macktintosh in 1920 to a
lighter scheme.

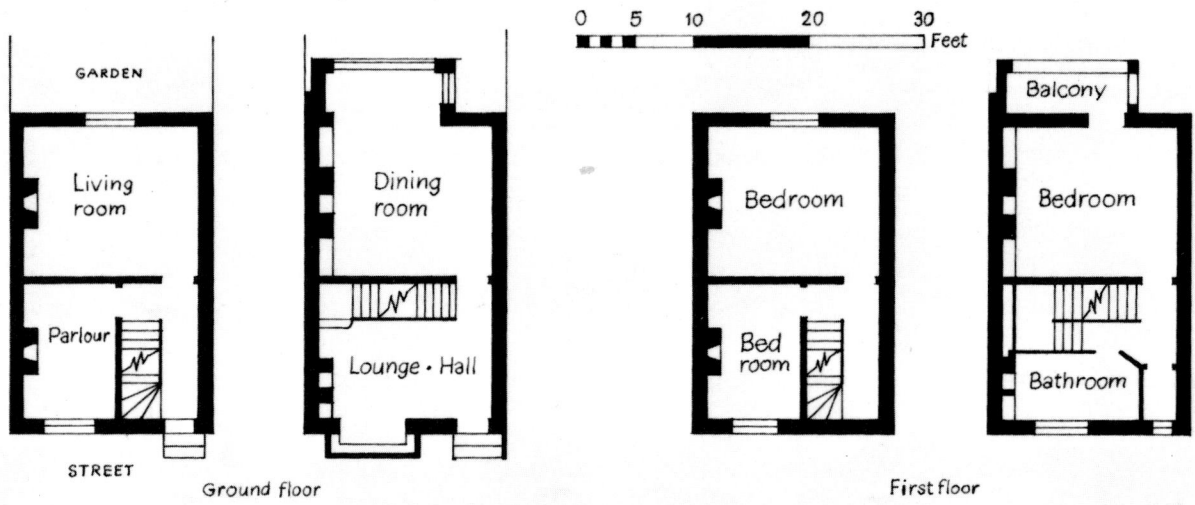

Plan of 78 Derngate

Right and below right
Second and final scheme
by Mackintosh for guest
bedroom at Derngate 1919.

Bassett-Lowke's bathroom
at 78 Derngate.

designed some minor items of furniture himself.

It seems that Bassett-Lowke finally made contact with Mackintosh towards the end of 1915. Although the job was relatively modest in terms of size, and the street facade may seem quite traditional, the garden front and extension were startingly modern for the time, and as such of great significance. Not only had such architecture not been seen in England before (although, of course, being on the garden side it wasn't seen that much), but the house also heralded an important departure in Mackintosh's own style, away from his previous sinuous curves and organic motifs as seen in various of his Scottish commissions such as Hill House 1903 or the Willow Street Tea Rooms.

The alterations to the street facade were slight, namely the insertion, to the left of the door, of a bay window which was tiled and glazed in a traditional way. There was a new front door, although the same frame was kept. At the back, on the garden facade, the changes were much more dramatic. Here the land sloped away steeply and there was thus greater height in the back elevation than the front. As the plan shows, an extension was built to the full height of the house and almost the entire width, thereby providing two balconies for the bedroom, and extra space for what otherwise would have been a very small dining-room and basement kitchen. Thomas Howarth was to write of the garden facade in his excellent book *Charles Rennie Mackintosh and the Modern Movement* 'Its functional simplicity, the form, proportions and disposition of the openings, the concept of the enclosed balcony on the second floor, and use of flowering plants and gay sunblinds all belong to the post-war period.'

Unfortunately, or fortunately as the locals would probably have said, the garden front of uncluttered white and simple, unadorned openings, was not visible from the street, and thus what was certainly the first building in England to incorporate such revolutionary features, was hidden from public view. Had the street facade been treated in similar fashion, there is little doubt that it would have caused a sensation.

Inside, the main structural change was the realignment of the staircase by 90° and into the centre of the house, thereby creating a simpler and more open plan and improving the size of the lounge. The decoration of the hall/sitting-room was stark and dramatic; black in overall colour and designed to create an immediate impression. The ceiling, walls and furniture were black, whilst the carpet was black and grey. To prevent the darkness from becoming too oppressive, Mackintosh employed bands of stencilling based on overlapping triangles of yellow, grey, vermillion, blue, green and purple. This use of the triangle motif which dominated the room, was new in Mackintosh's work, although he also employed a favourite motif, the lattice square and this may be seen in the staircase screen (parts of which were infilled and parts left open) and the backs of the chairs.

The dining-room was less exciting from the overall design point of view, but interesting in so far that Bassett-Lowke himself may have designed the plain walnut furniture. The wall-covering consisted of walnut veneer panels, relieved by strips of a dark wallpaper. In connection, with the furniture, it should be mentioned that unlike some of Mackintosh's designs, these were made up by excellent craftsmen, many of whom were German prisoners of war imprisoned on the Isle of Man and with whom Bassett-Lowke had various links.

The main bedroom was unremarkable in design: grey wallpaper, twin beds, grey sycamore furniture. The addition of the balcony was however a modern touch, and once again it would seem that it was Bassett-Lowke who designed its sturdy white furniture. Bassett-Lowke ever keen to be innovative was extremely proud of his modern bathroom, writing 'The equipment is entirely American and most modern in character, including as it does a Kohler Bath and a Pedestal wash basin with nickel fittings, dry cupboard and such labour-saving devices as glass shelves, etc.'

The decor of the guest bedroom which featured in an *Ideal Home* article on the house in August 1920 was in fact a second scheme executed in 1919, and from all accounts was more successful and innovative than the first. Its effectiveness lay in the use of black and white striped paper in bands across part of the ceiling and wall, with the curtains and bedspread picking up the motif. Touches of ultramarine and emerald green relieved the starkness. The furniture was very simple, a band of blue squares outlining the forms. Again, Mackintosh returned to his beloved square. This bedroom represents the last important interior design by Mackintosh and shows that he had lost none of his vitality or originality. George Bernard Shaw was a close friend of Bassett-Lowke and often came to stay. Bassett-Lowke showing Shaw to this newly decorated room, expressed some anxiety as to whether its startling decor might disturb his guest. However, the great man reassured him by saying 'I always sleep with my eyes closed!'

In 1920, Mackintosh was again recalled to change the perhaps over dramatic black hall. A pale grey was the new colour chosen and a smaller, lighter frieze was used, although the triangular motif remained predominant. Bassett-Lowke obviously liked this second scheme as he was to use the same frieze in his next foray into modern architecture at 'New Ways'.

In total, Derngate represents a plethora of new and exciting ideas squeezed into a small and unpromising site. After a break from architectural design of several years, Mackintosh was able to adapt his style to suit his knowledgeable and demanding client and in the process created a modern house, which he must have hoped would be the fresh start he needed and the source of new commissions. However, although Bassett-Lowke did put a couple of small commissions his way, Mackintosh did not achieve the recognition he deserved. It has been observed elsewhere in this book, that for all Whynne's good qualities, he was sometimes sparing in the recognition given to his many helpers and collaborators. Perhaps the same characteristic came into play here, for although Bassett-Lowke was very proud of his modern house he did not always mention Mackintosh as the architect, and indeed, the two *Ideal Home* articles of 1920 made no mention of his name. During the period in which Bassett-Lowke and Mackintosh were in contact, the latter also designed various advertising labels for the firm, but another major commission did not come his way. It is not known whether Bassett-Lowke intended Mackintosh to design his next house or whether he tried unsuccessfully to contact him. Thus Derngate, which many have regarded as untypical Mackintosh, but which could have been the start of a new period, was in fact the end of a great career.

## New Ways 1925–1926

By the early 1920s, Derngate was probably becoming too small and Bassett-Lowke decided that a new house was needed. As discussed above, he may or may not have attempted to contact Mackintosh in circa 1923. Whatever the result, Peter Behrens was in fact the architect chosen. The choice of Behrens is perhaps a curious one, for although he was extremely famous as a pioneer of modern architecture with such seminal buildings as the AEG factory of 1910–1913, he was no longer in the forefront of modern domestic design as were such architects as Walter Gropius or Le Corbusier. Bassett-Lowke was well-travelled throughout Europe and would have been aware of all current trends. However, Louise Campbell of Warwick University has kindly pointed out that it was as a result of looking through the 1913 Werkbund handbook illustrating the AEG factory that Behrens was chosen. The architect never visited the site, or came to England at all. The design being arrived at through an exchange of letters and plans.

The site was open and presented a much easier commission than that which had been given to Mackintosh. Again Bassett-Lowke wanted something which was obviously modern and this was certainly achieved, its free-standing cubic white silhouette being plainly visible for all to see. Although the original plans had envisaged concrete as the building material, local by-laws prohibited its use and eventually white rendered brickwork was used. As encapsulated in the *Architectural Review* critique of November 1926, Bassett-Lowke wished the house to achieve the following aims:

'After preliminary essays in modernity [a reference to Derngate], the present building was evolved by Mr. Bassett-Lowke with certain definite intentions. He was determined to incorporate into one building every modern aid to comfort and efficiency, to build a house which should express his idea of the spirit of the age, to limit the height to two storeys, and to include every room within the four surrounding walls, omitting the customary collection of odd outbuildings . . . there was to be a separate room for the maids, and their bedroom was to be fitted with hot and cold running water . . . other essentials included a spacious communal room, large enough for dancing, a dining-room reduced to a purely meal-taking apartment, and a study, or spare room, available if required as a nursery. There was to be electric power in every room, central heating in most rooms, but a coal fire in the living-room on account of its sentimental value and human appeal. Bedrooms with adjacent dressing-bathrooms, the provision of adequate built-in cupboards, and a spacious hall with modern conveniences were other requirements.'

As with Derngate, Bassett-Lowke clearly knew what he wanted from the house and was determined to achieve his aims. Once again, he was closely involved with the interior design. The study was a replication of the Derngate Mackintosh hall (second design) and the bedrooms, bathrooms, kitchen, the heating and other details of this nature were largely under Bassett-Lowke's design and control.

THE FOUNDATIONS OF THE EMPIRE ARE IN THE HOMES OF THE PEOPLE
KING GEORGE V.

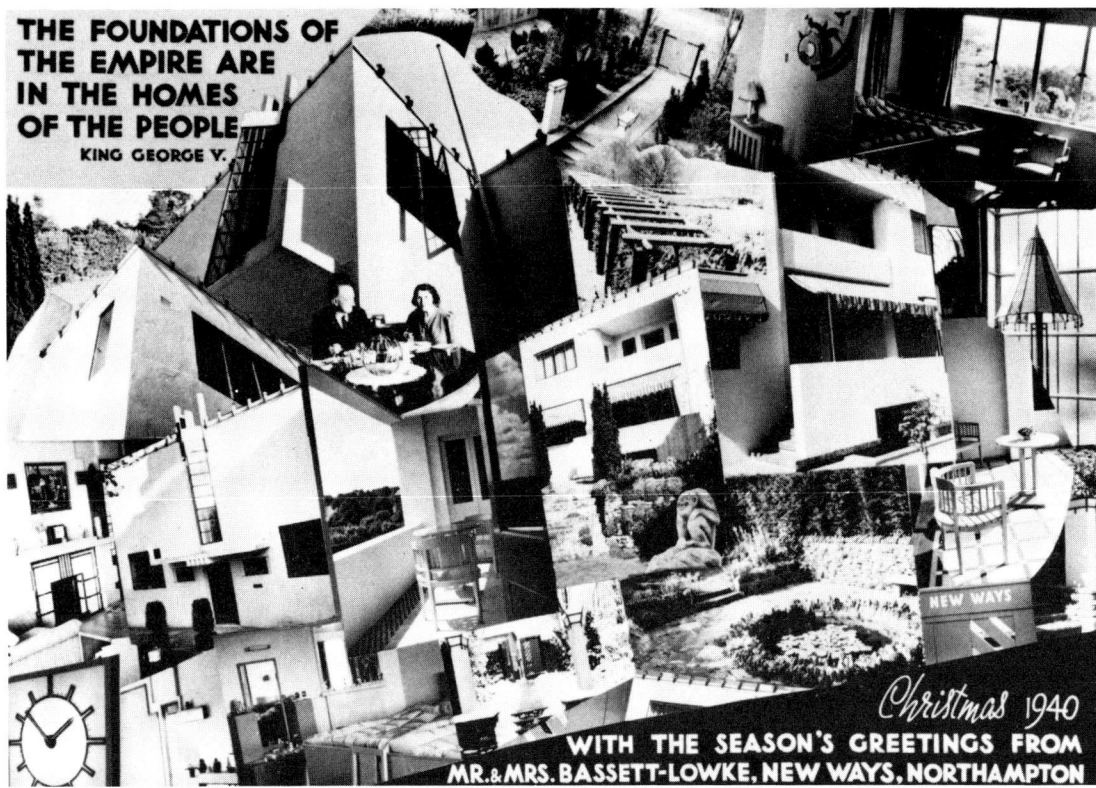

*Christmas* 1940

WITH THE SEASON'S GREETINGS FROM MR. & MRS. BASSETT-LOWKE, NEW WAYS, NORTHAMPTON

An amusing montage of 'New Ways' formed the Bassett-Lowke's 1940 Christmas card. A close inspection will reveal many interesting features such as the garden lamps and the hall lamp. The terrace furniture has been reused from Derngate. Mr. and Mrs. Bassett-Lowke are seated at a meal, top left. Front facade at left.

'New Ways' viewed from the back garden.

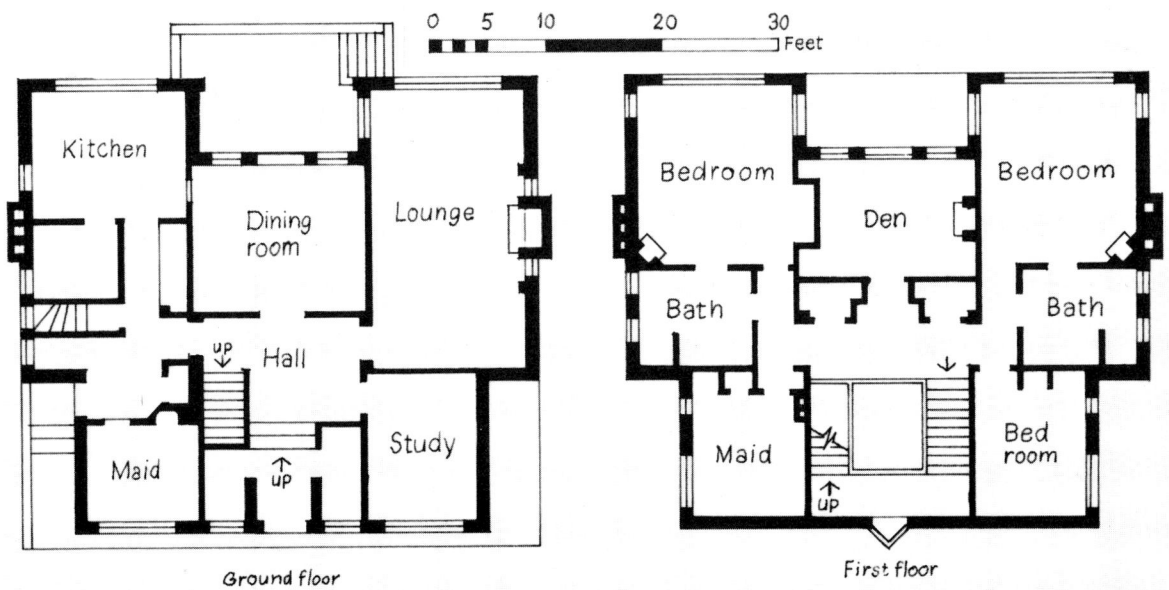

Ground floor

First floor

'New Ways' lounge.

'New Ways' view of dining room from the hall.

SOME OF OUR HAPPY MEMORIES OF 1951

Holidays snaps of 1951
give an example of Bassett-Lowke
as an ardent traveller. This had been
a favourite occupation throughout his life.

Set on the edge of Abington Park in a large spacious garden, the site presented no real problems. The plan was simple, symmetrical and even traditional. The rooms were self-contained, rather than free-flowing, and opened off the main hall. Upstairs the four good sized bedrooms open onto the main landing, the two principal bedrooms with access to a shared veranda overlooking the sloping garden. Indeed, the modernity of the building is only expressed in the facades.

The entrance facade was most striking; a cubic white structure pierced by three windows and the front door (painted ultramarine blue), the openings symmetrically arranged but in an unusual placement. The hall was lit by a tall vertical window which projected out in a triangular, and even expressionist manner. Indeed, other similarly expressionist features are incorporated in the exterior of the building, i.e. the black concrete crestings surmounting the parapet, the five notches above the front door, the verticals above the hall window, and the whole arrangement of the windows and door.

The garden facade was also symmetrical, but very different in spirit, being more in line with current international style buildings. Two large centre openings are flanked by four windows of equal size, creating a feeling of horizontality in two bands in marked contrast to the verticality of the entrance facade. Other exterior features of interest were the modern style gates in brilliant ultramarine; the miniature pylons with illuminated tops flanking the entrance path, various plant containers.

The interior was largely the work of Bassett-Lowke himself, although a striking feature was Behrens' hall floor with its intricate pattern of grey black and white tiles. The hall also contained a small fountain. The study, opening off the hall to the right utilised the ideas of Charles Rennie Mackintosh: the second frieze pattern from Derngate was copied and the lattice screens were reused. The lounge was very 'modern' in appearance. A large window overlooked the garden and a smaller one looked out on the loggia, which could be reached via the dining room. Either side of the fire place were two German-made stained glass windows composed of an asymmetrical arrangement of squares. A glass and steel rectangular light hung from the ceiling (the lighting throughout the house was very unusual). The ceiling was interesting in that it was composed of different levels. The carpet was of a bold, abstracted design. As at Derngate, the dining room

was walnut veneered. Double glazed doors opened onto the garden. Upstairs the rooms were less dramatic than, for example, the guest bedroom at Derngate, but there was a strong use of colour such as in Bassett-Lowke's own bedroom of cerise, blue and purple. The bathrooms were efficient and functional.

Although it can be argued that 'New Ways' lacked the overall cohesion of interior design which Mackintosh had brought to Derngate, not helped by the fact that the architect never visited Northampton or participated in the interior, it is clear that Bassett-Lowke achieved his aim of creating a house which was 'intended not only to be but to look a modern House.' Whilst later critics have sometimes minimised its importance, pointing out its traditional construction and plan, there is no doubt that at that time in England, 'New Ways' was quite unique and remarkable. One has only to glance at the photograph of the house surrounded by its neighbours to grasp the point. For many locals it must have seemed as if an extraordinary white box of a house had suddenly arrived from the Continent. Bassett-Lowke, obviously liked the house, remaining there until his death in 1953.

Just as he was the first real innovator in the field of model railways, so too W. J. Bassett-Lowke was the first to introduce modern architecture to this country. In the beginning, in a small way in the garden facade of his Derngate home, and in 1926 in the aptly named 'New Ways' – a new modern house for a new efficient approach to life. That Bassett-Lowke did not minimise the effect of environment on the individual or the importance of the home can be seen in the quote of King George V used for Whynne's 1940 Christmas card: 'The foundations of the empire are in the homes of the people'. To fully understand Bassett-Lowke and his approach to his model-making business it is thus extremely important to examine his approach to and patronage of modern architecture.

Bassett-Lowke did not commission any other houses for himself, nor did he ever build a new modern factory, the works managing to shuttle back and forth between various buildings in St. Andrew's Street. However, in the architectural model side of his business, he was to supervise the building of many interesting and intricate models, a notable one from the point of view of modern architecture being the Boots factory model in Nottingham.

# Contents
# of the 'Picture Album'
## (from original Bassett-Lowke archive material)

The dates given are those originally marked on the pictures by Bassett-Lowke staff and do not necessarily reflect the first date of manufacture.

1. 'Lady of the Lake' 2–2–2, g 1 Carette 1902.
2. GWR 4–4–0, 3″ g Schoenner 1903.
3. LSWR 4–4–0, 2½″ g Bing 1901.
4. GER 'Claude Hamilton' 4–4–0, 2½″ g Carette 1905.
5. MR 4–4–0, 3¼″ g probably Bassett-Lowke 1903.
6. 0–4–0 tank, g 0 Carette 1905.
7. SECR 'Wainright D' type 4–4–0, 3″ g Schoenner 1904.

8. GER version of 'Black Prince' 4–4–0, 2½″ g Bing 1903.
9. GNR 'Stirling Single', 2½″ g Carette 1903.
10. 'Sir Alexander' 4–4–0, g 1 with GC coach promo model Bing 1904.
11. 'Black Prince' 4–4–0, 2½″ g Bing 1905.
12. SECR Steam Rail Car, g 1 Carette 1905.
13. LNWR 'Experiment' 4–6–0, Carson 2½″ g c. 1910.

14. MR Steam Set 4–4–0, g 1 Bing 1907.
15. 'Black Prince' Bing in an Edwardian Garden.
16. 'Black Prince' 4–4–0, 2½″ g Bassett-Lowke 1909.
17. MR 0–6–0 Goods engine, g 1 Bing 1908.
18. MR 'Compound' 4–4–0, g 1 Bing 1908.
19. GNR Atlantic, g 1 Bing 1909.

20. LNWR 'Precursor' tank 4–4–2, g 1 Bing with Carette coaches 1909.
21. LSWR 'M7' 0–4–4, g 1 Bing 1909.
22. GWR 'Sydney' 4–4–0, g 0 Bing 1909.
23. GNR 'Saddle' tank 0–4–0, g 2 Bassett-Lowke 1910.

24

25

26

27

28

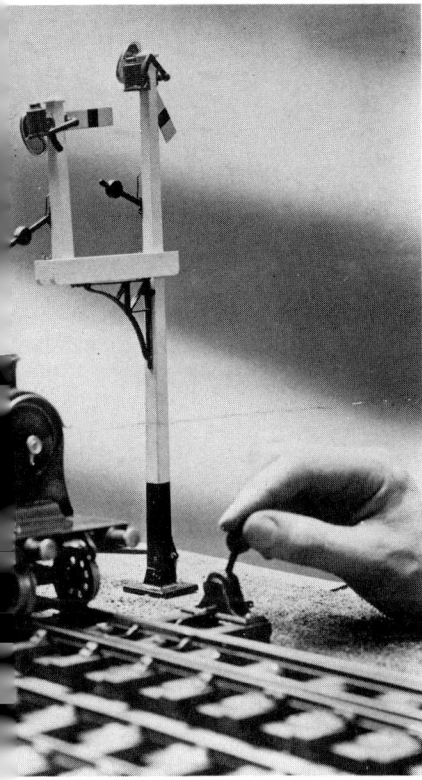

44

45

46

47

SE&CR    1630

48

SIR SAM FAY    423    GREAT CENTRAL

49

NORTH EASTERN

44. LT & S 'Tilbury' tank 4–4–2, g 1 Bing 1912.
45. NER 0–4–4, g 1 Bing 1912.
46. GWR 'County of Northampton' 4–4–0, 2½″ g set Bing 1912.
47. SECR 'Wainright D' 4–4–0, g 1 Bing 1912.
48. GCR 'Sir Sam Fay' 4–6–0, g 1 Bing in Bassett-Lowke finish 1912.
49. NER 4–4–0, 2½″ g Bassett-Lowke 1912.

50. NER 4–4–0 promo prototype, approx. g 0 probably Carette 1912.
51. GNR Atlantic, 3¼″ g Bassett-Lowke 1913.
52. GWR 'Gooch' 3¼″ g Twining 1912.
    Coaches by Winteringham's 1914.
53. CR freelance 4–4–0 tank, g 0 Bing 1912.
54. GWR freelance 4–4–0 tank, g 0 Bing 1912.
55. GNR freelance 4–4–0 tank, g 0 Bing 1912.
56. LNWR 0–6–0, 2½″ g Bassett-Lowke 1915.

57. Close-up of 3¼″ g 'Gooch' by Twining.
58. Commemorative 'Sir Gilbert Claughton' 4–6–0, g 1 Bing 1919.
59. 'Peckett' tank lithographed, g 0 wagons Bassett-Lowke/ Carette 1920.
60. Freelance 0–4–0 tank, g 0 Bing 1920.
61. GWR freelance 4–4–0, g 1 Bing 1920.

62. GNR tank 0–4–0, g 0 Bing 1920.
63. GWR 'County of Hereford' 4–4–0, g 0 Leeds 1920.
64. LSWR 'Urie' 4–6–0, g 1 Bing 1920.
65. LNWR 'Sir Gilbert Claughton' 4–6–0, g 1 Bing 1920.
66. GWR 'Titley Court' 4–6–0, g 1 Bing 1920.
67. GCR 'Lord Farringdon' 4–6–0, 2½″ g Bassett-Lowke 1921.

64

65

66

67

68

69

70

71

72

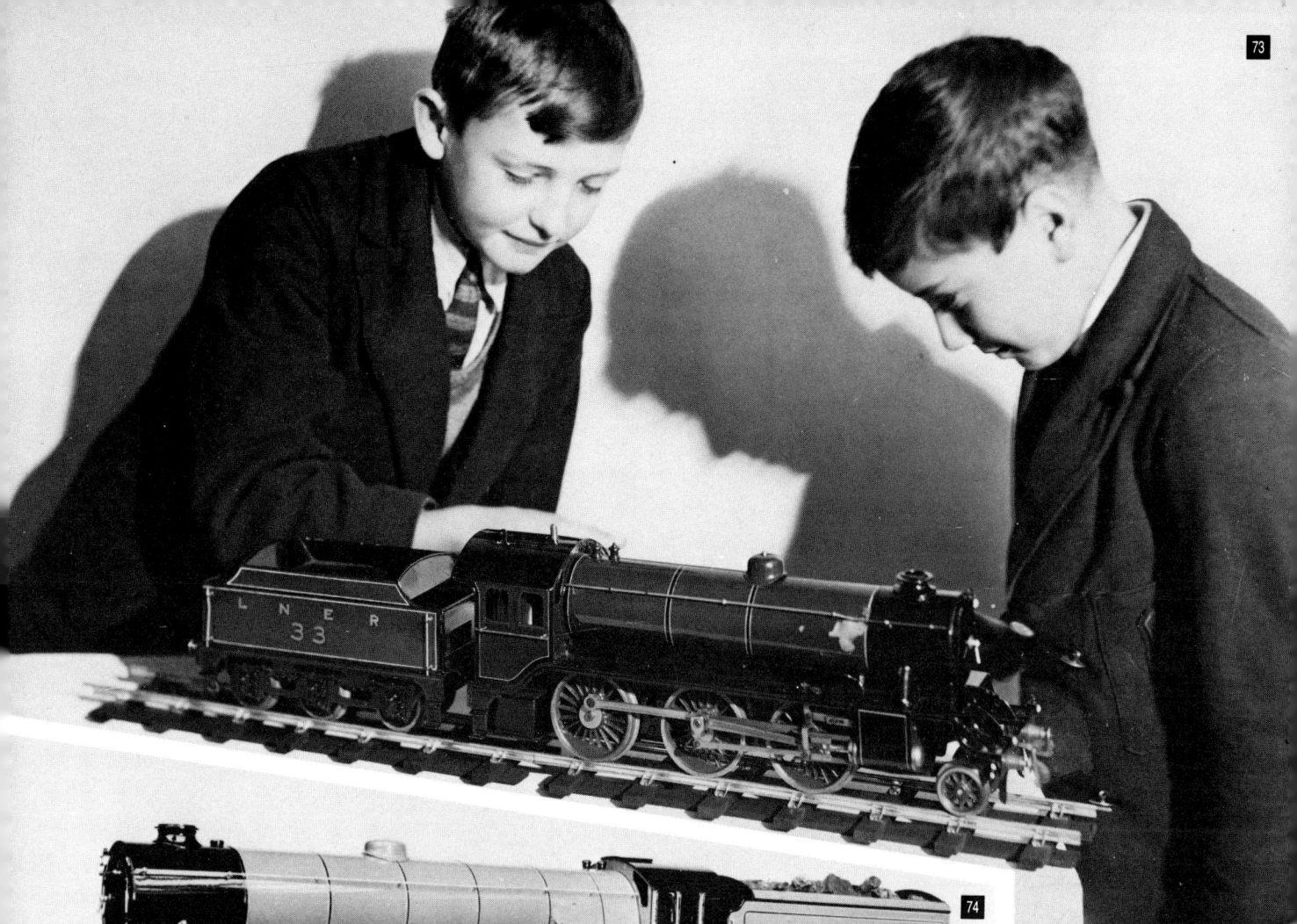

68. LSWR 4–6–0, 2½″ g Braunston & Walters 1922.
69. GNR 'Gresley' K1 Mogul, 2½″ g Braunston & Walters 1922.
70. GNR 'Flying Scotsman' Pacific, 2½″ g Braunston & Walters 1922.
71. Southern 4–4–2 tank, g 1 Bing 1922.

72. 'Challenger' 2–8–2, 3½″ Greenly Vs Lawrence 1924.
73. LNER Mogul, g 1 Bassett-Lowke 1925.
74. LNER 'Flying Scotsman' Pacific, Bassett-Lowke 1925.
75. GWR 'Prairie' 4–4–2 tank, 2½″ g Bing 1925.
76. 'Duke of York' coaches using Carette patterns, g 0 Bassett-Lowke 1925.

77. LNER '112' tank 0–4–0, g 1 with Bing coaches 1925.
78. PLM Pacific, g 0 Bassett-Lowke 1925.
79. LMS 'Prince of Wales' 4–6–0, g 0 Bing 1925.
80. LNER 'Lord Farringdon' 4–6–0, 2½″ g Braunston & Walters 1926.
81. CPR Pacific & rolling stock, 2½″ g special order Bassett-Lowke 1926.

82. SR Mogul, g 0 Bassett-Lowke 1927.
83. 0–6–0 tank (prototype) with Bassett-Lowke telephone no. reversed. 1928.
84. LNER set, g 0 Bing 1927.
85. LMS Mogul, g 1 Bassett-Lowke 1928.

86. LMS 'Royal Scot' 4–6–0, g 0 Bassett-Lowke 1930.
87. GWR 'Hurst Court' 4–6–0, Bing with Bassett-Lowke High Pressure Conversion g 1 1930
88. Southern 'Super Enterprise' 4–6–0, g 0 Bassett-Lowke 1930.
89. LMS standard tank 0–4–0, g 0 Bassett-Lowke 1930.
90. 0–6–0 standard tank production model, g 0 Bassett-Lowke 1930.

91. LMS 'Royal Scot' promo (non-working) model 4–6–0, Bassett-Lowke 1930.
92. LMS 'Royal Scot' 4–6–0, g 0 Bassett-Lowke 1930.
93. LMS 'Royal Scot' 4–6–0, g 0 Bassett-Lowke 1930.
94. LNER 0–6–0 tank, g 1 1930.

95. GWR 'Pannier' tank 0–6–0, g 0 Precision Models 1934.
96. LMS 'Royal Scot' super-detailed 4–6–0, g 1 Bassett-Lowke 1934.
97. LMS 'Royal Scot' 4–6–0, g 1 Bassett-Lowke 1935.
98. LNER 'Great Northern' Pacific, 2½″ g Bassett-Lowke 1935.

99. SR 'Lord Nelson' 4–6–0, g 0 Bassett-Lowke 1935.
100. SR 'Lord Nelson' 4–6–0, 2½″ g Bassett-Lowke 1935.
101. SR 'Schools' 4–4–0, g 0 Marklin 1935.
102. LMS 5XP 'Victory' 4–6–0, g 0 Bassett-Lowke 1935.
103. LMS 'Princess Elizabeth' Pacific, 3½″ g Bassett-Lowke 1935.

99

100

101

102

103

104. LMS Goods Engine 0–6–0, g 0 Bassett-Lowke 1935.
105. CPR Pacific, 2½″ g Bassett-Lowke 1935.
106. LMS 'Princess Elizabeth' Pacific, g 0 Bassett-Lowke 1936.
107. Cab of 2½″ g 'Princess Elizabeth' Bassett-Lowke 1936.

108. LMS 'Conqueror' 4–6–0, g 0 Bassett-Lowke 1936.
109. LNER 'Silver Jubilee' train, g 0 Bassett-Lowke 1937.
110. LMS 'Coronation Scot' train, g 0 Bassett-Lowke 1937.
111. LMS 'Silver Link' & 'Coronation' Pacifics, g 0 Bassett-Lowke 1938.

MODEL TRAINS WORKING ON THE BR...

THIS IS GUAGE "O" AND THE MODEL TRAINS WERE SPECIALLY MA...
AND ARE ALL ELECTRICALLY DRI...

MODELS BY BASSETT-LOWKE LTD., OF NOR...

L.M.S. CORONATION SCOT DRAWN BY L.M.S. PACIFIC LOCOMO...

THE L.N.E.R. CORONATION TRAIN

THE G.W.R. CORNISH RIVIERA DRAWN BY LO...

THE SOUTHERN...

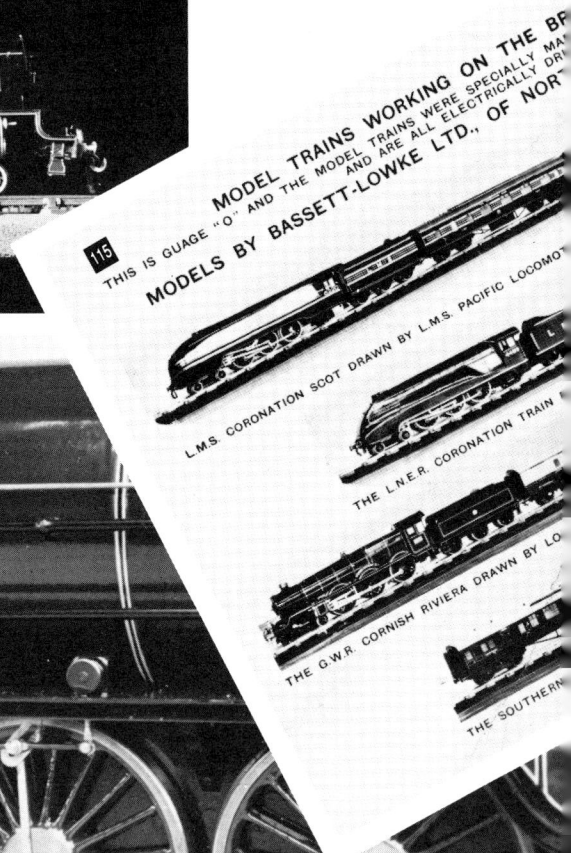

COCK O'THE NORTH

112. LMS 'Princess Elizabeth' and coaches 3½″ g
    Bassett-Lowke 1938.
113. LMS 'Duchess of Montrose', g 0 Bassett-Lowke with Trix
    00 locomotive and coach 1938.
114. LMS 'Duchess of Montrose' Pacific, g 0 Bassett-Lowke
    1938.
115. A special pamphlet for Glasgow exhibition.

116. LNER 'Cock-O-the -North' 2–8–2, 2½″ g Bassett-Lowke
    1938.
117. BR 'Flying Scotsman' Pacific, g 0 1950.
118. GWR 'Pannier' tank 0–6–0, g 0 Hunt 1950.
119. BR 'Stanier' 2–6–4 tank, Bassett-Lowke 1950.
120. LMS 'Fowler' 2–6–4 tank Bassett-Lowke 1932–1956.

117

118

GREAT WESTERN

5765

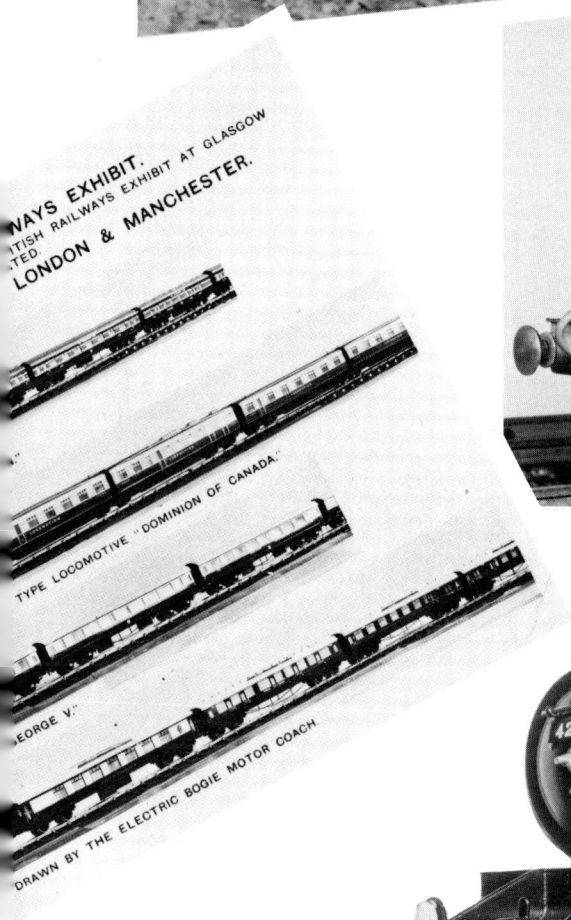

WAYS EXHIBIT,
...TISH RAILWAYS EXHIBIT AT GLASGOW
...TED.
LONDON & MANCHESTER.

TYPE LOCOMOTIVE "DOMINION OF CANADA."

...EORGE V."

DRAWN BY THE ELECTRIC BOGIE MOTOR COACH.

119

42608

42608

120

L M S    2603

121

122

123

124

125

121.   LMS Turbomotive Pacific, g 0 Bassett-Lowke 1950.
122.   LMS 'Royal Scot' 4–6–0, g 0 Bassett-Lowke 1950.
123.   BR rebuilt 'Royal Scot' 4–6–0, g 0 Bassett-Lowke 1955.
124.   BR 'Duchess of Montrose' Pacific, g 0 Bassett-Lowke 1955.
125.   BR 'Black Five', g 0 Bassett-Lowke 1955.

126.   BR Standard 0–6–0 tank, g 0 Bassett-Lowke 1955.
127.   BR Super Enterprise, g 0 Bassett-Lowke 1955.
128.   BR '8F' 2–8–0 Bassett-Lowke 1955.
129.   BR Mogul, g 0 Bassett-Lowke 1957. Showing amount of gold sent by purchaser to cover the price.

130. BR 'Evening Star', g 0 probably Hunt for Bassett-Lowke.
131. BR 'Britannia' Pacific, g 0 probably Hunt for Bassett-Lowke.
132. GWR 'Pannier', g 0 Hunt 1960.
133. GWR 'Prairie' tank, g 0 Bassett-Lowke 1962.
134. M & GN tank 4–4–2, g 0 Bassett-Lowke's last special order 1964.

135. NBR 4–4–0, g 0 special order Bassett-Lowke 1963.
136. CR 4–6–0, g 0 Bassett-Lowke 1963.
137 & 138. 'Burry Port' type 0–6–0 tank built as samples for Bassett-Lowke Railways, g 0 1969.

1. Unidentified 2–6–4 steam locomotive, g 1 c. 1925.
2. Unidentified American-style Pacific, probably 2½″ g live steam c. 1925.
3. Unidentified NER 4–6–0 tank, probably g 1 live steam 1920–1925.
4. 'Ivatt Single' g 1 or 0 (?) possibly by Bing 1915.
5. Unidentified ex-NBR Atlantic probably g 0 clockwork c. 1955.
6. Unidentified LNER Raven-style Atlantic probably 7¼″ g 1920.

7. LNWR 'Black Prince' type 4–4–0, 2½″ g Bassett-Lowke special order 1906.
8. CPR Pacific, 2½″ g Bassett-Lowke for Wembley Exhibition 1924.
9. GCR 'Immingham' 4–6–0, 7¼″ g Bassett-Lowke special order 1925.
10. Nigerian Rly 2–8–2, 5″ g under construction Bassett-Lowke 1925.
11. Nigerian Rly 2–8–2 finished model of above.

105

12. CPR Pacific, 2½″ g static model Bassett-Lowke special order 1924.
13. LMS 4–4–0 'Compound', 2½″ g Bassett-Lowke special order 1925.
14. Benquela Rly 'Garratt' type 4–8–2+2–8–4 Bassett-Lowke special order 1927.
15. LSWR Paddle box, 2½″ g Bassett-Lowke special order 1925.

16. GWR 'King George the Fifth', 5″ gauge Twining for Bassett-Lowke for GWR 1932.
17. United Dairies tanker, 5″ g Bassett-Lowke 1930.
18. GWR 'King', g 1 Bassett-Lowke for V J Harrison 1930.
19. LMS Dining car, 3½″ g Bassett-Lowke for Metropolitan Cammell Co. 1934.
20. Pullman restaurant car, 5″ g Bassett-Lowke for Pullman's 1935.
21. LMS dining car, 3½″ g Bassett-Lowke special order 1936.

22

23

24

25

26

22. Chinese National Rly 4–8–4, ¹⁄₂₀ full-size Bassett-Lowke for Vulcan foundry.
23. LMS 'Compound' 4–4–0, g 1 Bassett-Lowke 1936.
24. Rhodesian 'Beyer-Garratt' 4–6–4+4–6–4, 2½″ g Bassett-Lowke special order 1939–1945.
25. LMS re-built 'Royal Scot' 4–6–0, 2½″ g Bassett-Lowke for LMR 1948.
26. 'Class 5' 4–6–0, 2½″ g Bassett-Lowke for LMR 1949.
27. '2F' 2–6–0, 2½″ g Bassett-Lowke for LMR 1949.

28. E. African Rly Class S9 'Beyer-Garrett' 4–8–2+0–8–4, 3½″ g for Beyer-Peacock 1950.
29. E. African Rly Class S 7 'Beyer-Garrett' 4–8–4+4–8–4, 3½″ g 1950.
30. New South Wales 1000 hp Diesel Electric 3½″ g Bassett-Lowke for BTH Ltd 1952.
31. Bogie covered wagon, 3½″ g for Metropolitan Cammell 1954

109

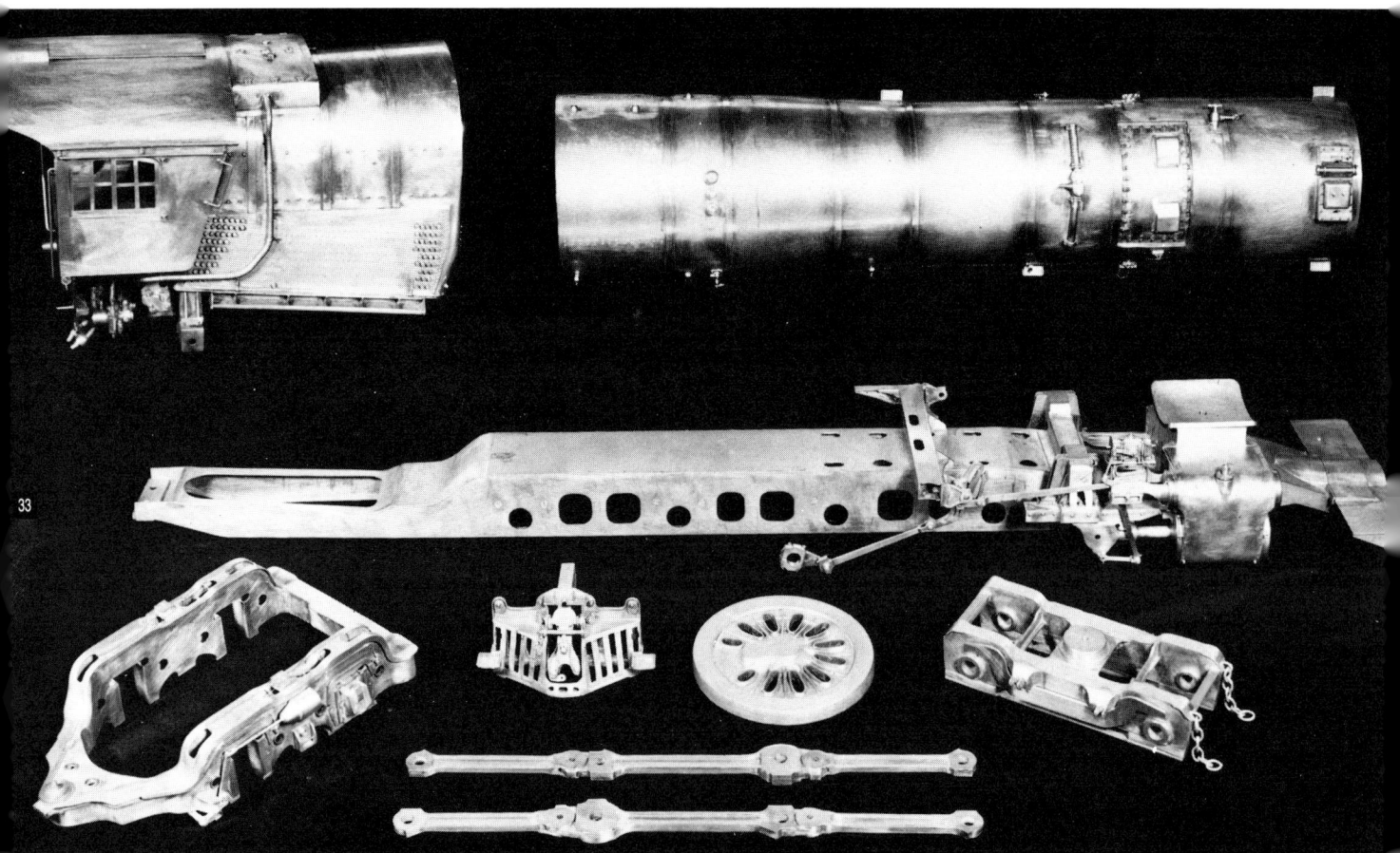

32. Wrecking Crane, 3½″ g Bassett-Lowke for Cowans, Sheldon & Co Ltd 1960.

33. Atlantic Coast Line 4–8–4, 2½″ g Hunt for Bassett-Lowke for Smithsonian 1960.

34. BR 'Evening Star' 2–10–0, g 0 Bassett-Lowke for Alex Issigonis 1960.

35–7. Further completed views of figure 33.

34

35

36

37

# THE BASSETT-LOWKE
# TWIN TRAIN
## TABLE RAILWAY

### THE *BIG* SENSATION IN MODEL RAILWAYS!

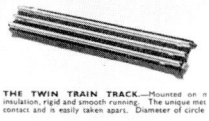

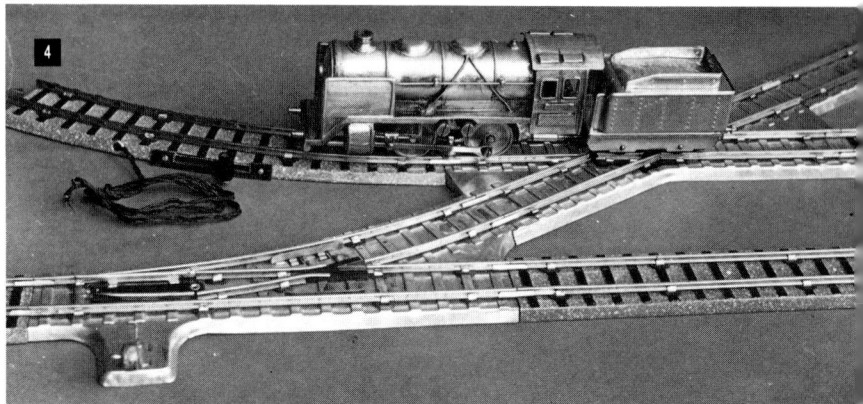

## ALL ABOUT THE "TWINS"!

Two electric trains running on the same line at different speeds, in the same or opposite directions, forwards or backwards, fast or slow !

These are some of the outstanding features of the Bassett Lowke Twin Table Electric Railway which has astonished the experts and sent thousands of boys wild with delight.

Here is something entirely new, and far ahead of anything of the kind ever attempted before, a scale miniature train as modern in many ways as the latest Southern Railway flyer and just as responsive ! The name "Bassett-Lowke" is indicative of its sterling quality.

One of the most astonishing things is the price—35/- only for the passenger train, 30/- for the goods—complete with track and controller—value absolutely unprecedented.

Another startling revelation is that a complete railway system can now be operated in one quarter of the space usually needed.

Another big thrill is that each train is actually fitted throughout with automatic couplings. The new and powerful motor is designed to run trains at all speeds. The special Resistance Controller with safety fuse gives perfect control and makes starting, stopping and reversing as easy as pressing a button and just as sure.

The steel rails are mounted on a patented moulded base, setting a new standard in track construction. These rails carry the trains round the sharpest curve, over points and crossings, safely and smoothly without jolt or jar. To join them firmly together is the work of a second and it is just as easy to take them apart. They are absolutely rigid and true, also impossible to bend.

Before being placed on the market one of the "twins" was subjected to the severest tests. With 15 coaches, one loaded with nails, she was sent on a run of over 100 miles. First at express speed, then dead slow, now forward and then in reverse, the powerful little engine proceeded to eat up the miles. At the end of the journey the train was pronounced as perfect as when she first left the terminus.

No description of these trains can possibly do them justice. You must put your hand on the switch before you can realise what a revolution has been created in model railways.

Be one of the first boys in your town to own a "Twin."

**THE TWIN TRAIN TRACK.**—Mounted on insulation, rigid and smooth running. The unique met contact and is easily taken apart. Diameter of circle
Straight Rail. No. 21/1. 7½" long. Price 9d.
Price 9d. Half-length Curved Rails 21/5) 3⅞
length Straight 21/3. 1⅞" long. Price 6d. a
7½" long. Price 1/-.

**CROSSING.**—Of new construction, mounted on moulded base as rails, with same method of connection. No. 21/9. 7½" long. Price 2/6.

10

11

20/103

12

13

Kühlwagen

20/61

112

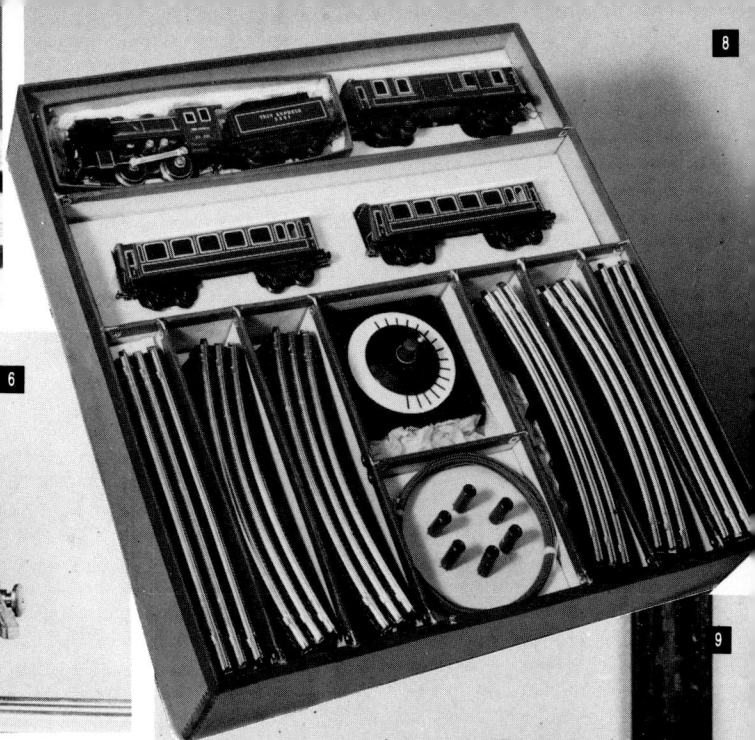

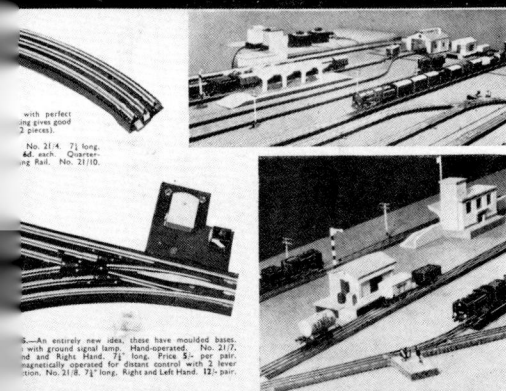

**BASSETT-LOWKE TWIN PASSENGER TRAIN 35/-**
The standard Twin Passenger Electric Train is made up of Engine and Tender, 2 Bogie Coaches and 1 Bogie Guards Van. Automatic couplings are fitted throughout. The electric motor is extra powerful, very strongly built and designed to operate at all speeds. The special Regulating Resistance gives perfect control. Sixteen rails are included, twelve curved and four straight. The rails set an entirely new standard of quality. Mounted on a moulded base they are as rigid as the real thing and cannot be bent or damaged. The train is finished in correct Southern Railway green with yellow lining and lettering. Length of train 24 inches. No. 11/2, Gauge 00. 14 volts A.C. and 12 volts D.C. complete with full instructions. Price 35/-

**BASSETT-LOWKE TWIN GOODS TRAIN 30/-**
The standard Twin Goods Electric Train is made up of Engine and Tender (the same model as for the Passenger Train), I Covered Wagon, I Open Truck, I Shell Oil Truck, I Goods Van. The new automatic couplings throughout add tremendous realism, especially when shunting operations are in progress !
The powerful electric motor drives the train at all speeds at a touch of the switch. Sixteen patented rails on bakelite base are provided, 12 curved and 4 straight. Finished in correct colours. Length of train, 20½ inches. No. 11/1. Gauge 00. 14 volts A.C. and 12 volts D.C. complete with full instructions. Price 30/-

1–17. Bassett-Lowke Twin Trains made by Trix in 1935. This system was later to become known as the Trix Twin System and the story of the association can be found on page 43.

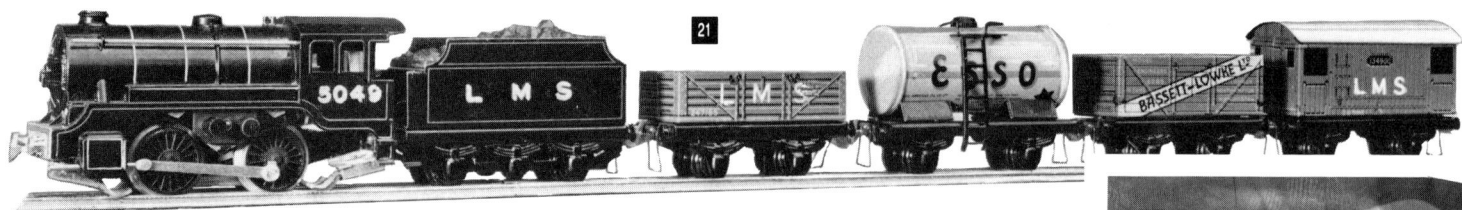

18–30. The range of Trix Twin equipment shown on this page reflects the variety that was available through Bassett-Lowke between 1936–9. The prototype 'Princess' (fig. 26) 1937 is particularly interesting and it should be compared with the production version shown in fig. 25.

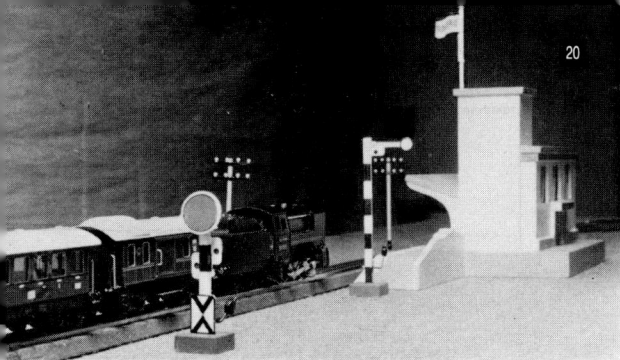

20

31

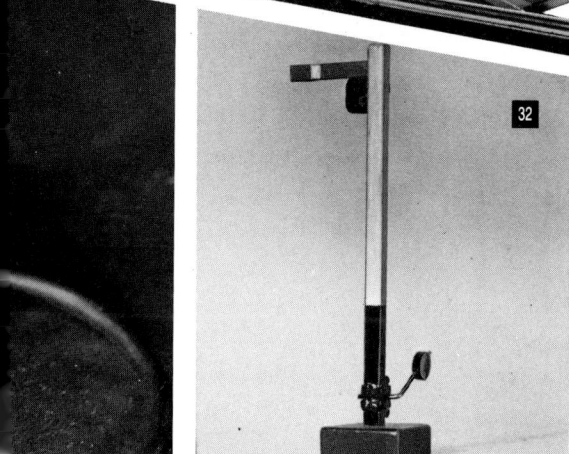

27

32

28

29

30

With best Wishes!
X mas 1936.
S. Kahn

This is the 4-6-2 Trix Twin
German Pacific Scale Model
in its present stage.
Many details are
missing yet, such as
spoked wheels, lamps etc,
but the photo gives some
idea of our plans.

TRIKSTADT

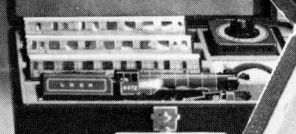

34. It is worth quoting the inscription on the back of the photograph of the prototype German pacific: 'With best wishes, Xmas 1930, S. Kahn. This is the 4–6–2 Trix Twin German Pacific scale model in its present stage. Many details are missing yet, such as spoked wheels, lamps, etc., but the photograph gives some idea of our plans.' An Americanised version of the Pacific (1937) may be seen in fig. 39. All other items on this page are pre-war Trix display sets and layouts.

117

40. A typical Trix rail formation indicating the relatively sophisticated circuitry available on the continental small 3-rail systems pre-war.
41. The departure side of the hall shown in fig. 42.
42. A simple arrangement for a terminus using 'Many Ways'.
43. 'Many Ways' terminal station Trix 1937.
44. Trix cranes, mobile and stationary 1937.
45. Facade by Trix, reflecting the modernist style favoured by Bassett-Lowke 1936.
46. SR motor coach Trix Twin 1937.
47. Driving unit for motor coach.
48. 3 car SR set Trix Twin 1937.
49. Side view of fig. 48.

118

44

45

46

47

48

49

50. The 'Mitropa' steams in on a foggy night somewhere in Europe! (1937).
51. The painted prototype Pacific with pre-production baggage car and second class German coaches 1937.
52. W. J. Bassett-Lowke and Prince Bira operating the layout.

53. Prince Bira's Trix Twin layout in 1941.
54–55. Prototypes of Trix 'Mitropa' (fig. 54) and standard German express coaches 1937.
56. The author operating a Trix layout at Waterloo Station, June 1937.

57–9.  Trix Twin American issues for 1948.
60.  Trix Twin LNER 'Flying Scotsman' Pacific 1938.
61.  Young enthusiasts at St. Pancras.

62.  Various Trix Twin structural series: bridges, viaducts, etc. in planning for Trix Twin Railways 1939.
63.  Trix display at British Industries Fair 1939.

62

63

1 & 2.  A Swiss customer's gauge 1 railway of the 1920s.
3.  A corner of a model railway laid with gauge 1 'Lowko' track 1914.
4.  A customer's LNWR railway in gauge 1 depicting York station 1923.
5.  Another view of fig. 4.

6.  A Maltese customer's model railway probably gauge 0, pre First World War.
7.  Scene on a typical gauge 1 garden railway of the 1920s.
8.  A 2½″ garden scenic line 1920s.
9.  W. F. Cushnie's extremely atmospheric gauge 1 railway in the 1920s.

10–22.  Victor Harrison (whose family were printers of Post
Office stamps) was a friend and customer of
Bassett-Lowke for many years. Several views of his
magnificent pre-war gauge 1 railway at Bishops
Stortford are shown here. Victor Harrison at left in fig.
14.

15

16

17

18

19

20

21

22

23

24

25

26

27

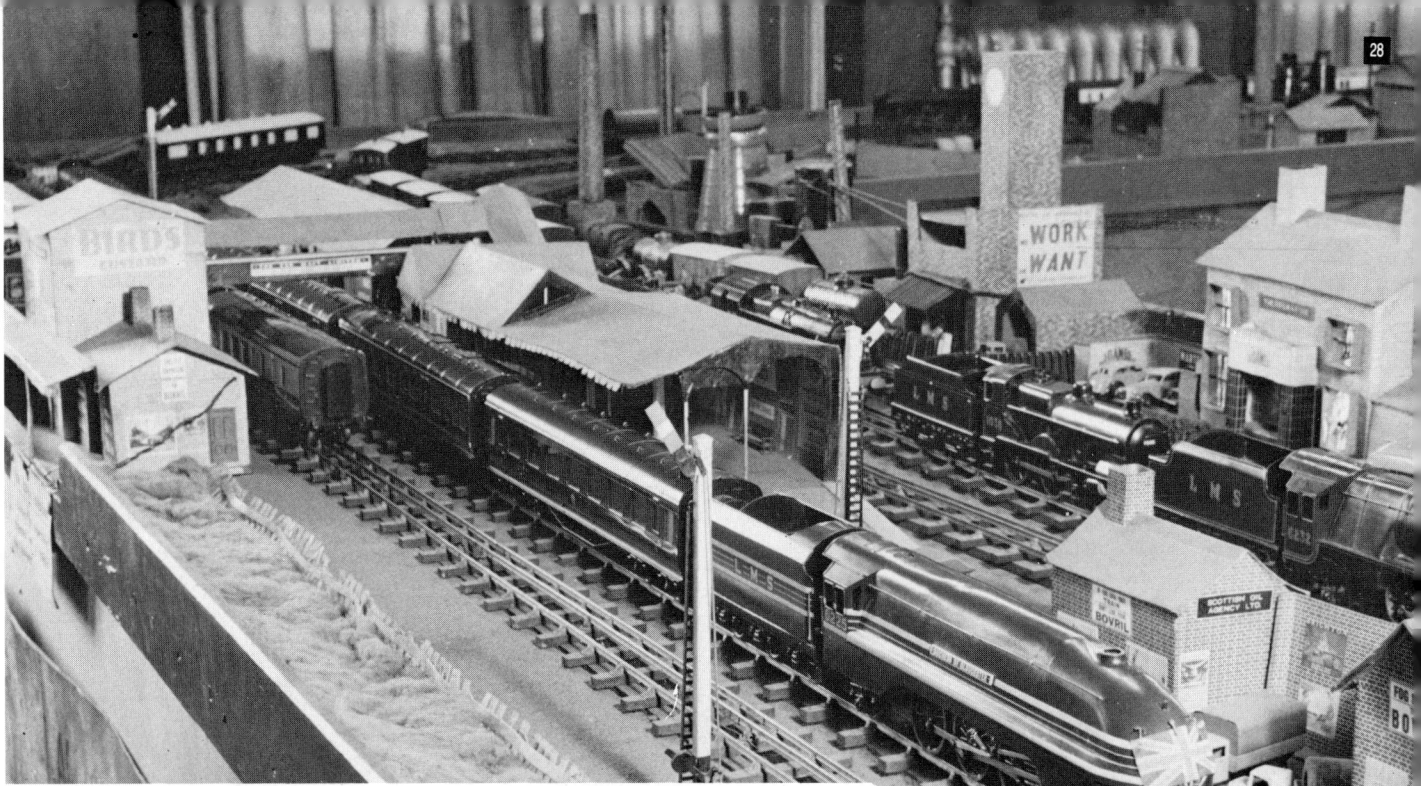

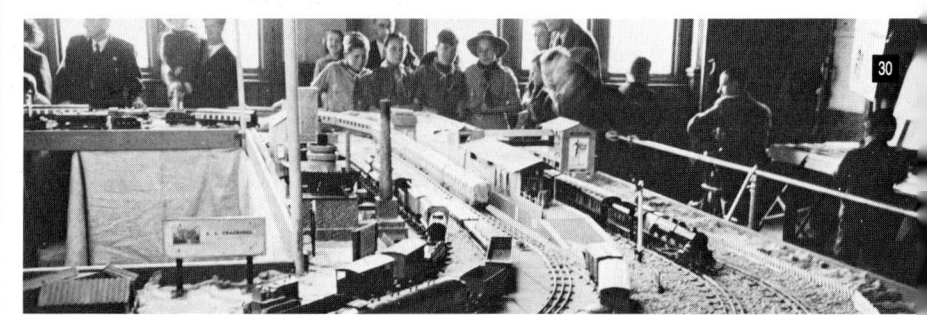

23. Cecil J. Allen's gauge 0 layout in 1935.
24–6. Other views of Mr Allen's layout.
27. Beaconscott model village for which Bassett-Lowke Ltd made the model trains.

28. Harold Elliott's famous portable gauge 0 railway, used for public exhibition work. It toured the country before and after the Second World War.
29–31. Other views of fig. 28.

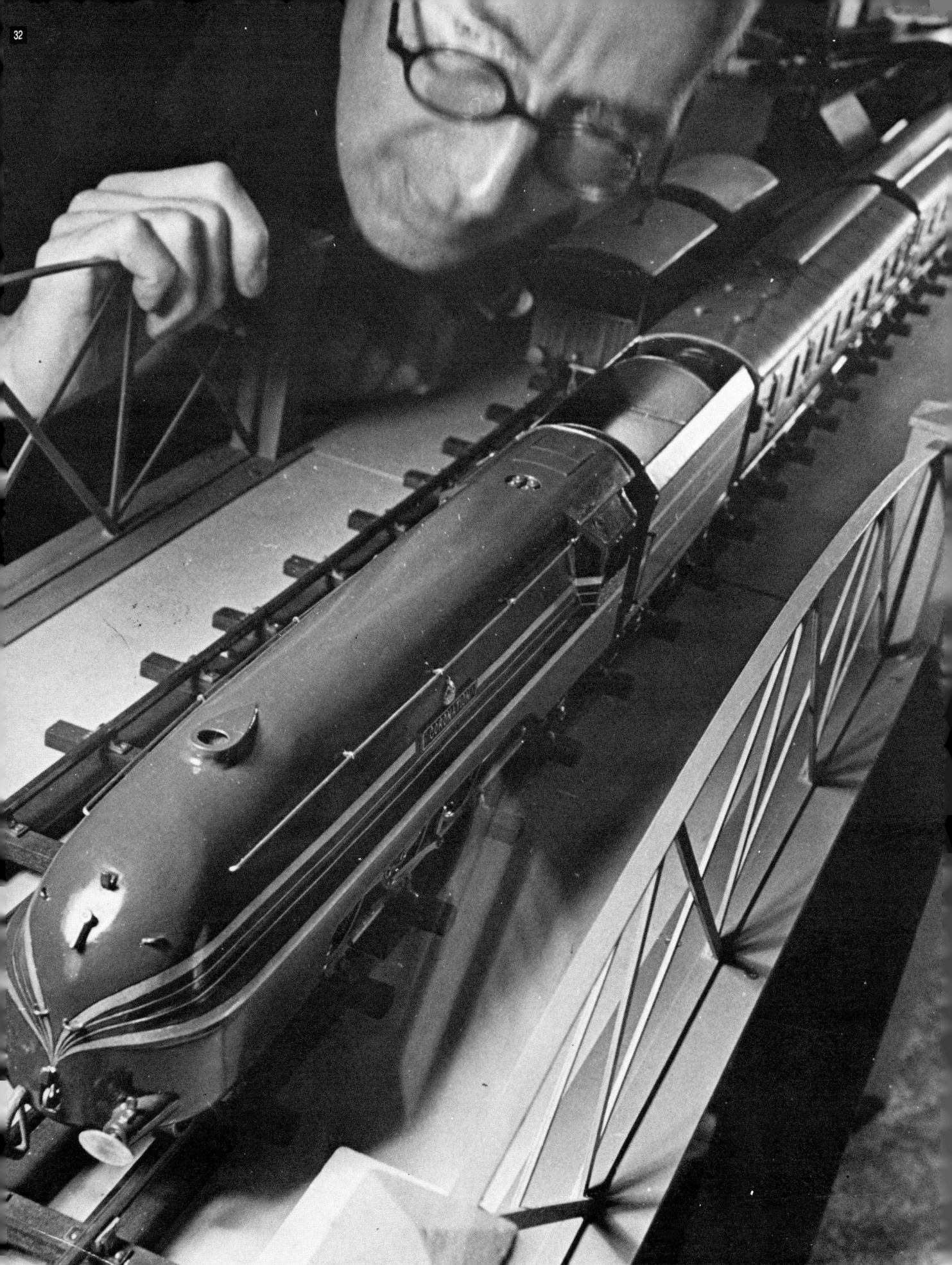

32. View of Gilbert Thomas' gauge 0 railway featuring Bassett-Lowke 'Coronation Scot' Pacific 1938.
33. Gilbert Thomas and his railway at Teignmouth in the late 1930s.
34. GNR train at 'King's Cross', gauge 1 1937.
35. Bassett-Lowke's magnificent gauge 1 GNR A1 1924, which ran on the layout shown in fig. 34.
36. Ivo Peter's electric gauge 0 railway of the 1950s.
37. Prince Bira steaming up his 2½" gauge 'Cock o' the North' 2–8–2 at Rock, Cornwall 1940.
38. An enthusiastic Bassett-Lowke customer, Ryoichi Kusano, displays his Bing/Bassett-Lowke 'King Arthur' 4–6–0 of 1926.

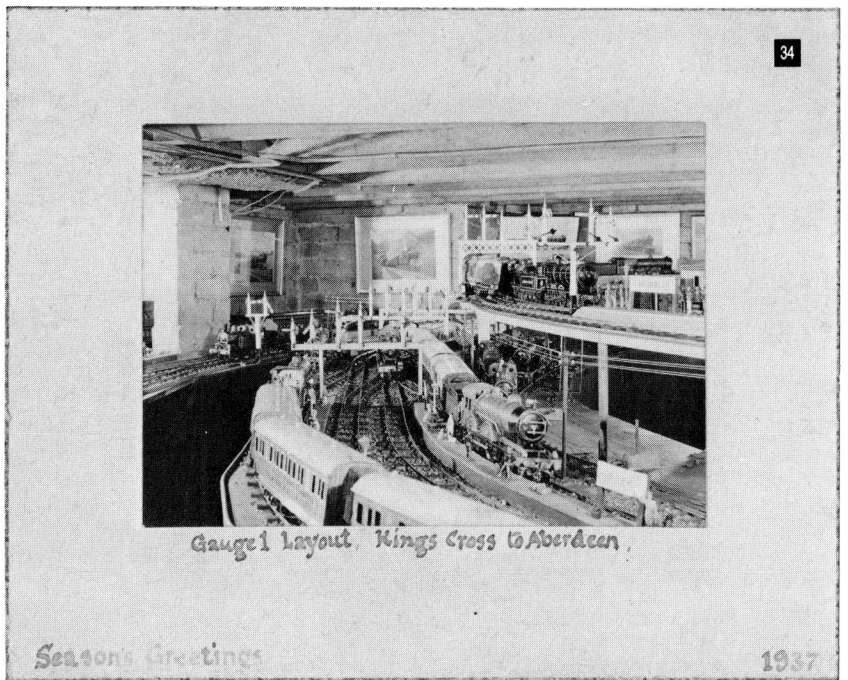

Gauge 1 Layout, Kings Cross to Aberdeen.

Season's Greetings 1937

39–41. Douglas Seaton's magnificent gauge 0 layout utilising only Bassett-Lowke items. It was built in 1945 and dismantled in 1970.

42. 15″ 'Little Giant' locomotive bound for the Franco/British exhibition at White City in 1908. Here standing outside the then new London Shop at 257 High Holborn.

43. 15″ 'Nipper' 1912.

44. An Edwardian family outing behind 'Nipper' c. 1912.
45. 7¼" passenger carrying vehicle produced from 1910 onwards.
46. 'Mighty Atom' 4–4–2, 15" gauge 1912.
47. GNR Atlantic in 9½" gauge on Captain Holder's famous railway at Beaulieu 1913.
48. John Terence's GNR Atlantic probably 10¼" gauge on his garden railway c.1914.
49. Atlantic on the Ravenglass & Eskdale 15" railway c.1914.
50. The Pacific 'Sir Aubrey Brocklebank' 15" gauge on the Ravenglass & Eskdale railway c.1914.

The Fairbourne Express at the Bathing Beach.

136

Miniature Railway, Marine Lake & Park, Rhyl.
Locomotive built by Messrs Bassett-Lowke, Ltd., London & Northampton.

51. Postcard.
52. Fairbourne 15″ gauge railway in 1915.
53. Ticket.
54. Unknown locomotives (possibly special orders) which formed the basis of a Bassett-Lowke postcard.
55. Carson 3½″ gauge 'Great Bear' Pacific in foreground, GNR Pacific (middle) and GNR 'Precursor' 4–4–0 (top) 1920.
56. Radwell Park 10¼″ gauge railway.

57. 1913 Bassett-Lowke Christmas card featuring the miniature railway at Rhyl.
58. 15″ Little Giant at Southend in 1922.
59. 10¼″ NBR A1, 'Stanley Baldwin' 1923.
60. 7¼″ LNWR gauge 'George the Fifth'; at right: Johnny Braunston, the builder of the model; at left: Mr. Kilburn. c.1920. Note bellows.
61. 7¼″ LNWR 'George the Fifth' 4–4–0 produced from 1911 to 1928.

62. The Brast brothers owned a garage in Zurich and were Bassett-Lowke large scale devotees. Here shown with 7¼″ gauge 'Flying Scotsman' in construction using Bassett-Lowke parts 1943.
63. 7¼″ gauge 'Royal Scot' in construction for Enrico Pardo of Peru 1951.
64. Mr. Kilburn's 'Royal Scot' complete.

65. Walter Mann working on 7¼″ gauge Bullied Pacific 'Winston Churchill' for Canadian customer in 1967.
66. The Brast brothers' 'Flying Scotsman' complete on their Lucerne railway in 1953.
67 & 68. 7¼″ gauge 0–6–0 tank built by E. K. Mackintosh of Narwee, Australia 1967.

65

66

67

68

1. Rare coach in gauge 2 by Schoenner for Bassett-Lowke 1902 – first scale proportion tin plate coach available.
2. Bing gauge 2, 3, or 4 SECR coach 1902.
3. GNR Third class hand-painted coach by Carette 2½″ g 1905.
4. One of a range of hand-made goods stock in 2″ gauge by Winteringham for Basset-Lowke in 1905. Sets of parts also available.
5. Other items in the same range as fig. 4.
6. Prototype lithographed goods stock by Carette for Bassett-Lowke 1905.

7. A typical production example of tin plate goods rolling stock by Carette in 0, 1 and 2″ gauge from 1905 onwards.
8. Examples of best quality wood goods rolling stock in gauge 2 by Winteringham's for Bassett-Lowke from 1907 onwards.
9. Four goods vehicles, gauge 1 Carette 1909.
10. Range of tin plate rolling stock in gauge 0, 1 and 2 by Carette for Bassett-Lowke photographed in 1909.
11. Flat printed tin sides for Great Western brake end by 1909.

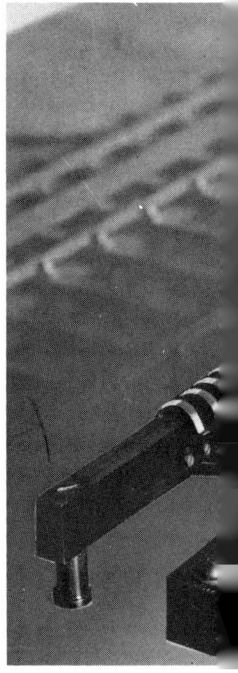

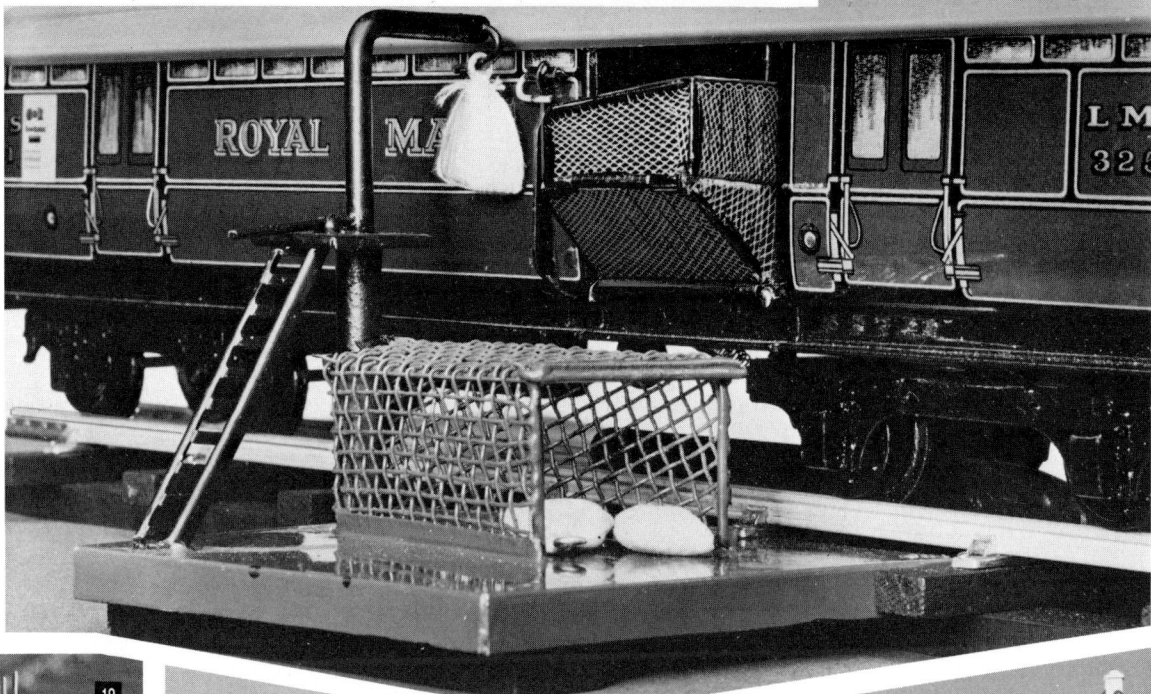

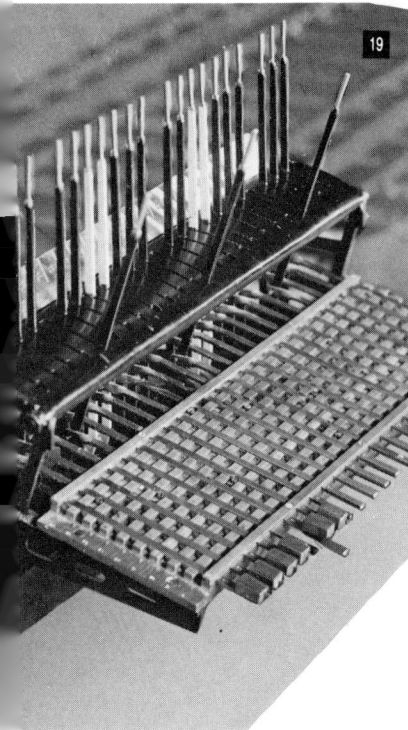

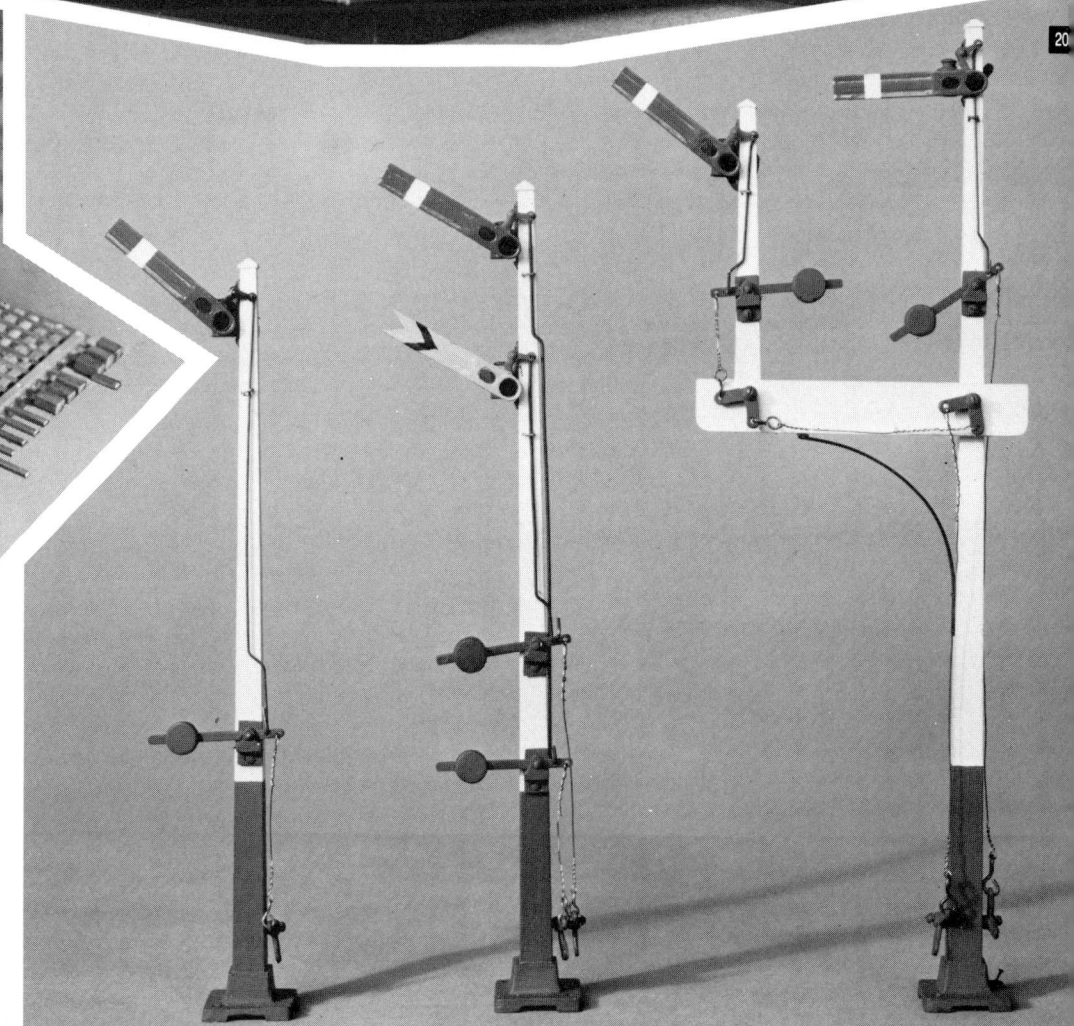

12. Mobil Oil tanker gauge 0 Bassett-Lowke 1925.
13. Colas tanker gauge 0 Bassett-Lowke 1925.
14. LMS van gauge 0 – one of final series of lithographed goods rolling stock by Bassett-Lowke in 1950.
15. Typical goods train comprising final series lithographed goods stock 1950.
16. Bassett-Lowke's close connection with the Derbyshire firm of E. Exley was reflected in the fine range of scale appearance passenger vehicles. These SR motorised units

were based on the standard SR brake composite.
17. Lithographed tin plate railway station, gauge 0 Carette for Bassett-Lowke 1910.
18. Post Office mail van and ground gear, gauge 0 Bassett-Lowke 1931.
19. Interlocking lever frame Bassett-Lowke 1920.
20. Standard 'Best Quality' signals for gauge 0, Bassett-Lowke 1912–63. They were made only in lower quadrant until 1923.

21. GNR Atlantic gauge 1 by Bing standing in front of one of Carette's finest lineside accessories, the Water Tower c.1909.
22. Luggage for gauge 1 of continental origin c.1910.
23. An accurate if somewhat stern Goods Terminus, gauge 0 by Bassett-Lowke 1925.
24. Wooden signal box, gauge 1, adorned with charming tin 'enamel signs' so typical of pre-war model railway series 1925.

25. Single road wooden engine shed Bassett-Lowke 1925.
26. Range of station accessories – figures for gauge 0 Bassett-Lowke 1925–39. The two figures on the left are Britains, Lloyd George and George Bernard Shaw.
27. Bookstall made up from printed card supplied by Percival Marshall & Co for gauge 0 1920.
28. Platform series, gauge 0 Bassett-Lowke available from 1925.
29. Original works drawing for book stall in fig. 28.

26

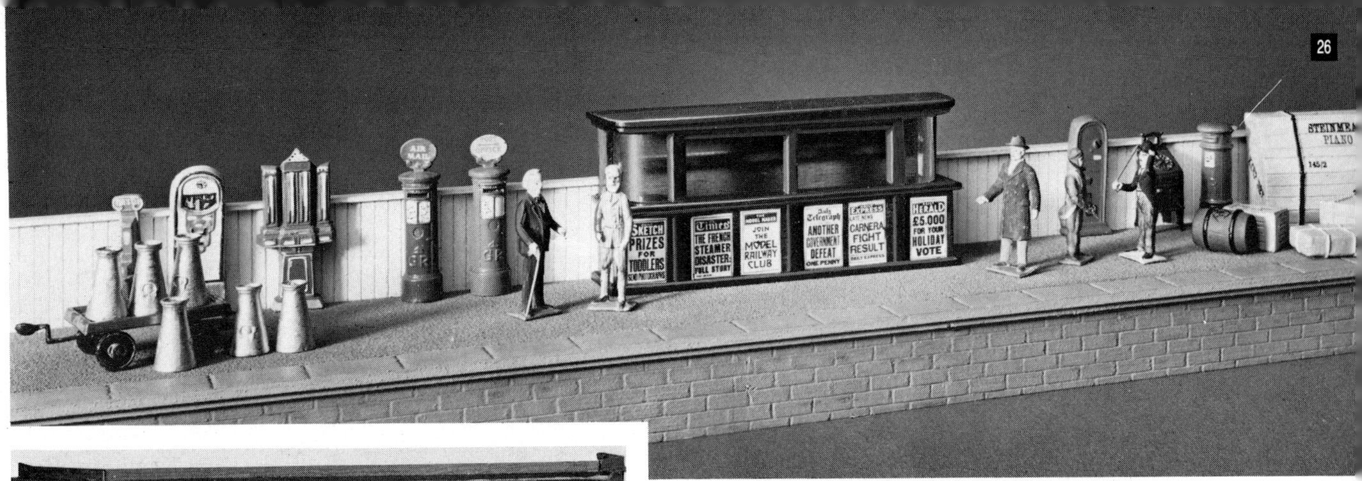
SKETCH PRIZES FOR TODDLERS
Times THE FRENCH STEAMER DISASTER: FULL STORY
JOIN THE MODEL RAILWAY CLUB
Daily Telegraph ANOTHER GOVERNMENT DEFEAT
Express CARNERA FIGHT RESULT
HERALD £5,000 FOR YOUR HOLIDAY VOTE
STEINMAN PIANO

27

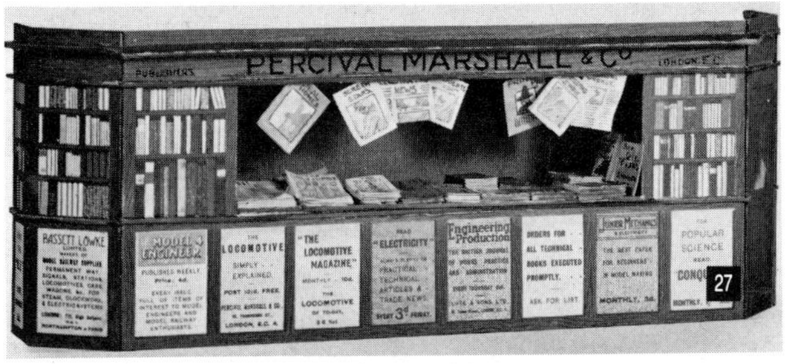
PUBLISHERS
PERCIVAL MARSHALL & Co
LONDON E.C.
BASSETT-LOWKE
"THE LOCOMOTIVE MAGAZINE"
Engineering Production
THE POPULAR SCIENCE

28

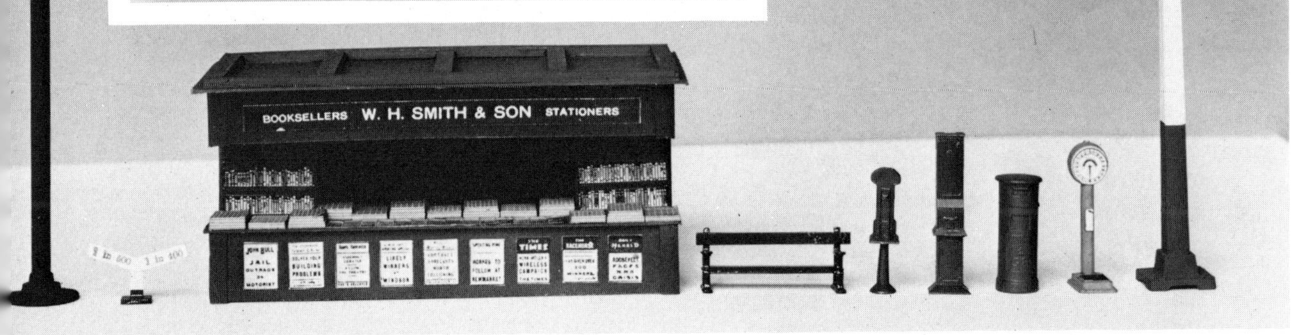
BOOKSELLERS W. H. SMITH & SON STATIONERS
JOHN BULL
TIMES

29

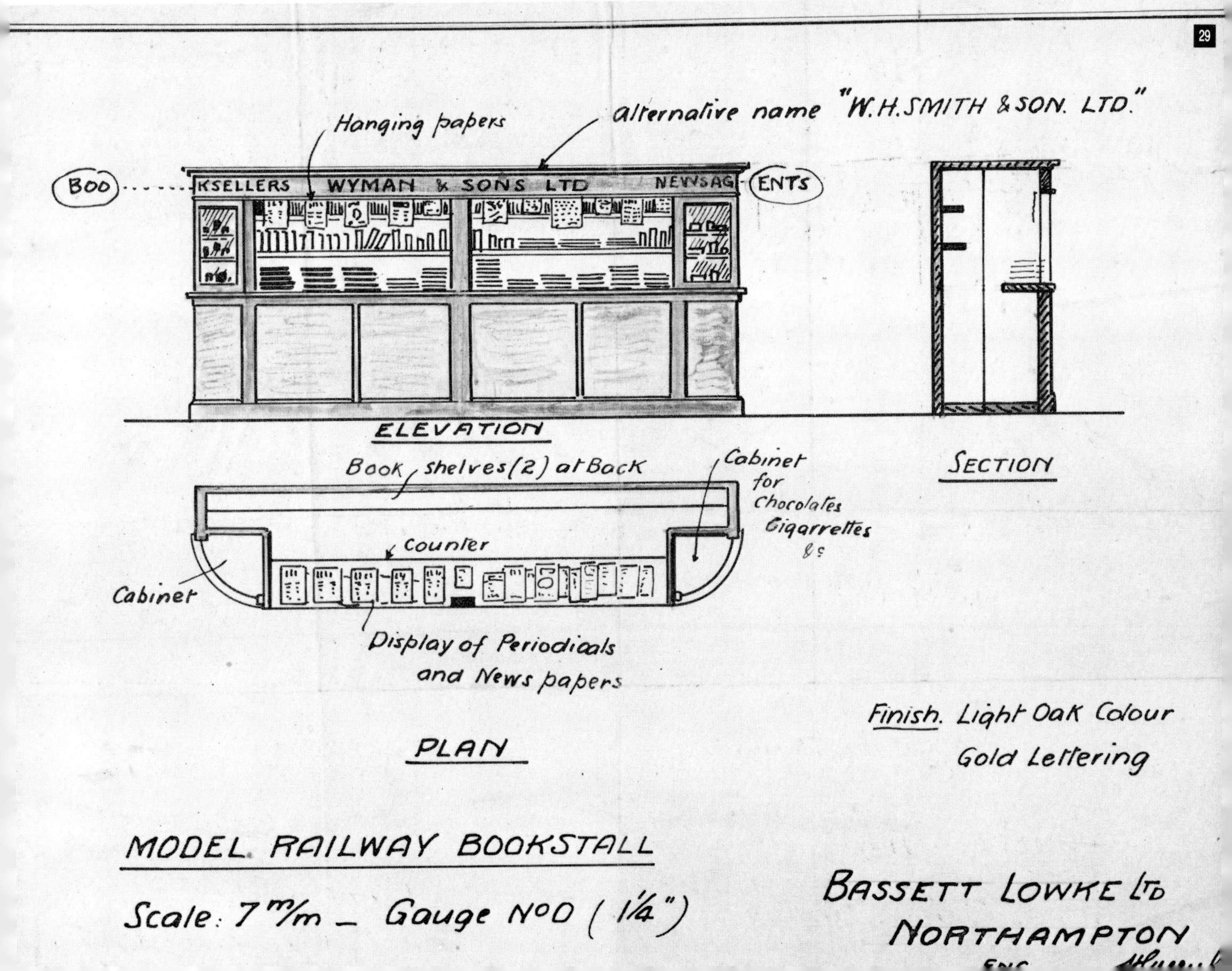
Hanging papers
alternative name "W. H. SMITH & SON. LTD."
BOO
KSELLERS WYMAN & SONS LTD NEWSAG
ENTS
ELEVATION
SECTION
Book shelves (2) at Back
Cabinet for Chocolates Cigarrettes &c
Counter
Cabinet
Display of Periodicals and News papers
PLAN
Finish. Light Oak Colour Gold Lettering
MODEL RAILWAY BOOKSTALL
Scale: 7 m/m – Gauge No 0 (1¼")
BASSETT LOWKE Ltd NORTHAMPTON

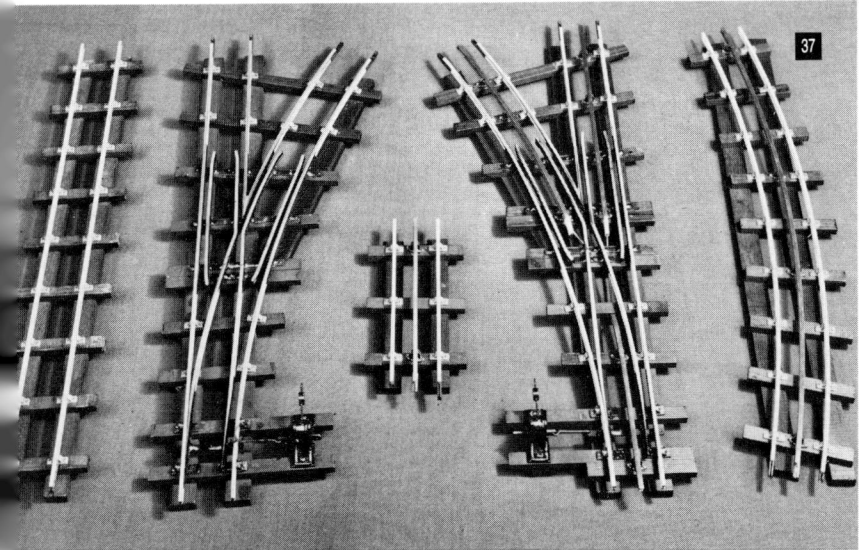

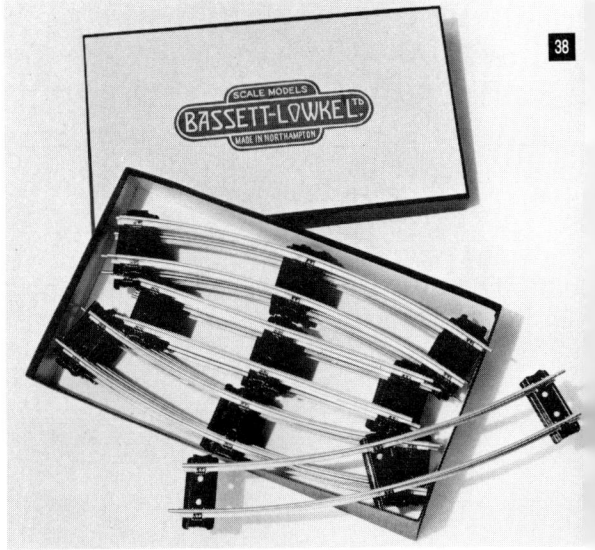

30. Wooden turntable gauge 0, Bassett-Lowke 1930.
31. Small wayside wooden station, gauge 0 Bassett-Lowke with tin 'enamel' signs 1920.
32. Wooden through station facade gauge 0 Bassett-Lowke 1925.
33. Track side facade of lithographed through station Carette available in gauge 0 and 1 1909.
34. Plate layers hut and buffer stop, gauge 0 Bassett-Lowke 1924.

35. Single road engine shed, gauge 2 Bassett-Lowke 1920.
36. 'Modern' prototype single road engine shed in wood, Bassett-Lowke 1935.
37. The final gauge 0 permanent way using slide on chairs and spring metal fishplates by Bassett-Lowke available until early 1960s.
38. Tin plate track used in post-war clockwork and steam sets, available until 1955.

48. Bassett-Lowke's new cast bogie frames c. 1930.

39. Shows a detail of the coach of the Euston–Watford set
    which was to be a unique lithographed motorised model in
    the Company's range.
39–47. Archive photographs taken on the introduction of new
    British-made tin plate rolling stock in 1930.

# Model 15-Rater Schooner.

## "VEDETTE BOA

This fine model is constructed to a scale of approximat
represents the latest type of "Pickett" Boat as used in H.M
the Model provides a good reliable boat that will steam ste
be

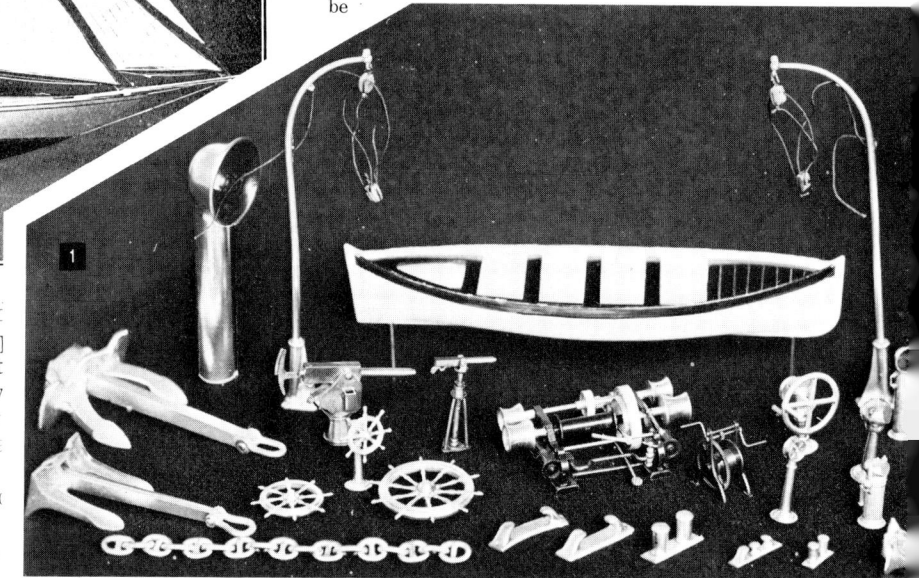

This schooner is modelled on the most mod
to compete in the model 15-rater class.  The disp
and being exceptionally light, is very spright
inherent difficulties of a model schooner hav
entirely eliminated, the result being exceedingly
of sailing.  The various centres of pressure a
properly considered.

The Specification is identical with the moc
page.

Price, £20 complete.

## Clockwork Boats.

### NEW MODEL TORPEDO BOAT DESTROYERS.

*Bing*

High-Class Scale

## Model Clockwork Batt

153

### SCALE MODEL TORPEDO BOATS.

#### H.M.S. "VANGUARD."

This Model is an entirely new introduction this seas
oubt the most up-to-date Clockwork Model Battleship
ver produced.  It is a model of the latest Englis

An entirely new Model for this season, fitted with strong Clockwork, Four
Funnels. Torpedo Tubes. Guns. and Railings.

# H.M. Cruiser "Minotaur."

## (WITH STEAM MACHINERY.)

Bassett-Lowke
London & Northa

## Scale Model
# .S. "Lord Nelson."
### (ELECTRICALLY DRIVEN.)

a foot, and
he design of

# High=Class Scale Model Steam Yacht.
### (With Electric Mechanism.)

Bassett-Lowke, Ltd.,
London & Northampton.

os.

# SCALE MODEL LINER.
### (ELECTRICALLY DRIVEN.)

Range of ships and boats available through Bassett-Lowke in
1910.
1. Standard Bassett-Lowke (Ship Models) ship fittings range
   1910.

3. HMS *King George* V ¹⁄₁₀″ to 1′, electric 1913.
4. HMS *Queen Mary* ¹⁄₁₀″ to 1′ electric 1913.
5. Steam plant.

6–9. The fighting fleet in miniature constructed for the Imperial Services exhibition at Earls Court 1913, featuring *Neptune, New Zealand, George V* and *Thunderer*. Boats measured between 18–20′ with weights from 2,400–2,700 lb each firing 10–13″ guns.

No130

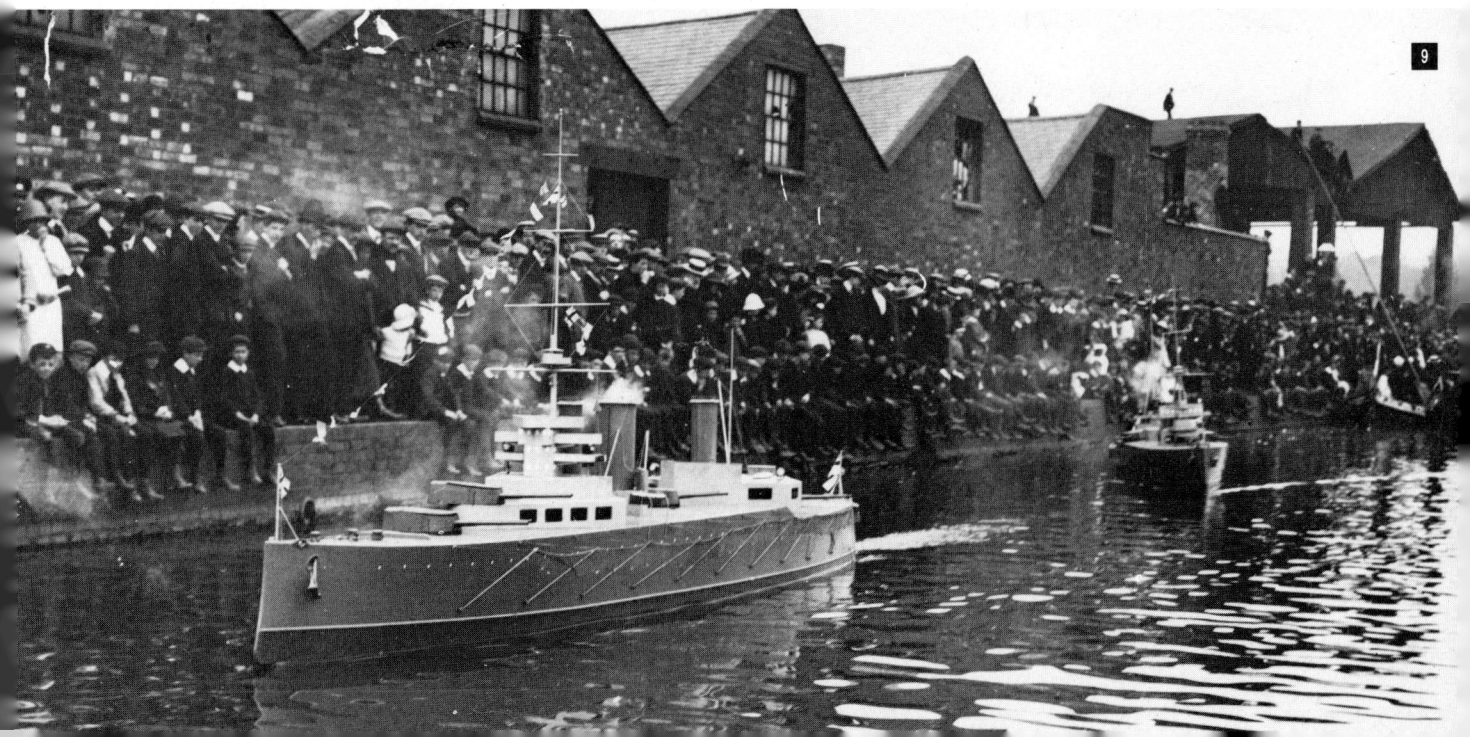

No 114    No 110

No. 92

10.   Super Dreadnought HMS *Thunderer* c. 1912.
11.   Super Dreadnought HMS *Colossus* with HMS *Neptune* in
      background c. 1912.
12.   Stern of HMS *King George* V under construction c. 1912.
13.   *King George* V at left and HMS *Neptune* at right under
      construction.

14.   HMS *Neptune* prior to launching.
15, 16.   Testing the hull of *King George V*.
17.   Hull of *Victoria and Albert*.
18.   HMS *Victoria and Albert* scale of 2/5" to 1' c. 1912.

A selection of boats imported by Bassett-Lowke.

19. Torpedo Boat Märklin 1910.
20. Dreadnought Bing 1912.
21. Destroyer Bing 1912.
22. Cruiser Bing 1912.

23. Launch Bing 1914.
24. Tug Bing 1920.
25. Riverboat Bing 1914.
26. Liner Bing 1914.

27–8. *Cutty Sark* Bassett-Lowke special order finished 1927 with and without sails.

29. A large hull being transported from the Northampton works 1950.

30. *Empress of Britain* ready for despatch 1935.

31. *SS Massillid* for Parisian shipping office. c. 1928.

32. *SS Josephine Charlotte* – one of a standard range of ship models made between 1922–1939 – this for member of Belgian royal family.

33–42. The above craft are a representative selection of the standard clockwork, electric and steam range made between 1920–1935. They appear in Bassett-Lowke's special ship catalogues which were usually issued on a bi-annual basis. All these were made by Bassett-Lowke Ships Models, commonly known as Bassett-Lowke SM Ltd.

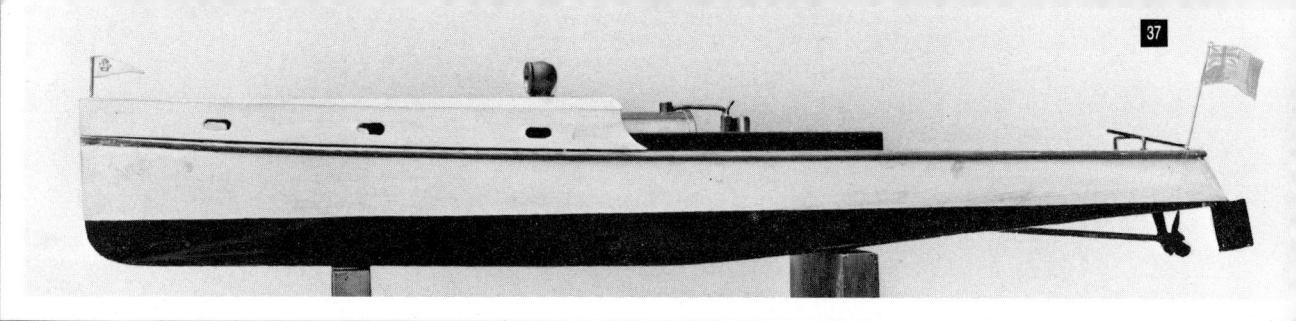

37

MARGARET ROSE

38

TURBINETTE

39

IOLANTHE

40

IOLANTHE II

41

MISS ENGLAND

42

43–9. A series of naval vessels made as standard lines between 1914–1939. Most had wooden hulls and metal superstructures.

50. 48″ steam-driven model of White Star liner 1932.
51. 30″ standard cargo boat available in clockwork or electric 1935.
52. 30″ *Iolanthe* electric launch c. 1930.
53. 39″ D 36 Destroyer steam-powered 1934.
54. *Streamlinia* steam-powered launch 1937.

55. Prince Chula Chakrabongse and royal visitors about to launch Bassett-Lowke *Europa* electric powered Bremen Nord Deutscher Lloyd liner 1939.
56. Bassett-Lowke cabin cruiser fitted with radio control being tested in July 1947.

54

55

56

57

## PERFECTION IN MODEL YACHT DESIGN

We have pleasure in presenting to connoisseurs of Model Sailing Yachts a new series for the coming season. The design of the " Southwold " Racer, as she has been christened, is based upon years of experience and backed by an expert knowledge of sailing craft both large and small. We guarantee this yacht to give every satisfaction, both in regard to speed and holding a course. To ensure these very desirable features each model is thoroughly tested on an open stretch of water. Anticipating the popularity of this model, we have kept the price as low as possible to enable every racing enthusiast to possess a real prize-winning yacht.

166

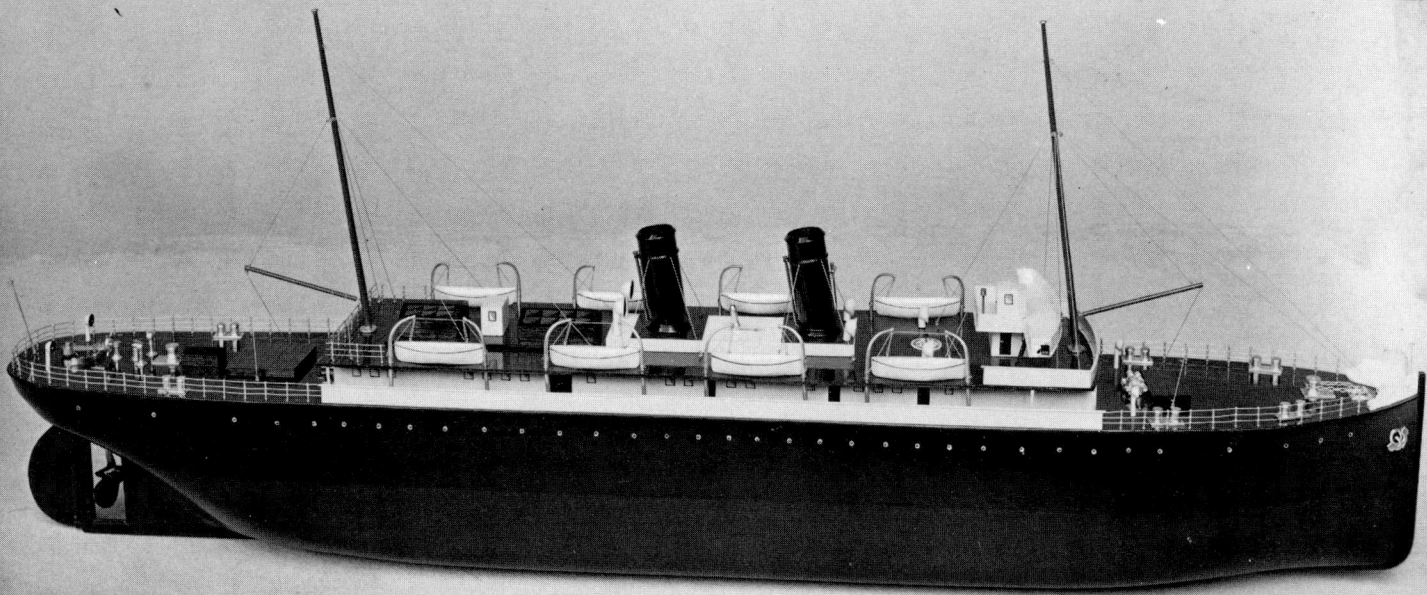

57. Part of the Bassett-Lowke Yacht range 1939.
58. Standard cargo ship c. 1925.
59. *Normandie* standard clockwork model 1936.
60. Standard liner 1930.

61. HMS *Vindex* ⅛″ to 1′ scale made for Swan Hunter 1947.
62. Detail of HMS *Anson* ⅛″ to 1′ scale for Swan Hunter 1947.
63. Atlantic Blue Ribbon holders (l to r): *Mauretania*, *Conte de Savola*, *Bremen*, *Normandie*, *Queen Mary* with *Mayflower* in foreground.
64. A view of the Mariners' Museum in the U.S.A. – models (l to r): *John D. Archbold*, *Strathnaver*, *The Cape Town Castle* and *President*.
65. *Arnhem* scale of 4 mm to 1′ for Messrs J. Brown & Co 1947.

168

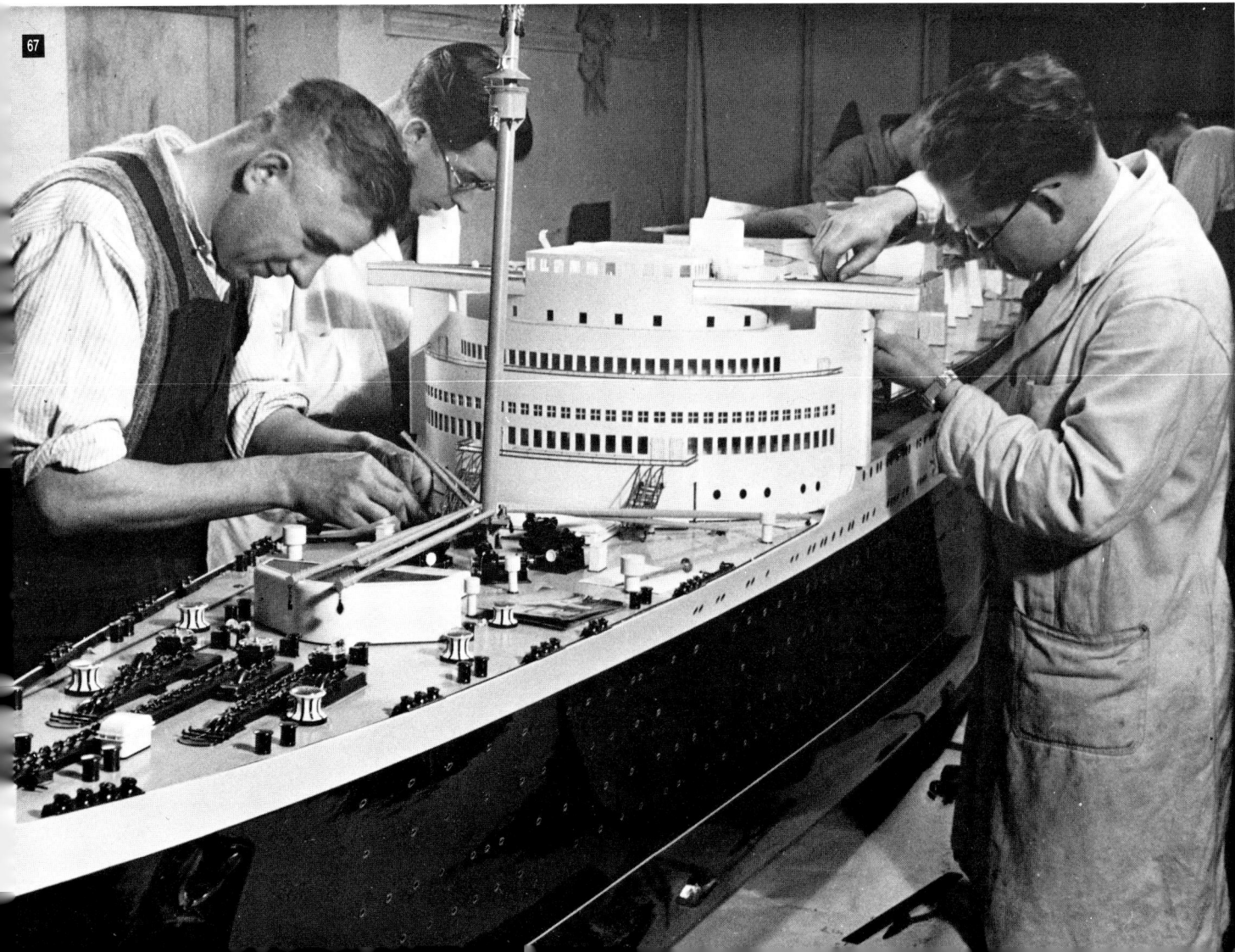

66. Working on hull of *Queen Elizabeth* ¼″ scale for Cunard
    White Star Line 1948.
67. Deck fittings being applied to *Queen Elizabeth*.
68. Waterline Models of *Queen Elizabeth* in scales of 100″, 50″
    and 25″ to 1′ alongside ¼″ scale model.

69. Committee of inspection including (extreme left) Lord
    Brookdale talking to the author; extreme right rear, Sir
    John Brown.

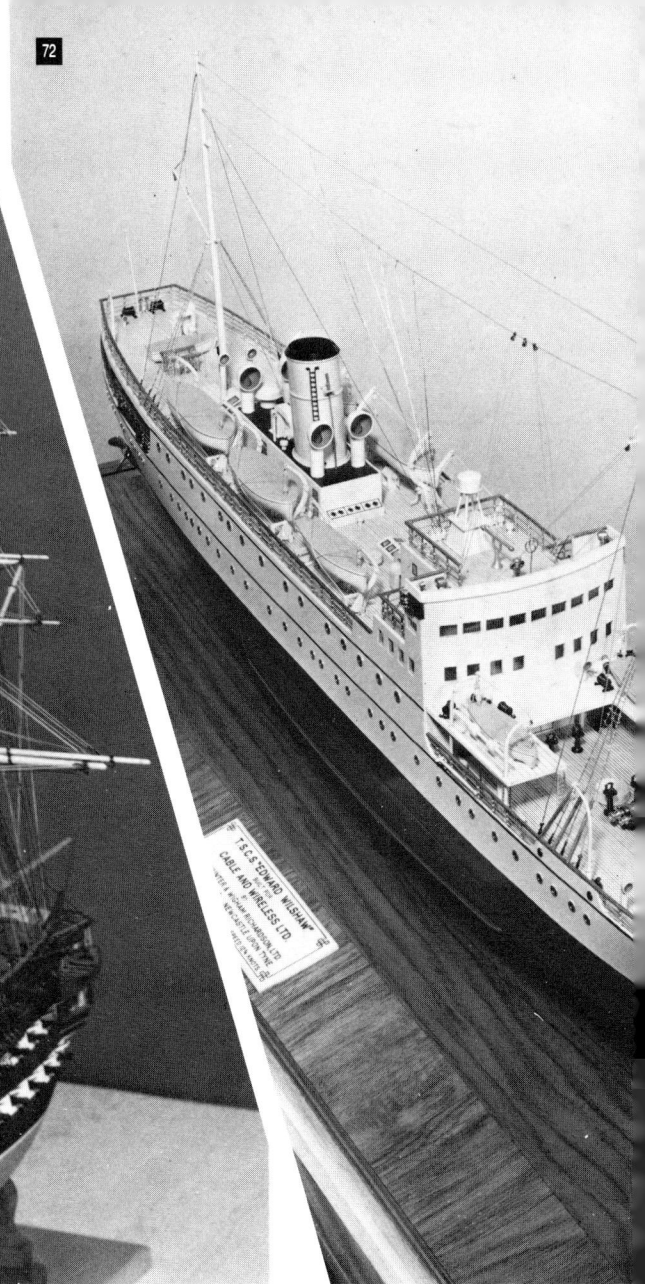

70. *HMS Cornwall* 1815 originally *HMS Wellesey* ¼″ to 1′ Bassett-Lowke for Admiralty 1949.
71. *King George V* ⅛″ to 1′ for the Admiralty 1949.
72. Ship no. 1862 TSCS *Edward Wilshaw* approx 2′ long for Swan Hunter 1949.

73. Ship no. 648 *Rangitani* ³⁄₁₆″ to 1′ for John Brown 1949.
74. Detail of LMS Holy Shaun-Ulster ferry 1950.
75. Model of two-berth cabin 3″ to 1′ for Blue Star Line 1950.

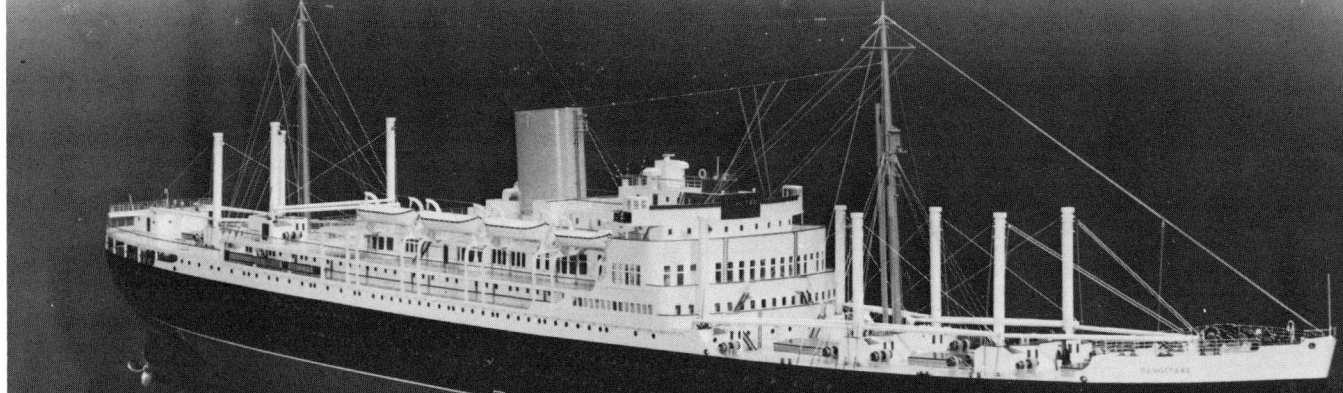

73

74

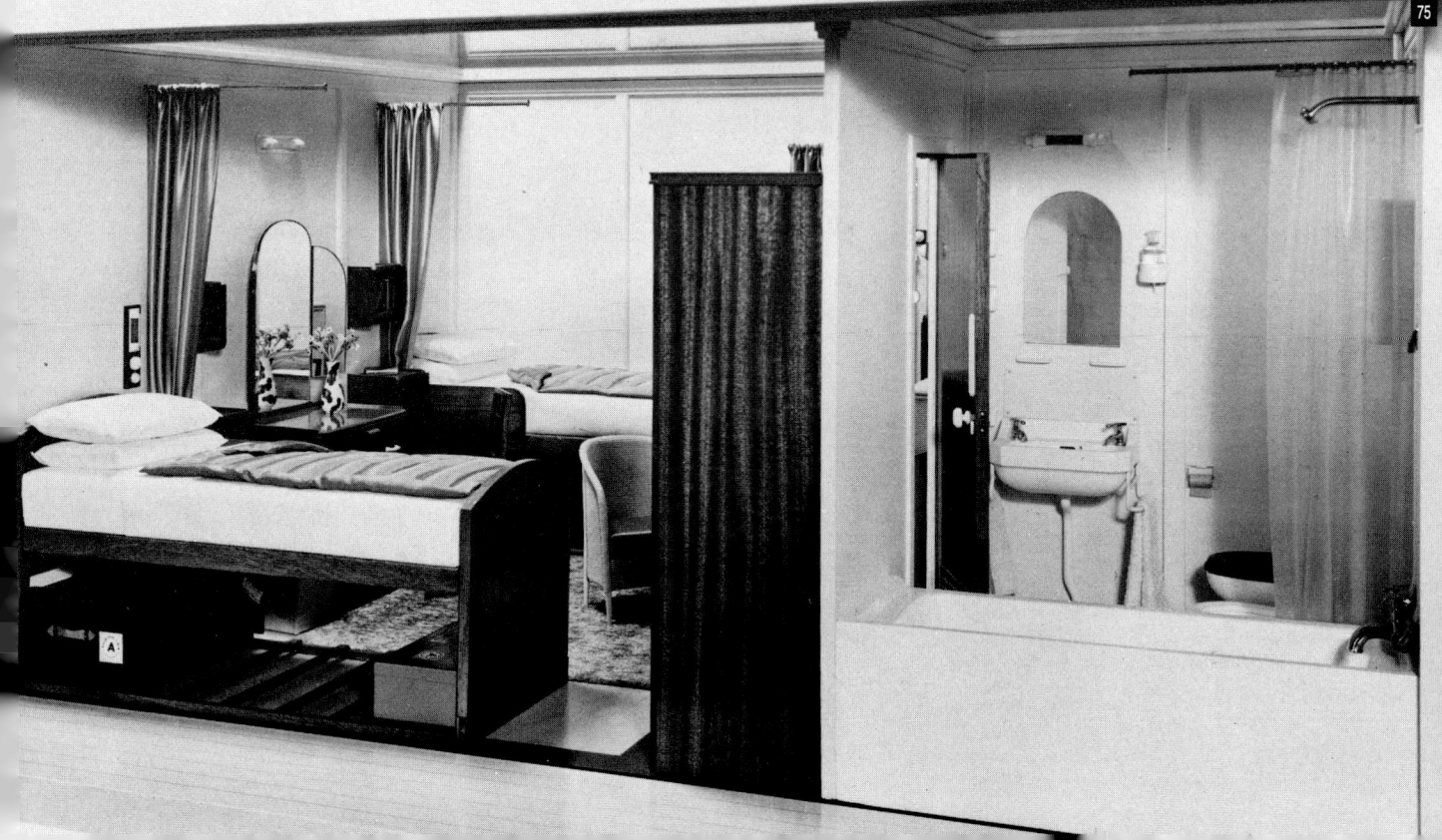

75

76

MODEL OF
S.S. COLOMBIE
HAVRE · PLYMOUTH · WEST INDIES · SPANISH MAIN SERVICE
COMPAGNIE GENERALE TRANSATLANTIQUE · FRENCH LINE
Makers of the model: BASSETT · LOWKE Ltd.

77

78

79

PATHFINDER

76. *SS Colombie* made for French line 1950.
77. *St. Patrick* ⅛″ to 1′ for BR Western Region 1950.
78. *Bloemfontain Castle* ¹⁄₁₆″ to 1′ for Union Castle Mail Steamship Company 1950.
79. Ore carrier *Pathfinder* ¹⁄₃₂″ to 1′ made for William Darvie & Co 1951.

80. *Vickland* scale of 1:96 for John Brown 1950.
81. Dredger no. 1111 ¼″ to 1′ for Lobnitz 1950.
82. Vessel no. 1203 *General Sam Martin* ¼″ to 1′ for Cammell Laird 1950.

83. 22 models of cable ships ¹⁄₃₂″ to 1′ for Swan Hunter 1951.
84. Battle class destroyer ⅛″ to 1′ for the Admiralty 1951.
85. Tri-structural model of *SS Velutina* ³⁄₁₆″ scale for Swan Hunter 1951.
86. Passenger liner *Vera Cruz* ¹⁄₇₅″ scale for John Cockerill 1951.

87. 350 ton barge ¼″ to 1′ for Mechans 1951.
88. Model of lifeboat renovated and rebuilt for I. R. Fleming 1951.
89. Vessel no. 1104 Grab Hopper Dredger *Mersey No 14* ¼″ to 1′ for Lobnitz. 1952.

86

87

88

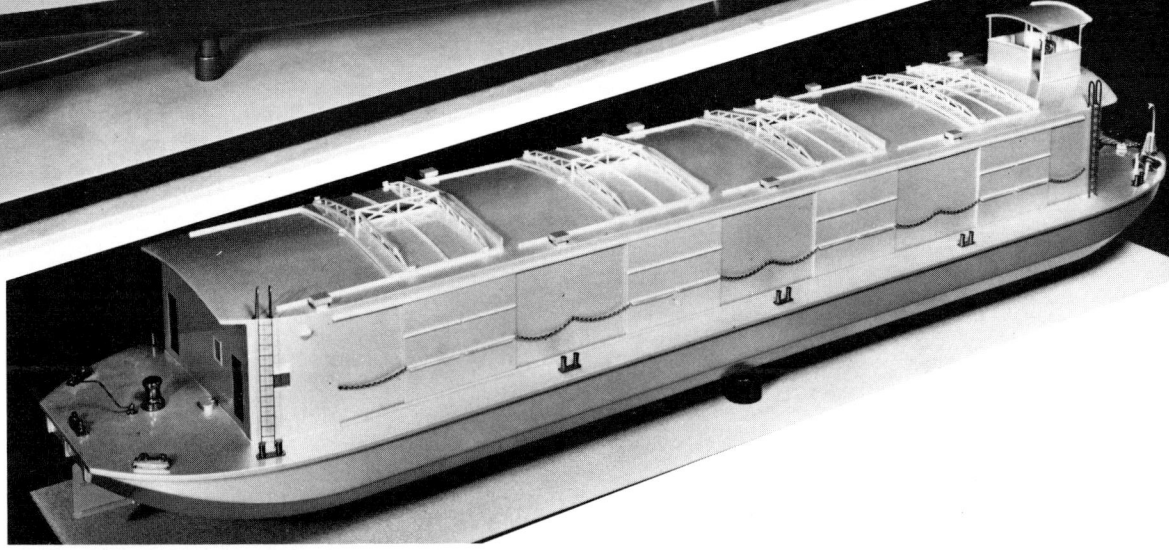

FLEMING PATENT THWARTLESS HAND PROPELLED LIFEBOAT
CONSTRUCTED OF DUMABRIGHT SEA WATER RESISTING ALLOY
LENGTH 30'0" BREADTH 9'6" DEPTH MLD 4'0"
SEATS 56 WITH FOOD WATER & EQUIPMENT
WEIGHT OF BOAT COMPLETE 2 TONS 18 CWT
SCALE OF MODEL 1 inch to 1 foot
MODELLED BY BASSETT-LOWKE LTD NORTHAMPTON

89

DIESEL ELECTRIC GRAB HOPPER DREDGE
MERSEY No 14
HULL DIMENSIONS ........ 245'0 x 48 x 18 FEET
HOPPER CAPACITY ........ 670 CUBIC YARDS
SPEED (LADEN) ........ 10.5 KNOTS
BUILT FOR
MERSEY DOCKS & HARBOUR BOARD
BY
LOBNITZ & CO LTD
RENFREW SCOTLAND

90. Bow detail of waterline model 1455 *Lord Warden* ¼″ to 1′ for William Denny 1952.
91. Aft view of *Lord Warden*
92. Pilot vessel no. 1114 *Jean Mantelet* ¼″ to 1′ for Lobnitz 1952.

93. Burmah Oil Vessel no. 1224 ¼″ to 1′ for Cammell Laird 1952.
94. Vessel no. 1813 *Helix* ½″ to 1′ for Swan Hunter 1952.
95. Ship no. 1226 *Elizabeth Holt* ³⁄₁₆″ to 1′ for Cammell Laird 1953.

96. *HMS Daring* ⅛″ to 1′ for Swan Hunter 1953.
97. No. 675 *Arcadia* 1/12″ to 1′ for John Brown 1954.
98. *SS Empire Viceroy* 1/12″ to 1′ for Pendelis Shipping Co. 1954.

99. Waterline Model of *Iberia* 1/12″ to 1′ for P & O 1954.
100. *Saxonia* 1/12″ to 1′ for John Brown 1954.
101. P & O Liner *Chusan* 1/12″ to 1′ for P & O 1955.

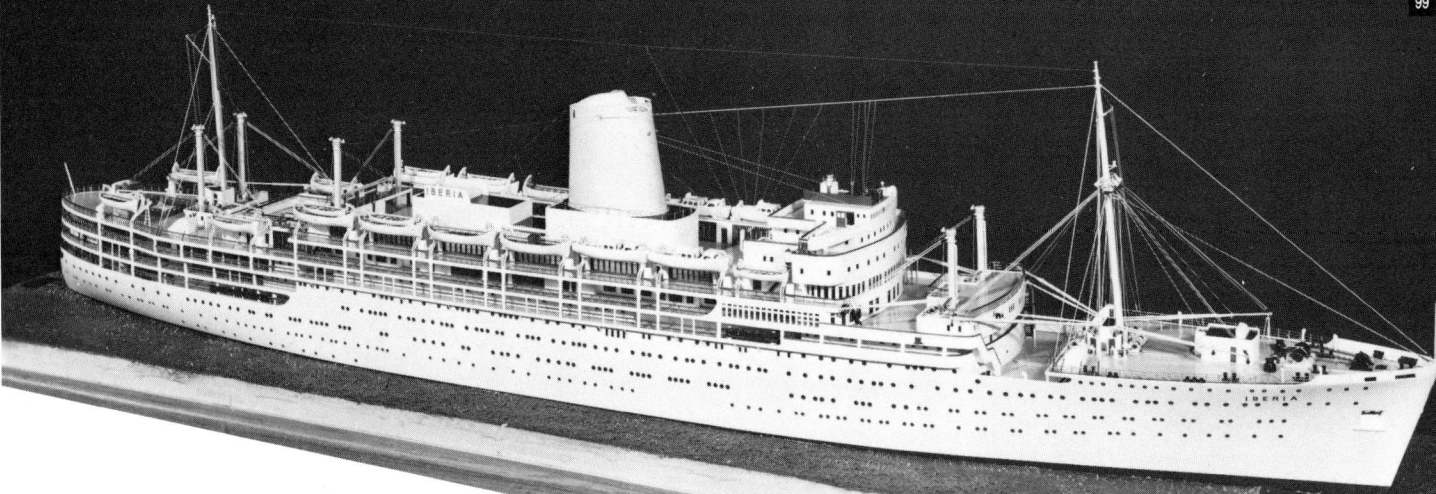

99

T.S. "IBERIA"
THE P. & O. STEAM NAVIGATION CO.
HARLAND & WOLFF LTD, BELFAST.

100

R.M.S. "SAXONIA"

101

T.S. "CHUSAN"
THE P. & O. STEAM NAVIGATION CO.

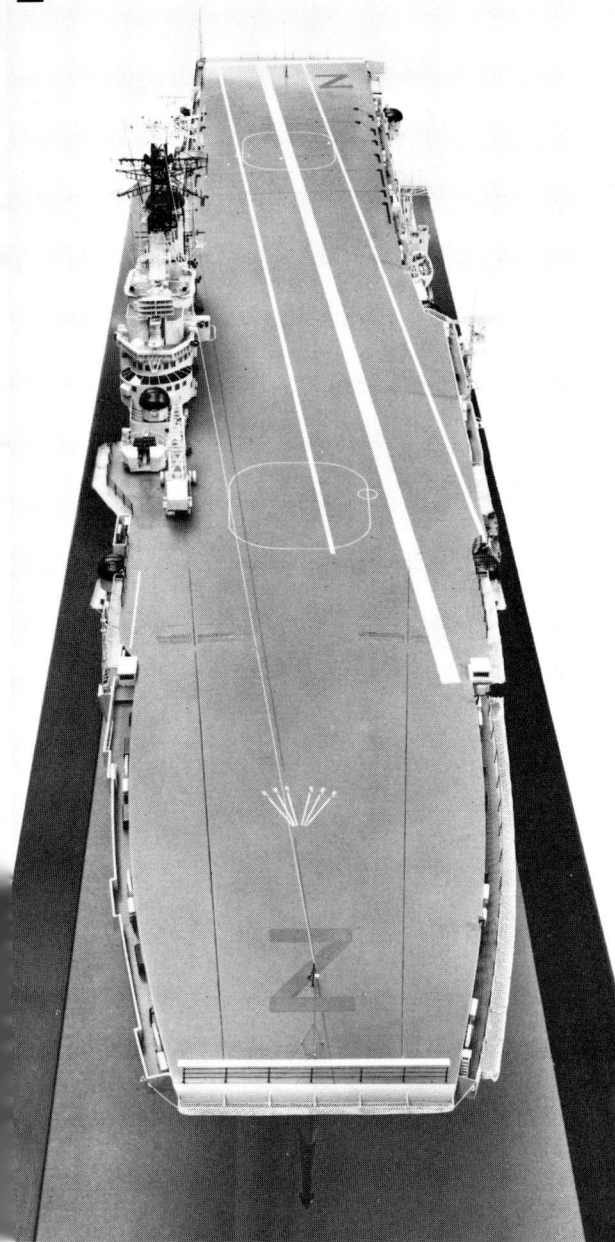

102

103

104

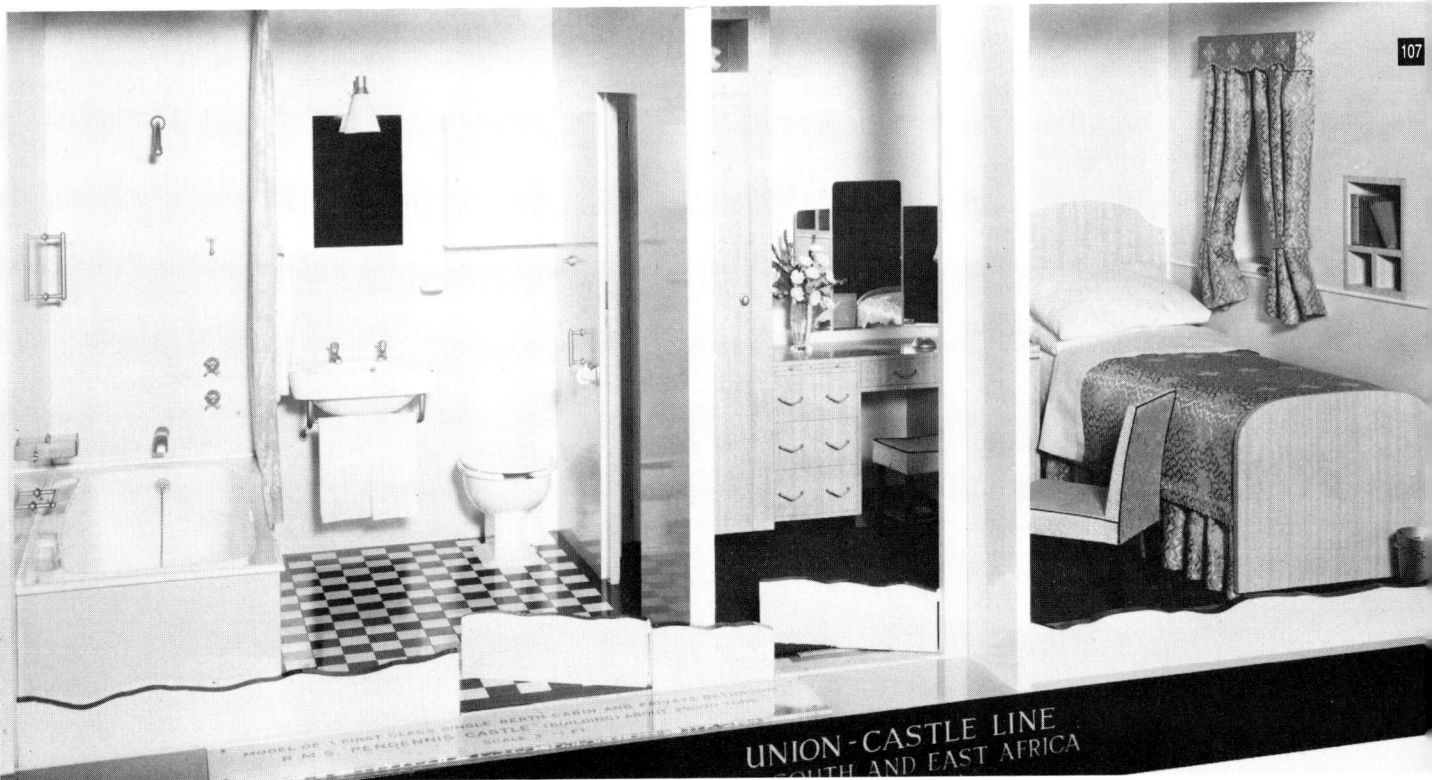

102. *HMS Albion* ⅛″ to 1′ for Swan Hunter 1955.
103. 100 ton floating crane *Atlas* ¼″ to 1′ for Lobnitz 1957.
104. Engine room of *Princess of Vancouver* ¾″ to 1′ for The National Gas & Oil Co. 1956.
105. Tanker *Zenatia* 3⁄16″ to 1′ for Shell Tankers 1957.
106. Motor Torpedo boat ⅛″ to 1′ for Vosper 1957.
107. First class single berth cabin and private bathroom on *Pendennis Castle* 3″ to 1′ for Union Castle Line 1957.

108. Cabin cruiser *Gwen Eagle* radio controlled for Tec Ltd. 1957.
109. Radio control equipment on *Gwen Eagle*.
110. Yacht *Gaviota IV* ⅛″ to 1′ for owner, Arturo Lopez Wilshaw 1958.

111. *HMS Ark Royal* ⅛th scale for Cammell Laird 1958.
112. 82′ 6″ Motor Torpedo Boat ¼″ to 1′ for Vosper 1958.
113. *Brave* class 'FPB' ¼″ to 1′ for Vosper 1958.

111

112

113

114

115

116

114. Full-rigged ship of 1859 period ⅛″ to 1′ for Singapore Harbour Board 1959

115. Waterline model of *Bristol Queen* ¹⁄₁₆″ to 1′ for private customer 1959.

116. Suction dredger *Peraki* ¼″ to 1′ for Lobnitz 1960.

117. Union Castle *Windsor Castle* ⅛″ to 1′ for Cammell Laird 1959.

118. ⁵⁄₁₆ scale *Windsor Castle* first class lounge for Union Castle 1960.

119. Top view of fig. 118.

120. De luxe cabin of *Windsor Castle* 3″ to 1′ for British and Commonwealth Shipping Company 1961.

121. ⁵⁄₁₆″ scale First class dining-room on *Windsor Castle* for Union Castle 1960.

122. Warship *De Brouwer* ex-HMS Spanker ½″ to 1′ for Baron de Brouwer 1961.
123. Dragon class yacht *Nerifs* for presentation to King of Greece by S. G. Embiricos Ltd. 1961.
124. 92′ fast patrol boat ¼″ to 1′ for Vosper 1961.

125. *Transvaal Castle* ¼″ to 1′ for British and Commonwealth Shipping 1961.
126. TSCS *Retriever* ⅛″ to 1′ for Cammell Laird 1961.
127. Bow view of *Transvaal Castle* ³⁄₁₆″ to 1′ for British and Commonwealth Shipping Co. 1961.

128

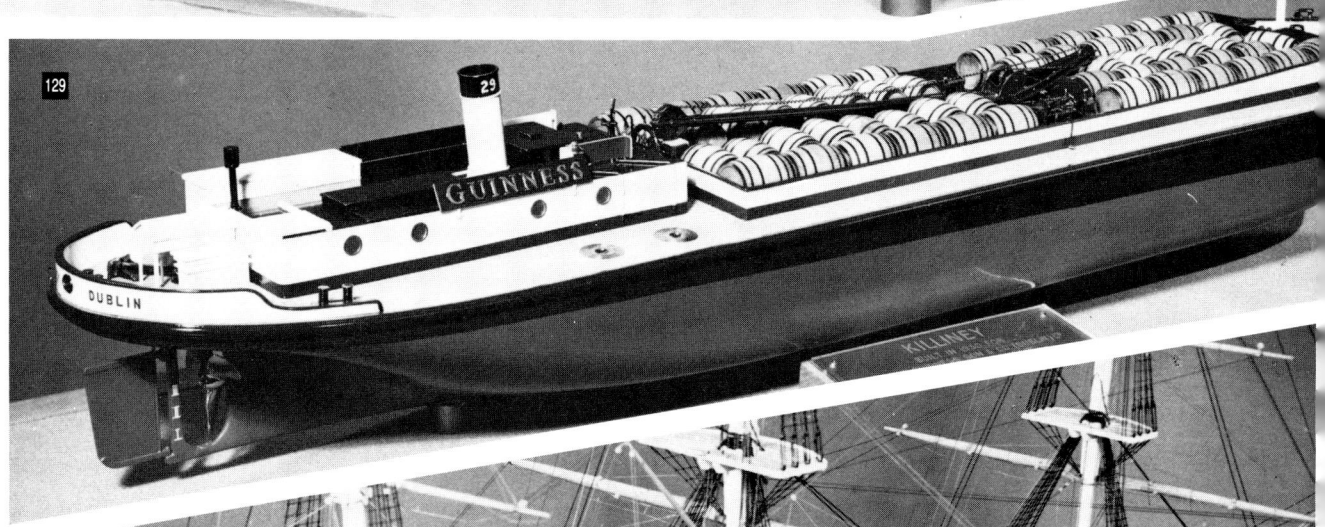

129

130

128.  Ship no. 1304 ¼″ to 1′ for Smithsonian 1962.
129.  Barge *Killiney* ½″ to 1′ for Arthur Greens Son & Co 1962.
130.  US sloop *Hertford* ¼″ to 1′ for Smithsonian 1962.

131.  Model of proposed royal barge ⅜″ to 1′ for Vosper 1963.
132.  Power boat *Termontana* 2′ ½″ to 1′ for Vosper 1963.
133.  96′ Danish FPB ¼″ to 1′ for Vosper 1964.

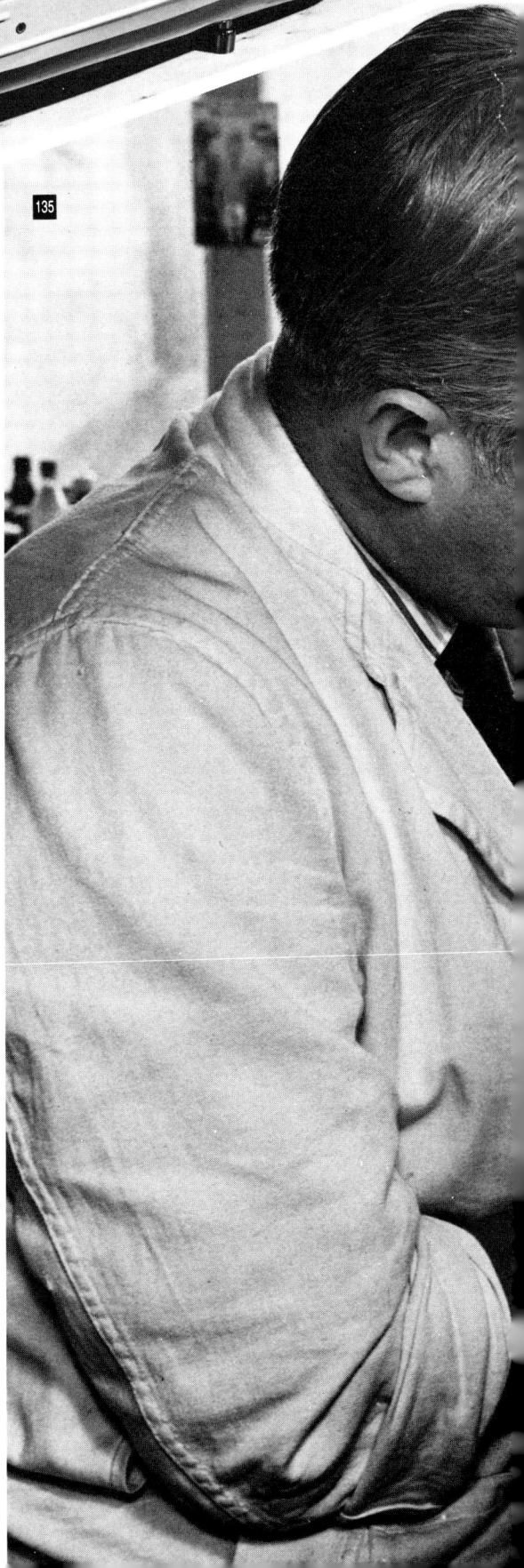

134. 110′ Peruvian Mine Layer for Vosper 1964.
135. Roy Stutley working on *Oriana* ⅛th scale in 1967.
136. Frigate *Constitution* ¼″ to 1′ for Smithsonian Institute 1965.

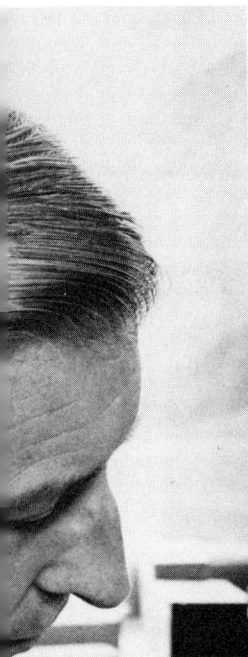

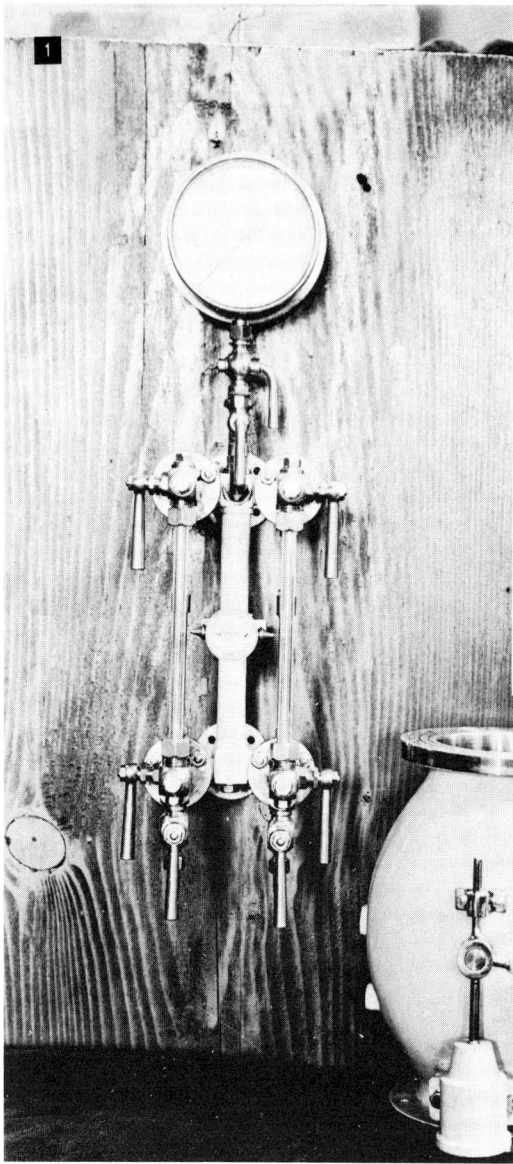

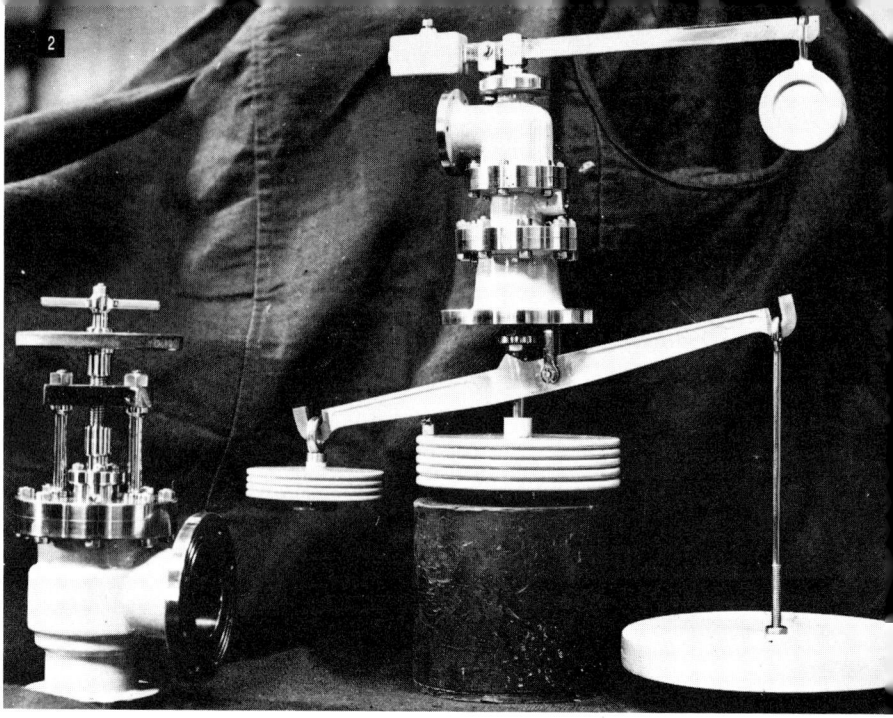

1. Nautical instructional model by Winteringham and Mackenzie 1905.
2. Industrial model by Winteringham and Mackenzie 1905.
3. Experimental marine engine (forerunner of the Swift) 1908.
4. Experimental 3-cylinder paddle engine 1906.
5. Oscillating engine and marine boiler 1930.

6. Blow lamp-fired single flu boiler 1930.
7. Marine boiler unit with final drive 1912.
8. Marine boiler installation and final drive installed 1910.
9. Marine engine for twin propeller drive using gauge 0 locomotive steam cylinders 1927.
10. Twin funnelled marine set 1912.

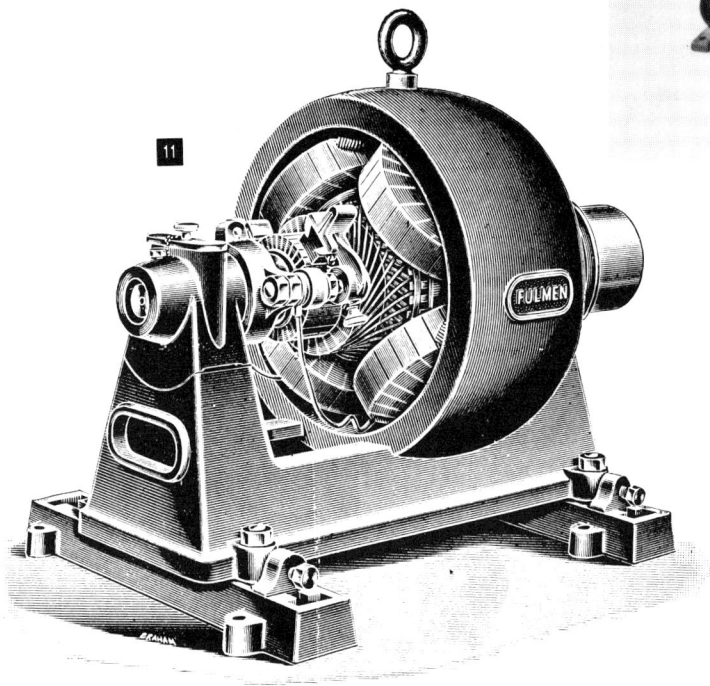

11. Typical electric motor sold by Bassett-Lowke from 1902–12.
12. Electric motors made by Bassett-Lowke 1903.
13. The 'lowko' motor. The first electric motor for model railways by Winteringham for Bassett-Lowke; in 4 sizes made from 1907.
14. A typical motor marketed between 1902–12.
15. 'Permag' marine motor. Standard unit as used in gauge 0 locomotives; ran on 4½ volts c. 1930.

16. 'Permag' 4 volt marine motor 1930.
17. Permanent field magnet motors (4½ volt/battery operation) for model boats 1920–35.
18. AC mains motor driving an air pump of German importation c. 1930.
19. Permanent magnet motor by Precision Models – part of instruction set range. Here mounted with pump 1937.

197

1 & 4.   ¾″ scale traction engine, parts for which were available until the end of Bassett-Lowke's proprietory model business. Many parts were supplied to Bassett-Lowke Railways, who continued with this model for a time.

2.   1″ scale Aveling & Porter 20 ton engine c. 1915.

3.   Pike engine supplied to the London branch from 1908.

5.   ¾″ scale 'Burrell' traction engine.

6–7, 9–12.   Component parts of fig. 5, 1939.

8.   'Caliban' traction engine scale unknown 1915.

CALIBAN

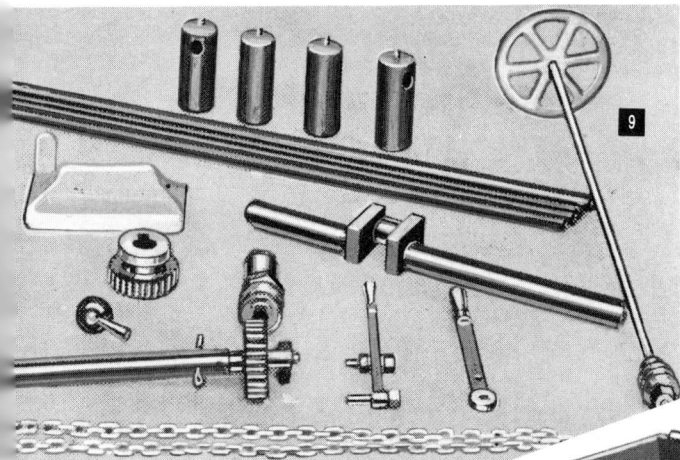

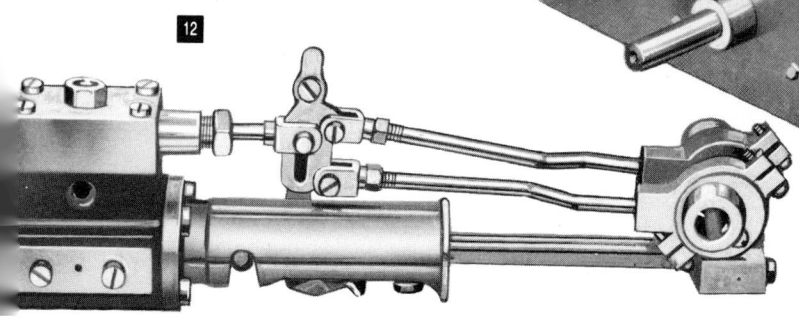

1. H7 Vickers AA gun 1″ scale 1935.
2. 'Dauntless' Scout car 1″ to 1′ 1947.
3. War Department tanker 1″ to 1′ 1947.

4. Crossley lorry 4-wheel drive 1″ to 1′ 1947.
5. Armoured Scout car for Rootes group 1946.
6. Churchill tank 1946.

7–14.  Model of Mulberry
Harbour – various
views showing all
the components
(see text page 49).

202

BRIDGE TOWING LINK

TANK LANDING SHIP PIERHEAD

STORE PIERHEAD

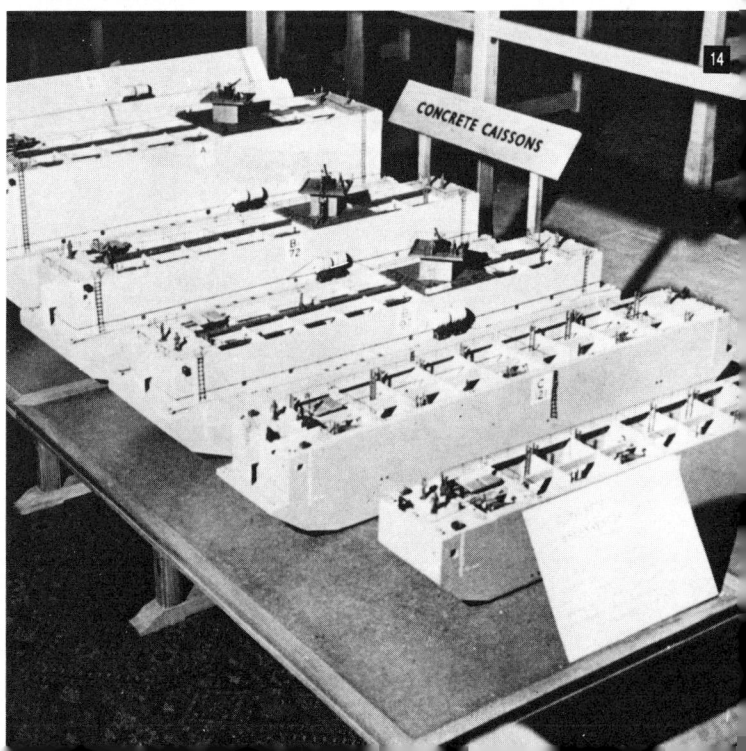

CONCRETE CAISSONS

15 & 17.   Bailey Bridge (see text page 49).
16.   Inglis Bridge – left: P. F. Claydon; right: J. Nutsford,
        metal shop foreman.
18.   Model for demonstrating handling equipment for
        Admiralty 1956.

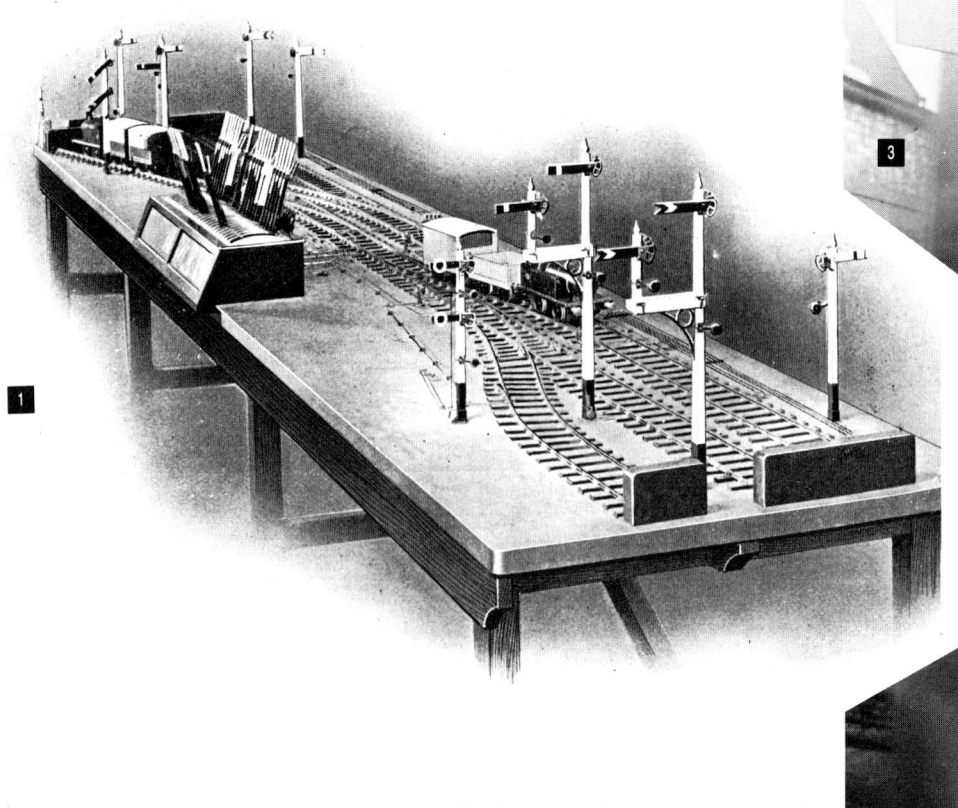

1. Scale model signal instruction set for GWR technical training class 1905.
2. Signal instruction model 2″ gauge for L.N.W.R 1908 – the locomotives are not motorized, movements being made by hand.
3. Signalling model ¼″ scale for L.N.W.R 1908.
4. Signalling instruction model ¾″ to 1′ for L.N.W.R 1910 – signals not in working positions.
5. Gauge 2 display exhibit of between 1910–14.
6. Gauge 2 railway for Brussels exhibition 1910, featuring GNR, NER and NBR electrically operated stock.

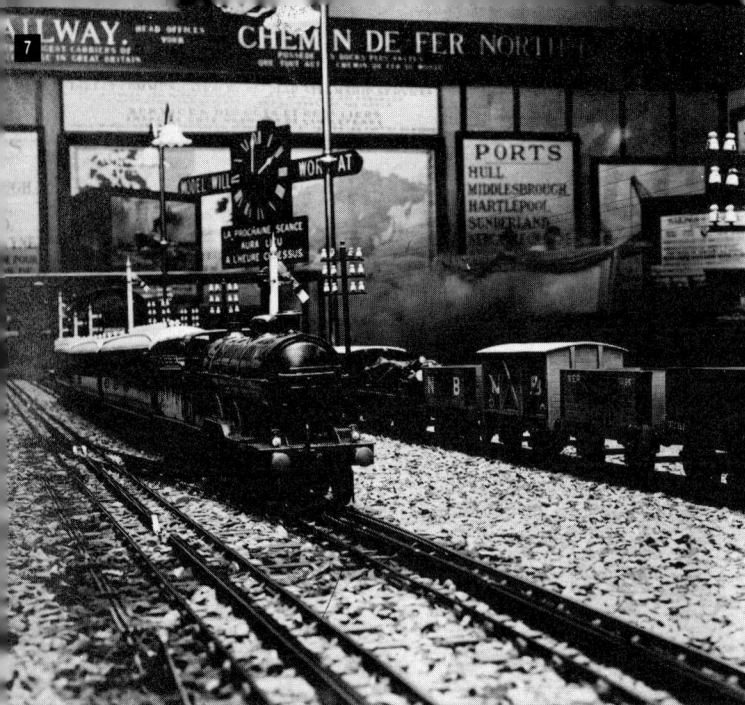

7.   Another view of the Brussels 1910 exhibition.
8 & 9.   The Brussels layout under construction.
10.   Part of the Ghent exhibition layout 1910.
11.   Bassett-Lowke Exhibition layout for the Canadian Northern System c. 1908.
12.   Elaborate display at Imperial Services Exhibition, Earls Court 1913 (see text page 26).

13.   Standard exhibition display of c. 1912.
14.   2″ scale 9½″ gauge model railway at the Children's Welfare Exhibition Olympia, London 1914. Mrs. Winston Churchill in white; W. J. B-L crouching; Mr. Cadbury with beard.

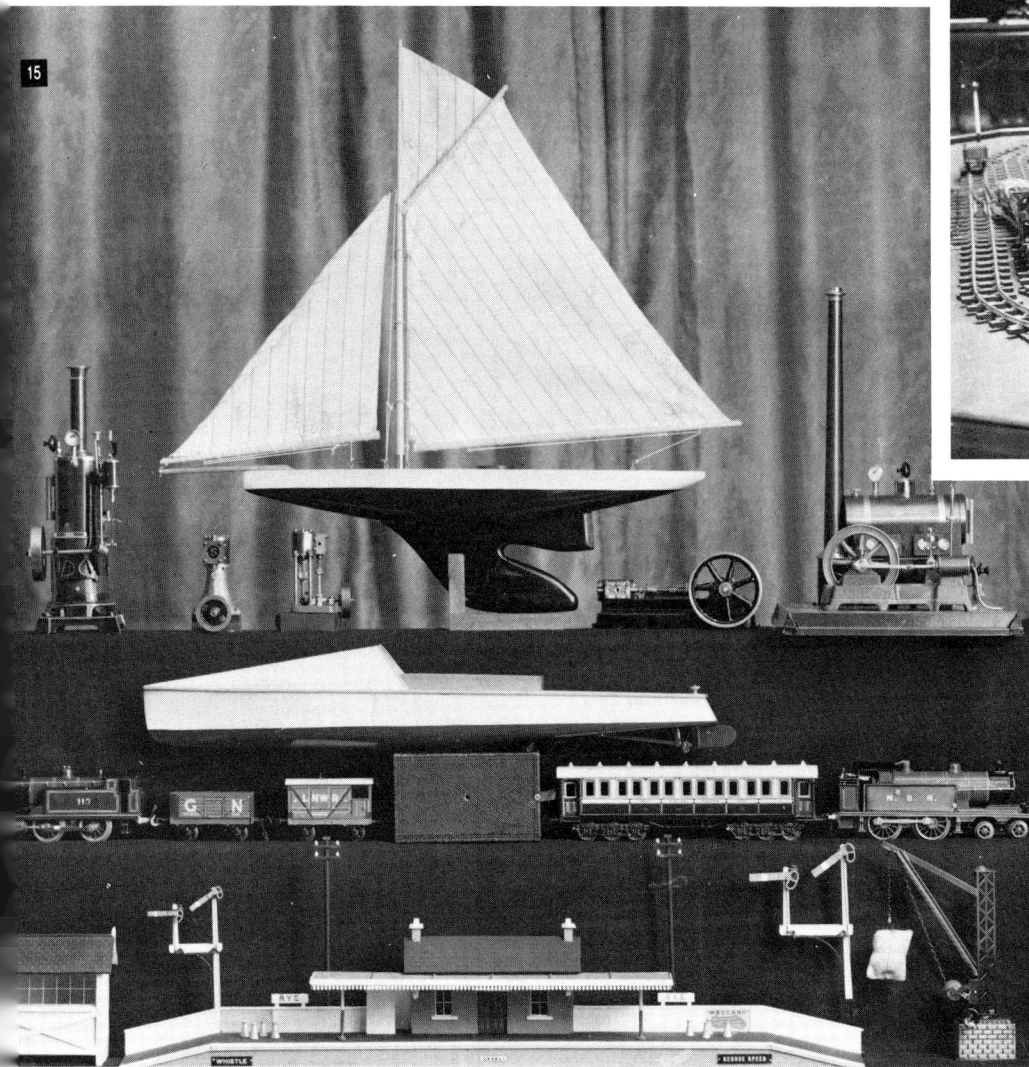

15. Display of a representative range of Bassett-Lowke offerings c. 1920.
16. 2½″ gauge model display for Canadian National Railways under construction for Wembley exhibition 1924.
17. Bassett-Lowke model railways display featuring *Black Prince* early 1920s.
18–20 Model Engineer Exhibition 1921 – various views.
21. Model Engineer Exhibition 1923.

LOCOMOTIVE "CHALLENGER."
WATER TUBE BOILER, METHYLATED SPIRIT FIRING,
THREE CYLINDERS 1⅛" X ⅝".
BASSETT-LOWKE, LTD. NORTHAMPTON.

22. Bassett-Lowke works first run of spirit-fired locomotive *Challenger* in locomotive trials at 1924 MEE. H. Greenly is central passenger (see text page 35).

23. Model Engineer Exhibition 1925.

24. Model Engineer Exhibition 1926.

25–30. Canadian Pacific gauge 1 electric locomotive with coaches 1924.

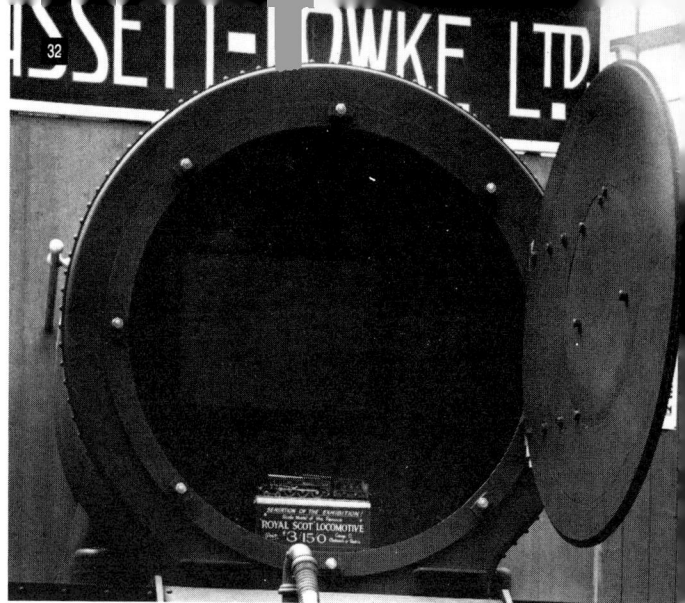

31. Bassett-Lowke stand at the Model Engineer Exhibition 1929.
32. The introduction of Bassett-Lowke's 'Royal Scot' gauge 0 in electric and clockwork was made with typical bravura at the 1929 Model Engineer Exhibition. The model can be seen in the smoke box of a full-sized replica.
33. Antwerp exhibition 1930.

34. Gauge 1 display of Post Office mail railway equipment for Radio Olympia 1934.
35. Another view of the GPO stand 1934.
36. ¼" scale model of a portion of the Underground system exhibited at Charing Cross, 1934.
37. Bassett-Lowke stand at model exhibition to accompany the Hastings carnival 1936.

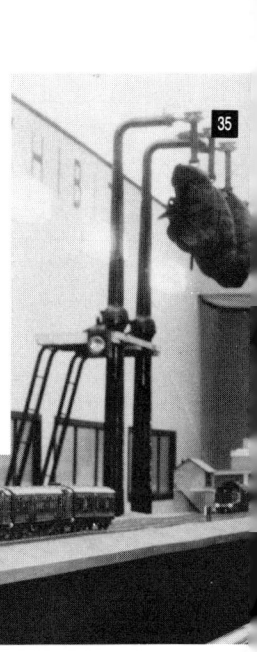

38

39

40

SCALE MODELS    BASSETT-LOWKE

BASSETT-LOWKE LTD
NORTHAMPTON

MODEL    RAILWAY ENGINES SHIPS

41

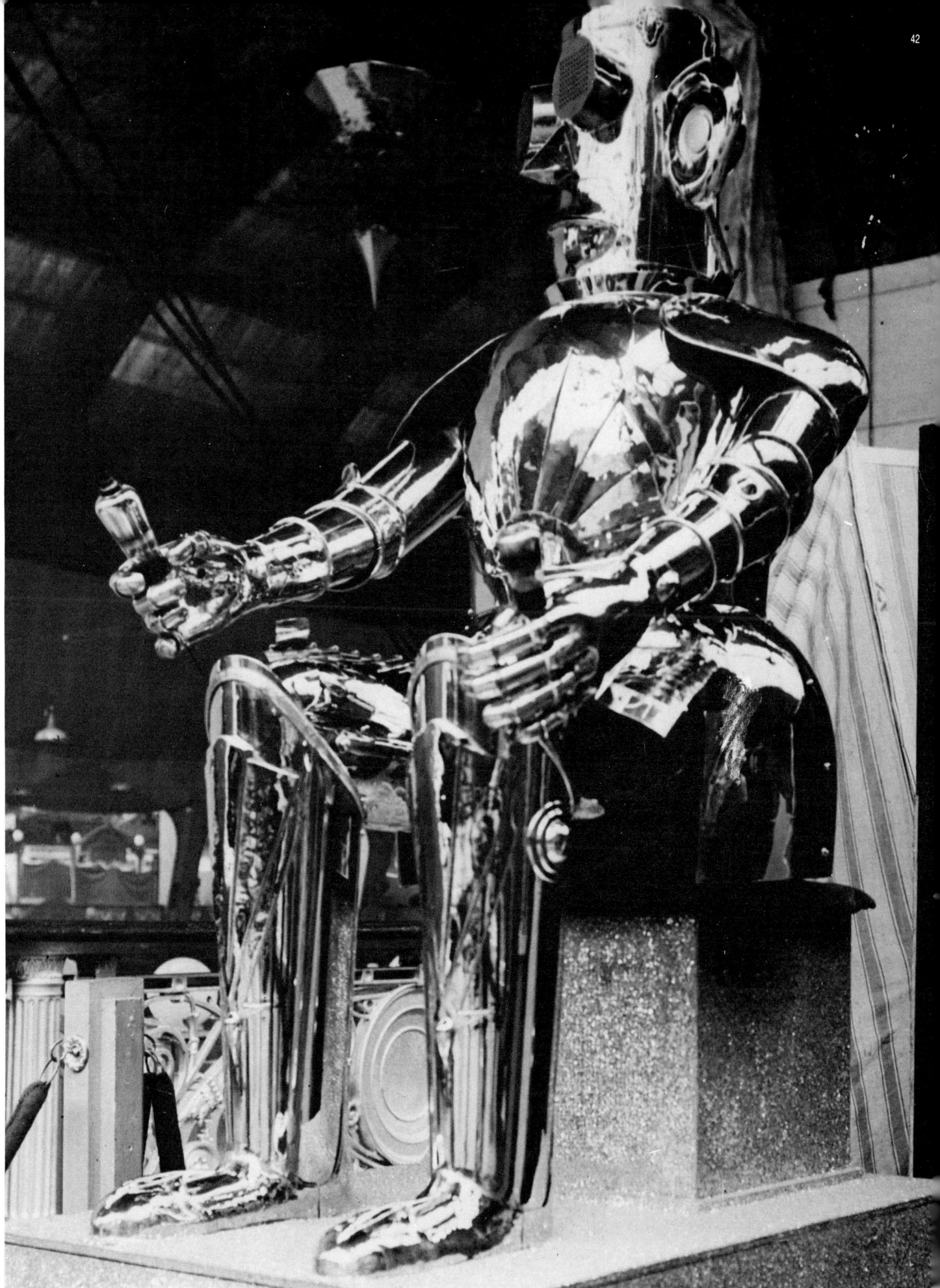

38. Euston station model for LMS centenary exhibition 1935.
39. Trix Twin layout for British Industries Fair 1936.
40. Bassett-Lowke stand for British Industries Fair 1938.
41. Gauge 0 layout by Bassett-Lowke at Waterloo station 1937.
42. Bassett-Lowke's famous pre-war exhibition robot.

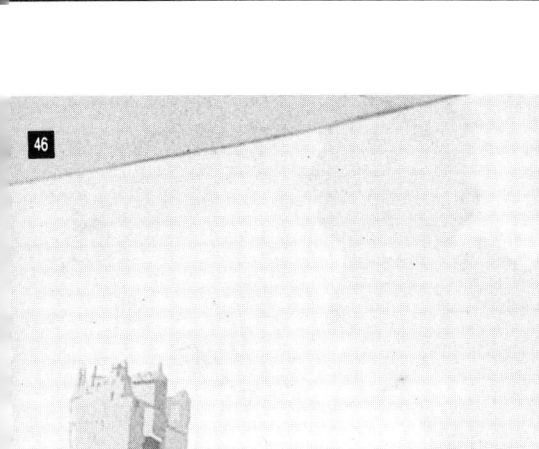

43. British Empire Exhibition, Glasgow 1938, featuring Bassett-Lowke gauge 0 railway.
44. A view of the exhibition layout at Glasgow.
45. Operating the gauge 0 railway at the Glasgow exhibition.
46. Another view of the Glasgow exhibition.
47. The superb 'turnouts' at Glasgow.
48. Panel for Cunard White Star display being taken from Kingswell Street en route for New York. 1939.

49. Detail of 1938 World Fair display in New York showing half section of *Queen Elizabeth*.
50. Detail of *Queen Elizabeth* half section – lounge 1938.
51. *Queen Elizabeth* half section prior to installation at New York World Fair.
52. ¼″ scale half section of *Queen Elizabeth* at the World Fair.

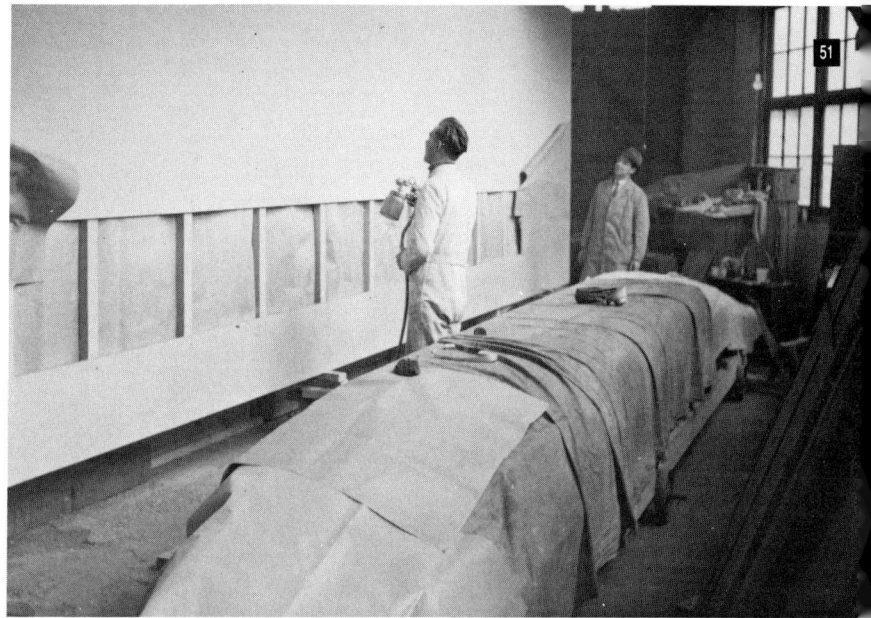

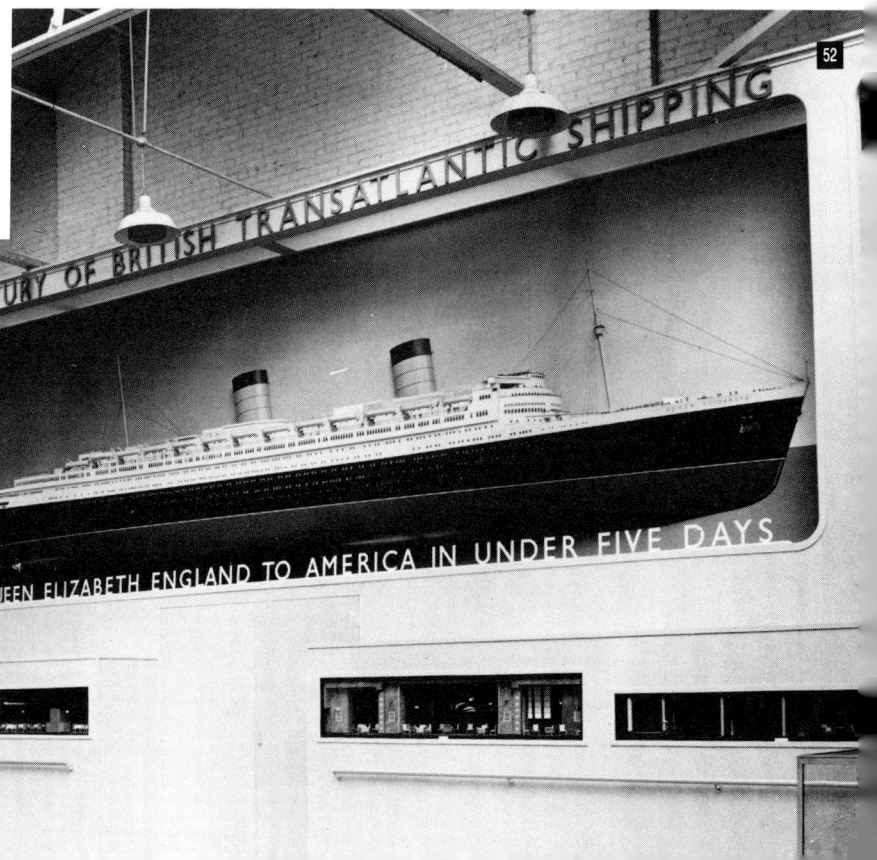

A CENTURY OF BRITISH TRANSATLANTIC SHIPPING

RMS QUEEN ELIZABETH ENGLAND TO AMERICA IN UNDER FIVE DAYS

53. Showroom in Western Australia using Bassett-Lowke
    gauge 0 equipment 1938.
54. W. J. Bassett-Lowke illustrating a variety of model trains
    on a BBC programme entitled 'Model Trains' 1946.
55. A further scene from the BBC programme.
56. A Bassett-Lowke architectural model of Finsbury Circus
    in a television programme entitled 'Models in Modern
    Planning' 1946.

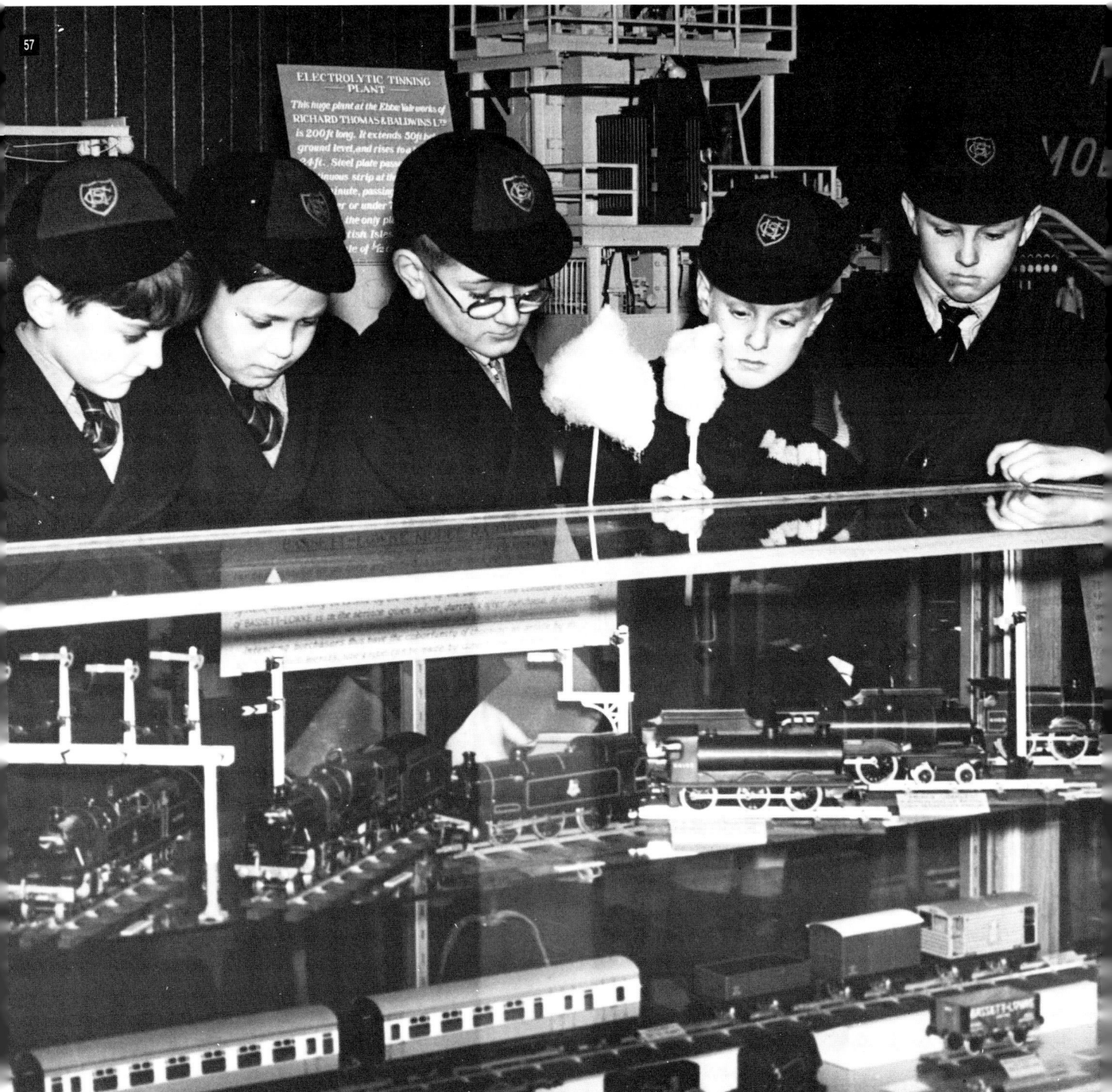

57. Bassett-Lowke gauge 0 equipment on display at the
    Birmingham National Trades exhibition 1954.
58. Exhibition model railway at Weston-super-Mare c.1955.
59. Bassett-Lowke stand at Model Railway Club exhibition
    1960.

HOLBORN,
ON, W.C.I.

BASSETT-LOWKE LTD

LONDON    MANCHESTER    NORTHAMPTON

28, CORPO
MANCHE

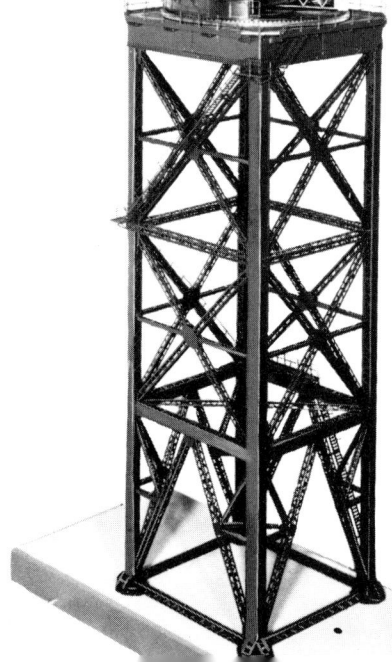

224

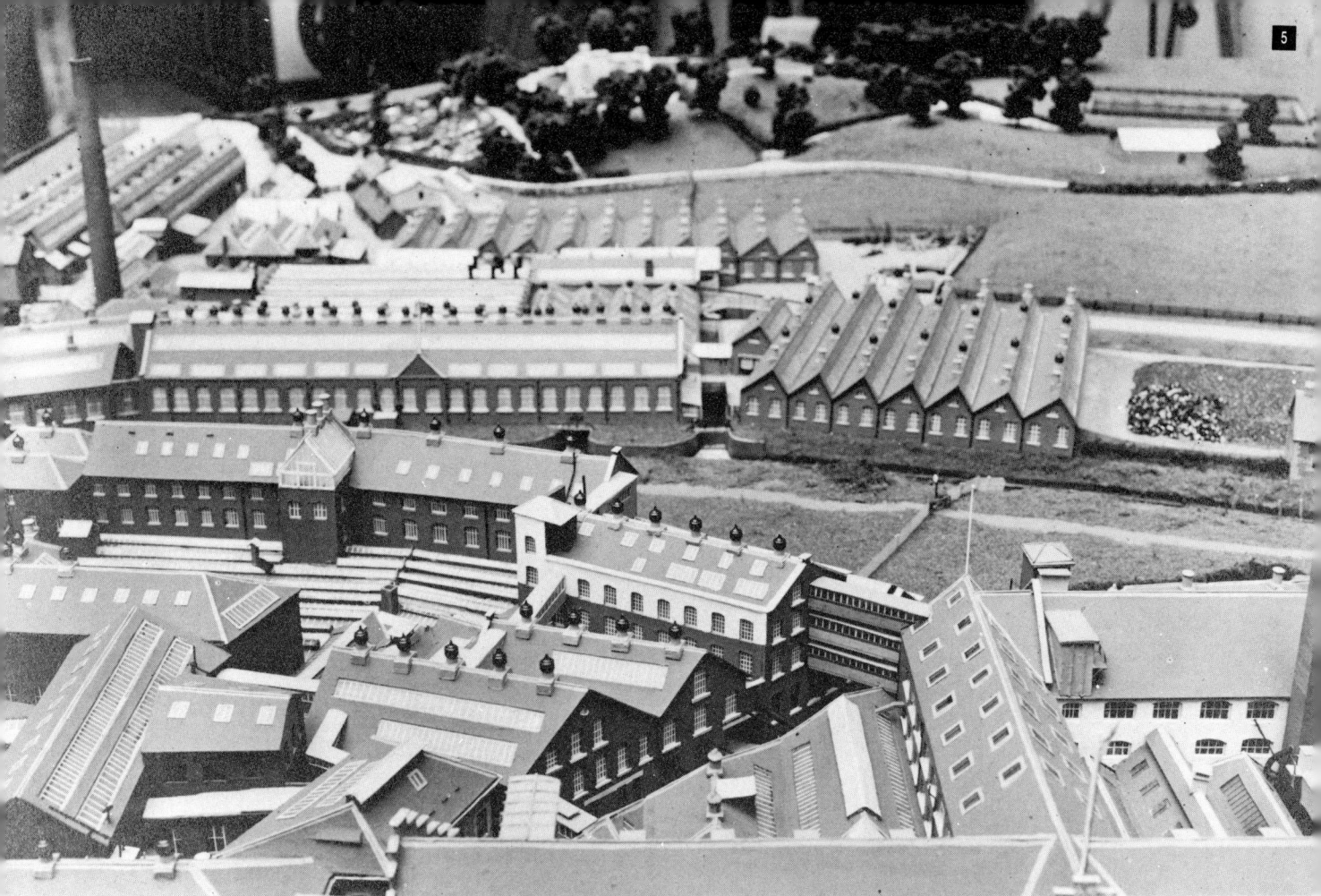

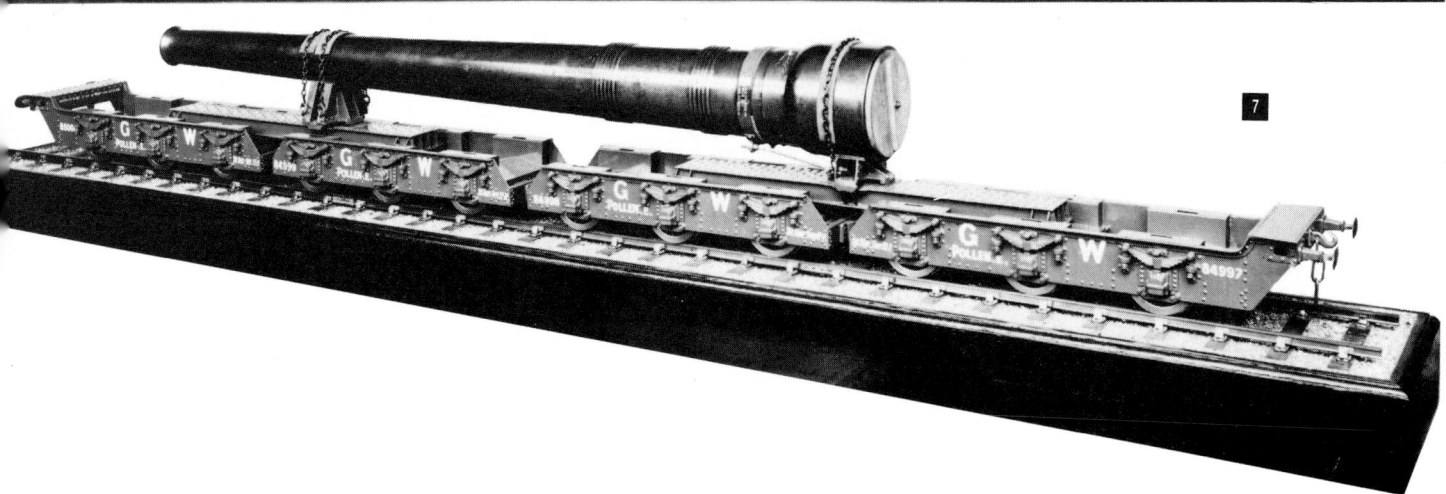

1. Bassett-Lowke's first architectural model built to the order of Blackpool Corporation in 1912 scale 40′ to 1″.
2. Portion of model of Lever Bros. works at Port Sunlight 1913.
3. Dolls house model for royal customer. Exact date unknown.
4. 250 ton crane for Vickers Armstrong 1926.
5. Model of Pullars Dye Works at Perth 1914.
6. Model of Harwich–Zeebrugge train ferry for LNER 1925.
7. ¾″ scale model for GWR 1932.

8 & 9.   Before and after pictures of a model tin dredger
         repaired by Bassett-Lowke in 1934.
10.      ¼″ scale milk pasteurising plant for United Dairies 1936.
11.      Architectural model for the new Coventry c.1943.
12.      Delegates viewing the partly finished model of Coventry
         at a planning meeting in May 1943.

13.      Model for Palestine University 1945.
14.      Model showing a development scheme for Nahalal village
         (birth place of Moshe Dayan) 1946.

9

10

13

14

15. Immingham Docks model.
16. Scale model of BSA Birmingham 1″ to 24′.
17. Working model of Kingston-upon-Hull Corporation Cottingham plant 1952.
18. 13′ ¹⁄₃₂ scale model of Carton board machine for Reed Paper which was presented to the Science Museum.
19. Formore whisky distillery model c.1955.

20–27.
A working model of Plymouth, portraying the seventeenth century life of the city, including the return of the Golden Hind, the repelling of the Spanish Armada, and the sailing of the Mayflower. 1963.

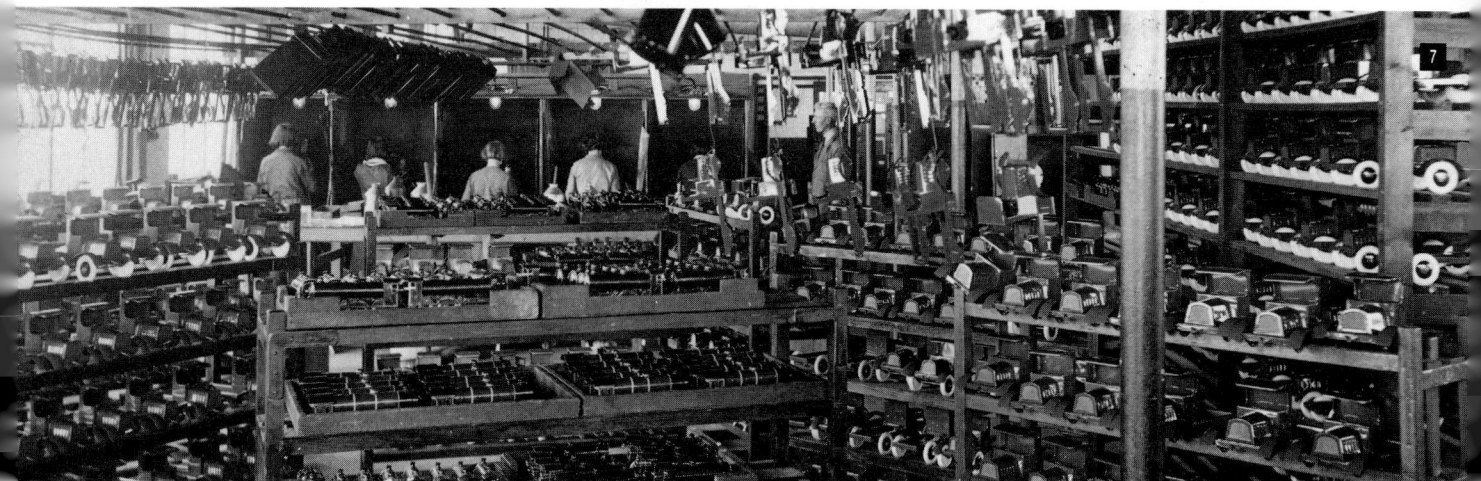

1. The machine shop for large scale locomotives c.1912.
2. Small scale assembly bench c.1912.
3 & 4. Gauge 2 electric railway for LNWR under construction in 1912.

5. Track assembly at Winteringham's 1913.
6. 'Duke of York' assembly bench in the 1920s.
7. The paintshop in 1922. The model lorries are interesting. It is not known whether they are of Bassett-Lowke manufacture.
8. Track making at Winteringham's in 1925.

8. 'Enterprise' 4–4–0 locomotives steam in gauge 0 being assembled at Winteringham's 1929.

9. Final testing of gauge 0 clockwork 'Compound' locomotives at Winteringham's 1925.

10. Testing clockwork and electric mechanisms before fitting to chassis at Winteringham's in 1925.

11. The paintshop at Winteringham's showing 'Enterprise' boiler barrels being formed in 1929.

12. Hull making at Kingswell Street 1925.

13. Architectural model assembly in the 1930s.

14. Waterline final assembly for 'Normandie' and 'Queen Mary' 1935.

15. Waterline model production 1935.
16. Tinplate coach assembly early 1930s.
17. Aircraft assembly bench, making model for Imperial Airways 1933.
18. Waterline naval models being assembled; at right: Mr. Blank 1930s.

19. Boiler fitting shop at St. Andrews Street 1935.
20. 'Queen Mary' hull 1936.
21. Chassis of 2½" gauge 'Flying Scotsman' produced as finished models from 1925 to 1939; parts available until 1968.
22. Assembling bodies for gauge 0 'Duchess of Montrose' 1937.

23. 'Winchester Castle' model in the works 1934.
24. St. Andrews Street premises from 1930–53; offices at left; warehouse at right.
25. *Mauretania* nearing completion, date unknown.

26. Precision Models, Stimpson Avenue.
27. The first premises occupied by Ships Models at Kingswell Street.

240

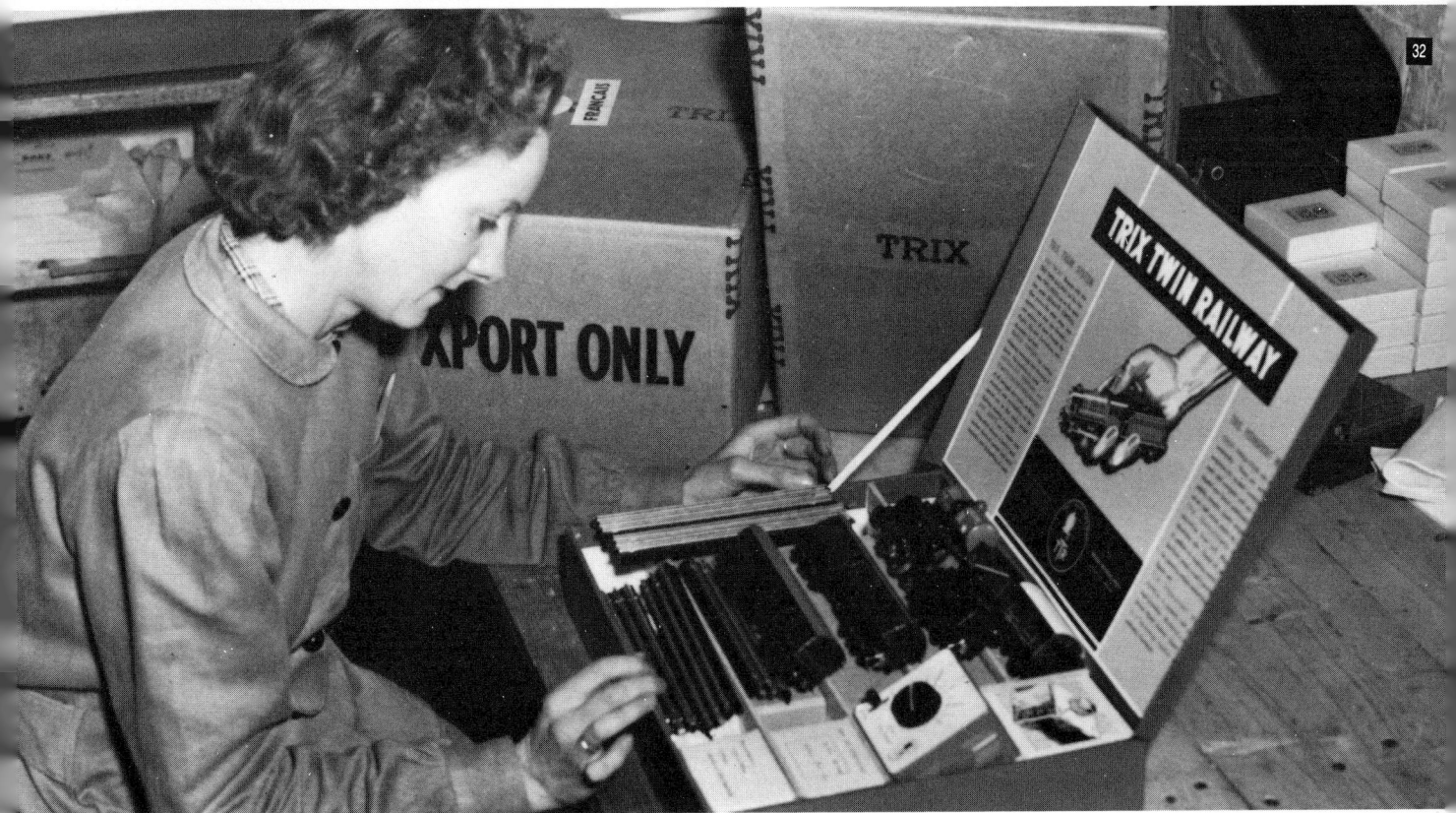

28. Assembling 'Enterprise' gauge 0 models at Precision Models in 1938.

29. Reassembling gauge 0 locomotives after painting at Precision Models in 1938.

30. Testing Trix Twin locomotives at Precision Models c.1950.

31. General view of Trix Twin assembly area 1950.

32. Packing Trix Twin train sets 1950.

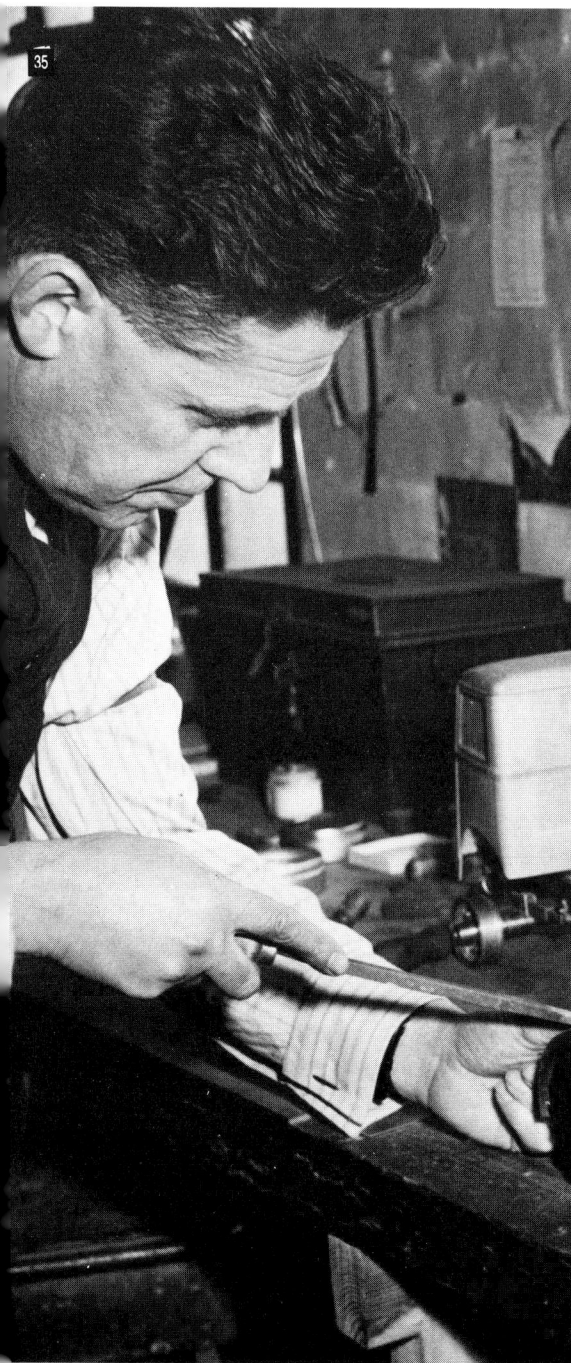

33. The architectural model shop 1942.
34. W. J. Bassett-Lowke examining various ship models in 1947.
35. P. F. Claydon working on vehicle model assembly for the Rootes group 1947.
36. R. Shrine working on vehicle model for the Rootes group 1947.
37. Vehicle models for Rootes group with J. Borsberry 1947.

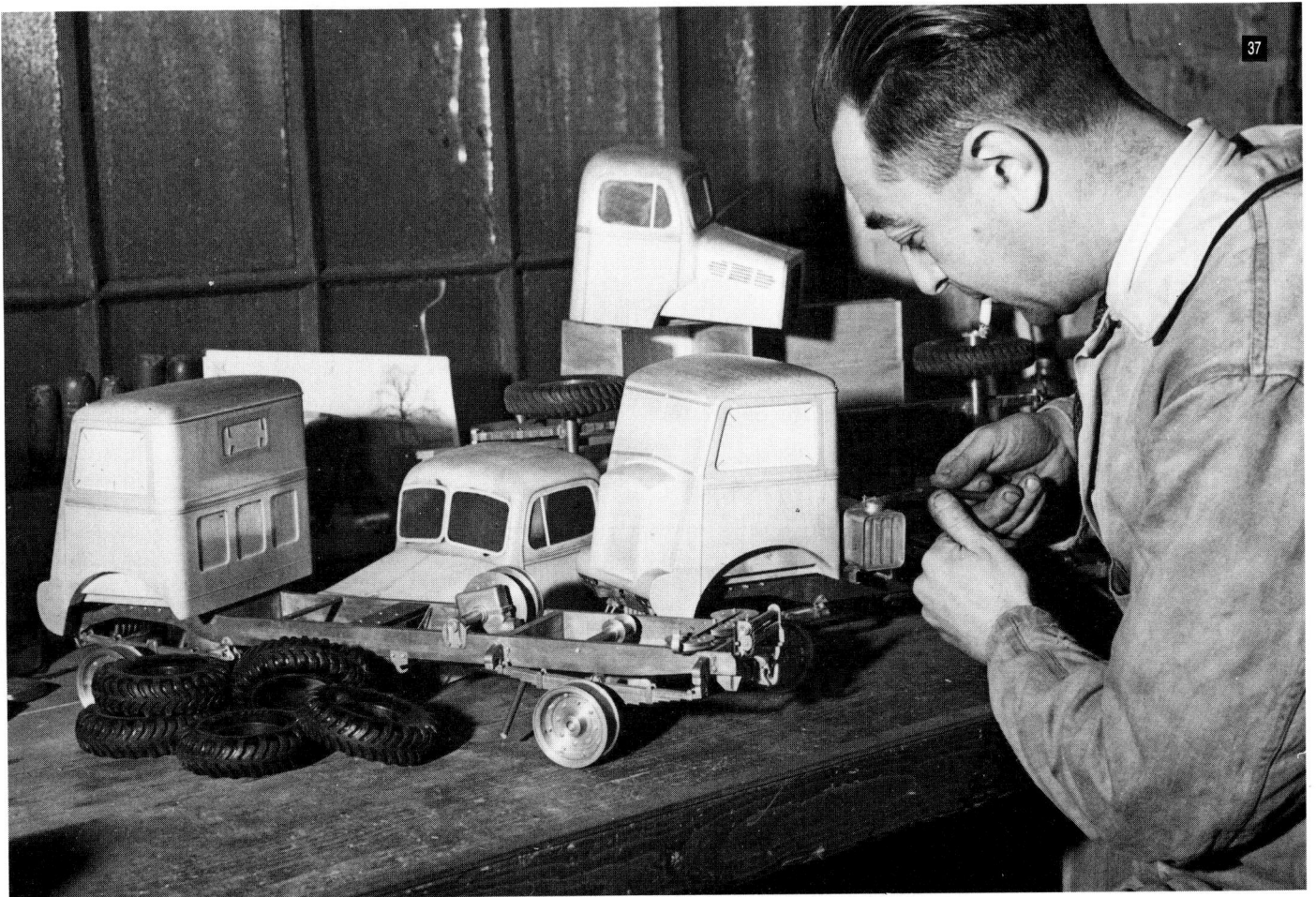

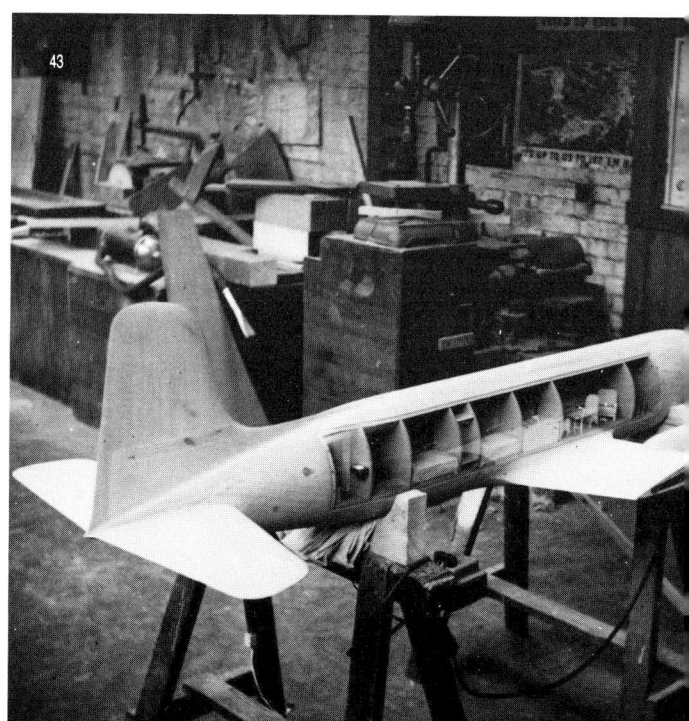

38. Bailey bridge model components 1949.
39. Repair shop in 1950, St. Andrews Street.
40. W. J. Bassett-Lowke inspecting the works in 1949.
41. The metal shop, St. Andrews Street. In background is J. Nutsford, the foreman in 1950.
42. The wood shop St. Andrews Street c.1942.
43. Model aircraft construction 1950.

44. The press shop at Precision Models 1951.
45. Paint shop April 1950.
46. Peter Marshall working on Pullman car, one of a set in gauge 0 for the Winston Churchill funeral train. 1965.
47. Some of the last special order gauge 0 locomotives being lined up 1965.

1. The first London shop at 257 High Holborn opened in 1908.
2. The first London shop staff from left: A. Walker, J. James, E. W. Hobbs (manager), Miss Freight, Miss Chalk. The two shop boys are unknown.

3. 112, High Holborn opened in 1910. This picture was taken in 1923. The two central figures are: left, the author and H. M. Sell.
4. 112, High Holborn in 1920. The painted panel in the foreground was by E. W. Twining.
5. 112, High Holborn in 1910.

**BASSETT-LOWKE LTD**

MODEL · RAILWAY · SPECIALISTS

6. Bing/Bassett-Lowke gauge 2 'Bowen Cooke' 4–6–2 tank on display at 112, High Holborn 1910.
7. LNWR 'Experiment' 2½" gauge steam, Carson/Bassett-Lowke photographed in 1910.
8. Bing/Bassett-Lowke 'Compound' steam gauge 1, 1910.
9. Clockwork version of Bing/Bassett-Lowke 'Compound' 4–4–0 gauge 1, 1910.

10. GNR Atlantic Bing/Bassett-Lowke gauge 1 steam 1910.
11. Bing/Bassett-Lowke 'County of Northampton' 4–4–0 gauge 3 steam 1910.
12. The 1913 Northampton works outing during which they visited the London shop.
13. The London shop Christmas 1919. On left: F. Underwood (manager) who was succeeded by H. C. Foreman.

249

14. The London shop in 1930 (interior). E. H. Sell at the counter.
15. The London shop in 1930 (exterior).
16. The restyled interior of 112 High Holborn 1932.
17. The most famous Bassett-Lowke shop front fitted in 1930.

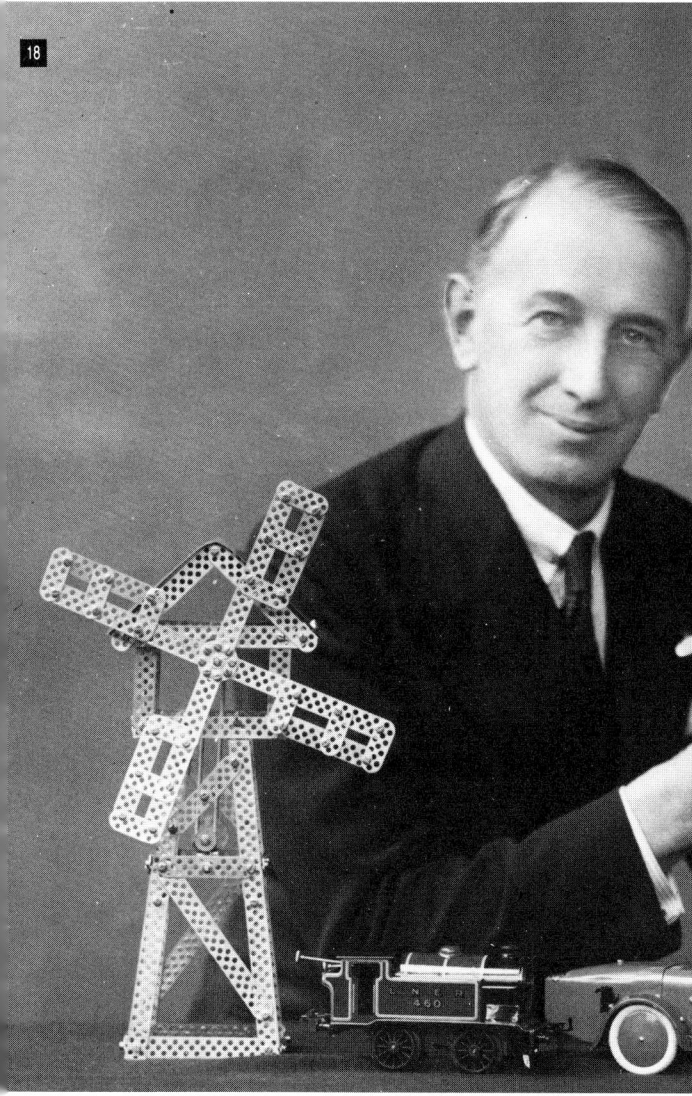

18. W. J. Bassett-Lowke with a selection of Hornby, Frog and Trix items on sale in the basement of 112 High Holborn in 1934.

19. Outside the London shop in 1940. Note window gazer carrying gas mask.

20. The shop front showing air raid precautions in 1940.

21. Typical Bassett-Lowke solution to a boarded-up fascia in 1941.

22. Opening the extension of 112 High Holborn on 11 December 1946.

23. The extended London shop in 1949. The lease of the right hand shop was relinquished in 1956.

24. The London shop taken in 1949 showing the new landlords' sign, namely the Boro Billposting company.
25. The London shop on 1 January 1959. 9 a.m. queue awaits the first Bassett-Lowke sale.
26. The Edinburgh shop in Frederick Street taken in the early 1920s.
27. The Edinburgh shop no 1, Frederick Street (taken in 1922). It was transferred to no 5 in 1927.
28. F. Royle's shop in Edinburgh, 1951. He was a Bassett-Lowke stockist.
29. Interior of F. Royle shop 1951.

30. Manchester shop early 1920s.
31. Manchester shop window 1929.
32. Manchester shop, another view.
33. Manchester shop 1930.

34. Northampton 1953.
35. Au Paradis des Enfants, rue de Rivoli, Paris, home of
    the Bassett-Lowke agency from 1912 to 1928.

With all good
wishes from
W. Smart

W. J. Bassett-Lowke
Model Railway
Northampton

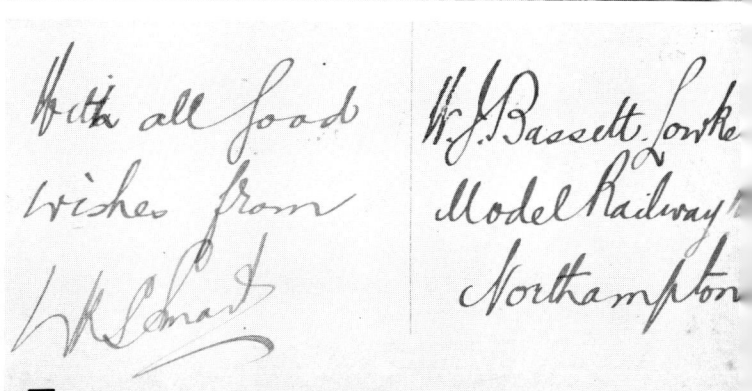

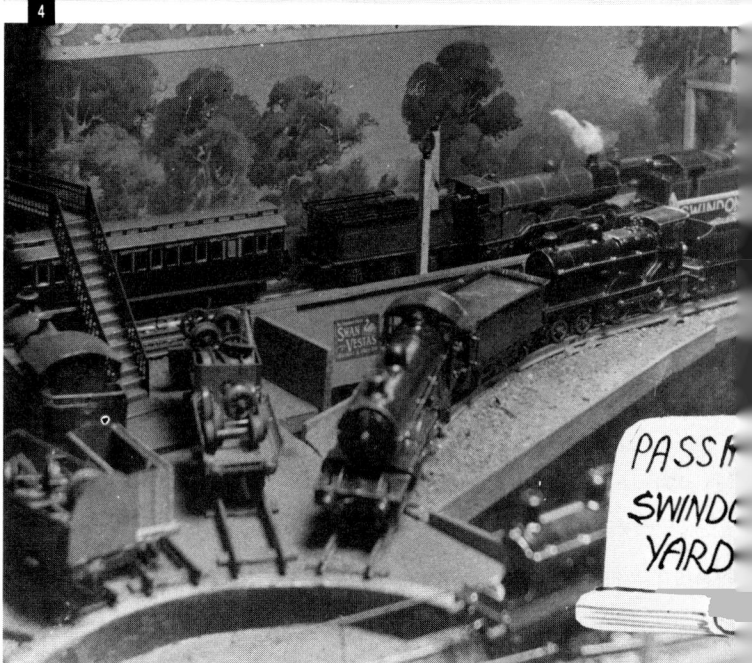

1. Bassett-Lowke's parents at left, 1883; pictured outside the engineering shop.
2. W. J. Bassett-Lowke in 1902 aged 25.
3. The daughter and grandson of the company's first chairman, Jack Sears, in 1908.
4. A Christmas card from W. Smart, one of the founders of the Model Railway Club, in 1911.
5. W. J. Bassett-Lowke with young members of the Sears family 1911.

6. W. J. Bassett-Lowke with W. J. Barnard (office manager) in 1913.
7. W. J. Bassett-Lowke with unknown playmates and the new 'Black Prince' 1909.
8. Bassett-Lowke staff outside the Children's Welfare Exhibition 1914.
9. W. J. Bassett-Lowke examines an exhibit at the Model Engineer Exhibition in the early 1920s.

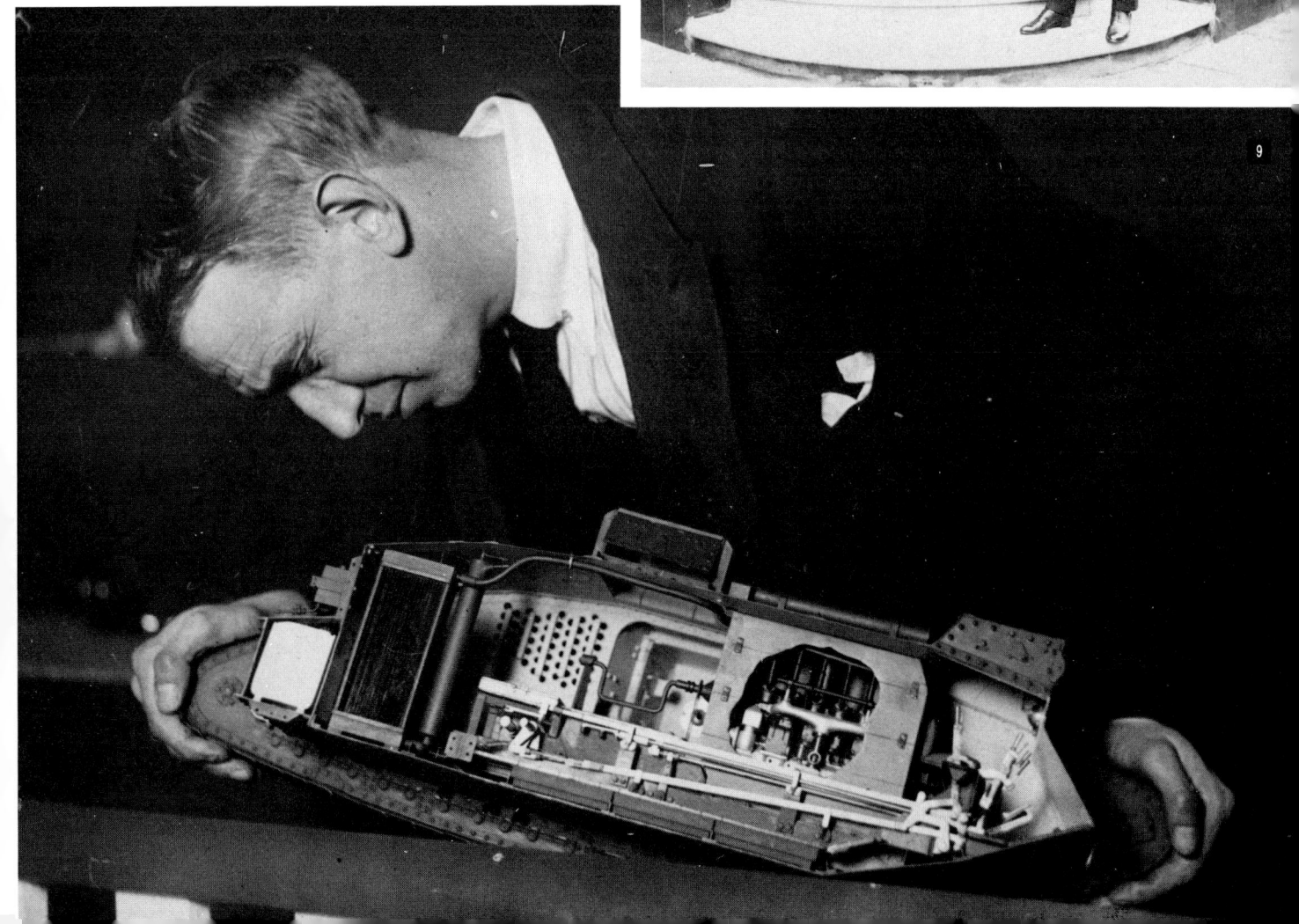

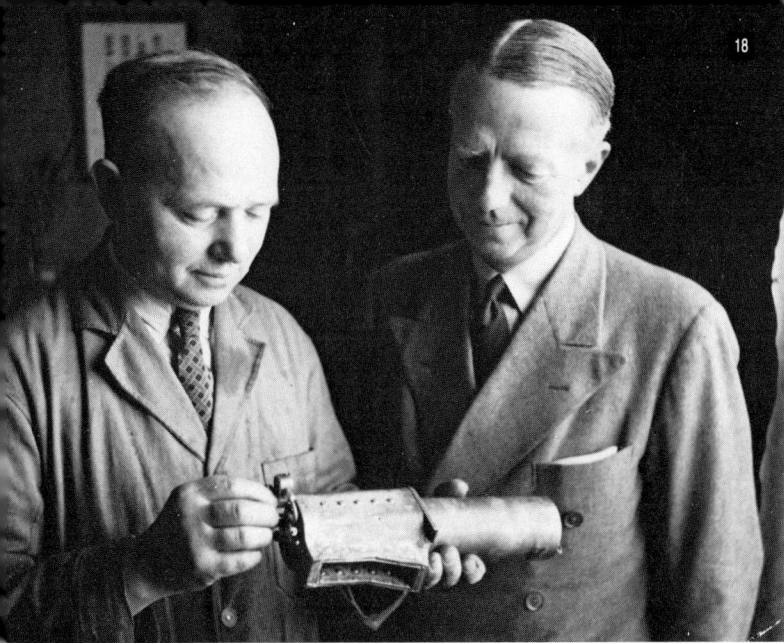

10. W. J. Bassett-Lowke in Norway 1925.
11. Train time at 'New Ways' in 1929.
12. Braunston driving the 3¼" 'Flying Scotsman' in 1924.
13. Brussels 1930; background: the author, C. Derry, G. Sell; front row: H. M. Sell, H. C. Foreman, W. J. Bassett-Lowke.
14. W. J. Bassett-Lowke on 'Children's Hour'.
15. Commander Lockhart at his home at Dunstone 1938.
16. Left: Commander Lockhart, right: R. Bindon Blood 1938.
17. J. M. Maskelyne, a key figure in the development of scale model railways 1938 (driver unknown).

18. J. Braunston and Commander Lockhart 1938.
19. Misha Black (with bow tie) inspects *Queen Mary* 1938.
20. Editor of *Model Engineer*, Percival Marshall; R. Bindon Blood; J. M. Maskelyne c.1939.
21. W. J. Bassett-Lowke, Mrs Keen and J. P. Keen.
22. Bassett-Lowke and J. M. Maskelyne, 1925.
23. Frau Bing, Stefan Bing and Mrs Bassett-Lowke at New Ways in 1939.
24. Franz Bing with father, Stefan, and Mr Harris on the Mitropa Express 1938 photographed by W. J. Bassett-Lowke.

25.  W. J. Bassett-Lowke, P. F. Claydon and Bindon Blood (1st, 3rd and 5th from left) with Ministry Inspectors examining a training device in the works in 1942.

26.  Lord Brabazon inspecting a Mirror device in 1942.

27.  Left to right: W. J. B-L, P. F. Claydon, V. King, W. H. Rowe, H. W. Franklin, the author, H. R. Franklin, May 1943.

28.  C. B. Cox (Manchester shop manager) c.1925.

29.  Percival Marshall at Skindles, Maidenhead 1944.

30.  St. Andrews Street, left to right: W. H. Rowe, L. Hartford (boiler fittings foreman), H. W. Franklin, V. King (bookkeeper), A. C. Palmer (auditor), P. F. Claydon, W. J. Bassett-Lowke.

31.  Clement and Mrs Atlee visiting the works in 1945.

32.  Outside the showrooms, St. Andrews Street, 1946; left to right: V. King, H. W. Franklin, W. H. Rowe, the author, W. J. Bassett-Lowke, E. H. Clifton (Twining Models), P. F. Claydon, R. F. Bindon Blood.

33.  W. J. Bassett-Lowke on the BBC, 25 October 1946, 'Models in Modern Planning'.

34.  META annual meeting, spring 1946. W. J. B-L at rear.

35.  W. J. Bassett-Lowke and Mrs Bassett-Lowke, Franz Bing and unnamed friend and H. M. Sell on Lake Maggiore 1946.

## 37

## HAMTUNE PERSONALITIES

# Design for living

IF a boy's best friend is his mother, next best for countless thousands who prefer engines to "Injuns," is Northampton's model-man, 71-years-old Alderman W. J. Bassett-Lowke, Englishman by birth, European by inclination. This tall, energetic and indefatigable traveller, whose favourite reading is surely Baedeker, Bradshaw and Bernard Shaw, may discard with scorn the charge that home-keeping youths have ever homely wits.

Businessman, author, traveller, Repertory pioneer, photographer and Fabian, his home is "New Ways,"

ALD. W. J. BASSETT-LOWKE

England's first modern house. So it was styled 22 years ago, when famous architect Professor Bernard and he transferred it from blue-print to reality. But he is, as always, as much at home in the lesser comforts of the transcontinental wagon-lit as amid the labour-saving pleasures of his Wellingborough-road model house. He was born not so much with a silver spoon in his mouth as with a model engine in his hand. Engineering is his background. It began with his grandfather's boiler-making business, begun in Kingswell-street as far back as 1859, developed into engineering, and, by stages of sublimation as it were, into a renowned business of model-making that has reached as far as the rocky fastnesses of Afghanistan itself. There, years ago, went a model Cunard liner, the Scytnia, for the ill-starred Amanullah. That's the part of his life most people know and know well. He is also Nonconformist, radical into Fabian, and on into the wider circles of Socialism, and a friend of G.B.S., about whom the famous playwright could say: "I forget everything now in 10 minutes or less, but not the happy days in Northampton."

His models need no introduction here. They're part of Northampton's contribution to internationalism, but we must not forget their part in the planning of World War I.'s strategy, nor the share they had in the D-Day programme.

In Northampton his politics have been practical enough: we owe him the health-giving delights of the Campbell-square baths, and a prodding, persuasive interest in good design as an increasing part of everyday living. He is an example of the tolerance that wide vision and sympathies can give. And who is there who cannot appreciate his sage suggestion that the best of all possible uses for the Guildhall is as a museum and art gallery? With, might I suggest, some live exhibits from "upstairs"!

36. W. J. Bassett-Lowke aged 70 in 1947.
37. *Chronicle & Echo* 1 July 1948.
38 & 39. Messrs Theophile and Jean Carette (sons of the famous George Carette) visiting Northampton in May 1948.
40. W. J. Bassett-Lowke during a lecture on model railways at the Royal Society of Arts, London on 31 December 1948.
41. Second left to right: F. Prior, F. R. Franklin, H. C. Clifton, Stefan Kahn, Franz Bing, H. M. Sell, C. B. Cox and H. C. Foreman at 50th Anniversary 1949.

42. Lord Brabazon speaking at the 50th Anniversary dinner.
43. Franz Bing, W. Lines and W. J. Bassett-Lowke at the Savoy dinner.
44. The Guests.

1. Lord Brabazon
2. F. J. Camm (Practical Mechanics)
3. George Dow (British Railways)
4. R. Bindon Blood (Precision Models)
5. J. D. Kiley, M.P.
6. C. E. Rowe (Town Clerk Northampton)
7. C. Courtice (Passport Office)
8. S. Kahn (Trix Ltd)
9. W. H. Rowe (First employee Bassett-Lowke Ltd)
10. V. Harrison (Harrison Printers and amateur model engineer)
11. J. C. Cribbin (Model Engineer)
12. J. E. Timmins (David Harcourt Ltd)
13. E. H. Clifton (Twining Models)
14. Chairman of Model Engineers Trade Association
15. H. M. Sell (London Manager of Bassett-Lowke)
16. E. W. Stogdon (Model Engineer Exhibition Manager)
17. H. C. Foreman (London Manager 1919–45)
18. G. L. Lake (Model Engineer Trade Association)
19. P. Oppenheim (Trix Ltd).
20. R. J. Hingley (Holders Ltd)
21. J. H. Saillil (I.C.I. Ltd)
22. Representative from The Daily Telegraph
23. R. A. Rautin (French Lines)
24. J. Aggett (Blue Star Line)
25. D. Caird (Royal Mail Lines)
26. F. Bing (Trix Ltd)
27. H. Glenn (builders for reconstructed 18–25 Kingswell Street)
28. R. Saunderson (Stuart Turner Ltd)
29. F. E. Courtney (Principal Northampton Technical College)
30. R. H. Fuller (Bassett-Lowke Ltd)
31. A. J. White (Harrap & Co, Printers)
32. J. R. Cox (editor, Boys Own)
33. G. Lewis (Bassett-Lowke shareholder)
34. A. Robson (Union Castle Co)
35. P. F. Claydon (Bassett-Lowke Ships Models Ltd)
36. A. H. Ridrup (Cunard White Star Lines)
37. G. Archer (Jarrolds, printers)
38.
39. B. W. C. Cooke (editor, locomotive magazine)
40. A. B. Storrar (Chairman of Society of Model Engineers)
41. E. Steel (Greenly's son-in-law)
42. H. W. Franklin (Bassett-Lowke Ltd, son of joint founder)
43. J. Maskelyne (Model Railway News)
44. The editor of English Mechanics

BASSETT-LOWKE LTD

**50**

*FIFTY YEARS OF MODEL MAKING*

THE

# BASSETT-LOWKE

# FIFTIETH ANNIVERSARY

# CELEBRATION DINNER

WHYTE MELVILLE HALL
NORTHAMPTON
3rd FEBRUARY, 1950

CHAIRMAN   -   MR. CYRIL DERRY

45. 1949 dinner for the London Staff. Round the table from left foreground: H. C. Foreman, Mr. and Mrs Sell, Mr. and Mrs Bassett-Lowke, Mr. and Mrs Derry, the author and his wife, Mr. and Mrs H. W. Franklin.
46. The author and Lord Brabazon at the dinner.
47. Henry Foldas R. Franklin.
48. Self-explanatory.
49. General view of staff celebration dinner at Northampton.
50. Directors at 50th Anniversary dinner at White Melville Hall, Northampton.

51. W. J. Bassett-Lowke in 1950 with products ranging over a lifetime of Bassett-Lowke models.
52. W. J. Bassett-Lowke, spring 1951.
53. Richard Dimbleby and members of the Bassett-Lowke staff in 'Down Your Way' May 1952.
54. META dinner, 1952.

55. Standing left to right: C. Derry, P. F. Claydon, H. W. Franklin, R. Bindon Blood, W. H. Rowe, the author; seated:
W. J. Bassett-Lowke and his niece, Janet.
56. The opening of the new Northampton showroom, 16 October, 1953. Cyril Derry gives the address.

57. Roland Fuller hands a cheque to Tom Chick on his retirement.
58. Dudley Dimmock.
59. H. M. Sell.

# Stock-taking - CLEARANCE CATALOGUE.

## MAY, 1904.

### Stationary Engines, Locomotives, Coaches, Rails, Points, and Railway Accessories

# W. J. Bassett-Lowke & Co.,

## Kingswell Street, Northampton.

LEA & Co., LTD., PRINTERS, NORTHAMPTON.

---

# MECCANO

## A NEW TOY EVERY DAY.

THAT'S what the Meccano boy gets. He never grows tired and weary like other boys. When he has played with a crane and hoisted loads up and down for a while, he builds up a lathe, and commences to turn all kinds of wooden handles and knobs and spindles; then he builds a battleship, and works the guns and fights the enemy; then an Eiffel Tower with the elevator going up and down. All days are bright to him. He just enjoys himself, and enjoys himself, and then goes on enjoying himself. This is the year to start to be a Meccano boy, when a lot of fine new models have been added, and there is a rare chance of picking up a big money prize in the

### MECCANO £200 PRIZE COMPETITION.

This happy boy has built a fine working model with Meccano, and now he is playing with it.

You can build exactly the same models yourself, and scores of others, including

| | | |
|---|---|---|
| Trucks | Aeroplanes | Motor Bus. |
| Wagons | Lathes | Big Wheel |
| Cranes | Windmills | Cliff Railway |
| Signals | Battleships | Tower Bridge |
| Towers | Lighthouse | &c. &c. |
| Bridges | Eiffel Tower | |

An important feature of Meccano is that any boy can invent mechanical models for himself with it. 133 models are shown in the Book of Instructions, but these form only a basis or starting point for inventing scores of others.

2. Extract from 1915 catalogue.

Model of Open Touring Car, presented to H.M. The Queen's Doll's House,
by the Sunbeam Motor Co., Ltd., made by Twining Models, Ltd.

Scale : 1 inch to 1 foot

Model of Limousine Landaulette Car, presented to H.M. The Queen's Dolls' House
by the Lanchester Motor Co., Ltd., made by Twining Models, Ltd.

Model of B type Omnibus,
made for the London General Omnibus Co.

Scale : ⅛ full size

Model of W.D. 3-ton Lorry,
Made for the Leyland Motor Co., Ltd.

Scale : 1½ inches to 1 foot

Model of Road Tank Lorry,
made for Messrs. Shell-Mex, Ltd.

Scale : 1 inch to 1 foot

Model Landaulette Car, presented to H.M. The Queen's Dolls' House
by the Rolls-Royce Co., Ltd., made by Twining Models, Ltd.

Scale : 1 inch to 1 foot

## PRIMUS BIG WHEEL OUTFIT

So many working models give twice the pleasure when wheels are incorporated. This useful outfit has been designed for this purpose, and enormously increases the scope of standard Primus Outfits. Each Outfit has ample parts to build four wheels of 4 in. dia., or two of 6 in. dia., or two of 8 in. dia.

Price (including Book of Instructions)

**13/6**

## PRIMUS MOTOR CHASSIS OUTFIT

This is the outfit for the model maker; it builds up into a complete chassis, upon which bodies of touring cars, lorries, tractors, etc., can be fitted. The Primus Clockwork Motor can be easily built in.

Price (including Instruction Manual)

**21/-**

## PRIMUS LOCOMOTIVE OUTFIT

Contains 109 separate parts which are required to construct the Locomotive. The finished model is one of the best examples of constructional toys ever offered. Complete with Primus Clockwork Motor, fitted with control levers and reversing gear.

Price (including Instruction Book)

**37/6**

| | | |
|---|---|---|
| No. 1S, 9d. | No. 3S, 9d. | Big Wheel, 9d. |
| No. 2S, 1/- | No. 4S, 1/3 | Wood Parts, 9d. |

**INLAND POSTAGE** on Primus Outfits, etc.

| | | |
|---|---|---|
| No. 1, 9d. | No. 3, 1/3 | No. 5 } Too heavy |
| No. 2, 9d. | No. 4, 1/3 | No. 6 } for post. |

---

# PRIMUS ENGINEERING

## STANDARD OUTFITS

At prices to **suit** all pockets—each outfit being complete in every respect and suitable for Boys and Girls of all ages.

Packed in strong useful boxes with illustrated instruction book.

| | | |
|---|---|---|
| No. 0 contains 122 wood and metal parts ... ... ... | 6/0 |
| " 1 " 140 " " " " ... ... ... | 8/6 |
| " 2 " 267 " " " " ... ... ... | 17/6 |
| " 3 " 473 " " " " ... ... ... | 32/6 |
| " 4 " 649 " " " " ... ... ... | 45/0 |
| " 5 " 1131 " " " " ... ... ... | 65/0 |
| " 6 Presentation Cabinet, 1189 wood and metal parts | 105/0 |

## SUPPLEMENTARY OUTFITS

Contain the parts which convert a lower priced outfit into a higher one.

| | | |
|---|---|---|
| 1S converts No. 1 into No. 2 ... ... ... | 10/0 |
| 2S " " 2 " " 3 ... ... ... | 16/6 |
| 3S " " 3 " " 4 ... ... ... | 16/6 |
| 4S " " 4 " " 5 ... ... ... | 25/0 |

4. Primus engineering kits offered in 1924 Section B Catalogue.

# THE "ANCHOR" ENGINEER CONSTRUCTIONAL TOYS

### NO Screws.  NO Bolts or Nuts, NO Auxiliary Tools.

**THE "ANCHOR ENGINEER" works with Two Elements only.**

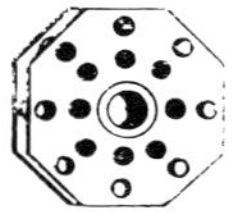

The Stay.

The Plate.

Magnificent Bridges, Cranes, Flying-Machines, Roundabouts, and all kinds of working models can be built with the greatest ease.

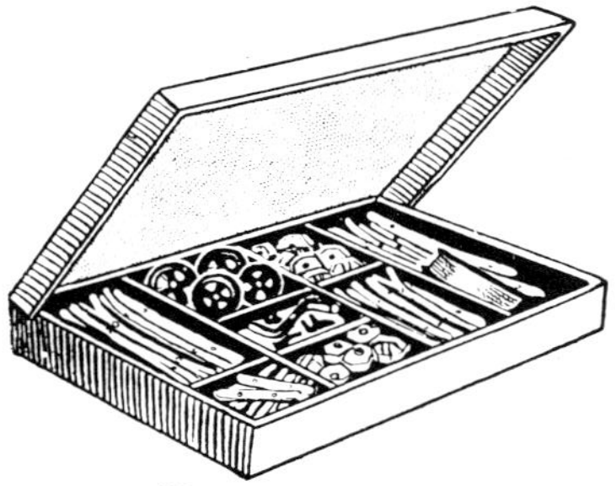

**No. o.**
This is the junior set of Anchor Engineer. Although it is a small and simple set, it contains parts, girders, pulleys and rods to make a great number of models that will fill endless hours with amusement and interest.

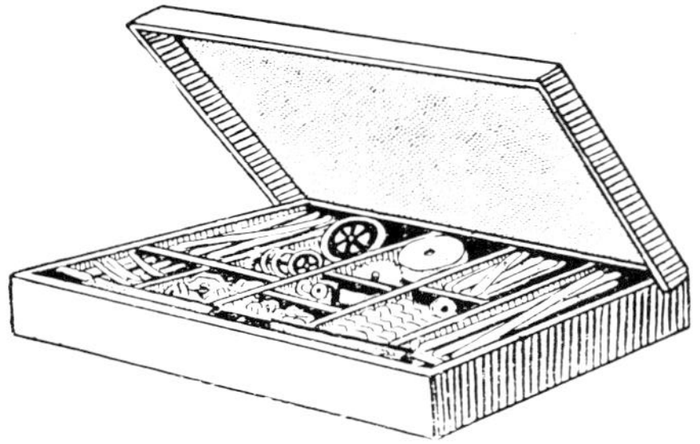

**No. 1.**
This is the next size set of Anchor Engineer—bigger and capable of building more advanced models than the junior with which it can be combined. This is the utmost value in toys that can possibly be offered.

|  | Price. |
|---|---|
| No. o Set. complete in box. makes 26 models ... ... ... | 4 6 |
| No. 1 „ „ „ „ 32 „ ... ... ... | 8 6 |
| No. 2 Set. larger than those illustrated. complete in box. makes 52 models ... ... ... ... ... ... ... | 16 6 |

Supplementary Boxes. for adding the above.

|  | Price. |
|---|---|
| No. oa ... ... ... ... ... | 4 /- |
| No. 1a ... ... ... ... ... | 8 - |

---

# THE "ANCHOR" ENGINEER CONSTRUCTIONAL TOYS

THIS system of metal parts for model engineering structures involves no bolts and nuts. It is devised with spring clip beams and struts fitting into joint units in such a way that when completed a rigid structure is obtained. The well-known principle of triangulation is adopted. The parts are more or less made to scale and are ingeniously proportioned so that they can form complete triangle girders of rigid form such as employed in all bridges and other engineering structures.

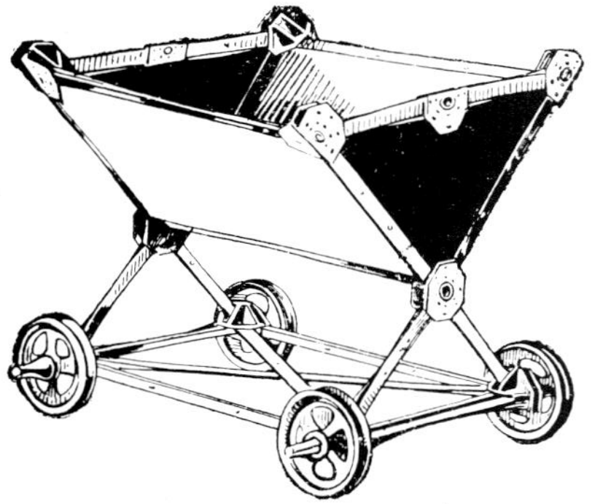

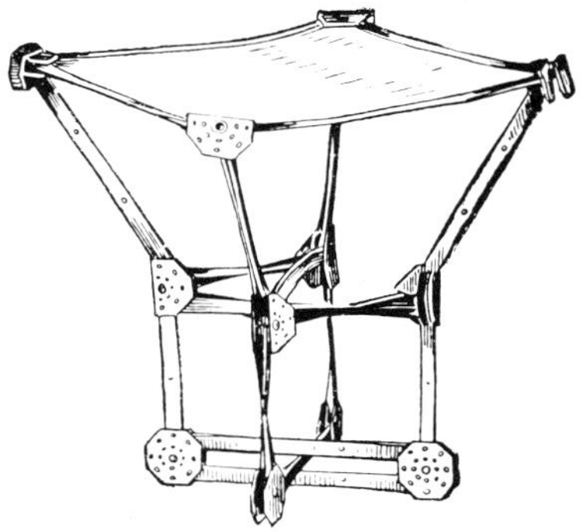

The real engineer rivets his beams together by connecting angles. In the "Anchor" Constructional Toy the nibs provided on the beams engage holes in the separate connecting pieces, two or four of these spring "rivets" being used as occasion may require.

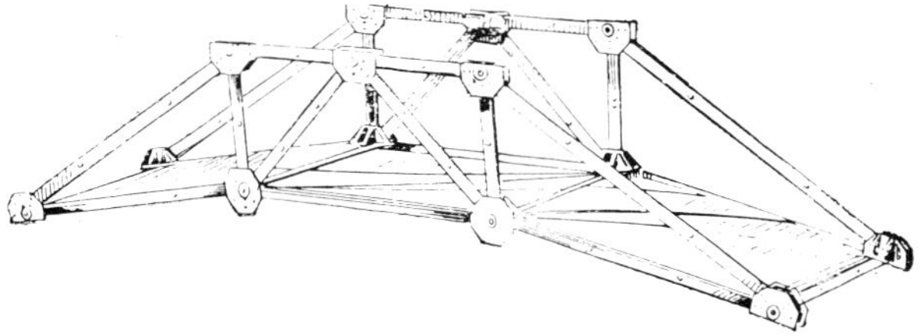

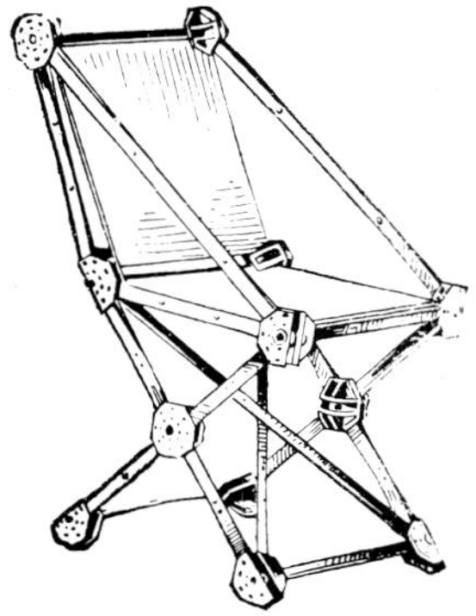

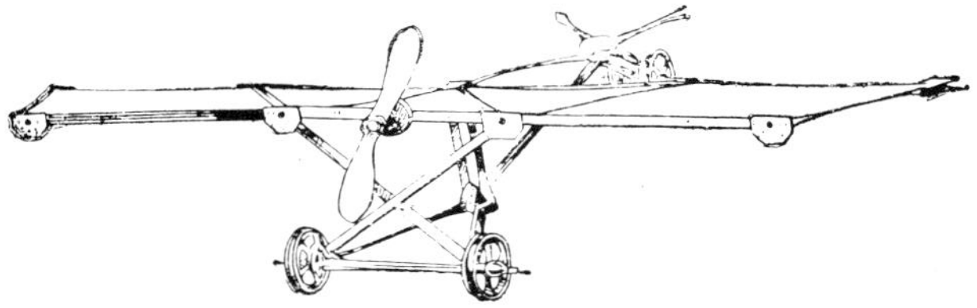

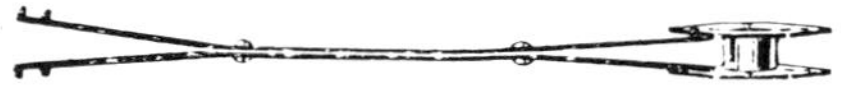

The parts are finished in a beautiful egg-shell black and are complete with shaft, wheels, pulleys and cords in varying proportions according to the value of the set purchased. The sets are progressive in character.

Instructions and scale drawings with photographic illustrations of the completed models are included in each set, and all sets form ideal Constructional Engineering Toys of an instructive character.

*The illustrations show some of the models which can be built with No. o set.*

5

5, 6. Examples of other manufacturers' products from the 1924 Section B Catalogue.

Bassett-Lowke, Ltd.,
London and Northampton.

# "STRUCTO" Touring Car, No. 12.

This is a model of a de-luxe Touring Car fitted with a heavy triple spring motor, cut steel gears, disc wheels, spare wheel, rounded wheel splashers, plate glass wind screen and other features of a high-class motor car. It has two speeds forward and one reverse, and proper motor car steering gear. The model is 16 in. long over all, with a wheel base of 12¼ in. Boxed in parts ready for assembly.
PRICE ... ... ... ... ... 57/6

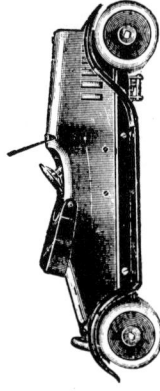

## "STRUCTO" De Luxe Construction Outfit No. 12.

# "STRUCTO" Commercial Car, Model No. 14.

This model Lorry carries a big load and is fitted with a tipping body and swinging rear door. It has a powerful triple spring motor, operating artillery wheels with a base of 12¼ in. The model measures 18 in. long over all, and is finished in red enamel with black and nickel-plated fittings. Boxed in parts as other models.
PRICE ... ... ... ... ... 63/-

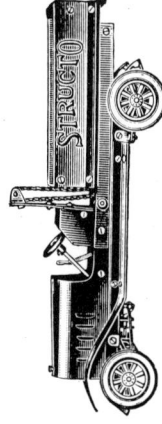

## "STRUCTO" Construction Outfit No. 14.
Commercial Tipping Lorry.

Bassett-Lowke, Ltd.,
London and Northampton.

# THE "STRUCTO" Constructional Motor Cars.

While the 'true to life' character of the "Structo" Model Cars has not been surpassed by any other make of mechanical toy, the system adopted by which the owner of the model builds it himself, gives it an additional fascination.

The "Structo" Auto Cars are miniature reproductions of the real thing. The motors are "clockwork" of exceptional power. The mechanism is arranged on the lines of the prototype, with the proper design of transmission and steering gear. Three types of cars are introduced in the series offered.

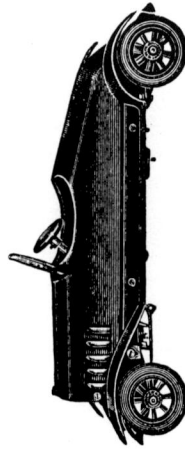

## BEARCAT MOTOR No. 10.
A smart sturdy motor car equipped with double-unit motor, which delivers ample power to the rear wheels to drive car at high speed for a long time. Direct shaft drive; die-cast gears on rear axle. "Start" and "Stop" lever. 16 in. over all. Wheel base 12¼ in. Finished in red enamel, nickel finish and black mud guard. Artillery type wheels, red hubs and spokes. This is an excellent model of a real motor car, ready to be constructed.

## BEARCAT MOTOR No. 10
In box ready to build.
Price ... ... ... 40/-
Complete in display box as illustrated,

6

**free** ...for **B.D.V** CIGARETTE COUPONS

## PURE SILK STOCKINGS

Ladies' 100% Pure Silk Hose, exceptionally fine quality silk coming well over knees, re-inforced double lisle tops, double ravel stops, spliced four ply lisle toes and heels, extremely durable.

*Fashionable Shades : French Nude, Flesh, Peach Bloom, French Beige, Light Grey, etc., also Black and White. State size and colour when ordering.*

PURE SILK STOCKINGS
**140 COUPONS**

**Non-Drip Lip THERMOS FLASK**
Latest model, with non-drip lip. Screw cup and handle. A Gift you should not fail to get.

**The Tournament STITCHLESS TENNIS BALLS**
With cemented seams, made of the finest materials, renowned for extreme durability. Three in a box.

**SCALE MODEL RAILWAYS**
This " George the Fifth " L.M.S. Scale Model Engine as sold by BASSETT-LOWKE LTD., Northampton, and all the equipment to build a complete Model Railway System—Free for B.D.V. cigarette coupons. Send to Godfrey Phillips Ltd., (Gift Dept. )55) 54 White Lion St. for the free B.D.V. train gift book worth 5 coupons) to-day. Every item for building a Model Railway is illustrated and the number of coupons for each part is shown.
Also BING Vulcan Engines Famous Clockwork trains and every necessary part for building up a Model Railway system.

*Simply collect the coupons (found generally at the back of every packet) of B.D.V. cigarettes. When you have sufficient number post to address below—stating gift required.*

GODFREY PHILLIPS LTD.
(Gift Dept. 155) 54 White Lion Street, E.1

Plain or Cork Tip.  **B.D.V**  10 for 6d, 20 for 1 ½d
**"—just like hand-made"**

**100 COUPONS**
The only Genuine Thermos in any Gift Scheme

GENUINE **THERMOS** REGD TRADE MARK FOREIGN VACUUM FLASK

THREE TENNIS BALLS **120 COUPONS**

**260 COUPONS** for ENGINE
Tenders free of coupons until further notice.

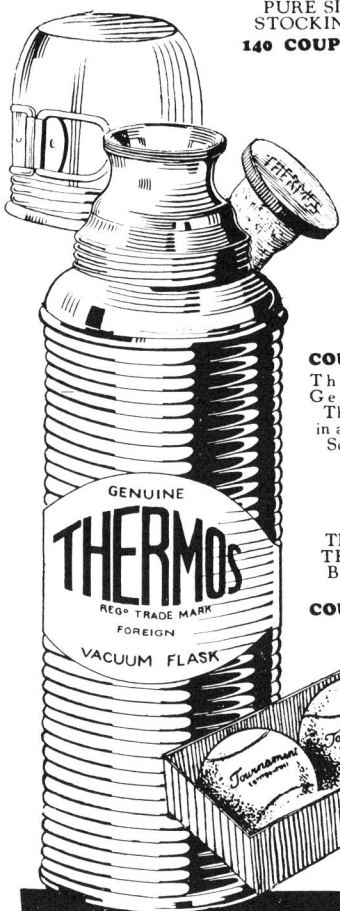

SCALE MODEL RAILWAYS

BASSETT-LOWKE LTD
NORTHAMPTON
LONDON WC MANCHESTER EDINBURGH

SCALE MODEL TRAINS

BASSETT-LOWKE L.TD
· LONDON ·
· NORTHAMPTON ·
· MANCHESTER · EDINBURGH ·

7. 1927 BDV advertisement.
8. Original artwork for catalogue cover, never published.
9. Further idea for a catalogue cover, unused c. 1938.

10. Extract from 1932 scale model furniture catalogue largely based on 'New Ways'.

in solid oak and finished to match chairs, with two cupboards to open and hinged writing flap. The three shelves are fitted with removable imitation books in effective colourings. Height 6 in., width 2½ in., depth from back to front 1½ in. Price **5/6**

**8500 4**   **Book or Smoker's Table.** A neat octagonal table made throughout in dark oak and fitted with shelves. Height 2 in., diameter 2 in. Complete with smoker's set. Price **2/9**

**8500 5**   **Chair.** Of modern design in dark oak, and with leather seat. Height 3½ in., width of seat 1½ in.   Price **1/6**

**8520 1**   **Club Chair** Upholstered and covered in real leather. Width over arms 3½ in., depth from back to front 2½ in. Price **4/–**

**8520 2**   **Settee, or Club Sofa** Of attractive design, properly upholstered and covered in real leather. Length 6½ in., width from back to front 2½ in., height to seat 1½ in. Price **6/6**

**8300 1**   **Standard Lamp** Made in metal throughout and fitted with translucent shade in unbreakable material. Complete with screw pea lamp and 14 in. of silk-covered flex. Height 5½ in., diameter of shade 2½ in.  ……   Price **2/9**
Spare pea lamps with screw socket, 3½ volts.   Price each **6d.**

**8510/1**   **Flower Stand** Specially designed for the Garden Room or Lounge. Complete with set of cacti plants and watering can. Price **2/–**

**8400/1**   **Picture** Lithographed in colour and fitted in metal frame. Size 3 in. × 2¼ in., either vertical or horizontal.   Price   **1/3** We can also supply, while the stock lasts, a series of 25 reproductions of celebrated oil painters, as issued with Army Club cigarettes. These are lithographed in correct colours, complete with gilded frame. Size overall 2⅛ in. × 1 7/16 in., assorted vertical and horizontal. Price per pkt. **1/–**

**8158**   **Tea Wagon** Complete with shelf underneath and metal handle. Height 3 in., width 3 in.  ……   Price **3/9**

**8521**   **Cushion** A necessary addition to the settee, stuffed, various colours. 1½ in. diameter  ……  ……   Price **8d.**

# L O U N G E

**8302**   **Fire Place and Mantelpiece** This is n exact replica of the well known Bell grate with Dutch tile surround and hearth. It is fitted with imitation fir illuminated with electric bulb when connected with pocket battery. Height to top of mantelpiece 3¾ in., width 4 in., projection of hearth from wall 1¼ in.   Price complete with electric bulb and flex ……  ……  ……  ……   **4/6**

**8303**   **Clock,** for overmantel  ……  ……   **6d.**

**8119**   **Fireside Companion** Consisting of shovel, brush, tongs and poker, complete with stand. Finished either oxidised or bronze. Height 2½ in.  ……  ……   **1/6**

**8450/1**   **Carpet,** of new design, being exact replicas as far as scale will permit of Persian design Wilton carpets, it Is made of good quality velvet fringed at either end. Stocked in four basic colours : blue, green, old rose and old gold. Size 13½ in. × 9½ in.  ……  ……   Price   **3/–**

**8450/2**   **Hearth Rug** Made especially to match above carpet, in same material, design and colour. Size 6½ in. × 3 in.  ……  ……  ……  ……   Price   **9d.**

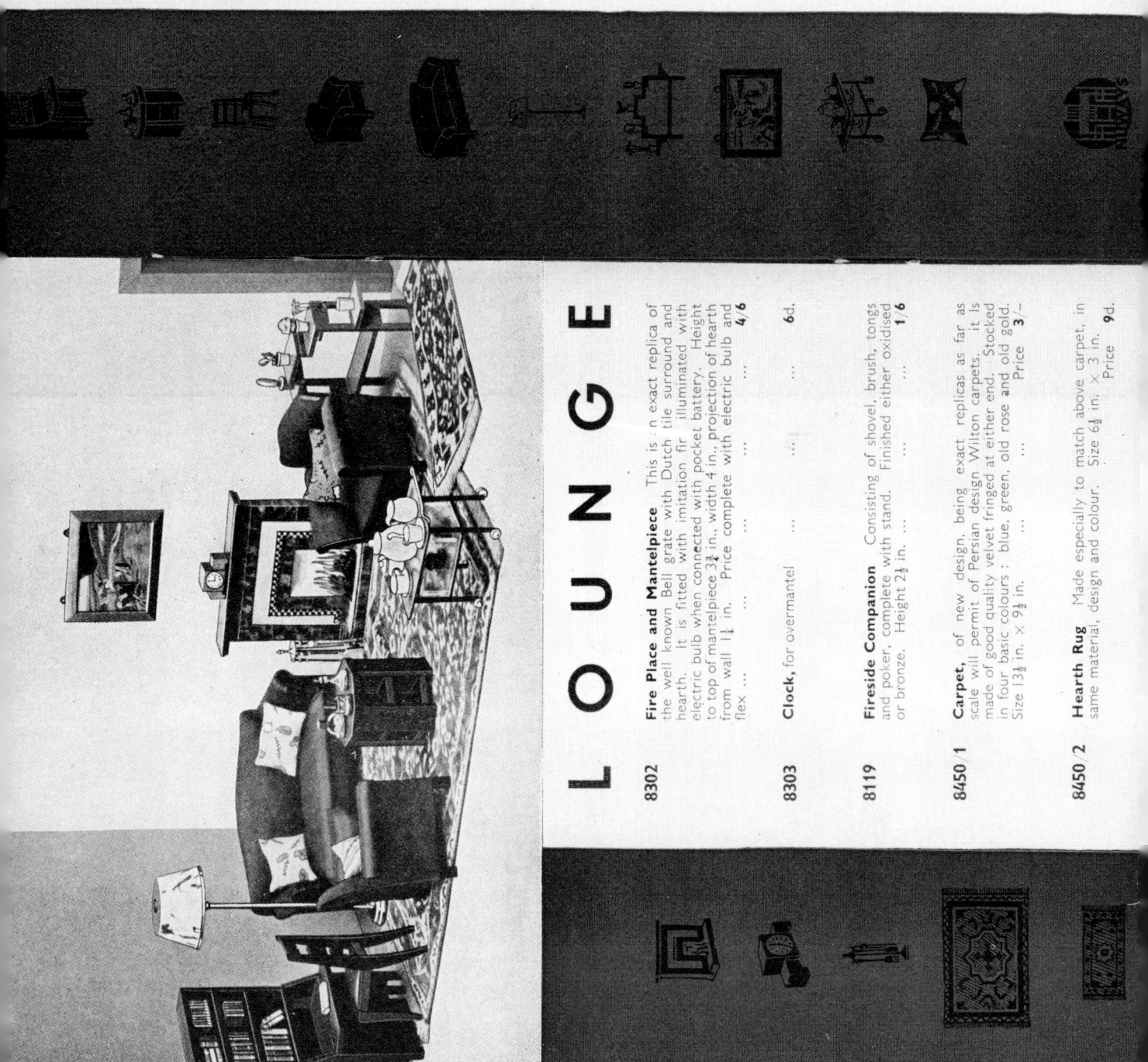

# BASSETT-LOWKE LTD
## GOODS TRAINS
### CLOCKWORK

For those who prefer operating freight trains, this is the best start. Packed in similar style to the Passenger Train sets, the models are of robust construction, and the six-coupled motors in the locomotives are especially powerful.

British Railways 6-coupled Tank Locomotive, with train of four all-steel body goods vehicles, comprising two open vans, 1 covered van and one Guard's Brake Van, and complete with Oval 7′ × 4′ having 12 curved and 6 straight lengths of tinned steel track.

Packed in two presentation boxes. Set No. 754/3. Clockwork drive.

Price No. 4

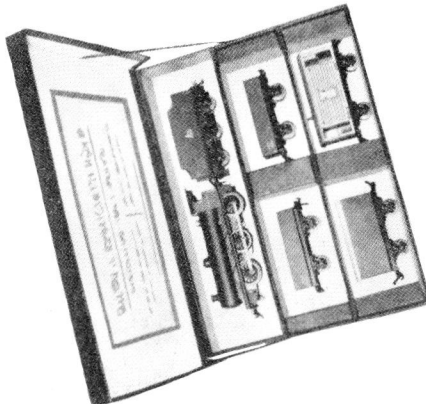

Six Coupled Tender Locomotive with train of four all-steel body goods vehicles and Oval 7′ × 4′ track formation as above.

Packed in two presentation boxes. Set No. 754/4. Clockwork drive.

Price No. 5

Scale Model Permanent Way track will improve both the appearance and performance of the trains.

Either of the above sets can be supplied with a 6′ × 10′ 6″ oval of first quality solid steel permanent way for an additional payment of Price No. 6.

All sets are supplied with full working instructions and winding key, lubricating oil and Valvespout leakproof oil-can.

Additional rails and points for these sets are shown on pages 23 and 24 or 32.

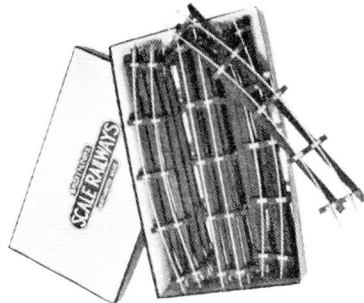

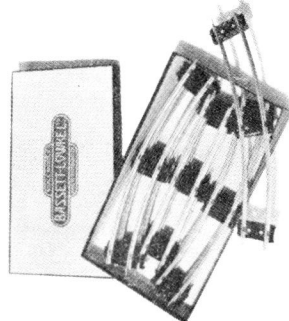

All Gauge "O" rolling stock and accessories shown in this catalogue are suitable for use with these

---

# NEWS OF THE MODEL WORLD

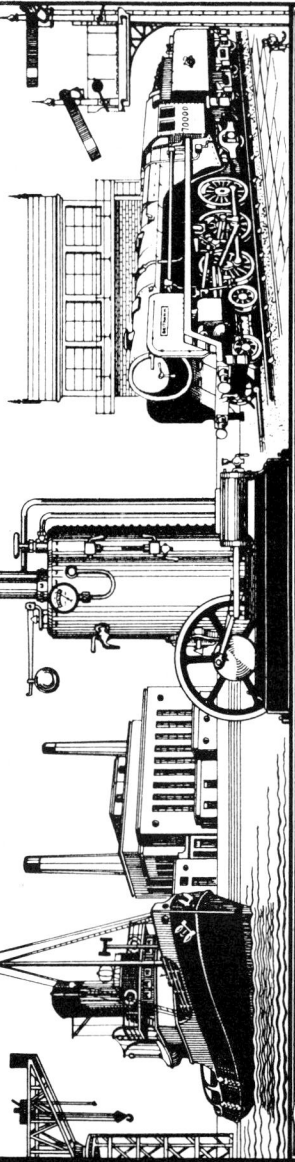

| No. 1 | BASSETT-LOWKE LTD | MARCH 1954 |
|---|---|---|

LONDON BRANCH
112 HIGH HOLBORN W.C.1.

HEAD OFFICE AND WORKS.
18–25 KINGSWELL ST. NORTHAMPTON.

MANCHESTER BRANCH
28 CORPORATION STREET. 4.

## THE 'ROYAL SCOT'

A FAMOUS ENGINE
'ROYAL SCOT'
No. 46100

PRICE £25 1s 8d
Incl.purchase tax

This is the newest model locomotive from the Bassett-Lowke works. The Royal Scot has been modelled for many years, but this 'O' version is vastly different in every respect to the 'first of the line'.

It was in 1933 that the first Royal Scot appeared in the Bassett-Lowke catalogue, and for its very modest price, it was indeed an outstanding product. History was made by it being the largest lithographed tinplate clipped-assembly model to be made in this country in gauge 'O'. It was well proportioned and was fitted with an accurate representation of the Walschaert valve gear and piston valvecylinders as fitted to its prototype.

From time to time, modifications were made and eventually, it became one of the series

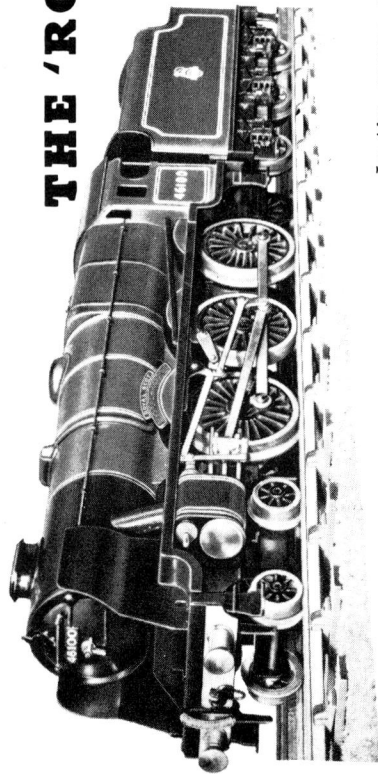

In the course of time, the real Royal Scot was very considerably rebuilt and there was a tremendous transformation from the first version with its massive parallel boiler and minute chimney to the current design with a graceful tapered boiler and double chimney. Some L.M.S. enthusiasts no doubt, regret the departure from classical style, but there is no doubt if one appraises the Royal Scot without comparing it to earlier versions, that it is a very handsome machine, and it looks particularly well in the British Railways green livery. Incidentally, the new model carries the special Royal Scot name plate which is such a distinctive feature.

Both clockwork and electric drive are available and a special feature is that the cylinders are mounted on a metal frame attached to the mechanism. This facili-

280

# PASSENGER AND GOODS SETS

## STEAM

Since Watt first evolved the principle of steam power, each succeeding generation has been attracted to the steam locomotive in greater measure than any other form of motive power.

Bassett-Lowke Live Steam models reproduce the fascinating atmosphere of quiet energy so typical of the prototype. They are easy and safe to handle, each locomotive being supplied with detailed working instructions.

"Enterprise" Goods set with 4-4-0 Locomotive and Tender, two open goods vans, one covered van, one Guard's Brake van, twelve curved and six straight tinned steel plate rails to form an oval track 7' × 4'.

Packed in two Presentation boxes.

Set No. 754/9     Price No. 11

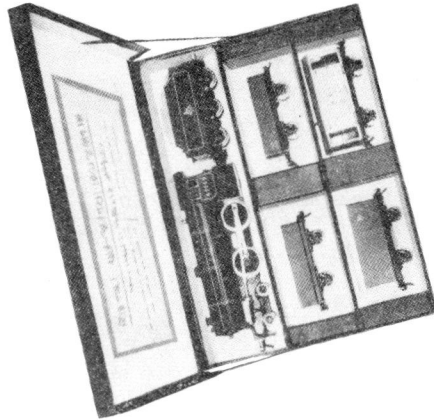

"Enterprise" Passenger set with 4-4-0 Locomotive and Tender, two passenger coaches, twelve curved and six straight tinned steel plate rails to form an oval track 7' × 4'.

Packed in two presentation boxes.

Set No. 754/10.     Price No. 12

Each set is supplied with instructions, spare wicks and washers, lubricating oil and a "Valvespout" leak-proof oilcan.

Scale Model Permanent Way track will improve both the appearance and performance of the trains.

Either of the above sets can be supplied with a 6' × 10' 6" oval of first quality solid steel permanent way for an additional payment of Price No. 13

Additional rails and points for these sets are shown on pages 23 and 24 or 32.

All Gauge "0" rolling stock and accessories shown in this catalogue are suitable for use with these trains.

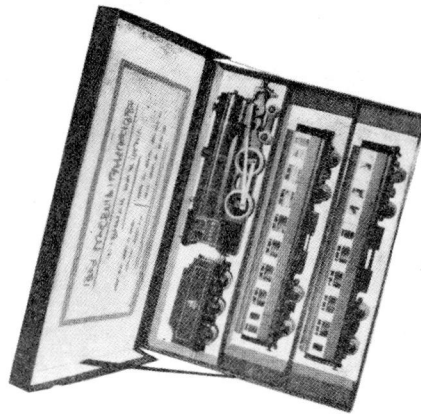

# PASSENGER TRAINS

## ELECTRIC

For power, performance and the interest of remote control, electric drive excels all. Bassett-Lowke Gauge "0" locomotives are fitted with efficient permanent magnet motors wired for running on 12 volts direct current. They may be operated from A.C. house mains by connecting through a rectifier-resistance unit, suitable apparatus being illustrated and described in this catalogue.

All Bassett-Lowke Electric Trains are absolutely safe to use—even by the very young.

British Railways Compound Locomotive with two all steel Passenger Coaches and an oval track 10' 6" × 6' of Bassett-Lowke Scale Model Permanent Way steel track complete with electric connecting rail.

Packed in two presentation boxes.

Set No. 754/5     Price No. 7

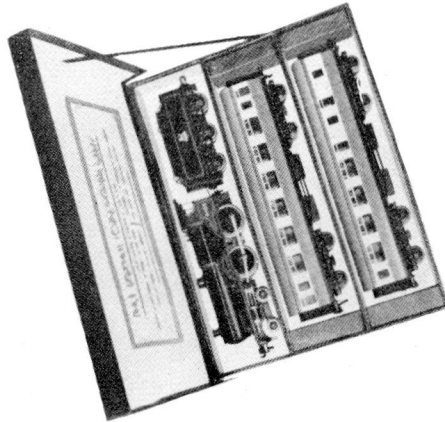

Prince Charles 4-4-0 Locomotive with two coaches and layout of Scale Model Steel Permanent Way as above

Packed in two presentation boxes.

Set No. 754/6     Price No. 8

*For operating sets from A.C. House mains, see pages 33 to 35 for details of suitable apparatus.*

11.   The company's last 'in-house' magazine.
12, 13, 14.   Extracts from 1957 gauge 0 catalogue.

# Super Detail
# Locomotive Models

**BASSETT-LOWKE LTD.**

*This photograph of a Gauge 'O' G.W.R. 0-4-0 Tank
is incapable of showing fully the
delicately reproduced detail and line of our Model
—that is why we usually have one in stock to
show our clients. Obviously models in this
class are higher priced than any of the standard locomotives
in the list, being individually hand
made throughout by master craftsmen.
Each is a unique collector's piece of
which their owner may justly be proud.
We welcome the opportunity of quoting for
any type in this same class of finish.*

By arrangement this specimen can be available for examination at our showrooms in London, Manchester or Northampton

MODELS BY
BASSETT-LOWKE

15.  The last super-detail gauge 0 model offered by
Bassett-Lowke which was still on offer until just before
the takeover of the retail shops by Beatties.

# Minutes

of the

## First Meeting of Directors

of

## Bassett-Lowke Limited

(incorporated the 11th of March 1910) held at the office of Messrs Dennis & Faulkners, Solicitors, Northampton, on the 22nd day of March 1910.

### Present.

Mr J. G. Sears.

   „   W. J. Bassett-Lowke.

   „   H. F. R. Franklin.

Mr W. A. Harmer also in attendance.

1. The printed Memorandum & Articles of Association with certificate of incorporation of the Company on the 11th of March 1910 were produced.

2. Resolved that Mr John George Sears be & is hereby appointed the Chairman of the Company until the first Annual General Meeting.

3. Resolved that the registered office of the Company be at the Company's premises in Kingswell Street, Northampton.

4. A lever press Seal designed for the Company was produced being in a circular form with the words "Bassett-Lowke Ltd London & Northampton" round the rim and on the inside thereof the words "Model Engineers" and a signal arm with the word "Lowko" thereon in the centre.

the Shares subscribed for by them to the
Company's Banking Account And that Shares
be allotted to them accordingly, viz:-

| Allottee | Nº of Shares | Denoting numbers of Shares. |
|---|---|---|
| W. J. Bassett Lowke. | 1. | 7201. |
| H. F. R. Franklin. | 1. | 7202. |
| John George Sears | 1. | 7203. |

12  Applications for 3375 Shares in the capital of
the Company from the under-mentioned persons
were considered  Resolved that 3099 shares
allotted & that to each of such persons there
allotted the number of Shares set opposite his
or her name in the third column below, viz:-

| Applicant | Shares applied for. | Number allotted | Denoting numbers of shares both inclusive | |
|---|---|---|---|---|
| | | | from. | to. |
| Jno Geo Sears. | 999. | 999. | 7204. | 8202. |
| James Bedington & Son. | 200. | 200. | 8203 | 8402. |
| Frederick C. Franklin. | 100. | 100. | 8403. | 8502. |
| William Henry Heggs. | 200. | 200. | 8503. | 8702. |
| Edward Walter Hobbs. | 100. | 100. | 8703. | 8802. |
| Ada Elizabeth Jones | 100. | 100. | 8803. | 8902. |
| Robert Charles Smith | 100. | To stand over until next Directors' Meeting. | | |
| Joseph Wakefield Hanson (Whitton) | 300. | 300. | 8903. | 9202. |
| Thomas D. Lewis. | 125. | 100. | 9203. | 9302. |
| H. A. Bassett Lowke | 50. | 50. | 9303. | 9352. |
| Eliza Lowke | 100 | 100. | 9353. | 9452. |
| Forward | | 2249. | | |

| Applicant | Shares applied for. | Number allotted. | Denoting Nºs | |
|---|---|---|---|---|
| | Brought forward | 2249. | from | to |
| Joseph Tom Lowke. | 150. | 100. | 9453. | 9552. |
| Henry Greenly. | 100. | 100. | 9553. | 9652. |
| Edward Lewis. | 500. | 500. | 9653 | 10152. |
| Fred. Green. | 50. | 50. | 10153 | 10202. |
| Tom Edward Black Lee. | 100. | To stand over until next Directors' Meeting. | | |
| Augustus C. Palmer | 100. | 100. | 10203. | 10302. |
| | | 3,099. | | |

**interingham** A letter from this company signed by
**Limited** Mr G. Winteringham, calling attention to the
agreement with us, + more especially as
to preference which they looked for, was
produced + read.

It was ordered that a letter should be sent
in reply stating that on no account can
we exceed the amount specified, as
unfortunately we are now overstocked.
Re competitive articles, preference will certainly
be given, but we should wish you to
reduce your supplies of stock goods for
the next three months to a sum not exceeding
£200. per month.

**ings Lt.** A letter from this firm calling attention to their
account, with suggestions as to payment, was
discussed; and it was agreed that
Mr Bassett Lowke should call upon them
and arrange payment by Drafts.

**solved** That Mr Meinhardt of Coventry be
appointed Sole Agent for Budapest
for Locomotives of 15" gauge . over
. Mr Lowke arrange with the Company's
Solicitor to . complete the Agency Agreement
The Question of Messrs Bassett-Lowke .
Franklin having an Interest in
Narrow Gauge Rlys Ltd was discussed
. the Chairman stated that he had no
objection provided always that no more
than the usual monthly credit be given
by the firm to N.G.R. Ltd without the
Chairmans permission.

285

# THE REPORT OF THE DIRECTORS

to be presented to the Shareholders at the THIRD ANNUAL GENERAL MEETING of the above Company, to be held at the Registered Offices, Kingswell Street, Northampton, 11th September, 1912, at Three p.m.

---

The Directors have pleasure in submitting herewith Balance Sheet and Profit and Loss Account for the financial year ending June 30th, 1912.

The Business done shows a satisfactory increase in the Sales and Profits, and the Directors have made arrangements for a Retail Agency for the sale of the Company's Goods in the city of Paris, which, they hope, will result in further increases next year.

All Expenses of Advertising and Catalogues (other than those in stock), which should be productive of further good business, have been written off the Revenue.

The Miniature Railways of Great Britain, Ltd. having gone into Liquidation, Messrs. W. J. Bassett-Lowke and H. F. R. Franklin have repaid to your Company the amount received by them on formation for Shares in the Miniature Railway Company.

The Nett Profit for the Year, after making due allowance for Depreciation, etc., amounts to £1,063 16s. 11d., which, with the balance of £208 14s. 2d., brought forward from last Account after payment of the Dividends, leaves £1,272 11s. 1d. now standing to the credit of the Profit and Loss Account.

The Directors therefore recommend the payment of a Dividend of 5% on the Subscribed Capital of the Company, which will absorb £606 2s. 0d., and that the balance be brought forward to the present year.

Owing to the increased cost of production during the past year and taking into consideration the special nature of the Company's business, the Directors consider the Gross Profits are insufficient, and have decided to advance all selling prices by about 10%. This should allow for the increased cost of the goods and at the same time provide a larger margin for Nett Profit in the future.

Dated this 2nd day of September, 1912.

By Order of the Board,

J. G. SEARS,

Chairman.

---

*Thanks.* A Vote of thanks to the Chairman concluded the Meeting

*J. G. Sears*
*Chairman.*

Applications for 1850 Shares in the Capital of the Company from the under-mentioned persons were considered, and it was resolved that to each of such persons there be allotted at par in exchange for cash the number of Shares set opposite to the respective names in the 2nd column below, viz:-

| Allottee. | No. of Shares allotted. | Denoting No. of Shares, both incl. From. | To. |
|---|---|---|---|
| Lewis, Thomas Davies | 100. | 14301. | 14400 |
| Hodgson, John Edmund | 50. | 14401. | 14450 |
| Franklin, Amelia Annie | 100. | 14451. | 14550 |
| Lowke, Florence Jane Bassett | 50. | 14551. | 14600 |
| Lewis, Edward | 250. | 14601. | 14850 |
| Jones, Ada Elizabeth | 100. | 14851. | 14950 |
| Forward | 650. | | |

| Allottee. | No. of Shares allotted. | Denoting No. of Shares, both inclusive. From. | To. |
|---|---|---|---|
| Brought forward | 650. | | |
| Carette, Georges. | 50. | 14951. | 15000 |
| Keen, Geoffrey Percy. | 200. | 15001. | 15200 |
| Eyden, William Edmund. | 100. | 15201. | 15300 |
| Cobb, Keightley. | 50. | 15301. | 15350 |
| Foreman, Hubert Charles. | 100. | 15351. | 15450 |
| Heggs, William Henry. | 100. | 15451. | 15550 |
| Franklin, Beatrice. | 300. | 15551. | 15850. |
| Lowke, Wenman Joseph Bassett | 300. | 15851. | 16150. |
| | 1,850. | | |

Certificates for the Shares in the names of the respective Allottees were thereupon sealed and signed, and directed to be issued on payment of the amounts due.

Edward Lewis

Chairman.

287

# TRIX LIMITED

*Makers of Electric Trains & Constructional Sets.*

DIRECTORS:
J. D. KILEY, J.P. (CHAIRMAN) H. OPPENHEIM, (GERMAN)
W. J. BASSETT-LOWKE. S. KAHN (GERMAN)
S. BING. (GERMAN)
SECRETARY: J. STEIN, BRITISH (BAVARIAN ORIGIN)

TRIX
TTR
TRADE MARKS

TELEPHONE: CLERKENWELL 1522
TELEGRAMS: TEETEEYAR, SMITH, LONDON.

· ST. JOHN'S HOUSE · 45 & 47, CLERKENWELL ROAD ·
· LONDON ·
E.C.1.

TRIX LTD. 45, CLERKENWELL ROAD, E.C.1.

20th October 1938.

Messrs. Bassett-Lowke Ltd.,
St. Andrews St.,
Northampton.

JS/SS

Dear Sirs,

In answer to your letter of February 3rd 1938 we have pleasure in informing you that our Board have now approved of the arrangement regarding the marketing of T.T.R. Scale Models as follows:

T.T.R. Scale Models of Locomotives and Coaches will be offered and sold by us, to the trade only, under the name of "Bassett-Lowke Scale Models" or under similar slogans.

For the use of your name in connection with these goods, and for any other assistance your Company may be able to give us from time to time, we reserve you a Royalty of 5% for a period of five years from January 1st 1938. This Royalty is payable for each calendar year not later than January 31st of the following year, on all net sales, excluding supplies to you, arrived at after deduction of trade discounts, cash discounts, returns and bad debts.

We shall supply you with these model goods for your own requirements at the regular terms agreed between us, and we are prepared to give you an extra discount of 10% in respect of all scale models which you will sell to your trade customers, provided you inform us about these sales in the same way as you are informing us regularly of your sales to the trade of Southern Railway Sets.

The first of the Bassett-Lowke Scale Models, the Southern Railway Set, will also come under this arrangement, and you will only take from us in future sufficient of this line for your retail trade.

It is understood that all models or articles sold by us as "Bassett-Lowke Scale Models", must have your approval before they are placed on the market, and it is also understood that you will not introduce any competitive lines during this arrangement, with the exception of special models you may build for private customers.

Yours faithfully,

J Stein

LADIES & GENTLEMEN,

THE NEWS I HAVE TO GIVE YOU TODAY IS BAD,
BUT PERHAPS NOT SO BAD AS IT SOUNDS ON THE SURFACE.,
YOUR DIRECTORS HAVE RELUCTANTLY DECIDED THAT THE
RETAIL SIDE OF THE BUSINESS MUST, BY THE END OF THE YEAR,
BE CLOSED DOWN ENTIRELY, AND THAT FOR THE TIME BEING
NO PENSIONS, DIVIDENDS AND THE LIKE CAN BE PAID, *
FOR WE HAVE LIVED TOO LONG ON AN OVERDRAFT. THEREFORE,
WE PROPOSE, IN THE FUTURE TO CONCENTRATE ALL OUR
ENERGIES ON THE SCALE MODEL SIDE OF THE BUSINESS.
WE HOPE AND BELIEVE THEREBY THAT IN THE FUTURE WE MAY
BE ABLE TO MAKE BIGGER PROFITS THAN WE HAVE BEEN ABLE
TO DO DURING THE LAST 15 YEARS, ON WHICH, OF COURSE,
WE COULD ONCE AGAIN PAY PENSIONS, DIVIDENDS, ETC.

IN MY OPINION THE PRESENT POSITION IS NOT
DUE TO BAD MANAGEMENT, ALTHOUGH THERE MAY HAVE BEEN
A CERTAIN AMOUNT OF THAT. ESPECIALLY IN THE LONDON SHOP.
THE FAULT HAS BEEN A WRONG POLICY, WE JUST CAN'T MAKE
TOY SHOPS PAY, PARTICULARLY IN BIG CITIES.   THIS
BUSINESS WAS FOUNDED AS A MAIL ORDER BUSINESS, IT WAS
ONE OF THE FIRST IN THE FIELD AND PRODUCED WITHOUT DOUBT
THE FINEST CATALOGUE, OFFERING MAINLY O GAUGE GOODS,
AND JUST THINK OF IT - WE ACTUALLY SOLD THE CATALOGUES!
O GAUGE UNFORTUNATELY, AND SPECIALISED LINES LIKE THAT,
HAVE FADED OUT OF FASHION.   FOR SOME YEARS NOW WE HAVE
BEEN SELLING LITTLE ELSE THAN OTHER PEOPLE'S GOODS,
MAINLY IN THE OO GAUGE TYPE;   REMEMBERING ALL THE TIME
THAT WE WERE NEVER MANUFACTURERS, ONLY RETAILERS.

INCIDENTALLY, WE SOLD MANY CATALOGUES
RECENTLY, IN FACT A MOST ENCOURAGING NUMBER, BUT
ONLY BEING ABLE TO OFFER GOODS SUCH AS COULD BE BOUGHT
IN ANY LOCAL TOY SHOP.  IN OTHER WORDS, THOSE INTERESTED
BOUGHT OUR CATALOGUE, DECIDED WHAT THEY WANTED TO BUY
AND THEN WENT TO THE LOCAL TOY OR HOBBY SHOP AND BOUGHT
THE GOODS, THEY DID NOT WRITE TO US.

I AM OF THE OPINION THAT MR. FULLER, FOR
EXAMPLE, HAS CARRIED OUT ALL THAT COULD REASONABLY BE
EXPECTED OF HIM AND NEXT YEAR MR. FULLER AND MR. CLAYDON
CAN CONCENTRATE THEIR WHOLE ENERGIES ON MAKING A REAL JOB
OF THE SCALE MODEL SIDE OF THE BUSINESS AND, I REPEAT,
VERY LIKELY MAKE A PROFIT.  AT THE PRESENT TIME WE ARE
ENDEAVOURING TO DISPOSE OF ALL THE STOCK IN THE RETAIL
SIDE THAT WE NOW POSSESS, AT EXCEPTIONALLY BARGAIN PRICES.

OUR ADVERTISING AGENTS HAVE TRIED FOR
TWELVE MONTHS TO SELL THE RETAIL SIDE AS A GOING
CONCERN BUT WITHOUT SUCCESS.  SOME THREE YEARS AGO OR SO
THERE DID LOOK A GLIMMER OF HOPE, UNFORTUNATELY ABOUT
THE SAME TIME THE WHOLE TOY TRADE TOOK A NOSE-DIVE.
SUCH FIRMS AS LINES AND HORNBY SUFFERED BADLY.
I REPEAT, WE ARE VERY SAD TO HAVE TO MAKE THIS CHANGE
OF POLICY, BUT THERE IS NO OPTION.  I HOPE YOU WILL
UNDERSTAND AND SUPPORT YOUR DIRECTORS ACCORDINGLY.

. . . . . . .

from Richard Derry

**Number Sixty**
**Vauxhall Bridge Road**
**London, S.W.1**
*Tate 7621*

H. Talbot-Butler Esq.,
55 Park Avenue North,
<u>Northampton</u>.                                    5th April, 1967.

Dear Sir,

Mr. Barry Riley and I would like to make a formal
offer for the Ordinary Share capital of Bassett-Lowke
Limited at 5/6 per share, subject to the following:

1.    That we obtain over 85% of the shares.

2.    Our acceptance of the 1966 profit and loss account
      and balance sheet.

3.    A signed declaration by all the Directors that
      there are no outstanding liabilities which are
      not disclosed in the balance sheet or profit and
      loss account.

We thank you very sincerely for the way in which you
have allowed us to examine your Company.

Yours faithfully,

SIGNED BY   BARRY RILEY
            RICHARD DERRY.

Notes for Specimen Chapter for "A LIFE OF MODELMAKING". (A. L. O. M

W.J.B.L. born 1877 - Childhood and schooldays.

18 months in an architect's office must have been about 1891,2,3, if W.J. left school at 13 years of age.

1893 of 4 he became engineering apprentice with his Father.
1899 - 1900, at Crompton, Ltd., Chelmsford, working on practical
electricity.
1899 - Advertised in Model Engineer & first catalogue appeared.

---

When I left school I thought I would like to be an architect.

The idea of designing buildings and drawing plans appealed to me.

But of course I was only about thirteen years old and after eighteen

months in a local architect's office I realised that this was not

the career for me, although I still had not any very definite

ideas on what I did want to do.   So my Father persuaded me to

enter his own business (of boilermaking and general engineering,)

xxxxxxxxpxxxxixxx and I became an engineering apprentice. to engineer

Describe here the business in Kingswell St. - See page 1A.

I started in the boilermaking department - in the black-

smith's shop.   I was then about fifteen and was put to working

the bellows for the fire and to helping the blacksmith generally.

This work was heavy for a lad of slender physical resources and

I found it tiring, grimy and uninteresting work.   Eventually it

proved too much for me and my Father transferred me into the

Pages 292–299   Original draft with amendments by W. J. Basset-Lowke
for one of his many lectures.

My Father's business was then known as J. T. Lowke & Sons

and was situated in Kingswell Street, Northampton - or rather

it was sprawled - for work went on in a number of variously-

*They were engineers & boilermakers, iron & brass founders*

sized buildings in the J. T. Lowke yard.    There was a small

blacksmith's shop, the boilermaking shop, the ~~fitting~~ ~~building where for~~ *fitting shop where fitting*

*& turning were done*

~~lathe and bench work~~ and a small iron foundry (where they made *among other castings*

cast iron ~~laths~~ *casts* for shoemaking, the staple industry of Nort-

hampton.    At that time J. T. Lowke & Sons had the sole agency

for Tangye Gas Engines.

*made Collier sandal moulder & Collier heel builder*
*for Collier who made shoe machinery — N'pton Machinery*
*Co.*

light engineering shop to learn bench and lathe work.    Here

I was much happier:  I could manage the work and what was more

found I liked it and at last I really began making progress in

a job that I found congenial and interesting.

Mr. William Vaughan was in charge of lathe and bench work

and I came under his supervision.    We were eventually to become

firm friends and it was Vaughan who first took an interest when,

as a result of learning to use a lathe I started a new hobby:
with the aid of miniature boilers that the boilermakers made up for

&lt;clean?&gt;

me, I made small stationary engines for my own amusement and I was

thrilled when I found I could make them work.

Gradually I became aware that other people were also

interested in this hobby and also in building model steam loco-

motives and other engineering models.    Many of these enthusiasts

were at a loss when it came to the very small fittings required

for these models, because this was over fifty years ago and not

many people building engineering models as a hobby pursuit had the

&lt;water gauges&gt;

tools for making such items as whistles, safety valves, bib cocks,

valves, hand pumps, etc., nor could they be bought easily for they

were certainly not manufactured for sale as standard modelmaking

fittings.

Here was an idea!  Why not start selling small fittings

and parts that I made in my spare time, to other enthusiasts,

who needed them for their modelmaking?  The premises in Kings _

well Street had a display window facing the street and adjacent

to the office.  It was used for displaying engineering parts

and I persuaded my Father to let me have some of the space to

show some of my model engineering ~~xxxkx~~ fittings.

Having decided to make some money out of my hobby, it

became necessary for someone to keep accounts and to look

after enquiries that were made at the office, so I enlisted

the help of my Father's book-keeper, Harry F. R. Franklin

to look after these things for me.  As I was still working for

my Father and only doing model work in my spare time, progress

was slow and somewhat uncertain.  Even so by 1899 we were

sufficiently advanced to produce our first catalogue:  not a

printed one, but a carefully compiled album containing actual

photographs of the model engines and parts we were offering,

with typewritten descriptions of each item.

Photography was another of my hobbies:  *although it has* ~~early photography~~

A.L.O.M.                    -4-

~~remained a recreational pursuit for me and, indeed, it is~~

~~ind it~~

remained a recreational pursuit for me even until today, I

found it most useful as an added accomplishment in the model-

making business, especially when photographs were required of

prototypes, for detail work on models.   Strangely enough, it

was photography that earned Harry Franklin and I a few pounds

in 1898 and encouraged us to start our spare-time business and

produce our first catalogue.   It happened thus.

On 2nd September 1898 a railway disaster occurred at

Wellingborough, a town some ten miles from Northampton.   A

platform barrow fell on to the line in front of a Midland Railway

express train, causing it to crash.   Harry and I visited the

scene soon afterwards and we took a number of photographs of

the smashed ~~xxxix~~ locomotive and ~~b~~roken, splintered coaches.

We found prints were much in demand and we sold a large number,

including some to the National press and so we pooled the proceeds

towards buying materials for our modelmaking venture.

~~Xeexxxxxxxxxxxfier~~ Having compiled our catalogue we felt justified in launching into advertising and it was in 1899 that our first announcement appeared in a newly-founded magazine, "The Model Engineer", which has since become the most widely read magazine of all among model engineers.

Shortly afterwards I was away for some months, having joined the firm of Messrs. Cromptons of Chelmsford, electrical engineers.   With this firm I gained experience in the general application of electricity and, of course, in particular,I had in mind electricity for model engineering .

1900 was the year of the big Paris Exhibition, an event that had a far-reaching influence on Europe in many ways, both culturally and commercially.   Accounts of the Exhibition in local newspapers ~~whetted my appetite~~ aroused my curiosity & interest, as I read that there was a good collection of mechanical toys and also some Continental scale models to be seen there.   Eventually I decided Iwould go ~~and~~ see for myself and off I went to Paris, accompanied by a Northampton friend, Frank Jones, of  a Northampton shoe company, who was going to look at the leather section in the Exhibition.

I was amazed at all I saw but especially I wondered at the
high class toy productions. Many of them were miniatures of
Continental railways with locomotives, coaches, wagons and other
accessories and these had a distinct superiority over other toys:
they were accurately built to scale, as far as was possible for
small, working models. One of the finest displays was that of
the German firm, Bing Bros. of Nuremberg. They showed metal
household utensils, model steam engines and clockwork, steam and
electrically-driven model railways. I made myself acquainted
with the late Stefan Bing, Governing Director of this Company,
who were known in their own country as "The toymakers of Nuremberg". I saw what possibilities there were in the idea of
having scale models to these standards made ~~byxthexexxexxeddextk~~
~~fexmanxxexkexsyxkmtk~~ to English designs. But we had no equipment
suitable for such precision work in such quantities. So it seemed
to me that the answer was to have them made in Nuremberg, by
these first class German toymakers. I asked Bing if they would
be interested in collaborating with me and if I provided the
design, if they would make me some model locomotives. He agreed

and I returned to England full of hope for a new venture.

One of the most popular railway Companies in Britain at that time was the London North Western Railway. We needed a popular prototype, so we decided on a steam-driven model of the L.N.W.R. xxxxx "Black Prince" locomotive, which was a favourite express engine of many railway enthusiasts. Drawings were borrowed from the Railway Company and we engaged a free-lance draughtsman, Henry Greenly, who sometimes did work for us, to prepare drawings scaled down to an appropriate scale for the mass production of such a locomotive, in modified form, but based on the actual official drawings for the prototype. The result was our 2½" gauge "Black Prince" locomotive model, which was the first attempt by a European firm to produce a model resembling an English prototype.

Editor's Note: There is some ambiguity in W.J. B-L's recollection of his and Greenly's influence over German-made models at the beginning of the century. Henry Greenly was certainly not involved in the design of the original Bing 'Black Prince' series introduced in 1901. The first attempt (at a British outline loco) by a European firm, i.e. Carette, was a model of 'Lady of the Lake'. It is unlikely that this was produced from the designs of Henry Greenly and it is probable that his influence did not begin to take effect on German-made items of British types until around 1905.

The L.N.W.R. 'Black Prince' (second series) which was certainly to the design of Henry Greenly was in fact introduced in 1909.

## Some Personal Reflections
by Dudley Dimmock

Looking back over the years, in which I was involved in the commercial world of model railways, I have no hesitation in stating that the years I spent at Bassett-Lowke were the happiest of them all.

I suppose that all men experience a peak in their lives, some place, or event in which they either excel themselves or reach heights of experience and excitement almost of happiness it could be said, which are never reached again. Such a time for me occurred during those halcyon days at Bassett-Lowke, when I lived through such peaks of excitement and experience, and had the pleasure of meeting people from all over the world, who were interested in models and in model railways in particular, and for whom Bassett-Lowke was the Mecca of all model enthusiasts.

As my story unfolds I want to make it quite clear, that in no way is it just another story about Bassett-Lowke, which has been covered so well in the previous pages of this book. Rather I wish to paint a picture of what I felt and experienced at Bassett-Lowke bearing in mind the circumstances in which I was appointed, and the reasons for that appointment.

If in the unfolding and on some occasions I may seem to be too critical of some person or party, or even of a system, please bear with me over these criticisms, since it is how I saw the situation or person at the time, and not necessarily as others would have reacted.

I believe that what I have to tell is worth the telling, and I hope that it will be found interesting and enjoyable, adding a further dimension to the Bassett-Lowke saga, so beloved by model enthusiasts all over the world.

The story so far has been told by the late Roland Fuller, better qualified than most of us to do so and those of you old enough to remember the Golden Years just prior and just after the Great War will have enjoyed the story even more and revelled in the nostalgia of those great days.

My first visits to Bassett-Lowke, Holborn, were in the early 1920s, when I purchased 0 gauge 'Lowko' track parts for my bedroom layout. I vividly recall being told by Mr. Bert Sell how I should go about the putting down of this track and thanks to his friendly advice, made a success of it, and laid the foundations of my later knowledge and expertise in track-laying.

I was to meet Mr. Sell many times in the years that followed, but little did I realise in those 1920 days, that one day I should succeed him as manager of the Holborn Showroom. Mr. Sell enjoyed a rather special relationship at Bassett-Lowke, with over 40 years of loyal service to his credit, first under the management of Mr. H. C. Foreman and in later years as manager himself. He enjoyed a special friendship with Mr. Bassett-Lowke and he accompanied him on many of his earlier trips abroad to Germany becoming something of a confidant, Bassett-Lowke valuing him for his opinion and judgement where models were concerned.

Mr. Sell's last, and my first week as manager were spent together so that he could acquaint me with the running of the showroom, which he did admirably. He never stopped talking during that week, and from him I learned a great deal about Mr. Bassett-Lowke and the company in particular. He told me how Mr. Fuller had come to the company in 1917 as a shy retiring lad, and how he had had the task of teaching him all about stock-keeping, selling, and the handling of models generally. Mr. Sell was at the time Mr. Fuller's direct boss under the eye of the Manager, Mr. Foreman. This image of Mr. Fuller was to remain with Mr. Sell for all time and he could never quite accept in later years, that Mr. Fuller had become his boss. Small wonder then, when Mr. Bassett-Lowke asked Mr. Sell in confidence if there was someone on the staff at 112, High Holborn who could be spared to help him with the paperwork at Northampton, he suggested the new junior Mr. Fuller. To Mr. Sell, Mr. Fuller was the natural choice as the lad was single and therefore more mobile, he had shown an aptitude for details and accuracy in his work and above all Mr. Sell did not get on too well with him, probably the deciding factor.

Those of you who ever had the privilege of knowing Mr. Bassett-Lowke will agree he was a man of tremendous vigour and enthusiasm; a sort of Churchillian character who could transmit his enthusiasm to others; a man of vision, who could instigate policies which would lead to success. But he needed someone after all the enthusiasm had died down, to carry out those policies, and make them work and become successful. Such a man was Mr. Fuller, and there is no doubt that he was just the right person for this work, with his remarkable attention to detail and accuracy and the keeping of all records relevant to the matter concerned.

As age took its toll on the Bassett-Lowke leader, Mr. Fuller became more and more essential to Mr. Bassett-Lowke, and no one was surprised that eventually Mr. Fuller was made General Manager. As Mr. Bassett-Lowke became weaker and unable to make decisions, Mr. Fuller gradually took over the running of the retail and manufacturing side of the business, leaving the industrial model side to be run by Mr. Claydon. On Mr. Bassett-Lowke's death, Mr. Fuller was a natural choice to become the Managing Director, since he had successfully run the company during long periods prior to Mr. Bassett-Lowke's death.

My first contact with Mr. Fuller came about following an approach I had made to the company, concerning power units and train controllers that my own company, of which I was a Director, were marketing and selling to the retail trade. The appointment had been made at 112, High Holborn for 11 o'clock, and at that time, armed with my samples, I met Mr. Fuller and Mr. Sell in the showroom. Before I could begin, Mr. Fuller suggested that he and I should go and have a coffee together at the nearby Carwardines Coffee House in Southampton Row. The ensuing conversation was a great surprise to me. He assured me that I would get an order for power units but that was not what he wished to discuss with me.

He congratulated me on the success of our business in Harlesden, and in particular for our splendid exhibition stand which had impressed him greatly. He seemed to be encouraging me to talk about our success and how we had achieved it, and he was obviously pleased at what he had heard. As I later learned, Mr. Fuller was a master in the art of diplomatic discussion, and I feared I had talked too much. However, he was still smiling when I finished talking and then asked me if I could see him again the next Thursday, our halfday at the shop, at the Cora Hotel at around 3.30 p.m. That was to be the first of many meetings we had together, at the same hotel.

At that first Cora Hotel meeting, over tea and toast, he outlined to me a picture of affairs at Bassett-Lowke that both intrigued and fascinated me. It seemed that the Manchester shop under

Mr. Cox was doing fairly well, but the company generally was not doing as well as it might, and that matters at Holborn were in rather a derelict state. Mr. Sell was approaching retiring age and was not keen to buy in any of the new smaller gauges which had proved so popular. He was very conservative in his choices, preferring to stick to the items in the Bassett-Lowke range and thus limiting his sales potential.

This worried Mr. Fuller as the Manchester shop, being less conservative was, as a consequence, more successful. Assuming Mr. Sell retired early, Mr. Fuller then asked me whether I thought the right person could make a success of things at Holborn, and if so would I agree to consider such an offer myself? The directness of his approach caught me unprepared, and I was unwilling to give an immediate answer, as there were a number of factors to be considered. I was aware of the Bassett-Lowke set up, and knew that all the executives had years of service behind them and that it was not customary to appoint an executive who had not come up through the ranks like themselves. What sort of salary and contract could I expect, and what assurances did I have that Mr. Sell would agree to an early stand down? I asked Mr. Fuller to give me time to consider this prospect. It would mean giving up my directorship with my own company, but on the other hand would be an easier journey and shorter hours.

In the event, I need not have worried unduly. The first stumbling block had been my remuneration which had not been acceptable to the Bassett-Lowke Board of Directors. The meetings went on and the weeks went by. Meanwhile, events in my own company conspired to make a possible transition easier. It began to look as if my company might break up due to internal family matters, and I realised that resigning as a Director would be a wise course. Mr. Sell, for reasons unknown to me, agreed to stand down. I agreed to a smaller salary, and a higher percentage commission on turnover, which was acceptable to the board. Everything was agreed and it was confirmed that I would start at 112, High Holborn on January 1, 1958. On that day, I passed once more through the portals that I had entered as a lad in the 1920s only, this time, I was the Manager.

I had timed my arrival at the Bassett-Lowke showroom to be slightly after 9 a.m. to enable the shop to be open and ready for business. Before entering the office with Mr. Sell, I looked around the showroom with a feeling of nostalgia rising within me. It seemed the same to me as it did those years ago in the 1920s – a gas fire burned between the counters and there was that same signal gantry at the back of the shop, albeit a little dusty. The same green baize still covered the counters to prevent damage to the beautifully painted models and the mahogany woodwork of the shop and glass showcases were unchanged, just a little worn and knocked about. I think the word 'tired' would describe the condition. There were the same chairs, they must have been Edwardian, the same stairs leading down to the basement, and the leaded glass behind the signal gantry. Time seemed to have stood still and I was lost in memories.

Mr. Sell's voice woke the dream, and we entered his office. I had never been in there before. Mr. Sell was talking, but I did not really hear him, my thoughts were far away, taking it all in – the leather topped desk and the swivel chair, the big iron safe at the other end, the tall windows letting in a modicum of light, filtering in from what I later learned to be a courtyard sandwiched between the buildings. In my mind's eye, I could imagine Mr. Bassett-Lowke unfolding his plans and ideas to a receptive Mr. Sell. I could feel his exuberance and enthusiasm still permeating that office, making me feel exhausted and excited. Mr. Sell was still talking but I was not listening. At last he said something I did catch, bringing me back to reality. He told me that Mr. Fuller had asked him to stay on for a week to show me the ropes and suggested that before meeting the staff we went and had a quiet chat over a coffee.

Carwardines Coffee House in Southampton Row was well known and patronised and Mr. Sell was apparently well known too, as a number of people nodded to him whilst we were there. Small talk ensued, the coffee came, and then Mr. Sell asked me straight out how I had got the job, and why I had given up a lucrative directorship to become a mere manager? I told him much of what I have just written, giving my reasons for making the change. I felt it was a challenge, and one I was proud to take, and I furthermore believed I could make it work. For his part he expressed amazement at the Bassett-Lowke directors choosing an outsider rather than someone who had come up through the ranks. He went on to say he had been with the company over 40 years, serving first under the management of Mr. H. C. Foreman, and then later on as a manager himself, and this was the first

time that an outsider had been brought in.

I did my best to reassure him, explaining that the company was worried about the changing market and clientele and the demand for smaller gauges. The company felt that there was no one in the Bassett-Lowke organisation that had the experience and knowledge to make the changes necessary to meet the new needs. [Ed. note: Ironic in view of Bassett-Lowke's foresight in encouraging the smaller gauges with Bing and then Trix.] As modestly as I could, I told him that I had many, many meetings with Mr. Fuller before I agreed to take on the new job, and that the directors knew from my record that I had the right qualifications for the position. To succeed I would need to have a fairly free hand on policy and buying. Mr. Sell ventured his opinion that this would not be forthcoming from the Northampton board. I veered the conversation round to Mr. Sell's position in the matter, and it appeared that the company had compensated him for his early retirement. Nevertheless, whilst this was fine as far as it went, it was difficult for him to imagine not being at 112, and not controlling the Bassett-Lowke interest in London.

He had come to Bassett-Lowke a couple of years or so after it had moved from 257, High Holborn to 112, joining the company as a lad and working his way up successfully until he became the manager in his own right. After 40 years of service, gaining the friendship and confidence of Mr. Bassett-Lowke himself, sharing business trips abroad with the great man it was little wonder that he felt sad and full of emotion at the thought that it was all going to end.

I like to believe that I convinced him that his beloved Bassett-Lowke was in good hands, and the early antagonism between us melted and he warmed towards me. We returned to the showroom and he introduced the staff to me, the senior assistant being Mr. Alan Fordham, whose speciality in the showroom was the 'Live Steam' department. Many readers will doubtless recall and remember with affection, his quiet attentive manner when dealing with a customer. He was a gentle man, I never saw him lose his temper at any time, even under provocation. Our tour of inspection and introductions took us down the stairs to the basement. In those days it was just a store room and I felt immediately that this lower area was not being utilised to its fullest extent but I said nothing to Mr. Sell.

And so the week passed pleasantly enough with Mr. Sell with me at all times, at coffee, at lunch, and at tea, which pleased me immensely, as his continual talking enabled me to build up a picture of all aspects of trade at 112, in addition to the general running of the business. On the last day, when he was leaving me on my own, he made quite a ceremony of handing over the keys and he left just before we closed for the day near to tears and full of emotion. Poor old Bert, what a way to go after 40 years of service.

### I GET STARTED

Walking through the doors on that second Monday morning, I realised that this time, I really was the manager, and that no longer could I turn to Mr. Sell for his opinion on how I should act and decide upon any situation that might arise. This in fact elated me and it was with some difficulty that I controlled my excitement and turned to the all important Returns Document, showing all the previous week's activities, which had to be posted early on Monday to be in the hands of the Directors at Northampton for their weekly meeting on Tuesday morning.

I had not been working long on this document, when I was interrupted by a knock on the office door and the entry of one of the junior staff. He had come to give in his notice, which if offered before midday Monday would enable him to leave at the end of the same week. It appeared he had not got on very well with Mr. Sell, and presumed that it would be the same with the new manager. I reasoned with him, and learned that he had never really been allowed to do anything constructive. When I suggested that he do the redressing of the window display, he informed me vehemently that no one but Mr. Sell had been allowed to touch the windows. Nevertheless, I asked him to have a go, after outlining some idea of what I had in mind, and he agreed. Mr. Sell had had very set ideas about window display, to such an extent that I could have drawn you a picture of his efforts which were always in the same pattern. Thus by a stroke of luck with so much to do, I was relieved of having to do the windows myself. Happily, the young assistant was a genius at display work and he did not give in his notice after all. I can only imagine how it would have looked to the Directors if the staff had started giving in their notices after one week of my management!

Naturally, that first week alone will always be remembered vividly by me. Unfamiliarity with the paper work chained me for long hours to the office, but I was determined to get out and meet the customers myself, and to go into the questions of alteration and change which I knew would have to be made. I quickly realised that the fixtures and drawers had been designed for the larger gauge locos and model engineering items and would be quite unsuitable for the 00 and TT gauge items I intended to introduce. I filled a notebook with plans and ideas I intended to submit to Mr. Fuller on his first visit.

Mr. Fuller telephoned me in the week, saying that he would be down the following Thursday and should be with me around 10.30 a.m. This was to be his weekly practice for many years with only holidays and special occasions altering this routine. On that first Thursday visit, we had morning coffee at Carwardines Coffee House in Southampton Row, followed later by a very nice lunch at the White House in Bloomsbury. Away from the showroom we could talk and discuss all the matters relevant to building up the business. I recall with great pleasure those happy luncheons together, and I have warm memories of Mr. Fuller who was not only the kindest and nicest person I have ever worked under, but also probably one of the most unflappable men I have ever met.

On that first occasion, as we lingered over our coffee, he expressed his pleasure at the new window display, and did not disguise his satisfaction that I was the new manager, it having made his task that much easier to have someone in charge at Holborn who shared the same views as himself with regard to possible expansion. We made arrangements to visit the Toy Fair together at the end of the month, so that we could see just what was available in the 00 and TT ranges we intended to introduce to the Bassett-Lowke customers and for which we would need to place early orders if we were to face the trade expansion we both envisaged. I was to buy what I needed for the London showroom, and following my choice as a guide, Mr. Fuller would order for the Northampton retail shop on a reduced scale as he had plans to develop a more lively and interesting retail section at Northampton. We came to an understanding with regards to the budgeting for the new purchases, so that I was quite clear in my mind as to the imposed limit and could plan accordingly.

Before we left for the showroom, Mr. Fuller told me it was the practice for the manager of the

London and Manchester showrooms to attend regular meetings with the Directors at Northampton. He suggested an early meeting following the Toy Fair visit, which I noted in my diary. Back at the showroom, I told Mr. Fuller of my misgivings with regards to the housing of the proposed 00 and TT items in the fixtures and drawers made for the bigger Bassett-Lowke items. He asked me to defer that request for alterations since it was not a good time to ask the Board for further financial expenditure, but that he would bear the request in mind. I mentioned also that I did not think that the best use was being made of the basement, and that I thought it would be a good idea to have all the 'live steam' and model engineering items down there, as a very special department in their own right. This would give greater scope for the display and for sales, as well as a better opportunity for Mr. Fordham to look after those specialist customers without rubbing shoulders with the 00 and TT gauge enthusiasts. At the same time, greater space would then be available on the ground floor showroom for the housing and better display of the 00 and TT items.

Mr. Fuller agreed that this would be a splendid idea but again urged a cautious approach, as the time was not right for the change. I was soon to learn why Mr. Fuller had been so tentative about these new innovations, and why there had been so much delay in settling the details of my appointment.

The days passed quickly enough. There was so much detail work to do in the office and I was impatient to get things moving and to improve the trading figures. All that I had been able to achieve so far, was a new window display and some better displays in the showrooms thanks to the efforts of our talented junior. I also realised it would take time for us to get a reasonable selection of the new 00 and TT items. The Toy Fair where orders could be placed was not until the end of January and orders were taken on the understanding that deliveries would have to be staggered over the following months. I felt I had very little to get excited about when the call came to report to Northampton, where I was to meet the other Directors for the first time.

After an early call at the showroom on the appointed day, to check that all was well, I was on my way to Northampton by train and was met at the station by Mr. H. W. Franklin the son of Bassett-Lowke's joint founder, Mr. H. F. R. Franklin. Mr. Franklin senior, had been the financial brains behind Bassett-Lowke in the early days, and without his great efforts behind the scenes, juggling with the accounts the company could not have survived. From what I gathered, it seems Mr. Bassett-Lowke gave him some very real headaches, and anyone who has had to handle the finances of a new small business will appreciate how troubles can be magnified when dealing with a genius like Mr. Bassett-Lowke, wanting to build faster than finances would allow. As time showed, he must have coped somehow because the business had grown from strength to strength.

Mr. Franklin's son had grown up in the midst of this success amongst a world of superb models. Unlike his father, his interests did not lie in financial matters, but in handling and living amongst the superb locomotives and models that were being produced. He was a kindly gentle man, an enthusiast like myself, and later I learned that he specialised in the factory in the repair and renovation department of the business, and on one occasion I was privileged to see him at work amongst his beloved models. As we left the station in his car, he explained to me that the usual practice on these special meeting days was for the Directors and managers to gather together in the lounge of the local hostelry for pre-lunch drinks and it was then that I would be presented to the assembled company.

In the main I enjoyed that meeting in the lounge and the lunch that followed, probably because I felt that I was now taking part in a sort of ritual that had been carried out from the very earliest days of the company up to the death of Mr. Bassett-Lowke and beyond. I also felt a warmth from most of the Directors, who seemed to be willing me on to be successful, despite that fact that I had not come up through the ranks. In particular, the Chairman, Mr. C. Derry singled me out. He told me he was based in London, and would come and see me and have a chat about things in the London showroom. This he did in due course, and many more interesting and constructive meetings were to occur in the months that followed. In the afternoon, we gathered again in the Boardroom in the factory, and I met Mr. Cox, the manager of the Manchester shop who I had not seen for many years since the days when I was with the Model Co. as their Market Research Officer. He treated me in a rather distant manner, and I began to wonder why, although later on the cause of his manner was apparent.

The atmosphere at the luncheon had been warm and friendly, a jolly good lunch and good wishes affair, but that was all gone and in its place, a cool, almost refrigerated atmosphere pervaded the afternoon meeting. The men who had smiled and had made me welcome, were now stern and anxious, and they fired question after question at me in an endeavour to assure themselves that they had made the right decision in my appointment. My experience stood me in good stead, and quietly but resolutely, I believe, my replies eased their minds and the ice was broken. All but one warmed to me, and that exception was Mr. P. F. Claydon, the joint-Managing Director with Mr. Fuller. Mr. Claydon was responsible for what we used to call the Industrial Model Section, the part of the business that made those wonderful showcase ships, advertising models, in fact any model made on special order for whatever purpose other than retailing in our showrooms. His antagonism to my appointment was obvious. It seemed he did not doubt that I could be the right person to introduce the new lines to re-vitalise the business, but questioned my ability to retain the Bassett-Lowke image, and to appeal to the customers who liked the old style and would resent a change. It was Mr. Derry, the Chairman, who came to my rescue, when he pointed out to Mr. Claydon that only time would tell and that it would be fairer to give me a chance before condemning me. Little did I realise then that there were many other unmentioned reasons for Mr. Claydon's opposition to my appointment.

When the meeting broke up, over a cup of tea, Mr. Cox, the Manchester shop manager came over to talk to me once more, and opened the conversation by suggesting that I had taken on an impossible task. In his opinion, not only did he consider there was more model railways interest in the north than in the south, but he also thought that his customers were the real model railway enthusiasts such as Model Club Members, whereas the London showroom customers were not genuine enthusiasts at all, but merely wealthy people indulging themselves with models whilst money was freely available, and whose interest in the hobby was purely a passing phase. I humoured him by not getting too involved in such a controversial subject, but it seemed to me there must be deeper motives behind this remark. It would seem that over the years there had been an almost antagonistic rivalry between Mr. Cox and

Mr. Sell, the Manchester shop being regarded as a sort of branch shop, quite wrongly in my opinion. Mr. Cox had worked very hard and with some success to raise the status of his shop. Like many people who have worked hard over a long period of time to achieve a goal, they sometimes become obsessed to the extent that any person seeming to threaten that goal, is regarded as a sort of enemy. With Mr. Sell gone, now an outsider was going to do all sorts of things to bring the London showroom into prosperity, challenging Mr. Cox's figures and setting himself up as a serious rival.

I returned to London that evening with many thoughts racing through my mind. As I went over the events of the day in retrospect, I began to line up the people I had met at the meeting, those who were for me, those apparently against me, and resolved that I had to tread carefully in the days ahead, realising how important it was for me to be successful. Any failure or bad result would give ammunition to those who wanted to see me fail, even if that would be a minor disaster for the company.

True to his promise, Mr. Derry, our Chairman, came to see me at Holborn many times. I like to believe that Mr. Derry was the one who swayed the Board of Directors and backed Mr. Fuller's belief that I was the one who could improve the London showroom's image and trade. Certainly he gave me support in almost every innovation I made or suggested, and on his initial visit, he tried to explain to me without divulging too much of the Board's business activities, the reason for Mr. Claydon's aggressive attitude. He went on to say that the cash flow in any business is vital, and that a problem existed in a business such as Bassett-Lowke, in as much as the Industrial Models section stretched these finances to the limit. Some of the models they made could take months to complete, entailing a heavy work in progress bill to be carried week by week. Even after the model had been delivered and approved by the purchasers, payment might still be delayed for some months, depending on the wording of the contract. Furthermore as the Industrial Models section was expanding its side of the business, more and more cash was needed to finance it. Bank loans or finances were not available unless the model was to be exported. In addition to my appointment, it would follow that my efforts if they were going to be successful would also need more capital outlay. Faced with this rising double demand for more and more capital, the Board had real problems on their hands, especially as Mrs. Bassett-Lowke had begun to give the impression that she might withdraw her financial support of the company in favour of a more lucrative return elsewhere.

As I saw the situation, it was essential that the retail section of which I was but a part, must try and increase its trade by every means, but as far as possible, without further capital expenditure. This could only be realised by faster turnover, so that the same money could earn several profits a year. Mr. Derry and I were in full agreement over this. He also divulged to me a very well kept secret, namely that he was also the Chairman and Managing Director of a company that manufactured women's foundation garments and where the same problem of cash flow existed. He asked me to keep this information to myself which naturally I did, the reasons for this request becoming obvious to me later on. He asked me whether I had any other ideas on how we could expand the London trade and I put to him the ideas I had outlined to Mr. Fuller. It speaks well for Mr. Derry's power of persuasion that he convinced the Board and Mr. Claydon, in particular, that these innovations were essential and that there was a very real need for the shop to be redecorated and refurbished.

There was an air of excitement about the showroom in the days that followed. Apart from the redecoration, the refurbishing was in the form of new green baize cloth covering the top of the counter, and french polishing of the mahogany counter fronts, showcases and chairs. The famous signal gantry at the rear of the showroom was also correctly repainted. Everything was dusted and polished or cleaned each day by a newly retired pensioner, who in addition, kept the floors polished and the brass handles and handrails gleaming. Fixture and alterations to the drawers were carried out and the downstairs basement was fitted out and became the 'live steam' department that I had envisaged. Exciting new window displays with working models were instigated, and these created tremendous interest. I was successful in getting a new commission scheme accepted by the Board, as an added incentive to the staff to further increase the volume of sales, but I failed when I tried to get some brighter, more adventurous advertising. The difficulty arose over the fact that the advertisements were intended to cover the entire field of Bassett-Lowke activities, and a branch of the retail section, such as the London

showroom, could not be specially singled out for advertising space, without the other sections feeling left out. However, I did get the advertising agents to agree to produce a small brochure showing the hand-made scale layout in TT I had built when with my former employer. We had shown this at the exhibition, with lists and pictures of the new 00 and TT items we were beginning to stock and by also mentioning this in the advertising attention was brought to the fact that we were now actively engaged in selling the smaller gauges.

Of course, there were the odd few customers who deplored the changes. The appearance of Hornby and Triang items on our shelves and in our windows was not to their liking. To them it was like Rolls-Royce showing and selling a cheap family car. The last bastion in the model world of the wealthy and privileged was being assaulted. It is hard for people to imagine today that special customers in the early days of the Holborn showroom would actually be taken into the Manager's Office while the staff brought in the various articles to be purchased. I must admit that I attended to some of the great personages of this world in this manner, but they were rare occasions. In the early days however, this was a common practice, more than half of the customers being handled in this manner.

Gradually, our efforts to increase the turnover bore fruit, not only did we enjoy the extra trade brought in by the 00 and TT gauges, but sharing the whole of the ground floor with the established 0 gauge items, gave a new look to the showroom. The 'live steam' and engineering customers, after some initial annoyance at having to go down to the basement for their requirements, afterwards expressed pleasure at the new arrangement and our figures in this section grew remarkably. The staff were behind me 100 per cent, the extra commission giving them the spur they needed, and it was for me a most uplifting period, feeling that one's enthusiasm was shared in the common goal.

EXHIBITION FEVER
Whilst all these improvements were being carried out, my efforts were also being directed towards the sort of showing we should put up at forthcoming exhibitions. I had already crossed swords with Mr. Claydon on my first visit to Northampton, and here I once again experienced his opposition to my ideas. Mr. Fuller had been reporting to the board on our showing at the Model Railway Club

Exhibition held at Easter time, the preparation of which had all been arranged and put hand before my appointment. Although Mr. Fuller appeared satisfied with the figures and general result of the exhibition, he also asked me for my opinion. I stated that I felt that a great model railway company like Bassett-Lowke should have achieved more. At the same exhibition, my old company had obtained figures thirty times greater than those given by Mr. Fuller, although in fairness, this was achieved mainly by the bigger stand and consequently longer frontage, so essential for big sales. I went on to say that at our next exhibition we should have a stand worthy of our great name, something around 60 feet long, with the name Bassett-Lowke in figures two or three feet high and the whole structure stretching right across the hall. With such a stand properly organised and run, we could expect figures forty times greater than those quoted by Mr. Fuller.

Following my remarks, there was a stunned silence, until Mr. Claydon broke in advising his fellow directors not to be carried away by fine theories, which could blind them and lead to possible disaster. At this point, Mr. Derry asked quite gently how, assuming I was given the go-ahead, could I staff such a large stand and run the showroom at Holborn at the same time. Even as I replied, I could envisage in my mind's eye the huge stand stretching right across the hall, telling the world of models that Bassett-Lowke was right back in business. I saw the stand as consisting of several sections (probably as many as five), all under the Bassett-Lowke banner, and I suggested that Peco, the famous track specialists should be invited to have one of the stands, providing their own salesman and all the stock on a sale or return basis. The cash taken would be handed to Bassett-Lowke each day and at the end of the exhibition, the unsold goods would be returned to Peco and we would be charged just for the goods sold over the exhibition counters. By this means, the Peco salesman would do his best to get as much sold as possible, with in addition a full range of Peco products being made available to the public. We would also be relieved of the responsibility of providing a salesman, and would be ensured of maximum cash sales in return for the space allocated. Other manufacturers could take other stands on similar arrangements, and our Bassett-Lowke products would be sold in the centre stand, rather larger than the others, with special en-gineering displays, a full range of our 0 gauge locomotives and accessories, graced on each side with TT and 00 items mainly in accessory form which would run automatically and not require an operator.

To a possible argument that there might be some difficulty in finding manufacturers willing to co-operate in such a scheme, I added that I had already approached several without commitment and the problem would rather be in choosing which ones to select, so anxious were they to have an opportunity to sell their products under our banner.

As to the approximate cost of setting up such a stand, and the ratio of costs against the expected takings, I had calculated that it would show a handsome profit. This was all based on my previous experience and took account of staffing costs and all the overheads. With regards to staffing the stand, I had worked it out carefully, and felt that three of our Holborn staff could handle everything, allowing for breaks and meals. The remaining Holborn staff had agreed to a rota system whereby they would come to the exhibition on alternate evenings, after closing. Saturday was the busiest day of the show, and all the staff agreed to come to the exhibition after the midday closing of the showroom. For myself, I would shuttle backwards and forwards to and from the showroom and the exhibition as required.

I suggested that a great deal of peg board should be used for our displays to show off to advantage the many hundreds of small but vital parts that modellers were always seeking. A system of letters or numbers would be used on the displays, enabling anyone on the staff to find the part required immediately. A great number of suitable shelves would be required to show to advantage our magnificent 0 gauge locomotives and coaches. I felt that the stand should be painted primrose yellow with black lettering, our company colours. Mr. Fuller had already had done some very neat and attractive cards in yellow with black lettering for our window displays, and I would require his co-operation in that direction, as a very great number of such cards would be needed. I proposed to make a plan or drawing of the stand to submit to the fitters, used to my requirements in my previous employment.

Finally, I asked the Directors to consider the drawing and plan, together with the estimated costs. Once, and if, the scheme was approved I intended to put my plans into immediate operation.

As I sat down the atmosphere was electric, a buzz of conversation, rising in a crescendo until Mr. Derry called the meeting to order. In his concise way, he summed up what I had said, and in a few moments the Board had agreed for me to get started on the basis I had suggested. Mr. Derry concluded by saying that he realised that not all the Board agreed with my proposals, but he believed that what I was advocating was the right course to follow if the company was to survive. He acknowledged the fact that we lived in a changing world. Whilst many more people had money to take up hobbies than in the past, smaller locos mean smaller gauges, and this exhibition should serve to convince the new generation of modellers that Bassett-Lowke were more than capable of meeting their present and future needs, to everyone's benefit.

The poetic and fine words were over. I now had weeks of hard work and preparation in front of me to justify my beliefs and claims. Mr. Fuller was wonderful in his support of me, creating the display cards I needed to back up the display boards, which he also got made to my specification. I built a special two track miniature gauge layout in TT in two levels, which went round one of the exhibition hall posts. This had to be made in two halves and then join-hardened so that it looked as if we had built the layout in the hall itself, fitting it round the actual post. It was quite automatic and was a double tracked figure of eight, one set of tracks passing above the other. The many tunnel entrances made it difficult to tell from which tunnel the train was about to appear. It created a great deal of interest yet at the same time, overcame the objection to having a great big post right in the centre of the stand.

I shall always remember the glow of success following that September 1958 exhibition. It was but the first of many great stands, comparable with the marvellous stands of the past that many will remember with nostalgia and affection. These later stands differed from the early ones in as much as those were real showpieces, but the latter were what the modelling public required, huge displays of all the bits and pieces, which were not always obtainable locally. Our shop trade increased tremendously following that exhibition, as well as our mail order business. I can still see in my mind's eye, that first primrose yellow stand stretching right across the hall, over 60 feet wide with those great two-foot letters in black, spelling out the magic words BASSETT-LOWKE. The takings were even greater than I had expected, and I shall never forget the satisfaction of seeing the eager modellers lapping up all we had to show, and revelling in the re-birth of a great name in modelling. It did not end at the exhibition and not only did our showroom trade increase accordingly, but we were back in the business at the top, where we should always have been.

NOTHING SUCCEEDS LIKE SUCCESS
Mr. Derry, our chairman, called at the London showroom to see me the week following the exhibition. He was delighted at our success, in fact stating that it had put a few nickels in our coffers without capital expenditure. All the takings from the exhibition were either on a sale or return basis, as had been our own stock takings, the stock for which had come from the showroom. In fact, the combined sales we enjoyed that week had actually reduced our overall stocks, so that true to our hopes, we were turning over the stock faster than hitherto – an enviable situation.

It was at this point that Mr. Derry told me that he was the Sheriff of the City of London, and as a consequence was present at the Old Bailey, whenever the courts were in session. It was better for his image that the learned judges who presided over the Courts at the Old Bailey should not know of his other business, women's foundation garments, and as far as the judges were concerned, Mr. Derry was only Chairman of Bassett-Lowke. I always respected that trust and on some occasions when one of the judges called at the showroom to see Mr. Derry, I had to explain that he was at Northampton that day and was not available, although in all probability, he was really in his factory supervising the output and mail order despatch of underwear.

On several occasions, I received telephone calls from him saying that a ticket was in the post for me to attend various City luncheons, such as those arranged by the Chamber of Commerce and other such bodies. These were held at the Connaught Rooms, or similar establishments, and this meant usually giving up about three hours of midday business to attend these long-winded affairs. Of course, Mr. Derry was always there as an important guest, and although I never sat next to him, I was always positioned on the top table.

The splendid lunch aside, I had to put up with hours of dreary speeches, and meet all sorts of important people both in commerce and politics. Mr. Derry was doing what he thought was the right thing for me, and when these personages called in the showroom as they did from time to time, they could ask for me and get personal attention.

I came to know many of the judges at the Old Bailey. Mr. Derry telephoned one day and said he had arranged for me to go to the Old Bailey, and had left a message with the Commissioner on the main door to expect me. I was to take with me sufficient track and points in TT to make a large layout with power units, locos and rolling stock in order to give a demonstration to the judges in their rest chamber. Alighting from the taxi, I struggled up the steps of the Old Bailey with all the TT gear, and the Commissioner on the door led me through a panel in the wall into the judges' rest room. There reclining on their black couches, were various elderly gentlemen, resting between sessions. A huge table in the middle of this vast room was available for the layout, which I did at some speed, having previously worked out a plan, following Mr. Derry's advice as to the size of the table. Before long three locos complete with either coaches or goods stock were rattling round the layout, which had station, signal boxes – in fact, everything. One by one, the judges left their couches and before long were operating the trains themselves. I stood back, it was a sight I shall never forget, so engrossed were they and so delighted and happy (we all know what fun there is in operating model railways). I was there for nearly three hours and made many new acquaintances and friends who in turn became customers of the Holborn Showroom and enthusiasts like ourselves. What a leveller is the hobby of model railways! Are we not all boys at heart in our love of the steam locomotive, irrespective of class or position, creed or religion, colour or race? I have met them all at the London Showroom during my time there; kings, dukes, earls, stockbrokers, clerks, warehousemen, admirals, and army generals, and people from the far corners of the earth.

Another vivid memory is of a tall Texan, with his huge hat which to my knowledge, he never removed, and his interest in a 5″ gauge loco that rested in a showcase on the floor. This had been bought in secondhand by Mr. Sell from a widow, at a comparatively low price. The locomotive had been there for years and there had never been any interest shown in it as far as I could gather from the staff. However, here was this Texan asking questions about its performance and price. He was clearly interested, and I suggested to him that as it had come into our possession before my time, perhaps Northampton could give further information. I was stalling actually, as I wished to talk to Mr. Fuller about it before offering a price. Over the telephone, Mr. Fuller could not help me at all, but he suggested that the loco should be sent to Northampton for tests and a valuation before giving a price. I put this to the customer and he agreed as his stay would be for several weeks and he would be back in London in about a month's time. He gave me a forwarding address, so that I could send him the details of our valuation before his return to London.

The next day our van called at the showroom and took the loco back to Northampton. A few days later, Mr. Fuller telephoned me and told me the engine had tremendous pulling power and was a remarkable machine. Under the old paint and grime, there was a fair amount of detail and he suggested a price to include a Bassett-Lowke repaint and burnishing of all the brass work. I advised our customer accordingly and not only did he confirm the purchase of the loco, but placed orders with Northampton for special trucks and a large quantity of track parts to be shipped to Texas. I learned the following year when he visited the showroom again, that he had made full use of this remarkable loco. He had track laid all over his ranch, and when more fencing wire was required by his 'hands', they radioed their needs to the ranch house, whereupon the required materials were loaded on to the trucks and the loco sent off towards the ranch 'hands'. By means of a 'trip' switch the loco whistle blasted off in time for one of the 'hands' to mount his horse, ride alongside the loco, bend down and close the throttle. After removal of the wire, the engine was reversed back to the ranch house, where the same procedure was carried out to stop the machine.

On Sunday and holidays, the trucks were used for the purpose of giving pleasure rides to his grandchildren and friends' children, joyriding all over the ranch. He showed me colour photographs of these activities, and expressed his great satisfaction in his purchase, saying that I would always be welcome in Texas. Later he invited myself and family to the ranch for our holidays, but unfortunately we could not make the trip.

Clearly the locomotive was not made by Bassett-Lowke, but is just one of many models which were labelled Bassett-Lowke by their ultimate owners. Although, it is true that it was tested, checked and possibly modified by our Northampton engineers, as well as being embellished beyond its orginal maker's dreams by the superb painting and lining carried out by the special department at Northampton. As a matter of interest it should be noted that no unauthorised person was allowed inside the paint shop, and the matching of the colours to line up with the great railways of the world was a trade secret.

Another superb model which came into this category of Northampton embellished models was a ¾″ scale, 3½″ gauge 'Flying Scotsman', made by a real craftsman in a tiny home-built workshop in his terraced house in North London. Following a call by a widow, Mr. Fordham, our engineering department expert at Holborn and myself, called on this old lady with the view to purchasing the loco if suitable for our requirements. It appeared her husband had spent every spare moment of his time in that workshop for the previous ten years before his death, working on this fabulous locomotive. In all my years I have never seen such a superb piece of model engineering. The poor woman seemed to be completely distracted, and said over and over again what a relief it was not to hear the locomotive building noises reverberating through the house. She begged me to take the model off her hands, and if possible also find a home for the superb workshop and tools that her husband had used to build the machine. I assured her that we would do our best for her but explained that until the loco was tested, we could not really give her a fair price. In the end to placate her and to meet with her insistence that we make the deal immediately, we came to a reasonable agreement on the price bearing in mind that we were buying it completely untested.

As promised we found a buyer for the workshop and tools, for which she was extremely grateful and wrote me a touching letter of thanks, in which she told me the room was now clear of all nightmares as she called them, and was a normal pleasant sitting room. Our van duly called for the locomotive and that was the last I saw of it, although Mr. Fuller was later to show me some fine colour photographs of the model in all its splendid L.N.E.R. livery. Apparently there had been quite a bit of work on the loco to finish, as well as the painting. In addition the results of the test were astonishing in the extreme, the engine just managing to pull eight big men on trucks in a very exciting test run. In all its glory when painted and lined out, it was a natural choice for a wealthy American to purchase, and the price he paid matched its wonder and beauty.

Mr. Fordham and myself purchased several such models from time to time, and if the model was not worthy of the Northampton treatment Mr. Fordham would renovate the model himself at home, for which he was pleased to get the extra money. In this way we were able to keep quite a variety of models passing through the showroom, thus helping to keep the old image of the Bassett-Lowke marque alive. In addition, especially at Christmas time, Mr. Fordham would prepare for customers all the components necessary to form a model workshop. Items included the boiler, sometimes coal-fired, and the engine unit with single or double piston and all the little workshop models, driven by the engine unit. Mr. Fordham mounted all these items on a baseboard and also fitted all the appropriate piping, pressure gauges and belting.

The sales of the 00 and TT items in no way affected the ever increasing demand for the Bassett-Lowke range of locomotives, coaches and model engineering items. A regular customer was Mr. Hugh Bean, at that time principal violinist of the London Symphony Orchestra, and he was always adding items to his fine 0 gauge layout. My father was a Professor of Music and a Fellow of the Royal College of Music, and from him I inherited a good love of music. Mr. Bean and myself had as a consequence two common interests, music and model railways. Another good customer was a stockbroker, who invited me to spend the evening at his home in the outer suburbs of London to see and run his 0 gauge layout. We had a marvellous evening and I think he must have had every current Bassett-Lowke model on that layout. The railway was in the boarded loft of his big house and I wondered what it must have sounded like in the lounge below where his ever patient wife sat all alone. Imagine an 0 gauge Bassett-Lowke Duchess Loco L.M.S., at full bore with eight Bassett-Lowke Exley coaches behind, then add an engine coach motor coach unit on the other track, with the noise ever increasing and reverberating when the points were negotiated – this going on for a full three hours.

I had another regular customer who also made his living on the Stock Exchange. Whenever there was a particularly good day on the Exchange, you could almost be certain that the telephone would ring at the end of the trading day, and my customer would be asking me to order another special locomotive for him. His layout was all clockwork, and he insisted on each model being a one off. He ordered super detailed models of certain types of locos running on the L.N.E.R., with hand painted bodies and lining, although the wheels had to be standard, so that the locos could negotiate the rather sharp curves on his layout. I suppose in all I ordered for him from Northampton twelve different locos, beautifully detailed and painted, yet rather spoiled by those steamroller wheels. Apart from that first visit, I never saw him again. All our business was conducted over the phone, and the goods when ready were posted to him direct from Northampton. I have often wondered whether it was his railway or whether he was acting for some other person, who for reasons unknown to me, did not wish to be known.

I mention this point because of another customer whom I never met or saw. This gentleman used to send his representative every fortnight or so to deposit £100 in cash with us to build up his credit, from which he would then order over the telephone any model railway items he might require. This went on for months and I never found out if the layout was ever completed, or where it was sited. I recall on one occasion entering a sum of £100 in the till, which was followed by a large sale entry in excess of £700 with a sixpenny (old money) entry in between for a small catalogue or leaflet. We were all amused by those three entries. Incidentally, the £700 plus sale was for a young American, the son of an oil magnate, who had seen our made-up model of a 1½″ scale to the foot traction engine in the window and wanted to buy it. In fact, the traction engine had been made specially for a customer, and was on display in the window so that would-be purchasers of castings and drawings (advertised in the catalogue) could see the finished result. The ultimate owner had agreed to let us keep it for this purpose as he was financially embarrassed at the time of completion, and could not take immediate possession. The American insisted on having it and, as the engine was already promised, on Mr. Fuller's instructions, I quoted a greatly inflated price for both the model and its box. Both prices

were accepted and Mr. Fuller realised with good grace that he would not only have to have another Traction Engine made, but a special box as well.

A few days later, the young American paid another visit and purchased a dozen of our Bassett-Lowke/Exley coaches, despite the fact that we pointed out that they would not traverse the sharp radius of his Lionel layout. Nevertheless he bought them for their aesthetic appeal. I certainly agreed with him on this point. A beautiful model is in itself sufficient satisfaction, and I am sure many have spent hours gazing at the wonder of a very splendid model, especially in the bigger gauges. It is not so easy to go into ecstasy with some of the modern miniature gauges, which have a tendency to look like something out of a Christmas cracker.

As I have written earlier, all sorts of people passed through the door of 112, High Holborn. One morning just before 9 a.m., as we were preparing to open for the day, a man came in and said he wanted to see the manager. As soon as I had settled in my office, I asked him to come in. He was dressed in a rather old hat and dirty raincoat, and his boots were muddy. Furthermore, it was clear that he had not shaved that morning, the black stubble standing out against the white skin. He apologised for his appearance, and said that he had been up most of the night and was very cold as a consequence. It transpired that he was a buyer at Covent Garden, had a chain of shops, and always preferred to do his own buying, even though this meant being up half the night. For a long time, he had thought about having a model railway, but lack of time had prevented him getting started. Finally he had come straight away that morning from the market, even though his boots were muddy and he needed a shave. I sent out for some hot coffee, and we were very soon lost in the planning of his layout and his requirements. In the end he had a splendid 0 gauge layout and one day some time later, he came to see me, properly dressed and shaved so that I hardly knew him. They say clothes maketh a man – how true it was in his case!

How different was the Marquis of Ailsa, who was the Laird of a huge slice of Scotland (some said you could have driven a car for an hour and still be on his land). It was in his castle home that the great American, General Eisenhower, stayed on a visit to this country, soon after the war. The Marquis sat in the House of Lords, and he frequently came in to see me whilst they were in session. He had a magnificent 00 model railway in one of the banqueting halls, and we discussed ways in which the locos themselves could actuate relays to work signals, etc. When we had anything special in stock in 00 gauge he was always interested. I had made for him some very fine Highland Railway locos such as the Jones Goods; these being made by super detail specialists rather than at North-ampton. The Marquis was the most charming of men, and I always entertained him in my office, where we could both indulge in our joint affection for model railways and all to do with them. He was extremely unaffected, with a sort of aura about him, and was able to be at home in almost any circumstance.

Many readers will recall Mr. Douglas Seaton, who had the tremendous 00 layout at Yeovil, as well as 0 gauge and other engineering items of a model nature. Mr. Seaton was a regular caller at the London Showroom, although previously he seemed to do all model business direct with Northampton. One day, however, he noticed in one of our displays, a model of a 00 loco he fancied. Having seen this perform on the test track, and being very pleased all round with its looks and performances, he decided to buy it. This was but the first of many such purchases, and later when I was in conversation with him, he told me that he liked these locos for their individual look. He was right of course, and this range of continually changing models, was made possible by an arrangement I had with Mr. E. Morris, of Eames, Reading. In the early days of the Eames model railway business, Mr. Morris came to see me at Bassett-Lowke and showed to me some of those special models which were being made for his company by a very talented model engineer. They were, in the main, detailed hand-made bodied locos fitted with the standard commercial chassis of Triang and Hornby, with the wheels converted to B.R.N.S.B. measurements, generally by the sub-stitution of those made by the Romford Model Co.

The arrangements with Mr. Morris worked very well for both of us. I was able to show a fine changing selection of very near scale 00 models at very reasonable prices whilst Mr. Morris taking other stock from us in exchange obtained a very good variety of the latest 00 items on the market. He was also able to secure special items for his individual customers from our vast stocks. Mr. Seaton's satisfaction with these special models, no doubt influenced his decision to ask me to have

made a special L.N.W.R. loco and coaches in 00 which he wanted on his layout for sentimental reasons. The choice was the L.N.W.R 4–4–0 'Precursor', and the coaches, eight in all, were to be L.N.W.R. stock of the 1908 period. Mr. Morris must have emphasised the importance of the commission to his engineer, because he turned out a superb model correctly painted and lined out. Mr. Exley of Bradford, an old friend of mine, finally consented to make these eight different coaches, when I filled him in with some of the details of why they were so special to my customer. The 'first', 'second' and 'third' coaches were all to have the correct interior decor and all the coaches were to light up. The detail was superb and the price reflected the quality. Mr. Seaton was so pleased that he ordered a further L.N.W.R. loco, this time a L.N.W.R. 4–6–0 'Prince of Wales' class and a further eight coaches as before. As I write, I have in front of me a photograph of Mr. Douglas Seaton and his two grandsons operating his layout with the two L.N.W.R. locos double-heading the front three of these superb coaches across a viaduct. Later I was able to do more business with Mr. Seaton, but more of that anon, when I shall deal with an unusual development at Bassett-Lowke.

I have fond memories of the great number of clergymen who had an interest in model railways, and in particular two bishops who became good friends of mine. My first encounter with one of the bishops, who shall be nameless, came about when he purchased a Hornby Dublo 0–6–2 tank loco for his nephew. He spent a great deal of time over his purchase insisting that we show him the mechan-ism inside the body shell, oil the same, and check it over our own test track. Some months later he returned, this time with his nephew. Although the assistant who had attended to him, had done everything possible to be of service to the Bishop, he insisted that I attend to him personally. It appeared that the nephew had been given a Hornby Dublo 'Duchess' class loco and was heartbroken, because the express loco was not as fast as the tank loco nor would it pull as many coaches. The express loco had not been purchased from us, yet the Bishop was asking my assistant to change the loco for an identical model which would perform to his satisfaction. I explained that we were under no obligation to do this, and that his complaint should be directed towards the Hornby Dublo manufacturers. However, I asked him to leave the loco with me, and promised him I would do what I could to help. I telephoned Mr. Parker, the London Sales Manager of the Meccano organisation (makers of Hornby Dublo models) and he came over to see me, bringing a replacement with him. I had known Mr. Parker during my previous employment in the model railway trade, and he always appeared very correct and very distant. I believe he was in the Guards at some time as many people called him Captain Parker. He always wore one of those small brimmed bowlers, very square and low down on his head, and in winter a military style camel coat and rolled umbrella. His distant attitude was to change, however, as we became friends, and I found him a warm generous man. Between us we did much to heal the very real breach that had existed between Mr. Bassett-Lowke and Mr. Hornby, which had continued right up to my appointment. The replacement loco was duly handed over to the Bishop, without charge of course, this being the sort of service we gave and were expected to give. After this incident, Mr. Parker made it possible for us to get better supplies of Hornby Dublo than hitherto. The enormous demand for model railways items had still not been met, even with the additional ranges of Triang, and Horby Dublo was in the throes of going over to two rail working with all the additional tooling that was entailed.

During these visits to me, Mr. Parker explained that all Mr. Sell had stocked of the Hornby range had been a few of the cheaper 0 gauge clockwork sets and some tinplate 0 gauge track and points which apparently had emanated from the Manchester branch via Northampton. Mr. Cox the Manchester manager, was nearer Liverpool, the home of Meccano, and had got on well with his local Hornby representative. During our conversations, I was able to question Mr. Parker as to why so many Hornby representatives were ex-servicemen and Mr. Parker explained that ex-officers were always chosen if possible. I found this to be a great disadvantage since my representative knew nothing about model railways and when the first delivery of the new two-rail curved set track proved to be faulty, due to bad tooling and drawing office error, he could not begin to understand what the problem entailed. The symmetry was in fact so bad that it was impossible to form a circle and the whole consignment had to go back to Liverpool and be scrapped.

We had another problem when the new two-rail points for Hornby Dublo arrived, in that the essential two-rail isolating rail had not been sent. Without this rail a short current would occur every time the point blades were moved. There are about eight ways of wiring two rail points, but Hornby Dublo had devised a ninth way, ingenious as far as it went, making even revised loops possible in two-rail, but so complicated that, with few exceptions, very few retailers knew how to use it, and the public certainly did not. Furthermore the illustrated detailed instructions were no help as they contained a great number of electrical wiring errors which played havoc with the modelling public's faith in the Hornby Dublo two-rail system. I edited a copy of the instructions, putting the errors right and sent it on to Liverpool, but they did not bother to acknowledge my efforts on their behalf. It was a most worrying time for me at Bassett-Lowke, because my staff although quite knowledgeable about model railways in general, could not be expected to grasp the exact details of the Hornby Dublo system, especially when the instruction leaflet was wrong. I spent days in the showroom explaining to customers how it worked, and many hours writing letters to customers with full explanations on the system. One irate Colonel in Warminster telephoned me, and finally to placate him, I had to get details of his layout, and make a drawing showing every point and where the insulated breaks must be put, explaining how these could be put in by do-it-yourself methods necessitated by the lack of Hornby Dublo isolated rails.

One of the letters I wrote about this problem, was to a Bishop in Hertfordshire, and this was to be the first of very many letters about Hornby Dublo and ways of using the different items available in the model railway accessories range. Many years later when he died, his daughter wrote me a very lovely and touching letter, thanking me for all the help I had given her father over the years, which she said had given him so much pleasure. Another Bishop, who always blessed me when he came into the office, used to thank me for my help in model railway matters, to such an extent, that I was often embarrassed. He purchased a very beautiful, very fully detailed loco, a Hornby Dublo 'Duchess', which had been specially converted with correct size Romford wheels. A good deal of detail had been added, including embossed nameplates, a repaint in true L.M.S. colours, and special attention to the motor to give superb slow running.

It was the sort of loco we specialised in at Bassett-Lowke and it was the apple of his eye. I shall always remember him buying it, since he was a very long time making up his mind. It seemed that his conscience was pricking him at spending so much money on pure pleasure.

Meeting people and talking about our great hobby, has always given me a great deal of pleasure and happiness, and in some cases, has been remarkably influential not only in bringing about some beautiful models and layouts, but also in changing peoples' lives. Such a situation arose when one of our customers, Mr. Bull, a Division Director of I.C.I., purchased one of the Bassett-Lowke ½″ scale 2½″ gauge L.N.E.R. 'Flying Scotsman' sets of castings and had difficulty in machining the cylinder castings. He could, of course, have purchased the two cylinders already machined, and ready for use, but he wanted to be able to say he had built the loco himself, a worthy and understandable sentiment. He purchased a fresh set of cylinder castings and between us, Mr. Fordham and I were able to help and advise him so that he could achieve his goal. On one of Mr. Bull's many visits to the Showroom, he asked to see me and inquired whether I would consider judging the models section of a display of handicrafts and hobbies that the members of his division were putting on at their headquarters just down the road in High Holborn. He went on to explain that the editor of a famous women's weekly paper was judging the knitting section and equally qualified people were judging the photographic section, the cookery section and so on. The event was to be held on a Thursday, Mr. Fuller's visiting day to Holborn, and Mr. Bull was happy that both of us could come provided Mr. Fuller agreed. There was to be a little get together of all the judges, where we could meet and talk over our drinks, followed by a luncheon.

At this luncheon, I sat next to a lady who was the Personnel Secretary, in charge of the secretaries and typing pool staff at I.C.I. and the talk came round to children. When she learned that my daughter was just about to leave school, with three A levels and nine O levels, she suggested that my daughter should apply to the Head Office for a position, as she was the type of girl for which they were always looking. If I skip a few years and tell you that my daughter eventually became one of the private secretaries to the then Chairman of I.C.I., Sir Peter Allan, who many will know from

his railway books, it will be seen that my early efforts to keep Mr. Bull happy resulted in my daughter's success in her career. However, back to Mr. Bull and the handicrafts and models. I was glad that Mr. Fuller was with me since the exhibits varied from Mr. Bull's half finished 'Flying Scotsman' to a variety of plastic kit models of aeroplanes and cars, as well as some 00 loco efforts and a number of paper and balsa wood model aeroplanes mainly from kits. There was no opposition to Mr. Bull's exhibit for first prize, but I was pleased Mr. Fuller agreed with me, as it could have looked like favouritism. But it was a very happy and entertaining day, and I know Mr. Fuller enjoyed himself. Once again I reflected on how lucky I was to have such an understanding boss as Mr. Fuller.

Many actors and television personalities are model railway enthusiasts and David Nixon, famous for his magic and tricks, was a frequent customer. He particularly liked to build as much as possible of his 00 model railway himself rather than buy the finished article. In live steam, too, we had a regular customer in Peter Cushing. Despite being well known for his creepy and horror films, in conversation he was a quiet, very pleasant gentleman, and always appreciative of the help that Mr. Fordham could give him. Lord Snowdon used our services on one occasion when he was designing his famous aviary for London Zoo and we were able to help him in the making of the model, by suggesting the use of our model ship stanchions for the walks above the ground in the aviary. The size of stanchion used for the ships railing proved to be just right for this purpose.

As a result of all this successful trading my visits to Northampton became more pleasant. The Directors began to see my efforts bearing fruit and undoubtedly made what followed possible.

THE GREAT SALE
It was during a visit to Northampton whilst Mr. Fuller and I were walking through the stock room part of the warehouse, that I noticed a very great number of items that I had not seen before. On enquiry Mr. Fuller explained to me that these were old discontinued lines in the main, the sort of accumulation that any business gathers after 60 years of trading. He said that these stocks were a continued source of irritation to the Board, as they took up considerable space and their efforts to get rid of them had failed, with even the dustmen

refusing them. I was extremely curious and begged Mr. Fuller to let me have a close look at them. Rather reluctantly he agreed that after the afternoon meeting I could have the full lights on in the stock room and inspect them properly. At the meeting I brought up the subject of these old items and suggested that subject to my closer scrutiny, they could be sent up to London and sold in a sale at the Showroom. Mr. Claydon was horrified at the suggestion and went on to say that companies like Bassett-Lowke did not have sales, which he considered lowered the tone of any organisation. However, I got my own way, backed up by Mr. Fuller and Mr. Derry, and after satisfying myself that these old bits and pieces of models had a saleable value, asked Mr. Fuller to send them to London by the van at their convenience. On their arrival, I got some of the better qualified staff to clean up the models and make any repairs and adjustments necessary. I was amazed at the quality and choice of what we had to offer. I telephoned Mr. Fuller full of enthusiasm and he agreed to go through any other slow-selling stock at Northampton and let me have them to offer in the sale at a reduced price. In the Holborn showroom we had quite a few items which had been there a long time and Mr. Fuller agreed that these should be included as well.

When Mr. Fuller called in on his weekly visit the following Thursday, I had all the items gathered together in one place in a room off the basement, where the main stocks were kept, so that he could see the volume of goods we had to offer. The prices charged were to be decided by myself and I estimated that the takings could reach four figures, if all the items were sold. Mr. Fuller was not so convinced, but I impressed him sufficiently for him to agree to take double spread advertisements in all the monthly model magazines giving us sufficient time to plan the campaign and get the necessary tickets made for the window. My young window dresser agreed to make them using bold blue and red crayon pencils on card. The time and date of the sale was fixed, the window was to be dressed a fortnight before the sale commenced and nothing was to be sold before the first day of the Great Sale.

I shall never forget the excitement outside the window as the sale items were placed in position, some with the words 'one only' or 'first caller receives' or 'few only' and the window became the centre of attraction for hours on end. It was soon apparent that the window could not hold everything we had to offer and we had to put in a card stating that there were huge quantities of further sale items inside and that nothing was to be sold until 9 o'clock on the first day of the sale. Despite that sign we had many callers who wanted to buy certain items before the sale commenced. I recall one such irate gentleman asking for the Manager and insisting that I let him have an item he had seen in the window, since as he put it, he had been a valuable and trusted customer of Bassett-Lowke for over thirty years. He felt this gave him the right to preferential treatment and if I did not accede to his request, he threatened to report me to the Directors. As patiently and as quietly as I could, I had to tell him that in fairness to all concerned, I could not concede to his wishes and in not doing so was carrying out the Boards' instructions.

On the first morning of the sale, I had left home earlier than usual so as to get everything ready for 9 o'clock and as I walked up High Holborn from the station, I saw a three deep queue right up to the showroom entrance, stretching past the shops and back round into Southampton Row, with a policeman doing his best to keep the queue orderly. Before going over the road to open the shop, I went to the corner and looked into Southampton Row and to my amazement the queue seemed to be endless. I spoke to the policeman and made myself known, asking him when the queue had formed. He told me that it had begun at around 5.30 a.m. and it was getting bigger and bigger and more and more out of hand every minute. The policeman had to accompany me to the head of the queue to let me in, assuring the queue that I was not trying to infiltrate to the front.

Once inside as the staff arrived, all having difficulty in getting in, I called a conference to plan tactics because of the queue development we had not foreseen. We decided that only eight customers should be allowed in at any one time. This was designed to stop the 'fighting' that might arise if any two customers wanted the same 'one off' item. Among the items in the sale were old locos with broken wheels, various and assorted old mechanisms, both electric and clockwork, early clockwork boat motors, parts for rear steering for yachts, old types of rolling stock, nearly always damaged in some respect, some old steam units and boilers no longer in the range. No doubt many of these items would be considered valuable by today's standard,

Douglas Seaton showing his grandsons the two LNWR '00'
locos double headed pulling the 1908 period coaches, all
supplied by Bassett-Lowke (text page 312).

A converted Hornby 00 Castle locomotive
with super detail by Bassett-Lowke c. 1960.

being regarded as antique models. In those days they had no such appeal.

The frenzy went on all day and the queue seemed to be just as long at lunch time. As fast as one item was sold out of the window it was replaced by another bargain. As the trading day wore to a close the length of the queue shortened until just before we closed for the day a friendly, satisfied customer showed me a copy of the *Evening News* with a big write up all about our sale and a large picture of the queue outside the showroom. The demand continued all that week, and only really fizzled out when there was nothing more to sell of the sale items. We had taken not only the four figure amount that I had quoted to Mr. Fuller but had doubled my estimate as I had not anticipated a total sell out. Our normal trading figures strangely enough were up as well, as I had arranged for a separate till for the sale items, and the only thing that concerned me was the natural aggravation and irritation felt by those customers who did not want sale items and still had to queue to get their requirements. Mr. Derry was delighted, saying it was like a miracle. He went on to say that the sale had put several thousands of pounds into the business, from items long since written off in the stock records, so that all the takings were 100 per cent profit at a time when the company was in real need of such a boost. As an afterthought, he mentioned that even Mr. Claydon was impressed. At the time I did not realise the significance of this remark, which later events were to make clear to me.

FURTHER IMPROVEMENTS

During one of the Thursday luncheons at the White House in Bloomsbury with Mr. Fuller, I mentioned that as our sales of Peco Products were increasing, sparked off by the Peco Stand incorporated under the Bassett-Lowke stand at the Exhibition, we ought to give more specialist thought to this matter. I explained that we should have a special section within the showroom devoted just to the sale of Peco parts and fittings. I envisaged a sort of 'Peco Bar' which would give as much display to the Peco items as possible and be staffed by members of our own staff, who could be trained not only to sell Peco products but be able to help customers with advice on track laying, etc. As usual, Mr. Fuller was in full accord, and said he would design a stand which could be made at Northampton, by our own workshop. The result

was marvellous, and from the front of the stand it looked exactly like a small shop within the showroom, complete with model striped awning. The project proved to be a great success, and Mr. Pritchard of Peco gave us all his support and help in the decorating of the 'Peco Bar' by supplying many superb display boards and display material. The result of all this splendid effort enabled us to carry the full range of Peco Products and customers were attracted from all over London and the suburbs. As one entered the showroom, the Peco Bar was sited at the far end, and was immediately visible.

Another innovation that proved partly successful was Mr. Fuller's idea to have a double-sided stand running down the centre of the showroom, carrying books on all subjects dear to the hearts of model railway enthusiasts and real railway enthusiasts alike. We sold a lot of books from this stand, but we also collected a lunch time showroom full of customers, or in fact browsers who fingered the books until they became unsaleable and we lost quite a few from actual theft, which was not quite so rife in those days as it is now.

I cleared out one of the longer glass display cabinets and fitted it out with better lighting to display our own very unique 'Waterline Models' at 50 feet to the inch for which Bassett-Lowke were famous. These models were accurate depictions of every visible detail of the original ships and were used by the Navy for instruction where foreign fleets were concerned. However, our greatest sales of these beautiful miniatures, were to the Americans. Every great liner and ship of renown had been modelled, and some of these American collections of Waterline ships may be worth thousands of pounds today, since they represent true models of some of the most famous transatlantic liners of all time, long since destroyed at the scrap yards. In my time at Bassett-Lowke, some of these beautiful models were priced from £10 each, a lot of money in those days. One American told me he had been offered half a million dollars for his collection but it was not for sale.

For a long time, Mr. Fuller and I had talked about the gradual and growing interest in fine scale 0 gauge locos, the term fine scale referring mainly to the tread and flange sizes being finer than the Bassett-Lowke standard. Also a greater back to back wheel measurement was used because of the reduced clearances between stock rails and check rails, and between the frog rails and the wing rails.

Mr. Fuller felt it would be too complicated to combine the sale of fine scale and standard Bassett-Lowke wheels, as customers would buy the wrong type of wheels for their track. I did not agree. I felt that provided our staff were instructed to enquire of the customers first before making the sale, the problem would not arise. Mr. Fuller countered this by stating that we should also have to provide all our rolling stock with both coarse and fine scale wheels and consider the manufacture of a new fine scale track system. I felt there was nothing wrong with that, if it opened up a new field of 0 gauge enthusiasts to us, with all the additional trade that would ensue. We reached a deadlock over this problem, and with hindsight it is clear that Bassett-Lowke was not in a position financially to launch a complete new range of fine scale locos, rolling stock and track. There had been a great deal of tardiness in setting up the 2-rail range of locomotives, rolling stock and track, and that had only come about due to the increased demand for 2 rail as against 3 rail. Mr. Fuller believed that he solved the fine scale problem by introducing what was known as 'nuscale', a term used to mean that all the wheels on the loco had smaller flanges and treads than those used on the standard locos but were so set on the axles to give a back to back wheel measurement that would work on the Bassett-Lowke standard track. Thus a customer could have a more scale appearance locomotive and yet be confident that it would perform without derailment on his standard Bassett-Lowke track and points. It was a clever move and did bring in some fresh custom. At the same time it did not require heavy financial commitment. However, in my opinion, it was running away from the real problem because the customers required scale locomotives and it should have been our aim to produce what the customer wanted. However, to be fair to Mr. Fuller, his nuscale did solve the problem in one way. Nuscale locos would work on Bassett-Lowke standard track and points but would also work on the new Peco 0 gauge points without derailment. It was claimed that the Peco points would also take the fine scale wheeled locos of other makes, so that by using Peco 0 gauge points you could use all the different scale wheel standards. Today everything is fine scale in 0 gauge, a step nearer to perfection, and I believe that if Mr. Bassett-Lowke had been faced with the same problem, he would have chosen to progress towards fine scale.

I now turned my attention to the marine section of our business. Older readers will remember the fabulous range that Bassett-Lowke carried, and will recall that a special catalogue covering this section was produced year after year. No doubt the demand for marine items was encouraged by the appointment of Mr. E. W. Hobbs, a distinguished marine architect, to the position of manager of the new showroom at 257, High Holborn and many of the designs of the finished models are attributed to his work. It is obvious with a manager biased towards marine models that the section flourished under his guidance and, of course, the whole range of battleships and liners from the well-established German toy industry were there for the ordering. When the management was taken over by Mr. H. L. Foreman, there was a marked fall off in the sales of the Marine section, no doubt accentuated by the absence of the German model ships ranges due to the Great War. After the war the old levels were never regained.

When I took over the managership, the marine section was almost dead. We still carried quite a large range of ship and boat drawings, a few medium priced yachts, one steam and one electric launch, and a range of boat kits by a well known maker but not exclusive to us. Stuart Turner could still provide us with steam units for boats and we ran an expensive and a cheap range of boat and ship fittings. In Mr. Hobbs' day, the majority of the battleships, liners, tugs and speed boats were powered by very strong, reliable clockwork motors, capable of giving long runs on one wind, and fitted with a governor so that the speed was reasonably to scale, and the length of run increased accordingly. No such models were available in my time, and the electric models which I had on offer used powerful electric motors, which ate up the current so quickly that the limited size accumulators were soon exhausted. In the case of steam models, it was almost impossible to get the steam unit to run slowly, and get adequate power to maintain steerage way, and it was ludicrous to see a model tug, steaming across the lake with a bow wave that would have graced a speed launch. Radio control was in its infancy, transistors were then not known and the dry batteries used to feed the greedy valves were soon exhausted with consequent loss of control.

Because of these problems I turned to yachts, and after much research found a yacht builder, who could provide us with that extra something which customers expected at Bassett-Lowke. I arranged with him that his small workshop should turn out variations of design and size, so that our own windows displayed continually changing models. The scheme proved a splendid success, and in addition my small builder was on occasion able to make up special orders for my customers, which pleased him greatly, as machine production tended to kill his art. This better quality yacht trade, stimulated a demand for serious model yacht builders, and we began to stock the very special parts required when making a racing competition model yacht. This in turn opened up another avenue of trade in yachts, as many of these builders, having failed to win their particular race, were glad to sell the yachts to us at reasonable prices, so as to recover their outlay on the model and have fresh funds to purchase further parts for the new model, which would definitely win next time! As a consequence of all this, our windows were graced with many fine yachts at prices people could afford and further helped in the restructuring of the Bassett-Lowke image.

Nothing succeeds like success, and because of this activity in the yacht section, the other sections of the marine department also picked up, helped by the additional ranges of the famous Web 6 fittings for ships. These included boxwood rigging blocks, some of them very tiny but all working, bollards, cleats and fairleads, and stanchions for deck railing, most of these in brass polished to a mirror finish. These were essential for the scale model ship builders and although relatively costly, turned over very fast, helping to build up this ailing section of the business.

Whilst all this activity in the marine section was going on, our engineering and live steam department had grown so much, that our orders for the Stuart engines and boilers were not being met with prompt delivery. It was the practice of Mr. Fordham to place before me his requirements for these Stuart items at least once a week and the order was sent to Northampton to be executed from their warehouse stocks. When I complained to Mr. Fuller that our orders and deliveries were getting very far behind, he told me that Stuarts had told him that the demand for their products from America was so great that all home orders had to be shelved. Mr. Fuller agreed that perhaps a personal visit from me to Stuarts might improve the situation. In due course, accompanied by Mr.

Fordham, we arrived at the Stuart factory at Henley-on-Thames. To our surprise the factory was much bigger than we had envisaged, but then we learned why. Most of the production went in the manufacture of marine boat engines (full-sized ones), and the making of rather special heart machines for hospitals. The section dealing with model engines was quite small, but we did see the small foundry where the castings were made and the machine shop where the parts were turned. We were made very welcome, but after showing us one of their upper store rooms bulging with steam units and boilers all awaiting shipment to the U.S.A., our hopes for better delivery were dashed, especially when the assistant said they were behind with their export orders as well.

All this was to change, however, and we were shown into a room to meet the Director immediately responsible for the models division. As soon as this Director and Mr. Fordham began talking about their beloved models and the Director realised that in Mr. Fordham he had a kindred spirit in the love of these live steam units, he promised that if we liked to give him an order on the spot to be delivered to the London Showroom, he would do the best he could to complete it. Of course, it was not only liking for Mr. Fordham that prompted the offer, but the fact that the goods delivered direct would carry a normal retail discount and not the special wholesale price they had to give to Northampton. When goods are in such short supply no manufacturer likes to send out goods to a wholesaler, when he can get better prices from retailers and exporters. Mr. Fuller accepted the arrangement with good grace and we continued this arrangement with Stuarts and never suffered again from shortages or poor deliveries.

The demand for the Triang 00 and TT items gradually increased, so that a few weeks before Christmas, we were in danger of selling out all we had ordered with very little chance of securing further supplies. I telephoned Mr. McKenzie of the Triang Sales Department who had always been able to help me in the past, and he suggested that if I could get down to Margate with a van there was a good chance of getting some supplies, but they were not in a position to send out deliveries before Christmas. I learned later why this was so, but it seemed strange to me that we could collect but they would not send. Mr. Butler, one of our senior sales assistants had a large shooting brake and he agreed to come down to Margate with me to collect what we could of further supplies. As we arrived at the works we noticed several large pantechnicons being loaded with what looked like boxed train sets. Whilst I had lunch with the Directors, I enquired about these pantechnicons and they explained that these were train sets ordered by one of the mail order catalogue companies and that to meet the order, all the despatch staff were needed in the first instance to make up the box train sets and then to help load them. This was one of the causes of the despatch department being unable to attend to fresh orders, the other reason being that it would have been impossible to complete any orders received due to the out of balance stocks.

Before lunch, I had handed in my list of requirements to Mr. McKenzie, and he explained to me that they could not do all I had listed, but that after lunch he would be able to tell me what we could have, and what alternatives he had to offer should I wish to take up any of these. It was whilst waiting for the goods to be loaded in the shooting brake, that a Triang Director spoke to me, and said he would probably be getting in touch with me by telephone in the very near future, but that he would leave the matter to be discussed until he actually telephoned.

It was the New Year before he telephoned and explained the problem he wanted me to solve. At that time, the famous toy shop in Regent Street, Hamleys, was in fact owned by Triang and some of the Triang Directors were Directors of Hamleys as well. It appeared that Hamleys had built the layout and supplied the locos and all the relevant gear for an extensive layout in a large country mansion at a place called Salem between Petworth and Midhurst. The layout was housed in a special building away from the house and had been commissioned by a Prince of one of the Arabian States, who lived in exile in the house. Apparently, the Prince refused to pay the bill, on the grounds that the layout did not work satisfactorily. As I was an exccecutive of Bassett-Lowke, the Arab had agreed to abide by my ruling one way or the other, if I was prepared to take on the commission and report my findings after inspection of the layout. I agreed to go down, and I must confess that I was as pleased as punch that the name of Bassett-Lowke still stood so high in the Trade's esteem. I was determined to justify that faith in my company.

Mr. Butler drove me down to Salem, and as we were about to enter the gates of the drive, an Arab came out of the shrubbery and held up his arm.

My letter from the Prince's secretary was our passport, but as we drove slowly up the drive, I could see dark figures in the shrubbery. Apparently, when the Prince was in exile his brother had been assassinated, and they were taking no chances. The Prince's male secretary, with whom I had corresponded, met us in the hall and conducted us to the layout building. He said the Prince would be joining us shortly, but on no account was I or my assistant to disagree with him on any point that might arise. I made no comment, but motioned that we would like to get started. The trackwork was made of the then popular Wrenn type in steel, and our first job, obviously, would be to clean the track. It was very oxidised and nothing would have run on it in that condition.

It did not take me long to realise that basically the layout was well laid by competent people, but the power supplies were inadequate. On the power units supplied, the trains made a very poor showing and some of the stationary working models did not perform as they should. We had brought with us some 12-volt heavy duty car type accumulators and after these were connected to the layout, everything came to life. At this moment, the Prince came into the room, and the pleasure on his face was remarkable, as he saw for the first time his locos and the dozen or so stationary models working as they should. He turned to me, and said that he had obviously chosen the wrong people to make the layout. He told me how delighted he was and asked whether I could guarantee that it would always work like that. I assured him that it could and we operated the layout together, chatting all the time, lost in the fun of operating model railways. At last, he turned, shook my hand in a warm firm grip and was gone. His secretary, who had come into the room unnoticed, stood in amazement. He had never seen the Prince so informal before.

In due course, I made out my report to Hamleys telling them about the shortcomings of the layout, and the remedies necessary to put matters right. I explained that the 12-volt big capacity accumulator had enabled the locos and static models to draw the current they required to give of their best. The necessary current was above the optimum load of the fitted power units, and I suggested two 6-amp power units for the layout, one for the locos and one for the stationary working models. Hamleys followed my advice to the letter, including all sorts of other improvements which I had suggested as well; the Prince was satisfied, and Hamleys got their money. I received a very nice letter of thanks from the Director of Hamleys, and a cheque for our out of pocket expenses with a little extra as appreciation. Many years later, I saw the layout again – but that's another story.

## THE OTHER SIDE OF THE STORY

This chapter is devoted to the other side of the story, which the ordinary modelling public knows very little about. I am referring here to the side of the business we used to call the Industrial Models. Ask anyone, not necessarily interested in models, whether they have heard of Bassett-Lowke, and they will probably answer that they were the people who made those beautiful ship models to be seen in the windows of various shipping and insurance companies. Of course, they would be right, but very few people really know the complexity and variety of models that have emanated from Northampton. In my time, it was Mr. Claydon who was the Managing Director of this side of the business, and great credit must be given to him for his efforts for the company, following on as he did from Mr. Bassett-Lowke, and the results he achieved, some of which one would have thought unbelievable. I know I crossed swords with Mr. Claydon many times, but I have nothing but respect and admiration for his devotion to his work, aiming always to maintain the Bassett-Lowke standard.

The models were extremely varied and each one presented problems to Mr. Claydon which had to be overcome. In the main, they were to the order of the great names in industry, although some were for teaching and tuitional classes and a few were to demonstrate inventor's ideas to clients. At other times the models represented scale model railways for clients who were exhibiting them to the public. Various commissions stand out particularly in my memory: the beautiful gauge I 10 mm 2–2–2 Great Western Loco, built to the order of Messrs. Beyer Peacock and Co. Ltd, and then from another age and type, the superb model of a mid-eighteenth century stage coach scale ¾″ to 1′ made to the order of The White Horse Distillers. There were models of ships of all types and sizes, of course, but I especially remember marvelling at the model of a yacht, a replica, ¼″ to 1′ of the famous Camper Nicholson Ltd's own vessel No. 843. Then mention must be made of the

Bassett-Lowke-made window displays, put on by the Union Castle Steamship Co. Ltd. in their Bond Street Showrooms. These showed a huge section of the Southern Hemisphere with South Africa and the Indian Ocean on one side and the Southern Atlantic Ocean on the other, with miniature Union Castle liner models in the foreground, all made to a scale of ¹⁄₆₄″ to 1′. This was to be followed by the huge 21′ long models of the RMS *Windsor Castle*, the pride of the Union Castle's fleet, magnificently detailed, with parts of the ship cut away to reveal the fully detailed first class lounge, the first class cabins etc., all fitted with miniature ships' furniture and beautiful hand painted figures. The figures were made for Bassett-Lowke by K's Ltd., the famous model loco and accessory kit manufacturers, and all had to be cast individually, a mammoth task which K's did so well.

Not quite so glamorous were the purely industrial models such as the Slabbing Mill, ½″ to 1′, to the order of The Steel Company of Wales, the Twin Drive for Rolling Mill, ¾″ to 1′ for British Thomson Houston, and the Grace Thorough Boiler at Margam for Simon-Garves Ltd., or the delightful sectional model for educational purposes of a petrol 4-stroke engine made to the order of United Africa Ltd.

There were also the models made for inventors, and I recall one in particular with which I was personally involved. It was on show in South Africa House, and consisted of a large baseboard, about 8′ × 6′, upon which had been modelled an African jungle. Rising above the tree tops on pillars was a railway/roadway upon which ran a motorised truck. Everything worked automatically; the truck was loaded and eventually unloaded by remote control, and was intended to show a way in which goods and materials could be transported through jungles or remote areas, without the need for cutting down trees and building roads. The whole idea was quite ingenious, although I doubt whether the idea ever came to fruition. However, I do know that the model used to go wrong resulting in frantic phone calls from South Africa House for me to come and put it right – I was glad when the demonstration ceased!

Another very interesting demonstration model used two ships in a tank, one fitted with the inventor's stabilizers and one without. The water was agitated, so that the two models rolled about on miniature waves and, in model form at least the stabilisers seemed to work. Another instructional model which intrigued me consisted of the stern of a whaling ship, mounted with a dummy harpoon gun. The model, although not in the water, simulated the roll and pitch of a ship in a rough sea and beyond the ship's stern was a model of a whale rising above the water. The idea of the model was to instruct would-be harpoonists in the art of hitting the whale while allowing for the pitch and roll of the ship. The harpoonist had to press a button and, bearing in mind the 'sea', use electronic means to hit the whale. A hit was shown by a bulb lighting up. No light and he must try again.

A superb model was made to the order of the Kariba Dam authorities, with certain parts of the structure cut away for the benefit of the engineers working on the dam. Another model, which I did not see but was partly involved with, was a model of Singapore Harbour, in which the dock side cranes had to work much like the real thing, in that they had to be capable of loading and unloading the goods from the holds of the model ships. This was to be done by magnets, other than permanent magnets, and I scoured London to find a suitably fine wire, strong enough to carry the current needed and the weight of the load, yet thin enough to be unobtrusive. Eventually I found the right type through the help of a colleague from earlier days. Mr. Claydon, who had failed to find a source of the wire personally thanked me for my efforts and I like to believe that from that moment, he began to think that perhaps I was an asset to Bassett-Lowke after all.

This change of heart was further heightened when Mr. Claydon's department took on the task of installing an 0 gauge model railway in the gardens of a park run by the Clacton Corporation. The area covered was quite extensive and there was considerable voltage drop as a consequence. The first locos did not survive long, and the track soon became oxidised and electronically dirty. This caused poor performance and the flow of heavier currents than normal caused havoc with the motor windings. I suggested using 24 instead of 12 volts, as this higher pressure would cut through the dirty track problem, enable finer wire to be used in the armature windings and thus lower the current in the circuit. This was done and reasonable results were achieved, but the inexperienced operators at Clacton would run heavily laden trains at full bore, which took a heavy toll on the motor brush

gear. We overcame the problem however, by keeping identical chassis, complete with motors, oiled and ready to be rushed to Liverpool Street Station and on to the first express to Clacton, to be collected at the other end by the Clacton Corporation employees. These fresh chassis replaced the ailing ones which were returned to London to be serviced and oiled, and if necessary fitted with new brushes. The trains ran all day, 12 hours a day in high season, and it speaks well for the Bassett-Lowke motor units, and chassis generally, that they stood up to the gruelling task so well, after the initial gremlins had been eliminated.

There was another very beautiful Bassett-Lowke installation with which I was involved. This was a really splendid layout with magnificent scenic effects, and was sited on the pier at Weston-super-Mare. However, the owner was not happy with the finished result, as he said it was failing to bring in the expected numbers. As I was holidaying in the area, I was asked to go and inspect the layout and make myself known to the owner. Unfortunately, the owner was right. One could not fault the layout itself, but it was too sophisticated for its audience. It was in fact an enthusiasts layout with scale 00 locos and scale speed running. What the crowds wanted was great speed and I was not surprised to learn later on, that the owner had scrapped the installation for one using Triang track and points, with dozens of engines racing round a speed equivalent to a real speed of 300 mph! It is what the kids love and want and if there is an occasional crash, so much the better. You can't win them all!

Bassett-Lowke built the first locos for Disneyland; 100 per cent American, of course, in 15″ gauge, and I saw these before they went. Later, Walt Disney started his own workshops and had his locos built there to his designs.

The Admiralty used our Industrial Models section, not only for models of the warships themselves, but for all sorts of instructional models for the Navy. Invariably the first contract always came through the manager at High Holborn. Fortunately, for me, I was well versed in nautical terms, and so was able to understand their requirements.

One of my favourite Northampton models which was duplicated so that it could be shown as a sample of their work, was a double track layout of around 8′ long. It consisted of one 'Up' and one 'Down' road with crossovers at each end. It was correctly signalled including ground signals and was all operated from a lever frame with locking bars just like the real thing. I loved working this with the two locos and I imagine that the young lads training to be signalmen must have got quite a thrill out of learning their trade on this particular track. Just to have played a very tiny part in the industrial model side of the Bassett-Lowke story makes me feel very honoured and proud and I salute the craftsmen who made it possible, but it is to Mr. Bassett-Lowke above all that credit must be given for turning his visions of such models into reality, and giving us all such wonders to look upon.

## WHAT HAPPENS NOW?

Things were going well for us at Holborn, and there was a real air of optimism. Our sales of Triang and Hornby 00 railways had increased beyond our wildest dreams, and fortunately, so had the demand for our own Bassett-Lowke range of 0 gauge locos and accessories. The only sad thing that worried me, was the fact that rumours were flying that the Trix Company was in financial difficulties. As sales of Triang, and Hornby 00 railways rose, so Trix sales declined, and this was understandable when the reasons were examined. Trix models were very much dearer, not so reliable in matters of control and reversing, and in the main were still very toylike with their coarse over-scale track and wheels. Whilst the model railway shortages after the war were rampant, Trix had had their share of the trade, but as more and more items became available to the model railway public, their share declined. I had no idea how much this situation affected us, until Mr. Fuller came to Holborn on his Thursday visit, looking very worried and distraught.

Over coffee at Carwardines, he explained what might happen to us if Trix collapsed. Apparently many years ago, Mr. Bassett-Lowke together with several other gentlemen interested in the manufacture of the Twin Train System, as Trix was known then, formed a separate company called Precision Models Ltd., to manufacture the engine parts and lithography of the coaches and wagons and most of the engineering parts need for this Trix system. As Bassett-Lowke no longer had factories in Germany making models and parts, it was agreed that Precision models would make similar parts for the 0 gauge range and many will have noticed that the lithographed 0 gauge wagons of the later years

looked much like the bigger brothers of the Trix range. Mr. Fuller explained that if Precision Models no longer had the Trix orders, they could not exist on the Bassett-Lowke requirement alone.

In addition, Mrs. Bassett-Lowke had intimated that she needed to get a better return for her money, implying a withdrawal of support from Bassett-Lowke and Precision Models. He did not enlarge on this possibility but stated that the ultimate result of these happenings would mean the closing down of the Precision Model factory. The following week, he told me that the factory would have to close, although they would try and keep it going as long as possible. The closing down would mean the end of a number of items, and his list included most of our standard locos and their attendant chassis, wagons, wagon wheels, couplings, etc. – in fact, almost all of our model railway engineering items, other than the one-off scale hand-built models at the top end of the scale. He said he had been scouting around to see what could be made elsewhere, and he asked me if I could help, as he understood I had many connections in the trade. I determined exactly what was needed and promised to make enquiries.

Mr. Fuller told me that he intended to put up the prices of all our standard locos on the assumption that if they were going to be in short supply, those who really wanted them would have to pay the increased prices. He said they were going flat out to produce from existing parts as much of our model railway engineering range, including the locos, as possible before the closing date.

Bassett-Lowke were worried about coach bogies and the motor bogie for the new diesel deltic loco they were in the process of producing, and he asked me to see if I could help in this direction. It was a sad Mr. Fuller that returned to Northampton that night, with the prospect in his mind that all we had worked for together, was collapsing around us. Perhaps I was not so easily discouraged, and the next days started moves which were to have a tremendous impact on my future, and to a lesser degree, the future of Bassett-Lowke. I telephoned an old acquaintance of many years, Bill Mathews, who had a small engineering business in Potters Bar, where he specialised in sub-contract work. I arranged an appointment with him, so that I could show him samples of the model railway accessories that would be affected by the closure of the Precision Models factory. The high standards demanded for the finished work did not bother him, but the price that could be paid did. I took this up with Mr. Fuller, explaining that it was generally accepted that work put out to subcontract would invariably be more costly than if produced in house. He was impressed with the high standard and agreed to put up the retail price to meet the extra costs involved. From the word go, the scheme worked well, and a large portion of Mr. Fuller's worries with regards to accessories were over.

Over the next few weeks, I arranged to get made or built a great many more of the items that Precision Models had originally fabricated – wheels, couplings, buffers, and bogie frames. Most of these items were made by small engineering firms similar to the one belonging to my acquaintance at Potters Bar, with quite a number of industrial people being drawn into the scheme. Naturally, these small concerns and the individual modellers required immediate or almost immediate payment for their work and did not want to have to issue detailed invoices to Bassett-Lowke and then wait weeks for payment to be met. They wanted cash which, if I wished to keep their services I would have to pay them out of the till, as the petty cash was not sufficient for this purpose. The new accountant at Bassett-Lowke was up in arms about this policy and said it would have to stop. I was shattered. I felt that, on the one hand I was moving heaven and earth to help Mr. Fuller and the company overcome a problem which if not solved could close the business, whilst on the other, the accountant was making a stand and stating that my methods were not permitted.

I think Mr. Fuller must have realised how much the accountant had upset me, because at the first opportunity during one of our luncheons at the White House, he raised the subject again. He said there must be a way round the problem, because in these last few weeks I had become a sort of miniature Precision Models company. He suggested that I paid these workers myself by my own cheque, the workers would then endorse the cheque and I could pay the cheques into the till and take out the equivalent in cash. To compensate myself, I could then invoice the goods to Bassett-Lowke, plus a small commission, and I could present a statement to Bassett-Lowke each month which the accountant would settle. The tills each day would not be affected and the takings would not be subject to deductions as had existed under the original scheme. I did not accept the idea straight away as I wanted time to see if there were any snags. Finally I agreed to the scheme, and called the service, which began in March 1961, Dudley Enterprises. This was the best solution, enabling us to cope with the tremendous increase in the volume of trade that followed.

Over the months that followed, I gathered together such an array of small business concerns and outworkers, that it surprised even me. Under the banner of Dudley Enterprises I was able to use the services of toolmakers, machinists, loco builders, kit builders, repairers, etc., covering all aspects of our Bassett-Lowke trade. So big did the business become, that I realised that I would have to apply for a Purchase Tax Certificate, but, fortunately for me, when the inspectors called at my home to discuss this possibility, they decided it was unnecessary as the majority of the work was processing and not actual manufacturing. I was very relieved at this decision, as can be imagined, because this would have added to the paperwork, which was already assuming mammoth proportions for a one man service.

One of my best people was a retired toolmaker in Torquay, who had worked in a company noted for its finely engineered products. The amount of work that man got through was beyond belief, especially as his retirement had been an early one through ill health. So good and accurate was his work that through Dudley Enterprises, he made the Deltic 6-wheeled loco bogies used in the Bassett-Lowke model, their first diesel loco. Some parts for these came from Northampton, of course, but the main work was his. Another motor bogie, used in our motorised electric coach stock, proved extremely difficult to substitute. To overcome this problem, I designed a new 4-wheeled motor bogie using two 00 Triang motor units, each motor unit worm driving the worm wheel on the separate axles of the bogie so that each single motor bogie had two motors, one for each axle. My Torquay tool maker made a superb job of these, and we made many hundreds of them, our clients asserting they were just as powerful as the original and had the advantage that should the motor unit fail, a replacement Triang unit could be fitted in a few moments, and did not cost a fortune.

We always had a great demand for the Stuart engine units made up and ready to be connected by piping to a boiler and main. This demand accelerated in the summer months when so many Americans came to the Holborn showroom.

Looking through my records, I see that Mr. Butterfield of Torquay, made dozens of each type. In fact, he was always behind in his deliveries and as fast as they came from him, all beautifully finished and turned out, they were sold. Two particular models he made for Dudley Enterprises, for Bassett-Lowke, were the Triple Expansion Engine and the Beam Engine, and these were so magnificently made and put together that everyone who saw them marvelled at the workmanship. The Beam Engine was to the order of Douglas Seaton of Yeovil as a present for his grandson, and he was delighted with the result.

Locos for Bassett-Lowke were getting in short supply, so I arranged with Mr. Butterfield to put together the well known C.C.W. 0 gauge white metal kit for an 0–4–2 G.W.R. tank loco, the type used in the push-pull model, with him adding detail, making a brass chassis and fitting the Bassett-Lowke motor unit and worm and worm wheel, as well as utilising the Bassett-Lowke wheels which he could supply in 2 rail or 3 rail, as required. The model was then painted in the Northampton paint shop and first appeared in the Holborn showroom window going backwards and forwards with one coach on a piece of straight track reversing automatically. The result was sensational and we made a great number of these as a consequence. In addition, we made many more chassis for this model, for those modellers who bought the C.C.W. white metal kit to build and paint themselves, but who did not have the skill to make the chassis and motor unit.

Other outworkers employed by Dudley Enterprises consisted of a yacht builder who also rigged a number of customer's own yachts. There was another young man who had a flair for building boat kits of the type we stocked in the shop, one of the popular models was the 'Titan' tug, which he put together many times, sometimes with steam units and boilers, or with electric motors with batteries as required by the customers. Many of the loco repairs and conversions which in the past had been carried out at Northampton, and now were no longer possible, were done by Mr. Fordham in his spare time at home. Through the formation of Dudley Enterprises I was able to offer a unique service to Bassett-Lowke customers in the form of a repairs service backed by spares for the ever-growing demand for Triang and Hornby model railways. This is commonplace today, but was a real innovation in those days, and the news that we

could offer this service spread throughout the modelling world, and items came by post for repairs, so that my outworkers were pressed hard to meet the demand for their services.

Mr. Franklin, about whom I have written earlier, telephoned me one day and asked me about the wheels used on the C.C.W. 0–4–2 loco, which as mentioned were for 3-rail and 2-rail working. He asked me if I could let him have a sample of the wheels in 2-rail and 3-rail and that if these were acceptable he would need a continuous supply. My records show just how many Mr. Butterfield supplied, the 2-rail type predominating. These were made by turning the wheel casting, removing the flange and tread, and forcing fresh turned tread and flange over the flange-less wheel with an insulating material between the two, these being known as loco wheels with insulating rims.

There is no doubt that the Dudley Enterprises set-up under the Bassett-Lowke framework was rather unique and might have gone on forever, except for two things. One reason was that in July 1962 Mr. Butterfield passed away. He had been living on borrowed time and we all knew it had to come. His passing left a big hole in Dudley Enterprises, which no-one could ever fill. I salute his memory for his skill and patience. Many times he was racked with pain, yet the standard never fell; what guts the man had, I am proud to have known him. The second reason comes later in the story, so you, dear reader, must be patient.

INNOVATIONS AND PROBLEMS
Earlier in the story, I explained how I had come to Bassett-Lowke, and how Mr. Fuller had first talked to me when I came to Holborn to sell him power units and train controllers which my own company were marketing. My old company had since gone out of business. The power unit and controller manufacturers had had to find other means of distributing their product. The directors of the power units company came to see me at Bassett-Lowke to see if there was any way in which Bassett-Lowke could run their range for them. As you will have gathered, Bassett-Lowke were in no position to take over a range of electrical products for distribution to the trade, but I suggested to the two directors the name of a well known wholesaler who could handle their products. For a time, this worked well enough, but finally these directors realised that they must do their own marketing, and as shortage of money was the problem I

introduced them to an industrialist that I had known for some time, a Mr. Zang.

Mr. Zang had come to this country many years ago, and brought his skills with him to produce fabulous Herald model soldiers so beautifully painted that in a previous employment I had been a significant buyer. Mr. Zang had then sold out to Britains, making a sizable profit. It was through Mr. Zang's brother-in-law, who had sold me the Herald soldiers in the early days, that I met Mr. Zang, and we often had lunch together whilst I was at Bassett-Lowke. I suggested to him that perhaps he would like to join forces with these power unit manufacturers and put up the capital. He agreed provided I became a sort of Technical Director of the proposed new company so that I could keep an eye on the two power unit directors. To this I agreed, and a splendid range of train controllers and power units followed of which we had a good share to sell at Bassett-Lowke. The new lines were to my design and specification and were the first train controllers ever made with a printed circuit, on what was, for the time, a very modern production line.

We were experiencing a very great number of enquiries from customers concerning the running of two trains on a layout. Over the years Bassett-Lowke had advocated the split potential system which worked well enough with the 3-rail system but was more difficult to understand and use with the 2-rail system. On the TT layout, which I had exhibited with my old company at Harlesdon, I had used a system I had devised myself and which had mystified many of the onlookers, as we appeared to run two trains on the same track, independently controlled. I discussed this design with both Mr. Zang and Mr. Fuller and the outcome of our discussion was that I was instructed to design a power unit and controller for Bassett-Lowke, incorporating two controllers to give the same results as we had obtained at the exhibition. However, this unit was to be in one case and have all the relevant switches contained within the case as well as the two controllers. The result was the famous Bassett-Lowke 'Trainsmaster' unit which we demonstrated to the trade and model press at the Cora Hotel near Euston. As I write, I still have this first model which we used for the demonstration and even today it is still technically in advance of many of the power units and controllers on the market. It incorporated variable transformer control, superior to resistance

control, and each controller working with its own transformer was completely isolated from the other controller/transformer. There was a flexi control so that it was sensitive to both 00 and 0 gauge locos and incorporated the then new half wave if required for shunting. Only seven wires to the case were necessary to give full train selection over six independent areas and, of course, 16-volt AC was provided for point operation and accessories, all outputs being protected by thermal cutouts. Inside the casing there were only two wires from each transformer to the printed circuit panel, a revolutionary step in those days.

Of course, it was a great success, but could have achieved even greater sales if Mr. Fuller had not priced it so high as to be out of reach of many modellers. A really good profit would still have been made by Bassett-Lowke if the price had been two-thirds of the chosen price. I was very annoyed about it, since so much effort had gone into producing this unique instrument and it is a shame that so many were denied the use of such a revolutionary two train model loco control. It upset Mr. Zang as well, as he had financed the tooling and it was essential to have big sales to recoup his outlay which had been considerable. It was galling to realise that Bassett-Lowke was making twice as much profit in selling the unit as the manufacturers who had done all the work. In hindsight, I think that Mr. Fuller was guided by his experience with the Bassett-Lowke locos where the inflated prices due to limited stocks had not stopped buyers. On this reasoning, perhaps he thought he might as well get a good price for the Trainsmaster Power Unit as well. It is dreadful to reflect that when I joined the Company, the famous mogul steam 2–6–0 loco and tender used to retail at £12.12s and it was £48.15s at the time of the Trainsmaster.

In an endeavour to fill the gap that would arise when all the Bassett-Lowke range of locos were sold out, Mr. Fuller started to create a range of super-detailed locos which were hand-built throughout by master craftsmen, individuals not actually employed at the Northampton factory. The first of these, as a sample to show customers the type of loco they could expect, was an 0–4–0 G.W.R. tank loco in 0 gauge. Three of these were built, one for display at each of the showrooms, London, Manchester, and Northampton. They were very pricey and as sales did not come up to expectations it was decided to make a slightly less detailed model range covering the G.W.R. region, which included the 5700 class Pannier Tank, the G100 Prairie Tank, the 'Castle' express loco and the famous 'King' class loco. The catalogue of the period explained why they were being offered and stated that the locos were being produced in an endeavour to satisfy the demand for locos superior to the standard range quantity produced models, but without the costly fine detail of the exhibition model. They were priced rather high but the demand was quite good, and was probably just about the demand that could be met by the builders. All these innovations helped to offset the falling output from Precision Models, as the raw materials available which could not be replaced were used up, and with the items made available through Dudley Enterprises, the figures were maintained and all seemed well at the Showroom.

However, Mr. Fuller had to face up to a time, in the not too far distant future, when a great part of our Bassett-Lowke range would not be available. I am sure he gave a great deal of thought to various options, but on this occasion I was not consulted beforehand. Unfortunately Mr. Derry passed away about this time, and his good advice was sadly missed. In an attempt to keep a reasonable range of goods in the showrooms, Mr. Fuller launched into other spheres of the model world, filling the showroom with cheap aircraft kits, aircraft diesel engines, glow plug engines with all the appropriate accessories (propellers of various sizes and pitches), radio control systems for the do-it-yourself merchant and a huge variety of plastic kits and made-up models of cars and aeroplanes, many of them so-called working models. There were microscopes for the junior enthusiast and a number of scientific toys, most of these items being the products of various toy companies. In the showroom we did our best to present these as well as possible, arranging glass showcase displays and featuring them in our window. Despite our efforts they turned out to be a great flop and huge stocks remained on the shelves unsold. There were a number of reasons for this, each one contributing to the failure. In the first instance, none of the staff had any knowledge or training in the selling of these kits. Not one of the staff had even made up a model himself from a kit, so it was impossible for them to offer advice and assistance. Not one of the staff had ever tried to start a model diesel engine or the glow plug type engine, and had no idea how these should be fitted in the plane or boat. But the

main cause of the failure lay in the fact that Mr. Fuller himself did not know anything about the items he was buying, and, as hindsight showed, he had been misled by the clever salesman, and did not realise he had bought items which were already out of date when purchased. At that time developments in diesel and glow plug engines were happening so fast that what was popular and saleable in one year, was out of date the next. This also applied to the radio control gear, and as I know from many years of experience in the trade, the modelling public are very much more aware of what is a good buy and what should be left alone than the trade give them credit for.

When it became apparent that these latest goods were not going to sell, the atmosphere at Bassett-Lowke began to change. We were turning customers away because we could not supply the 0 gauge locos they wanted, the overall sales were beginning to fall and because our shelves were stocked with unsaleable goods, we were not turning over our own stocks fast enough. Limits were imposed on what I could buy and the accountant came more and more into the fore in controlling purchases. The staff became impatient and resentful as their commission fell, and I felt I was helpless to do anything to improve matters. The death of Mr. Butterfield and subsequent closing of his workshop, left Dudley Enterprises without its major supplier, which could have done much to help the falling sales at Bassett-Lowke. I racked my brains to find a solution to the problem we were facing, but without coming to any conclusions as to how to proceed. I knew that economists would view the situation as a cut and dried affair – either reduce your costs and overheads or increase your turnover, or both. Thinking along these lines, I came to a novel conclusion, which I decided to put before the Board of Directors the next time I was in Northampton.

THE BEGINNING OF THE END
Before I was able to go to Northampton, however, Mr. Fuller told me during his weekly visit, that the Board had had some lively sittings, weighing up the pros and cons of the situation. He revealed to me for the first time that the showroom leases at both Holborn and Manchester were due for renewal in about 2 years time, and that most of the discussions had centred around the renewal or otherwise of these leases. There were those who

were 'against any renewal' and for the subsequent closure of the London and Manchester premises, letting Northampton deal with any retail trade by post or over the counter. They argued that renewal of the leases would mean greatly increased rents, adding to our overheads at a time when these needed to be reduced. Their reasonings were sound as far as they went, but they had overlooked that in London we had a centre where a lot of business, which did not go through our books, was conducted on behalf of Northampton and that this outlet would now be lost. There were others on the Board who thought that it was essential if the name of Bassett-Lowke was to survive that a London showroom be maintained, even if it meant a higher rent, which they argued could be offset by staff reductions and other economies.

Mr. Claydon, of course, figured prominently in the discussion since his department was doing very well, despite fierce competition from abroad and Sweden and Denmark in particular. He argued that if his department was to expand and survive, it would be necessary for him to have enough ready cash to pay his wages bill and raw material accounts. He felt it was better that money should go towards this side of the business, rather than to bolster up what he described as a failing market. Naturally he was biased towards his own interest, but there was a lot of sense in what he said. A few weeks passed before I went to Northampton, and this enabled me to go into further details concerning the project I proposed to put before the Board.

There was a glum look about the Board as we sat down for that final afternoon session. At last, with the preliminaries dealt with, we came round to the all important question of how to improve the sales in the showrooms. I asked if I could say a few words, and revealed to them that I was aware of the lease problem, explaining that Mr. Fuller had thought it fairer if I knew all the facts and problems facing the Board. I went on to say that I felt that the London showroom should be retained if possible, quoting the reasons stated above, and that furthermore we should look to expansion rather than retraction to get us out of our troubles. I proposed that we should cash in on our great name and background by opening four shops in the London Suburbs, say one in Enfield, one in Ilford, one in Kingston and one in Croydon. In addition we should gradually open new shops in all the major centres of Britain so that the effect would be a saturation of the country with Bassett-Lowke shops. I went on to say that we should create a situation similar to that enjoyed by Cooks, whereby when one thought of a travel agent their name automatically sprang to mind. There would be central buying, with systems involving easy exchange of stocks between the branches so that stock would turn over very fast, while central buying would ensure manufacturer attention and keen buying prices. I suggested that properly handled the necessary finance could be found. Mr. Bassett-Lowke had been able to do this many years ago and I thought that we should at least make some initial efforts to seek this finance, stating the reasons why it was necessary, and what we proposed to do.

I had exected a lot of opposition to this idea, and to my astonishment I saw a gleam of hope in the eyes of the members of the Board. How wonderful it would have been if Mr. Derry, our late Chairman, could have been alive. I knew he would have endorsed the scheme, and probably was the one man who had the contacts and who could have found us the finance. However, the meeting broke up and I was instructed to look around the suggested venues in the London suburbs for suitable shops. I found an excellent site at quite a reasonable price in a main shopping centre in Croydon, but the scheme never really got off the ground. I could see Mr. Fuller was only lukewarm about it, and Mr. Claydon was dead against it, of course. How wrong they were can be seen today, when one looks at the Beattie shops under the direction of Mr. Kohnstann; one at Southgate, one at Lewisham, one in all the major cities of Britain and the main one at High Holborn. It is ironic when one reflects on those days and how the great name of Bassett-Lowke was allowed to drift away into oblivion.

As the days passed I began to realise that all the sparkle had gone out of the words Bassett-Lowke, more and more we were run by the accountant's office, and I spent many long hours in the office coping with their requirements, rather than getting among the customers and revitalising sales. There were brief periods, of course, when some of the old magic returned, and one of these followed a visit to the Model Railway Club Exhibition, where we were not exhibiting for financial reasons. On the Graham Farish stand they were showing some grand G.W.R. locos, one a Pannier 9700 class, the other the 6100 class Prairie. I was particularly impressed with the Pannier model and in April 1962 ordered quite a few because I knew they would help to stimulate sales which they duly did. Through these new models and the interest I had shown in them, I met Mr. Graham Farish, the Chairman and Managing Director of Graham Farish, and finally in August 1962 joined that company as General Manager, my interest and enthusiasm fired once more at the prospect of creating a new 00 trackwork system that was quite revolutionary.

My story is not quite finished, however. My successor to the management of 112, High Holborn, I had known for quite a time and he was a gifted modeller in his own right. Nevertheless, I believe he would agree with me, if I state that the pressures of management proved too much for him, especially with the 'bogey' that the showroom might not continue, and could close down when the lease expired. I know he experienced very great difficulties in maintaining the sales and the morale of the staff. Saturdays often found me outside No. 112, High Holborn; it still used to draw me, and I nearly always found an excuse to go inside, and have a few words with the staff and with my successor. A few months after I had joined Graham Farish, Mr. Farish showed me a letter he had received from Bassett-Lowke offering the shop stocks at London and Manchester at very reduced prices, and on which he asked my opinion. He agreed with me that in no way could we handle these products in our own set up, which was purely manufacturing and distributing to the model retail trade.

When Graham Farish who made full sized motor cruises as well as model railways moved to Poole in Dorset to be near water for testing their boats, I was unable to move there because of family reasons, and I joined the Beatties Organisation as a Director on November 1, 1964. It was whilst there that Colonel Beattie, the then Chairman and Managing Director, told me that Bassett-Lowke had offered him the same dregs of stocks in the showrooms, and we agreed one of us ought to see these before taking any decision. He decided to go up to Northampton to see Mr. Fuller, and on his return the next morning, he greeted me with the remark, 'I have bought Bassett-Lowke'. Of course, this was an exaggeration but he had bought the remains of the stocks at 112, High Holborn and at Manchester for a mere song on the understanding that he took over the remaining time left on the leases of the two shops, with a view to extension if he so wished. As soon as the deal was settled, Colonel Beattie asked me to go to 112, High Holborn and do my best to dispose of the remaining stock which having been bought cheaply could be offered at sale prices. It could have been history repeating itself, but it was not the same. Most of the sale items were goods Mr. Fuller had bought some years before and having been unsaleable then, remained unsold.

Walking through the door at 112, High Holborn was not the same either. The atmosphere had changed, and in my absence the office had been turned about and looked awful. Each time Colonel Beattie visited us at Holborn we had some disagreement. It was like two people trying to drive the same train and every time he answered the phone he would say, 'Bassett-Lowke-Beatties here' which irritated me so much that I could have screamed. How dare he call his enterprise Bassett-Lowke! As you may imagine I did not stay long with Beatties and soon after opened my own business with a Mr. Howell, calling it Howell Dimmock of Tottenham, a name which may be familiar. For the record, Dudley Enterprises did not die, it just lay sleeping over the years and appeared again a few years ago as the heading of a retail model business here in the Bournemouth area where I have now retired and sold up to write this story.

Bassett-Lowke continues today at Northampton, in a less diverse way. Mr. Fuller remained an executive right to the end of his days, in December 1980, and many times we conversed on the telephone in recent years whenever he thought I might be able to help him with regards to some item of model railway equipment and where it could be obtained. As many of you will know Beatties renewed the lease and after the improved management of Mr. Kohnstann made itself felt, they took over the shop next door to 112, High Holborn in addition and completely refurbished the insides of the two shops. They are fine emporium of models and model railway equipment, but it is not the same. The magic has gone and only the fine granite pillars each side of the window remain to remind us, especially the older ones, of what once used to be regarded as a 'shrine' to which all modellers flocked in their thousands to pay homage to the great Bassett-Lowke.

## EPILOGUE

At the end of the story such as the Bassett-Lowke saga, there are a great number of unanswered questions on which unfortunately no one is qualified to give an answer, but only an opinion. One I am asked constantly is whether Bassett-Lowke could be revived as a model train business comparable with the days of old. My opinion is not because the factors operating in the early days of Bassett-Lowke no longer exist. Before the First World War there were no models of any of the industrial machines of that era and certainly no locomotive models that looked anything like the prototype. Then suddenly a man of vision, Mr. W. J. Bassett-Lowke, organised the German toy manufacturers into making scale model loco-motives to his specifications and assuring them that a market existed for them before he even knew there was one. In my opinion Mr. Bassett-Lowke 'conned' these manufacturers into believing that a larger market existed than was the case, because when one reads the histories and accounts of some of these famous models, only 1500 or 2000 were made, which was nothing in terms of the production set-up in a factory. The market that existed in Mr. Bassett-Lowke's mind was com-posed of the wealthy and privileged classes, the landed gentry and industrialists of that day called by many 'County People'. In addition the models were so superb there was nothing to touch them and it took several decades before manufacturers could offer anything in competition.

Hornby was, of course, Bassett-Lowke's rival, not in quality but in quantity production of near-scale locos which suited the pockets of the middle classes better. The battle raged right up to the start of the Second World War between these two giants and as it became more and more possible for the mass-produced article to look nearer to scale, so Hornby leapt ahead. Today if one has the money to indulge in scale model railways, everything can be obtained without a concern such as Bassett-Lowke and the wonderful fine scale layouts and locos all over the country attest to this. There are more craftsmen than ever and the standard of work is higher than of yore. With the right contacts and money a unique fine scale layout can be achieved. As an example of this, one could quote Colonel Hoare's fine scale 0 gauge layout in Bournemouth, and, as one who has been privileged to see it, I can truthfully say that it is one of the most wonderful model railways that I have ever seen, not only scenically but for the fantastic locos and rolling stock, working signals etc.

People ask me about the magic myth that surrounds Bassett-Lowke. There is no doubt that Mr. Bassett-Lowke fostered the illusion. Even his name was not strictly his, his father was Mr. Lowke, his mother, Miss Bassett. The magic referred to existed more in the customer's mind. Even allowing for this, I think one must agree that all the projects fostered by Mr. Bassett-Lowke in total add up to something approaching magic, bearing all the facets in mind – the retail shops, the special Industrial Models section and the depart-ment that built all those wonderful layouts at seaside resorts, at Wembley and in the grounds of the stately homes of England. Mr. Bassett-Lowke was like a magnet, drawing to him all the best craftsmen, engineers, draughtsmen and designers. Mr. Henry Greenly's (dubbed 'the father of model railways') oft quoted saying is as true today as it was then, when referring to scale and accuracy: 'It all depends on the size of the engine driver's hat'. The magic really comes from the gift and ability of Mr. Bassett-Lowke to choose and select the greatest and finest and most gifted men for the job in hand and weld them all into a unit that literally mesmerised the whole model world.

Industrial Models are still made by Bassett-Lowke today, for instance, they installed the model railway at Tucktonia Christchurch, Bourne-mouth, but in my opinion the model was not up to the standard we have come to expect from Bassett-Lowke. Of course, not knowing the full facts perhaps the price would not allow for better models. When I left the Company the Industrial Model section was flourishing but as I have been given to understand, the increasing competition from Europe has made it more difficult for Bassett-Lowke to compete and may account for the situation that exists today, where this side of the business is very much reduced. This has also been aggravated by the fact that the recession in world trade has meant that fewer of the big com-panies and concerns have models made of their products today since this is one of the economies that has to be imposed in this present era. Fare-well then to an era which we shall never see again; for all we are left with are our memories and our catalogues and if you are lucky some-thing with the Bassett-Lowke stamp on it such as a vintage Bassett-Lowke loco.

Boys Own Paper - Nov-09.

# A DREAM COME TRUE

## Uncle Wynne's Christmas Story
### By W. J. BASSETT-LOWKE

CH-WHEEE!—the struggling safety valves of the magnificent 4-4-0 express engine could no longer stand the rising pressure of steam getting up. A double cloud of white, super-heated vapour rose to the roof, and so shrill was the whistle of its escape that people standing nearby on the platform put fingers to their ears to shut out that piercing sound. That is, all except Dick Ridgway.

He stood just by the huge, panting locomotive that was soon to pull its heavy load of passengers bound for London and the Christmas holidays, eagerly eyeing Jim, the fireman who, with cotton waste in hand, was going round with his oil-can giving her the final look-over.

Presently Jim climbed back on to the footplate. Wiping his sooty face with a clean corner of the cotton-waste, he glanced at the signals still set at danger, and then down at Dick, who stood, schoolcap perched on the back of his head, eagerly taking in all the details of the iron monster.

"Well, young feller-me-lad," he grinned, "off home for your Chris'mas pudding, I suppose."

"You bet!" answered Dick shortly.

He was absorbed in all the "gadgets" in the cab, the water and pressure gauges, valves of all descriptions, and the throttle lever, which seemed to have a special fascination.

"Wish I could come up there and look," he shouted above the din. "'Spect you do, son," answered the fireman, with a twinkle in his eye, "but Company's regulations, you know—nobody allowed in the cab without a special permit."

"Yes, I know," Dick sighed, then puffing out his chest, "but I'm going to be an engine driver myself one day, and then I'll show *all* the chaps who are keen on engines how to drive."

Jim smiled at such enthusiasm as he flung open the furnace door and proceeded to shovel coal into the leaping flames, for he was thinking how much more like hard work than fun a driver's or a fireman's job was.

"Take your seats, please," came the guard's shout, and Dick had reluctantly to leave his newly-found friend to board the train.

Determined to miss nothing he had got into the carriage nearest the engine, and as he leaned out he could see the red lights change to green as the signals fell with a thud. The guard's whistle blew once more, and then the first deep-throated chug of the exhaust was heard—she began to move.

Amid a shower of sparks the long train drew out of Peterborough—"London first stop."

Dick, settled in his corner, watched the whiteclad landscape flying by in the darkness, and the flurry of snow against the window. How glorious it would be, he thought, to have a real engine to drive, able to stop her or make her do sixty miles an hour just by your own skill.

Musing thus, his head began to droop, and soon he was fast asleep—to dream of his great ambition.

He seemed to hear the roaring of a mighty wind that, strangely puzzling at first, presently resolved itself into the rushing of the freezing, snow-laden air past the protecting roof of the locomotive cab.

Here, too, beside him, stood the grizzled driver, his cap pulled well down over his eyes fixed intently on the green lights of "distant" signals beckoning him on with their welcome message that the line was all clear. Jim, the fireman, clanging open the fire-hole door ever and anon, fed coal, shovel after shovelful, into the ever-hungry white-hot heart of the monster.

"Think you could do it?" presently asked Jim, "you watch."

Then Dick saw, for the first time, the amount of care necessary to keep the fire burning properly. Firing did not consist, as he had thought, in just opening the fire-hole door and throwing in shovelsful of coal now and again, just anyhow.

The locomotive boiler has to produce steam at a quicker rate than any other type of boiler that you could mention, of equal size; and the firing has, therefore, to be carried out scientifically if the engine is to do her work properly.

This means placing the coal in just the right positions on the fire-grate, whilst the engine rocks like a mad thing round curves, over points, ever and always hurtling on.

"Splendid!" cried Dick, after one of these firing jobs, admiration gleaming in his eye. Jim laughed—it was his job, and he took pride in doing it well.

"Do you ever have to watch the pressure and water gauges, too?" asked the ever inquisitive Dick. "Surely, sonny," answered Jim, "or I shouldn't know just when to fire her up." Dick now

WHAT DICK'S DREAM WAS MADE OF. THE COMPLETE L.N.E.R. 4-4-0 EXPRESS TRAIN.

turned his attention to that magical throttle lever which the driver kept so continually under his hand.

It controlled the steam from the boiler down to the cylinders, that much he knew. But adjusting the working of the engine by the reversing gear and the "cut-off," and manipulating the regulator and "cut-off" to meet every change of gradient, load and booked speed were quite beyond his idea of what an engine driver had to do.

When, therefore, the silent figure, watching the track ahead so closely, beckoned him to put a hand on the throttle lever and feel how she answered its slightest movement, he felt as though no more wonderful experience could ever happen to him.

Colder and colder it grew as the miles sped by. Over long bridges she roared and swayed; through blinding tunnels where the suction of the cab drew all the soot and cinders in on to the toilers in the cab.

Presently Dick began to feel so numb that not even the opening of the fire-hole releasing a shaft of warmth seemed to make the numbness less acute.

The sudden grinding of brakes brought him back to reality with a start. Gone were the gleaming gauges and levers of the locomotive cab.

Instead, the icicle encrusted window met Dick's eyes, still heavy with sleep. Hastily he rubbed them. Alas! it was all a dream after all. And now he noticed the gentle motion of the train, and the arc lamps that gleamed fitfully through the coating of mingled snow and ice that covered the window. London—they would arrive at King's Cross in a few minutes. What a short journey it had seemed. Had he really dreamed all that about driving the wonderful express, it was so real, it *must* have been true. Suddenly he had a bright idea—he'd ask Jim, the fireman, he'd know for sure then.

Slowly the long train slid over the points; up the platform; and then stopped.

Out jumped Dick to fling himself upon dear old Mums and the Pater, waiting for him on the platform, just opposite his carriage.

"Hullo, Mums! Hullo, Pater! I've had a ripping journey, but I've got a most important question to ask the engine driver."

Mr. Ridgway smiled down upon his son and was promptly hauled over to where Jim and the driver, their job done for the moment, lolled on the rail of the cab.

"Jim, do you really have to shovel a ton of coal an hour?" he asked eagerly. "Yes," answered the fireman slowly, "it would be about that." "And did I really ride on the footplate?"

"In your dreams, sonny, I guess," came the answer, with a wide grin. Dick turned away with a nodded good-bye. How strange that Jim should have said just that. There must have been something in it after all.

However, the business of loading luggage on to a taxi soon brought him back to reality, as also did his Pater's next remark.

"Dick, old son," he said, "Mums and I have decided to give you a model of some sort for Christmas, as you are so awfully keen on them. So we are going to take you to a very good shop in High Holborn to choose what you would like!"

Dick caught his breath. Would it be *the* shop, where they had such wonderful locos, he wondered.

Yes, there were the magic initials "B-L," symbol of really good models, made as well as they possibly could be just for the joy of it.

But the best was yet to come.

For there, standing out from all the splendid Pacifics, Atlantics, and Precursors, was, in miniature, the very train he had so lately longed to drive—had driven, in fact, as Jim had said, " in his dreams."

There it was—a regular 4—4—0 Express of the Great Northern Section of the London and North Eastern Railway—with four-coupled driving wheels, two bogie corridor coaches, one first and the other third class, all

A CLOSE-UP VIEW OF THE LOCO, SHOWING THE PERFECTION OF THE DETAIL WORK IN THIS MODEL.

painted the correct colours and exact in every detail. A bogie passenger brake van completed the train—as pretty a model as you could hope to find.

To add the finishing touch, its powerful clockwork motor could be reversed from cab or rail, and even be started automatically from the track by means of a special device.

Dick fell a victim to its charm immediately.

This and no other was what he had dreamed of and wanted for so long.

"This one, please, Pater," he cried, " and let's take it home *now* ! "

"A whole year's pocket money gone west," laughingly chaffed his father. But £50 could not have brought Dick such joy as this modest fifty shillings—all the set actually cost—did.

"A special 'Christmas Box, " said the man in the shop, who, of course, always knows.

And so that evening Dick, in the seventh heaven of delight, took his first lesson as a model engine driver and fireman—to say nothing of traffic superintendent—all rolled into one.

As the Pater remarked quietly to Mums :" There is not a doubt that the Bassett-Lowke people have hit on just the very thing for young people who are setting up as model loco engineers, and, of course, it is the very best way of beginning a new railway set. For Dick, it is his *dream come true* ! "

MESSRS. BASSETT-LOWKE LIMITED, the well-known model railway engineers, have just published their catalogue for the Christmas season. As usual, it is full of interest to all lovers of model locomotives and railways. It has been increased to 188 pages and describes many new models, among which may be mentioned the 2-6-0 L.M.S. and L.N.E.R. "Mogul" type locomotives, in 1¾-in. gauge, arranged for both steam and electric drive ; a range of new goods vehicles of the Southern Railway ; L.N.E.R. corridor coaches and brake thirds in gauges 0 and I ; and a fresh series of railway posters, reproduced in miniature from some of the latest ones issued by the leading railway companies. All who are wanting a suitable Christmas present for a boy of a mechanical turn of mind cannot do better than call at Messrs. Bassett-Lowke's London or Edinburgh shops, or send 6d. to their head office, Northampton, for a copy of this publication.

rly mag:
Dec: 1926

# TABLE A.

THE CLASSIC RANGE OF LOCOMOTIVES PRODUCED BY BING FOR BASSETT-LOWKE

| RAILWAY COMPANY | NAME OR CATALOGUE DESCRIPTION | TYPE | NUMBER | 1904 | 1905 | 1906 | 1907 | 1908 | 1909 | 1910 | 1911 | 1912 | 1913 | 1914 | 1915 | 1916 | 1917 |
|---|---|---|---|---|---|---|---|---|---|---|---|---|---|---|---|---|---|
| LNWR | 'Precursor' | 4-4-0 | 513 | | 1 | 1 | 1 | 1 | *11 | 1 | 1 | | | | | | |
| LNWR | 'Black Prince' | 4-4-0 | 1902 | | | | | | 123 | 0123 | 0123 | 0123 | 0123 | 0123 | 3 | 3 | 3 |
| LNWR | Precursor Tank | 4-4-2T | 44 | | | | | | | | 0101 | 0101 | 0101 | 0101 | | | |
| LNWR | 'George The Fifth' | 4-4-0 | 2663 | | | | | | | | 00 | 0101 | 012012 | 1212 | 22 | 22 | 22 |
| LNWR | 'Queen Mary' | 4-4-0 | 2664 | | | | | | | 00 | | | | | | | |
| LNWR | Goods Locomotive | 0-6-0 | 930 1269 | | | | | | | | 1 | 01 | 01 | 01 | 1 | 1 | |
| LNWR | Six-Coupled Tank | 4-6-2T | 2670 | | | | | | | | | 2 | 22 | 22 | 22 | 22 | 22 |
| LNWR LMS | 'Sir Gilbert Claughton' | 4-6-0 | 2222 5900 | | | | | | | | | | 1 | | | | |
| LNWR | 'Patriot' | 4-6-0 | 1914 | | | | | | | | | | | | | | |
| LMS | 'Prince of Wales' | 4-6-0 | 5600 | | | | | | | | | | | | | | |
| NLR | North London Tank Second Series | 4-4-0T | 88 | | | | | | 1 | 1 | 1 | | | | | | |
| LYR | Express Locomotive | 4-6-0 | 1510 | | | | | | | | | 1 | 1 | 1 | 1 | 1 | |
| CR | Dunalastair IV | 4-4-0 | 142 | | | | | | | 01 | 01 | 01 | 01 | 01 | 01 | | |
| MR LMS | Deeley Compound | 4-4-0 | 1000 1047 | | | | | | 1K | 1K1 | 1K1 | 01K1 | 01K1 | 01K1 | 11 | 1 | |
| MR | Express Locomotive | 4-4-0 | 999 | | | | | | | 0 | 0 | 0 | 0 | 0 | 0 | | |
| MR | Goods Locomotive | 0-6-0 | 3044 | | | | | | | | 1 | 1 | 1 | 1 | 1 | 1 | |
| MR | 2P Class Locomotive | 4-4-0 | 483 | | | | | | | | | | | | | | |
| MR | Tilbury Tank | 4-4-2T | 2178 | | | | | | | | | | | | | | |
| GNR | Atlantic | 4-4-2 | 1425 1442 | | | | | | | | 1 | 101 | 10101 | 10101 | 011 | 11 | 1 |
| GNR | Single | 4-2-2 | 266 | | | | | | | | 1 | 1 | 1 | 1 | 1 | 1 | |
| GNR | Condensing Tank | 0-6-2T | 190 | | | | | | | | | 1212 | 1212 | 22 | 22 | 22 | |
| NER | Passenger Tank | 0-4-4T | 441 | | | | | | | | | | | 01 | | | |
| GCR | 'Sir Alexander' | 4-4-0 | 1014 | 1 | 1 | 1 | 1 | 1 | 1 | 1 | 1 | | | | | | |
| GCR | Six-Coupled Tank | 4-6-2T | 165 | | | | | | | | | | 22 | 22 | 22 | 22 | 22 |
| GCR | 'Sir Sam Fay' | 4-6-0 | 423 | | | | | | | | | | | 11 | 1 | | |
| GWR | 'Sydney' | 4-4-0 | 3410 | 012 | 012 | 012 | 012 | 012 | 012 | 012 | 12 | *12 | 12 | 12 | 1 | 1 | |
| GWR | 'County of Northampton' | 4-4-0 | 3410 | | | | | | 123 | *123 | 123 | 123 | 123 | 123 | 3 | 3 | 3 |
| GWR | Tank Locomotive | 2-4-2T | 3611 | | | | | | | | 0 | 0 | 00 | | | | |
| GWR | 'City of Bath' | 4-4-0 | 3433 | | | | | | | | | | 0 | 00 | 0 | 0 | |
| GWR | 'Saint George' | 4-6-0 | 2923 | | | | | | | | | | 2 | 2 | | | |
| GWR | 'Titley Court' | 4-6-0 | 2936 | | | | | | | | | | | | | | |
| LBSCR | Passenger Tank | 4-4-2T | 11 | | | | | | | | 0101 | 0101 | 0101 | 0101 | | | |
| SECR | Express Locomotive | 4-4-0 | 516 | | | | | | | | | | 11 | 11 | 1 | 1 | |
| LSWR | Passenger Tank | 0-4-4T | 109 | | | | | | 01 | 01 | *01 | 01 | 01 | 1 | 1 | 1 | |
| LSWR | Express Locomotive | 4-6-0 | 736 | | | | | | | | | | | | | | |
| SR | 'King Arthur' | 4-6-0 | 453 | | | | | | | | | | | | | | |

**STEAM** GAUGE 0123 — START OF ADDITIONAL PRODUCTION RUN*

CLOCKWORK **KIT** **K**

*ELECTRIC*

**NOTE**
Bing-made locomotives and rolling-stock were imported by Bassett-Lowke from 1901 onwards. Several of these pre 1910 items are not included in these tables because they were not exclusive to Bassett-Lowke or designed to Bassett-Lowke's specification, e.g. the first 'Black Prince' series. Virtually all the locomotives listed above were built to the design of Henry Greenly.

Table based on Catalogues, Press Reports and Advertisements of the period.

| 1918 | 1919 | 1920 | 1921 | 1922 | 1923 | 1924 | 1925 | 1926 | 1927 | 1928 | 1929 | 1930 | 1931 | 1932 | 1933 | 1934 | 1935 | 1936 | 1937 | 1938 | 1939 |
|---|---|---|---|---|---|---|---|---|---|---|---|---|---|---|---|---|---|---|---|---|---|
|  | 0 |  | *0 | 0 | 0 | 0 |  |  |  |  |  |  |  |  |  |  |  |  |  |  |  |
|  | 01 | *0101 | 11 | 11 | 11 | 11 | 1 | 11 | 11 | 11 | 11 | 11 | 11 | 11 |  |  |  |  |  |  |  |
| 2 | 1201 | 1 | *11 | 11 | 11 | 1 | 1 | 1 | 11 | 11 |  |  |  |  |  |  |  |  |  |  |  |
| 22 | 22 | 22 | 22 |  |  |  |  |  |  |  |  |  |  |  |  |  |  |  |  |  |  |
|  | 1 | 1 | *1 | 1 | 1 |  | *1 | 1 | 1 | 1 | 1 | 1 | 1 | 1 | 1 | 1 | 1 | 1 | 1 | 1 | 1 |
|  |  | 1 | 1 | 1 |  |  |  |  |  |  |  |  |  |  |  |  |  |  |  |  |  |
|  |  |  |  |  |  | 0 | 0 |  |  |  |  |  |  |  |  |  |  |  |  |  |  |
|  |  |  | *01 | 01 | 01 | 1 | *1 | 1 | 1 | 1 | 1 | 1 | 1 | 1 | 1 | 1 | 1 | 1 |  |  |  |
|  |  |  | *0 | 0 | 0 | 0 | 0 | 0 | 0 | 0 | 0 | 0 |  |  |  |  |  |  |  |  |  |
|  |  |  | 1 | 1 | 1 | 1 | 1 | 11 | 11 | 11 | 11 | 11 |  |  |  |  |  |  |  |  |  |
|  |  | 1 | 1 | 1 | 1 | 1 | 1 | 1 | 1 | 1 | 1 | 1 |  |  |  |  |  |  |  |  |  |
| 1 | 11 | *001 | 011 | 011 | 11 | 11 | 1 | 11 | 11 | 11 |  |  |  |  |  |  |  |  |  |  |  |
|  | 1 |  |  |  |  |  |  |  |  |  |  |  |  |  |  |  |  |  |  |  |  |
| 22 | 1212 | 212 | *1212 | 1212 |  |  |  |  |  |  |  |  |  |  |  |  |  |  |  |  |  |
|  | 01 |  |  |  |  |  |  |  |  |  |  |  |  |  |  |  |  |  |  |  |  |
| 22 | 2 | 22 | 2 |  |  |  |  |  |  |  |  |  |  |  |  |  |  |  |  |  |  |
|  | 11 | 1 | 1 | *11 | 11 | 11 | 11 | 11 | 11 | 11 | 11 | 11 | 11 | 11 | 11 | 11 | 11 |  |  |  |  |
|  | 1 | 1 |  |  |  |  |  |  |  |  |  |  |  |  |  |  |  |  |  |  |  |
|  | 2 |  |  |  |  |  |  |  |  |  |  |  |  |  |  |  |  |  |  |  |  |
|  |  |  |  |  |  | 1 | 1 | 1 | 1 | 1 | 1 | 1 | 1 | 1 | 1 | 1 | 1 | 1 | 1 | 1 | 1 |
|  | 0101 | *0101 | 0101 | 0101 | 0101 | 0101 | 011 | 11 | 11 | 11 | 11 | 11 | 11 | 11 | 11 | 11 | 11 |  |  |  |  |
|  | 1 | 1 | 1 |  |  |  |  |  |  |  |  |  |  |  |  |  |  |  |  |  |  |
|  |  |  |  |  |  | 1 | 1 |  |  |  |  |  |  |  |  |  |  |  |  |  |  |
|  |  |  |  |  |  |  |  | 1 | 1 | 1 | 1 | 1 | 1 | 1 |  |  |  |  |  |  |  |

N.B. After the 1923 Grouping the following gauge 1 locos were offered suitably repainted:

| Precursor Tank | LMS | 6810 |
| 'George the Fifth' | LMS | 5320 |
| LBSCR Tank | SR | 596 |

Note. After 1925 Bassett-Lowke usually installed their own electric motors in place of the Bing electric and in some cases clockwork mechanisms. Except for this one digression the above list only contains items as produced by Bing.

# TABLE B.

BING 'FREELANCE' LOCOMOTIVES SOLD BY BASSETT-LOWKE

|  | STEAM | CLOCKWORK | ELECTRIC |
|---|---|---|---|
| Standard Tank No. 112 0-4-0T | GNR 1 Kit (grey) } 1911–14 | GNR 1, 2* 1912–14<br>MR 1, 2*<br>CR 1 1919 |  |

| STEAM | CLOCKWORK | ELECTRIC |
|---|---|---|
| LNWR<br>CR<br>MR } 0, 1 1921–29<br>GNR<br>NER | LNWR<br>CR<br>MR } 0, 1 1920–29<br>GNR<br>GWR<br>LMS<br>LNER | LNWR<br>CR } 0, 1 1920–29<br>MR<br>GNR |

| STEAM | CLOCKWORK | ELECTRIC |
|---|---|---|
| LNWR<br>CR<br>LMS } 1 1930–40<br>LNER<br>GWR | LNWR<br>CR<br>LMS } 1 1930–40<br>LNER<br>GWR | LNWR<br>CR<br>LMS } 1 1930–40**<br>LNER<br>GWR |

| 4-4-0 Tank | | |
|---|---|---|
|  | LNWR<br>CR<br>MR } 0 1920–26<br>GNR<br>NBR<br>GWR | |

| 4-4-0 Bogie Express | GWR 0, 1 1911<br>LNWR 1 1920<br>LMS<br>LNER } 0, 1 1924–26<br>GWR | | |
|---|---|---|---|

| Standard Express 4-4-0 | LNWR<br>CR<br>MR } 0 1922–29<br>GNR<br>GWR<br>LSWR | | |
|---|---|---|---|

| Standard Express 4-6-0 | LNWR<br>CR<br>MR } 2 1922–27<br>GNR<br>GWR | | |
|---|---|---|---|

* gauge 1 loco with extended axles
** between 1933–36 these locos were available with Walschaerts valve gear (from the gauge 0 'Royal Scot') and were fitted with a permag motor, these alterations were carried out by Bassett-Lowke.

# TABLE C.

CARETTE LOCOMOTIVES SOLD BY BASSETT-LOWKE

| GNR | Stirling Single | 4-2-2 | 776 | 3 | S | 1902 |
|---|---|---|---|---|---|---|
| LNWR | 'Lady of the Lake' | 2-2-2 | 531 | 12* | S | 1903 |
| NYC | Vauclain Compound | 4-4-0 | 2350 | 012 | C, S** | 1905 |
| GER | 'Claud Hamilton' | 4-4-0 | 1870 | 1 | S | 1905 |
| NER | Smith Compound | 4-4-0 | 1619 | 3 | S | 1906 |
| GNR | Atlantic | 4-4-2 | 251 | 01 | C, E | 1907 |
| LNWR/GNR/<br>MR | Peckett Saddle Tank | 0-4-0ST | 101 | 012* | C | 1907 |
| GER | 'Claud Hamilton' | 4-4-0 | 1870 | 2 | E | 1910 |

* gauge one loco with extended axles
** steam available in gauge one only
N.B. The GER and NER locos were available in either livery, although the gauge one NER was not listed. The gauge two version was made of non-ferrous castings to the same pattern and was only supplied in GER livery.

CARETTE LITHOGRAPHED LOCOMOTIVES SOLD BY BASSETT-LOWKE

| MET | Electric Loco | BO-BO | No 5 | 1 | E | 1907 |
|---|---|---|---|---|---|---|
| SECR | Motor Coach | – | No 1 | 01* | S | 1907 |
| SECR | Rail Coach | – | No 1 | 1 | S, E | 1909 |

| CR | 'Cardean' | 4-6-0 | 903 | 0 (floor) | C | 19 |
|---|---|---|---|---|---|---|
| GNR | Atlantic | 4-4-2 | 1442 | 0 | C, E | 19 |
| LNWR | 'George the Fifth' | 4-4-0 | 2663 | 0 | C, E | 19 |

* gauge one not available until 1910

# TABLE D.

MÄRKLIN LOCOMOTIVES SOLD BY BASSETT-LOWKE

| RAILWAY | NAME OR DESCRIPTION | WHEEL | NUMBER | GAUGE | PROPULSION | YEA INT |
|---|---|---|---|---|---|---|
| CLR | 2d Tube | 0-4-0 | (23) | 012 | C, E | 190 |
| LNWR | Charles Dickens | 2-4-0 | 955 | †012 | C, E, EB | 190 |
| L & M | Rocket | 0-2-2 | – | 1 | S | 190 |
| GNR | Suburban Tank | 0-4-4T | – | 0 | C | 190 |
| LNWR | Precursor* | 4-4-0 | 513 | 0 | C | 190 |
| LNWR | Precursor Tank | 4-4-2T | 44 | 01 | C, E, S†† | 190 |
| SR | Merchant Taylors | 4-4-0 | 910 | 0 | C, E | 193 |
| DR | German Pacific | 4-6-2 | – | 0 | E | 193 |
| NYC | Commodore Vanderbilt | 4-6-4 | – | 0 | E | 193 |
| ETAT | Mountain | 4-8-2 | – | 0 | E | 193 |
| SBB | Pantograph Electric | 4-6-2 | – | 0 | E | 193 |
| SBB | Pantograph Electric | 4-4-2 | – | 0 | E | 193 |
| SBB | Pantograph Electric | 0-4-0 | – | 0 | E | 193 |
| – | Der Adler | 2-2-2 | – | 0 | E | 193 |
| LMS | Jubilee | 4-6-0 | 5573 | 0 | C, E | 193 |
| LMS | Stanier Tank | 2-6-4T | 2524 | 0 | C, E | 193 |
| GWR | King George V | 4-6-0 | 6000 | 0 | C, E | 193 |
| LMS | Class 5** | 4-6-0 | – | 0 | C, E | 193 |

† gauge 0 not listed until 1907
†† steam in gauge 1 only
* listed with Bing gauge 1 Precursor
** Bassett-Lowke rebuild of 5573

# TABLE E.

BASSETT-LOWKE LOCOMOTIVES GAUGE 1

**High Pressure Steam**

| AMERICAN | Pacific | 4-6-2 | – | 192 |
|---|---|---|---|---|
| LNER | 'Flying Scotsman' | 4-6-2 | 4472 | 193 |
| LMS | 'Royal Scot' | 4-6-0 | 6100 | 193 |
| GWR | 'Titley Court'* | 4-6-0 | 2936 | 193 |
| LNER | Mogul** | 2-6-0 | 33 | 193 |
| SR | 'Lord Nelson' | 4-6-0 | 850 | 193 |
| LMS | 'Sir Gilbert Claughton'* | 4-6-0 | 5900 | 193 |

**Low Pressure Steam**

| LMS | Mogul | 2-6-0 | 13000/2943 | 192 |
|---|---|---|---|---|
| LNER | Mogul | 2-6-0 | 33/69 | 192 |
| LNER | Mogul (Kit of parts) | 2-6-0 | – | 193 |

**Electric**

| LMS | Mogul | 2-6-0 | 13000 | 192 |
|---|---|---|---|---|
| LNER | Mogul | 2-6-0 | 33 | 192 |
| LMS | 'Royal Scot' | 4-6-0 | 6100 | 193 |
| LMS | 'Princess Royal' | 4-6-2 | 6200 | 193 |
| LNER | 'Flying Scotsman' | 4-6-2 | 4472 | 193 |

**Clockwork**

| (Green) | Peckett saddle tank | 0-4-0ST | 810 | 192 |
|---|---|---|---|---|

* High pressure conversion of Bing product.
** High pressure version of low pressure model.

# TABLE F.

BASSETT-LOWKE LITHOGRAPHED GAUGE 0
(also included are the locos that are 'tab' constructed and painted)

| LMS/LNER GWR/SR | 'Duke of York' | 4-4-0 | 1927/1930/1931 | C, E | 192 |
|---|---|---|---|---|---|
| LMS/BR | Midland Compound | 4-4-0 | 1108/1063/1082 41109 | C, E | 192 |
| LMS | 'Royal Scot' | 4-6-0 | 6100 | C, E | 192 |

| | | | | | | |
|---|---|---|---|---|---|---|
| LMS | Watford Set | – | – | | E | 1930 |
| LMS/LNER | 'Princess Elizabeth' | 4-4-0 | 2265 | | C, E | 1932 |
| LNER/BR | 'Flying Scotsman' | 4-6-2 | 4472/103/60103 | | C, E | 1933 |
| LMS/LNER SR/BR | Standard Tank | 0-6-0T | 5374/78/947/335 68211 | | C, E | 1933 |
| LMS | Class 2P** | 4-4-0 | 601 | | C, E | 1936 |
| LMS/LNER BR | Goods Loco | 0-6-0 | 4256/1456/63871 64193 | | C, E | 1936 |
| LMS/LNER SR | Short Standard Tank | 0-4-0T | 25/36/63 | | C, E | 1937 |
| BR | 'Prince Charles' | 4-4-0 | 62453/62078 | | C, E | 1951 |

** Altered Compound. In 1935 the Compound was also available in GWR livery.

N.B. Several of these locos had their numbers applied after lithographing thereby allowing variety.

## BING LITHOGRAPHED LOCOMOTIVES SOLD BY BASSETT-LOWKE GAUGE 0

| | | | | | |
|---|---|---|---|---|---|
| MR | Midland Single | 4-2-2 | 650 | C, E | 1914 |
| LNWR | 'George the Fifth' | 4-4-0 | 2663* | C, E | 1919 |
| LNER | Ivatt Express | 4-4-0 | 504/4390 | C, E | 1924 |
| LMS | 'Royal Scot' | 4-6-0 | 6508 | C | 1928 |
| LNER | 'Flying Fox' | 4-6-0 | 4472 | C | 1928 |
| GWR | 'Windsor Castle' | 4-6-0 | 4460 | C | 1928 |
| SR | 'King Arthur' | 4-6-0 | 773 | C | 1928 |
| LMS | Goods Loco | 0-6-0 | 6508 | C | 1928 |
| LNER | Goods Loco | 0-6-0 | 4472 | C | 1928 |
| GWR | Goods Loco | 0-6-0 | 4460 | C | 1928 |
| SR | Goods Loco | 0-6-0 | 773 | C | 1928 |

* also available as 'Queen Mary' 2664 (overpainted and detailed)
    LMS    'George the Fifth'    5320
    LNER    504
    GWR    'City of Bath'    3433
    and also an 0-4-0 version

## BING TABLE TOP RAILWAY

| | | | | | |
|---|---|---|---|---|---|
| MR/LNWR LMS/LNER/GWR | | 2-4-0T | 513/3302/2536 | C, E | 1922 |
| LMS/LNER/GWR | | 2-4-0 | 504/3433 | C, E | 1925 |

# TABLE G.

## BASSETT-LOWKE GAUGE O LOCOMOTIVES

| | | | | | |
|---|---|---|---|---|---|
| LNWR | Precursor Tank | 4-4-2T | 44/6810 | C, E | 1921 |
| GNR/MR | Short Precursor Tank | 0-4-0T | – | C | 1921 |
| GWR/ ? – | Peckett Saddle Tank | 0-4-0ST | 4481/1017 | C | 1924 |
| CR | Dunalistair | 4-4-0 | 142 | C, E | 1925 |
| LMS | Mogul | 2-6-0 | 13000/2700 | C, E, S | 1925 |
| LNER | Mogul | 2-6-0 | 33/1864 | C, E, S | 1925 |
| GWR | Mogul | 2-6-0 | 4431 | C, E, S | 1925 |
| SR | Mogul | 2-6-0 | 866 | C, E, S | 1926 |
| LMS | Goods Loco | 0-6-0 | 4072 | C, E | 1927 |
| LNER | Goods Loco | 0-6-0 | 1448 | C, E | 1927 |
| GWR | †Pendennis Castle | 4-6-0 | 4079 | C/W | 1930 |
| (Red/Green Black) | Enterprise (also Kit) | 4-4-0 | 6285* | S | 1931 |
| LMS/BR | Stanier Mogul (also Kit) | 2-6-0 | 2945/42980 | C, E, S | 1934 |
| LMS | 'Princess Royal' | 4-6-2 | 6200 | C, E | 1935 |
| ‡SR | Lord Nelson | 4-6-0 | 850 | C, E | 1935 |
| LMS | 'Princess Elizabeth' | 4-6-2 | 6201 | C, E | 1936 |
| LMS | Turbine | 4-6-2 | 6202 | C, E | 1936 |
| LMS | 'Conqueror'/ 'Victory' | 4-6-0 | 5701/5712 | C, E | 1936 |
| LNER | 'Arsenal'/ 'Melton Hall' | 4-6-0 | 2848/2838 | C, E | 1936 |

| | | | | | |
|---|---|---|---|---|---|
| LNER | 'Silver Link'** | 4-6-2 | 2509 | C, E | 1936 |
| LMS | 'Royal Scot' | 4-6-0 | 6100 | C, E | 1937 |
| LMS | 'Coronation'/ 'Duchess of Gloucester' | 4-6-2 | 6220/6225 | C, E | 1937 |
| GWR | Prairie Tank | 2-6-2T | 6105 | C, E | 1937 |
| LT | Underground Set | – | – | E | 1937 |
| LMS/LNER SR/BR/ (Black) | Super Enterprise | 4-6-0 | 5524/2871/851 45295/2495 | S | 1937 |
| LMS | 'Duchess of Montrose' | 4-6-2 | 6232/46232 | C, E | 1939 |
| GWR | 'Pendennis Castle' | 4-6-0 | 4079 | C, E | 1939 |
| LMS | Suburban Tank | 2-6-2T | 78 | C, E | 1940 |
| LMS | Suburban Tank | 2-6-4T | 2603 | C, E | 1940 |
| BR | 'Royal Scot' (rebuilt) | 4-6-0 | 46100 | C, E | 1953 |
| GWR | 'Spitfire' (Castle Class) | 4-6-0 | 5071 | E | 1955 |
| GWR | Suburban Tank | 2-6-2T | 6100 | E | 1955 |
| BR | 'Britannia' | 4-6-2 | 70000 | E | 1958 |
| BR/GE | 'Deltic' | Co-Co | | E | 1959 |
| BR | Class 5MT | 4-6-0 | 45126 | E | 1959 |
| BR | Class 8F | 2-8-0 | 48209 | E | 1960 |
| GWR | 'King Richard 1' | 4-6-0 | 6027 | E | supplied |
| GWR | Pannier Tank | 0-6-0PT | 5765 | E | to |
| GWR | Dock Tank | 0-4-0T | 1106 | E | order |

  * Phone number of Bassett-Lowke shop in High Holborn.
** Also available as:  'Quicksilver'    2510
                          'Silver King'    2511
                          'Silver Fox'    2512
                          'Dominion of Canada'    4489
                          'Empire of India'    4490
                          'Sir Nigel Gresley'    4498
† Using existing GWR mogul parts
‡ Rebuilt from lithographed 'Royal Scot'

# TABLE H.

## LEEDS LOCOMOTIVES SOLD BY BASSETT-LOWKE

| | | | | | | |
|---|---|---|---|---|---|---|
| CR | Pickersgill Express | 4-4-0 | 77 | 0 | C, E | 1922 |
| GWR | 'County of Middlesex'* | 4-4-0 | 3800 | 0 | C, E | 1922 |

* other Counties also available.

# TABLE I.

## CARETTE COACHES

| | | | | | | |
|---|---|---|---|---|---|---|
| 13 | 2 | 1 | 01 | GNR | Coach | |
| | | 2 | 0123 | LNWR | " | |
| | | 3 | 01 | MR | " | |
| | | 4 | 012 | GWR | " | |
| | | 5 | 3 | NER | " | |
| | | 6 | | ——— | | |
| | | 7 | | ——— | | |
| | | 8 | 01 | LSWR | " | |
| | | 9 | | ——— | | |
| | | 10 | 01 | LNWR | Dining Saloon | |
| | | 11 | 01 | GNR | 'Clemenson' Coach | |
| | | 12 | 012 | LNWR | " | " |
| | | 13 | 01 | MR | " | " |
| | | 14 | | ——— | | |
| | | 15 | | ——— | | |
| | | 16 | | ——— | | |
| | | 17 | | ——— | | |
| | | 18 | | ——— | | |
| | | 19 | | ——— | | |

| | | | | |
|---|---|---|---|---|
| | 20 | | —— | |
| | 21 | 01 | GNR | Short Coach |
| | 22 | 01 | LNWR | " " |
| | 23 | 01 | MR | " " |
| | 24 | 01 | GWR | " " |
| 13 3 | 1 | 01 | GNR | Brake Van |
| | 2 | 0123 | LNWR | " " (incorrectly numbered in Gauge 1 as 1334.) |
| | 3 | 01 | MR | " " |
| | 4 | 012 | GWR | " " |
| | 5 | 3 | NER | " " |
| | 6 | | —— | |
| | 7 | | —— | |
| | (8) | 01 | LSWR | " " |
| | 9 | 01 | LNWR | TPO " |
| | 10 | | —— | |
| | 11 | 01 | GNR | 'Clemenson' Brake Van |
| | 12 | 012 | LNWR | " " " (also 'Clemenson' Brake Third) |
| | 13 | 01 | MR | " " " |
| | 14 | | —— | |
| | 15 | | —— | |
| | 16 | | —— | |
| | 17 | | —— | |
| | 18 | | —— | |
| | 19 | | —— | |
| | 20 | | —— | |
| | 21 | 01 | GNR | Short Brake Van |
| | 22 | 01 | LNWR | " " " |
| | 23 | 01 | MR | " " " |
| | 24 | 01 | GWR | " " " |

# TABLE J.

CARETTE GOODS WAGONS

| | | | | |
|---|---|---|---|---|
| 13 4 | 1 | 012 | LNWR | 10 Ton Goods Brake Van (Crewe) |
| | 2 | 012 | MR | 10 Ton Goods Brake Van |
| | 3 | 012 | MR | Cattle Truck |
| | 4 | 012 | LNWR | Covered Goods Wagon |
| | 5 | 012 | LNWR | Refrigerator Van |
| | 6 | 012 | LNWR | Open 7 Ton Goods Wagon |
| | 7 | 012 | MR | Open Goods Wagon |
| | 8 | 012 | GREAVES | Lime or Cement Wagon |
| | 9 | 012 | —— | Tar Wagon |
| | 10 | 012 | LNWR | Timber Truck in Pairs |
| | 11 | 012 | ANGLO-AMERICAN | Oil Wagon |
| | 12 | 012 | GNR | Covered Goods Wagon |
| | 13 | 012 | BASSETT-LOWKE | Private Owner's 10 Ton Open Goods Wagon 012   012   0 (RED/BROWN/GREY) |
| | 14 | 012 | GWR | Brake Van |
| | 15 | 012 | GWR | Covered Goods Wagon |
| | 16 | 012 | GWR | 8 Ton Open Goods Wagon |
| | 17 | 012 | MR | Bogie Coal Wagon |
| | 18 | 01 | W. H. HULL | Private Owner's 10 Ton Open Goods Wagon |
| | 19 | 1 | TRUE FORM BOOT CO | Private Owner's Covered Wagon |
| | 20 | 012 | GWR | Refrigerator Van |
| | 21 | 012 | GNR | 10 Ton Brake Van |
| | 22 | 012 | GNR | 8 Ton Banana Wagon |
| | 23 | 012 | GNR | 15 Ton Open Goods Wagon |
| | 24 | 012 | GNR | 5 Ton Covered Fish Wagon |
| | 25 BL | 01 | BASSETT-LOWKE | Private Owner's Covered Wagon |
| | 25 M | 01 | COLMAN'S | Private Owner's Covered Wagon (Mustard Traffic) |
| | 25 S | 01 | COLMAN'S | Private Owner's Covered Wagon (Starch Traffic) |
| | 26 | 012 | LNWR | Fruit Van |

| | | | | |
|---|---|---|---|---|
| | 27 | 012 | LNWR | Horse Box |
| | 28 | 01 | CITY OF BIRMINGHAM | Open Coal Wagon |
| | 29 | 012 | LNWR | Open Carriage Truck |
| | 30 | 01 | BIRMINGHAM CORPORATION | Coke Wagon |
| | 31 | 01 | NBR | 8 Ton Open Wagon |
| | 32 | 01 | GCR | 8 Ton Open Wagon |
| | 33 | 01 | MR | Loco Coal Wagon |
| | 34 | 01 | LYR | Ballast Wagon |
| | 35 | 01 | LB & SCR | Open Wagon with Tarpaulin and Bar |
| | 36 | 01 | MR | Ventilated Covered Wagon |
| | 37 | | | |
| | 38 | 01 | MR | Ballast Wagon |
| | 39 | 012* | NER | Boiler Trolley (with boiler) |
| | 40 | | | |
| | 41 | | | |
| | 42 | 01 | MR | E.D. Ballast Wagon |
| | 43 | 01 | CR | Low Sided Wagon |
| | 44 | 01 | LNWR | Gunpowder Van |
| | 45 | 01 | LNWR | Motor Car Wagon |
| | 46 | 01 | GER | 10 Ton Open Wagon |
| | 47 | 01 | LNWR | 10 Ton Goods Brake Van (Camden) |
| | 48 | 0 | LNWR | Covered Goods Wagon |
| | 49 | 0 | LNWR | Loco Coal Wagon |

* Re-gauged

# TABLE K.

THE BING '1921' SERIES LITHOGRAPHED COACHES FOR BASSETT-LOWKE

| RAILWAY | TYPE OF CARRIAGE | GAUGE | YEAR OF INTRO |
|---|---|---|---|
| LNWR | 1st class coach & 3rd brake | 0 & 1 | 1921 |
| GWR (lake) | " " | 0 & 1 | 1922 |
| MR | " " | 0 & 1 | 1922 |
| LMS | " " | 0 & 1 | 1926 |
| LNER | " " | 0 & 1 | 1926 |
| SR* | " " | 0 & 1 | 1926 |
| GWR (cream/brown) | " " | 0 | 1928 |
| SR | " " | 0 | 1929 |

* Bassett-Lowke repaint of GWR (lake).
  Also available was a Southern Electric Set, this too was a repaint with a motor bogie fitted.

# TABLE L.

BASSETT-LOWKE SERIES LITHOGRAPHED COACHES

| RAILWAY | TYPE OF CARRIAGE | GAUGE | YEAR OF INTRO |
|---|---|---|---|
| LMS | Suburban Electric Train (Watford Set) | 0 | 1930 |
| LMS | 1st class Corridor Coach | 0 | 1931 |
| LMS | 3rd/brake " " | 0 | 1931 |
| GWR | 1st class Corridor Coach | 0 | 1931 |
| GWR | 3rd/brake " " | 0 | 1931 |
| LMS | 1st/3rd Suburban Coach | 0 | 1931 |
| LMS | 3rd/brake " " | 0 | 1931 |
| LMS | TPO | 0 | 1933 |
| LNER | 1st class Corridor Coach | 0 | 1933 |
| LNER | 3rd/brake " " | 0 | 1933 |
| SR | 1st class Corridor Coach | 0 | 1934 |
| SR | 3rd/brake " " | 0 | 1934 |

LITHOGRAPHED COACHES USING CARETTE TOOLING

| RAILWAY | TYPE OF CARRIAGE | GAUGE | YEAR OF INTRO |
|---|---|---|---|
| LNWR | 12 wheeled Diner | 0 | 1921 |
| LMS | 12 wheeled Diner | 0 & 1 | 1924 |
| LMS | TPO | 0 & 1 | 1923 |

# APPENDIX I

## Wenman Joseph Bassett-Lowke

Born   December 27, 1877.
Died   October 21, 1953.
Father – Joseph Thomas Lowke. Mother – Eliza (nee Goodman.)
Brother – Harold.
Grandfather – Tom Lowke.

Address at birth – 13, Kingswell Street, Northampton.

Father's business – Agricultural Engineer, founded by Abraham Bassett and later owned by his stepson Joseph Tom Lowke.

Following Tom Lowke's death, his widow went, with her son Joseph Tom, to live as housekeeper to the widower Abraham Basset, whom she later married.

Educated at All Saints Commercial School, and Kingswell Street College, until 13 years old, attended evening classes in advanced Engineering Drawing.

Apprenticed by his father, but later felt a desire to become an architect, spent 18 months 1894–1895, in a local architect's office (name not known) but decided this was not to his taste.

Returned to the family business, where his father permitted him to build miniature steam engines. In this he was joined by his father's bookkeeper, Harry Foldar Robert Franklin.

The venture into the business of model engineering continued through the years of apprenticeship, even in the two years student apprenticeship with Messrs. Crompton Parkinson of Chelmsford during which time he was attached to their outdoor staff on site work at Hunslet Goods Yard and York Corporation Electricity Works. According to notes made by W. J. Bassett-Lowke, not later than 1910, the apprenticeship was during 1901–1902, but it is hard to equate this with the intense developments following his visit to the Paris Exhibition in 1900. Notes made by W. J. Bassett-Lowke in 1920, put the period as 1898–1900.
Married Florence Jane Jones 1917.
Lived at 13, Kingswell Street until marriage, then at 78, Derngate until 1927, when 'New-Ways' was completed.
Member –   Institute of Locomotive Engineers 1911.
          – Junior Institute of Engineers 1904.
          – Design and Industries Association.
          – Institute of Amateur Cinematographers, later Vice-President.
Founder Member Rotary Club of Northampton, President 1934.
Fellow of the Royal Society of Arts.
Founder and Director of Northampton Repertory Theatre.
First President Model Engineers' Trade Association.
Member of Kingsley Masonic Lodge 1907.
Member of Labour Party in 1912 through membership of the Fabian Society.
Town Councillor for St. Lawrence Ward 1930 and for St. Georges' Ward from 1932.
Chairman of the Baths Committee.
Deputy Chairman Town Planning and Development Committee.
Member of Housing, Library and Finance Committees.
Alderman in 1945.
Resigned from Council in 1952.
Author (with George Holland) of 'Ships and Men' 1950.
Author of 'Model Railway Handbook' 1906.
Joint producer and co-editor (with Henry Greenly) of the magazine 'Model Railways and Locomotives' 1909
Founded Miniature Railways of Gt Britain Ltd 1904.
Opened London branch at 257 High Holborn 1908. (Moved to 112 High Holborn in 1910).
Created Winteringham Ltd 1908.
Formed Bassett-Lowke & Co. into Limited Liability Co. 1909.
Founded Narrow Gauge Railways Ltd 1911.
Re-created Ravenglass & Eskdale Railway 1915.

## Harry Foldar Robert Franklin

Born 1875   Died January 1965.
Born at Chesterfield. The family moved to Bedford when he was quite young. Thence, some years later there was another move to Northampton where Franklin Senior joined the firm of accountants A. C. Palmer & Co. His son joined him in this employment when he left school.

Palmers were called in to J. T. Lowke & Sons to set up an accounting system, after which young Harry was retained to act as bookkeeper. It was then he met the young Bassett-Lowke and shared his interest in models, cycling and photography – thus starting a life-long friendship and business partnership.

In contrast to Wenman, Harry was a retiring, almost shy, personality quite happy to be concerned with the day-to-day activities of the business to leave his partner to travel and build up business connections and deal with all publicity matters.

Again in contrast, Wenman had not time to continue practical model-making or model-running whereas Harry maintained his interest in steam power. At his home in Leicester Parade, Northampton, he installed a 2″ gauge model railway and, in later years, had a 10¼″ gauge track laid in the grounds of his intended retirement home at Radwell in Bedfordshire.

For a number of years he owned a 'White' steam car, ceasing to run it only when replacement parts were unobtainable and even the expertise of the Bassett-Lowke works could not keep it in efficient running order. The car, registration No. HH 1878 is now in the vintage collection at Beaulieu.

A third contrasting feature in Harry's make up was that, unlike Wenman, he was prepared to undertake direct responsibility for manufacturing and thus set up 'Ships Models' in 1921. (Bassett-Lowke S.M. Ltd.).

When he retired in 1938 'Ships Models' continued as a separate entity although more directly supervised by Bassett-Lowke, whose new Director, Captain Lockhart, took a special position until recalled to the Navy in 1938.

'Ships Models' became a wholly owned subsidiary company of Bassett-Lowke, and eventually the name was changed to Bassett-Lowke (S.M.) Ltd.

In the General Strike of 1926 Harry demonstrated his loyalty to the Government by driving a train on the L.M.S. Northampton to Euston run. In this he was joined by his son, Harry, who acted as fireman.

Harry Senior had another interest – a steam launch *Iolanthe* which he bought at Brentford and navigated along the Grand Union Canal, via Blisworth branch to Becketts Park, Northampton. It was kept in a boathouse at Midsummer Meadow and, in the Great War, was used on many occasions to take parties of wounded service men on trips along the River Nene.

Harry was very active in this field and also took parties to various entertainments in his steam car.

# APPENDIX II

## Bassett-Lowke Ltd.

Authorised Share capital 20,000 Ordinary Shares of £1 each.

At the first meeting of the newly registered company on March 22, 1910. John George Sears, Boot Manufacturer, was elected as Chairman. Wenman Joseph Bassett-Lowke as Managing Director and Harry Foldar Robert Franklin as Director. The above were the only members present.

On the same day shares were allotted to–

| | |
|---|---|
| W. J. Bassett-Lowke | |
| H. F. R. Franklin | |
| J. G. Sears | |
| E. K. Bedington | Manufacturer |
| W. P. Bedington | ” ” |
| F. C. Franklin | Brother of H. F. R. F. |
| W. H. Heggs | Gentleman |
| E. W. Hobbs | London Manager |
| Mrs. A. E. Jones | Sister in law of Florence, later Mrs. Bassett-Lowke |
| J. W. Whitton | Gentleman |
| T. D. Lewis | Boot Manufacturer |
| H. A. Bassett-Lowke | Brother of W. J. |
| Mrs. Eliza Lowke | Mother of W. J. |
| J. T. Lowke | Father of W. J. |

Henry Greenly
E. Lewis              Boot Manufacturer. Later Chairman Bassett-Lowke Ltd
F. Green           Engineer. Works foreman of Bassett-Lowke Ltd
A. C. Palmer     Accountant

Further applications for shares continued at intervals over many years. Some of particular interest were –

Ernest Hull, the Birmingham toy importer and retailer; C. W. Bartholomew owner of the 15″ gauge railway at Towcester which inspired W. J. to manufacture in that size; R. Procter Mitchell who was so much involved with 15″ gauge railways; J. A. Holder who had a 9½″ gauge railway at Broome; George Carette the toy manufacturer and supplier of many special B.L. items; Paul Josephthal, partner of Carette; Florence Jane wife of W. J. B. L.; G. P. Keen who later became Chairman of B.L.; H. C. Foreman, London Manager; Beatrice Foreman (formerly Mrs. H. F. R. Franklin); Cyril Derry who became, and remained Chairman of B.L. for 31 years; Theophile Carette to whom his father's shares were transferred; V. B. Harrison who became a Director of B.L. for a short time and whose experience with gauge 1 steam models was so valuable to B.L.; A. B. Lockhart whose untimely death cut short his general management of B.L.; R. Bindon Blood who produced at Winteringham's a fine series of gauge 0 models.

In 1930 there was an issue of 1,000 £1 5% Preference Shares which were mostly taken up by existing shareholders.

## The newly Incorporated Company

Bassett-Lowke was incorporated as a Limited Liability Company on March 11, 1910 when A. C. Palmer & Co were appointed Auditors, Dennis, Faulkner & Allsop as Solicitors and Alfred Harmer as Secretary.

Henry Greenly was given a four year contract as Consulting Engineer (resigned January 30, 1913).

The first General Meeting was held on April 29, 1910.

The first Annual General Meeting was held on September 30, 1910.

On October 21, 1910 Bassett-Lowke and Harry Franklin were deputed to represent the Company in the Miniature Railways of Great Britain, Ltd.

On February 27, 1912 F. J. Allsop was appointing Secretary in succession to Alfred Harmer. H. F. R. Franklin was designated as Cashier and Bookkeeper at £5 per week. E. W. Hobbs' salary as London Manager was fixed at £3.5s.0d. per week plus commission.

Malaret was appointed as sole Paris Agent.

The London Shop to be instructed to remain open until 6 p.m. on Saturdays (7.30 other days).

On April 1, 1912 the salaries of W. J. B. L. and H. F. R. F. were fixed at £12.10s.0d. per month plus commission.

The London Shop to close at 2.30 p.m. on Saturdays.

April 25, 1915. Tools of steam loco. dept. transferred to Winteringham.

October 21, 1915 B.L. assumed 'controlling influence' over Winteringham.

Nett profits for the years 1910 to 1917 were steady, ranging from the lowest in 1914 of £939.17s.0d. to £2529.0s.9d. in 1918.

Dividends of 5% were paid, excepting 1914 when no dividend was declared. Ten per cent was paid in 1917 and 1918.

Dividends remained generally at these modest levels until the busy years following the Second World War when for a few years nett profits permitted a more generous distribution.

## APPENDIX III

## Principal Exhibition Class Ships made by Bassett-Lowke

Until 1908 the company showed little interest in ship models. Imported products were sold but no attempt was made to manufacture until the advent of E. W. Hobbs as manager of the new London shop. There was an almost immediate burst of activity resulting in an extensive range of sailing and power boats being produced. These were all relatively simple models designed for practical use on the water. The fine quality exhibition models were to evolve later.

The list that follows is of exhibition and showcase models unless otherwise described.

1909
'NIMROD' Exploration ship. Scale 1:48. Made for a private client for presentation to Sir Ernest Shackleton.
Fleet of waterline models of warships scale 1:1200 for the Navy League.

1910
'DEUTSCHLAND' Scale 1:96 Hamburg Amerika Line

1911
Bucket Dredger Scale 1:48 S.F.D. Ltd.
'OLYMPIC' Scale 1:96 White Star Line

1913
Fleet of manned working models of warships ranging in size from 12 to 20 feet long for Imperial Services Exhibition at Earls Court.
'CARMANIA' Scale 1:120 Cunard Line
'AQUITANIA' Scale 1:96 Cunard Line

1914
'QUEEN MARY' Scale 1:96 Steam-powered working model for Lord Howard de Walden
'ISHERWOOD' Steamer. Scale 1:96 for the Inventor
'ANDES' (later 'ATLANTIS') Scale 1:192 R.M.S.P. Co.

1915–1918
No exhibition quality work was done during the First World War but a very large number of waterline models of warships of all nations was made for the British Admiralty for recognition training.

1919
'NONESUCH' Charter carrying ship c. 1670 Scale 2½″ to the foot for the Hudson Bay Co. Canada
'FRANCONIA' Scale 1:144 Cunard Line

1920
'STUYVESANT' Scale 1:20 Nederlandsche Sheepsbouw-Maatschapy
'FRANCE' (Ten models) Scale 1:96 Compagnie Generale Transatlantique

At this time Winteringham closed down their model boats department and all future production was carried out by the newly formed SHIPS MODELS Company created by H. F. R. Franklin.

1921
'OLYMPIC' Scale 1:44 White Star Line
'PARIS' Scale 1:96 Compagnie Generale Transatlantique
'OHIO' Scale 1:96 R.M.S.P. Co.
'ALMANZORA' Scale 1:96 R.M.S.P. Co.

1922
'MASSILIA' Scale 1:96 Compagnie Sud Atlantique
'ARCADIA' Scale 1:96 R.M.S.P. Co.
'ORCA' Scale 1:96 R.M.S.P. Co.

1923
'ORDUNA' Scale 1:96 R.M.S.P. Co.
'MAJESTIS' Scale 1:96 White Star Line

1924
'MAURETANIA' Scale 1:96 Cunard Line
'BERENGARIA' Scale 1:96 Cunard Line

1925
Harwich-Zeebrugge Train Ferry Scale 1:384 L.N.E.R.
'CUTTY SARK' Scale 1:120 for private client

1926
'ASTURIAS' Scale 1:96 R.M.S.P. Co.
'SHRIMP' Scale 1:120 Lord Louis Mountbatten

1927
'CERAMIC' Scale 1:96 White Star Line
'ILE DE FRANCE' Scale 1:96 Compagnie Generale Transatlantique

1928
'DORIC' Scale 1:96 White Star Line
'ALCANTARA' Scale 1:96 R.M.S.P. Co.
'JOHAN van OLDENBARNEVELT' Scale 1:96 Netherlands Royal Mail Line

1929
H.M.S. 'HOOD'  Scale 1:120  Steam powered models for Lord Howard de Walden and Maharajah of Patiala
'CARNARVON CASTLE'  Scale 1:96  3 models for Union Castle Line
'BERENGARIA'  Scale 1:192  Half-section model for Cunard Line

1930
Harwich–Zeebrugge Train Ferry  To a larger scale than the 1925 model, this was a working display for the Antwerp Exhibition by the L.N.E.R. Co.
'EMPRESS OF BRITAIN'  21 ft long waterline model for the Canadian Pacific float in the Lord Mayor's Show
'LLANGIBBY CASTLE'  Scale 1:120  3 models for Union Castle Line
'EMPRESS OF BRITAIN'  Scale 1:96  Canadian Pacific Co.

1931
'BERMUDA'  Scale 1:48  Shaw, Savill & Albion
'L'ATLANTIQUE'  Scale 1:100  29 models for Chargeurs Re-unis, Paris
'EMPRESS OF BRITAIN'  Series of models at scale of 1:6 of main rooms and cabins  Canadian Pacific Co.
'J. SEBASTIAN de ELCANO' training ship  Scale 1:50  Camper & Nicholson Ltd.
'L'ATLANTIQUE'  Scales 1:48 and 1:92  Compagnie Sud-Atlantique

1932
'CHAMPLAIN'  Scales 1:600 and 1:1200  200 of each waterline models  French Lines
'MARNIX van St. ALDEGONDE'  Scale 1:192  Nederlands Royal Mail Line
'STRATHMORE'  Scale 1:144  P. & O. Co.
'WINCHESTER CASTLE'  Scale 1:96  3 models  Union Castle Line
'GEORGIC'  Scale 1:96  Cunard White Star Line

1933
'BRITANNIC'  Scale 1:96.  Cunard White Star Line
Cabin models of Heysham–Ulster route ships.  Scale 1:66 for the L.M.S. Rly. Co.
'JOHAN Van OLDENBARNEVELT'  Scale 1:48  Stoomvart Maatschappij Nederlands
'ISLE of SARK'  Scale 1:48  Southern Railway

1934
'ORCADES'  Scale 1:96  P. & O. Co.
'ATLANTIS'  Scale 1:48  R.M.S.P. Co.
'CHAMPLAIN'  Scale 1:96  French Lines
'COLOMBIE'  Scale 1:96  French Lines
GRAND UNION CANAL  Scale 1:48 Working model of a short section with locks  Grand Union Canal Co.

1935
'CAPETOWN CASTLE'  Scale 1:96  Union Castle Line
'STRATHMORE'  Scale 1:96  8 models for P. & O. Co.
'NORMANDIE'  Scale 1:1200  1000 waterline models French Lines
'NORMANDIE'  Scale 1:100  Waterline model with interior lighting  French Lines
'QUEEN MARY'  Scale 1:48  Cunard White Star Line

1936
'QUEEN MARY'  Scale 1:96  Cunard White Star Line
'AWATEA'  Scale 1:96  New Zealand Shipping Co.
'ARANDORA STAR'  Scale 1:48  Blue Star Line

1937
'ENDEAVOUR' Yacht  Scale 1:96  T.O.M. Sopwith
BRITISH MERCHANT NAVY  Scale 1:600  Panoramic display for the Paris Exhibition.  Shipping Consortium
'STRATHMORE'  Scale 1:144  P. & O. Co.

1938
'HAMPTON FERRY' Train ferry  Scale 1:96  Southern Rly
'PHILANTE' Motor Yacht  Scale 1:48  T.O.M. Sopwith
'DOMINION MONARCH'  Scale 1:96 3 models  Shaw, Savill & Albion
'STRATHMORE'  Scale 1:96 3 models  P. & O. Co.
'STRATHAIRD'  Scale 1:9 3 models  P. & O. Co.
'MAURETANIA'  Scale 1:64  Cammell-Laird Co.
H.M.S. 'HOOD'  Scale 1:64  John Brown, Clydebank
'QUEEN ELIZABETH'  Scale 1:48 Half model mounted on a panel with historic Cunard and White Star ships for the 1938 New York World Fair.  Cunard White Star Line

'ORCADES'  Scale 1:96  P. & O. Co.
'ORION'  Scale 1:96  P. & O. Co.

1939
'ANDES'  Scale 1:96  R.M.S.P. Co.
'DOMINION MONARCH'  Scale 1:96  Shaw, Savill & Albion
'ORANJE'  Scale 1:192  Stoomvaart Maatschappij

1939–1945
Quite early in the Second World War Ships Models Ltd. was heavily engaged in the production of waterline models of warships of many nationalities for the recognition and tactical training of Naval and Air Force personnel. Orders continued right through the war years and were supplemented by contracts for Observation Mirrors, various types of bridging (including the famous Bailey), the complete Mulberry Harbour assemblies and invasion craft of every kind. As new types of Tanks and service vehicles were created large numbers of models were made for familiarising service men and women under Combined Operations Command.

The only interruption permitted in this long work programme was for making a model of the new Coventry after that city had been devastated.

1946
'ABILITY'  Scale 1:100  Everard & Sons
'PHILANTE'  Scale 1:48  Camper & Nicholson
Tank Landing Craft Mark VIII  Scale 1:64  Motherwell Bridge and Engineering Co.

1947
H.M.S. 'VINDEX'  Scale 1:96  Swan, Hunter & Wigham Richardson
H.M.S. 'ANSON'  Scale 1:96  Swan, Hunter & Wigham
H.M.S. 'VANGUARD'  Scale 1:48  John Brown
'QUEEN ELIZABETH' turbine installation  Scale 1:48  John Brown
'HELECINA'  Scale 1:96  Swan Hunter & Wigham Richardson
'ST. ESSYLT'  Scale 1:96  South American Saint Line
Five classes of Cruisers  Scale 1:96  Admiralty

1948
'NORGE'  Scale 1:48  Camper & Nicholson for presentation to King of Norway
'MEDIA'  Scale 1:64  John Brown
'HAPARANGI'  Scale 1:96  John Brown
'HUNTINGDON'  Scale 1:96  John Brown
'CUMBERLAND'  Scale 1:96  John Brown
'HURUNUI'  Scale 1:96  John Brown
'HERTFORD'  Scale 1:96  John Brown
'ARNHEM'  Scale 4 mm to the foot  John Brown

1949
'EDWARD WILLSHAW'  Scale 1:120  Swan Hunter & Wigham Richardson
'ANGOLA'  Scale 1:96  Hawthorn Leslie
Battleship stern section  Scale 1:16  Admiralty
H.M.S. 'CORNWALL' (1815)  Scale 1:48  Admiralty for the Bombay Museum
'Campeche' suction dredger  Scale 1:48  Lobnitz
'CHAMPAVATI'  Scale 1:48  French Lines
'KARANJA' Cabin models (6)  Scale 1:6  British India
H.M.S. 'KING GEORGE V'  Scale 1:96  Admiralty
'MAID OF ORLEANS'  Scale 1:48  Wm. Denny
'RANGITOTO'  Scale 1:64  New Zealand Shipping Co.
'RANGITANI'  Scale 1:64  John Brown
'RANGITOTO'  Scale 1:96  Vickers Armstrong
'QUEEN ELIZABETH'  Scale 1:64  John Brown
'FALAISE'  Scale 1:48  Wm. Denny
'CHAMPAVATI'  Scale 1:48  Harland & Wolff

1950
'BLOEMFONTEIN CASTLE'  Scale 1:192  Union Castle
Suction Dredger  Scale 1:48  Lobnitz
'GENERAL SAN MARTIN'  Scale 1:48  Cammell Laird
'NORDBO'  Scale 1:128  Lithgow
'QUEEN ELIZABETH'  Scale 1:48  Cunard Line
'VIKLAND'  Scale 1:96  John Brown
'ST. PATRICK'  Scale 1:96  British Rlys. (S.R.)
Landing Craft LST 3  Scale 1:96  Van Leer Equipment
'ROYAL IRIS'  Scale 1:48  Wm. Denny
'COLOMBIE'  Scale 1:100  French Lines
'J. D. WHITE' Tug  Scale 1:48  Charles Hill & Son
Tanker No. 651  Scale 1:96  John Brown

1951

'PATHFINDER'  Scale 1:384  Wm. Harvie
Bucket Dredger  Scale 1:48  Lobnitz
'VERA CRUZ'  Scale 1:75  John Cockerill
350 ton Barge  Scale 1:48  Mechans Ltd.
'SUSSEX'  Scale 1:192  New Zealand Shipping
'VELUTINA'  Scale 1:64  Swan Hunter
Battle Class Cruiser  Scale 1:48  Admiralty
'PROVENCE'  Scale 1:96  Swan Hunter
Cable Ships (22 types)  Scale 1:384  Swan Hunter

1952

Burmah Oil Carrier Scale 1:48  Cammell Laird
'GOTHIC' No. 1224  Scale 1:96  Shaw Savill
'CAPETOWN CASTLE'  Scale 1:48  Union Castle Line
Grab Hopper Dredger  Scale 1:48  Lobnitz
'RUAHINE'  Scale 1:96  New Zealand Shipping Co.
'JEAN MANTELET'  Scale 1:48  Lobnitz
'VELLETIA'  Scale 1:96  Swan Hunter
'HELIX'  Scale 1:96  Swan Hunter
'ST. ESSYLT'  Scale 1:96  John Brown
'LORD WARDEN'  Scale 1:48  Wm. Denny

1953

'MARKLAND'  Scale 1:96  Wm. Denny
'ISOLDA'  Scale 1:48  Liffey Dockyard
Engine Room and Generating Compartment of Tug-boat  Scale 1:96  J. Samuel White
'ANDES'  Scale 1:96  Royal Mail
H.M.S. 'DARING'  Scale 1:96  Swan Hunter
'LEDA' (4-models)  Scale 1:96  Swan Hunter
'ELIZABETH HOLT'  Scale 1:64  Cammell Laird
'SOUTHERN CROSS'  Scale 1:300  Shaw Savill

1954

'BENREOCH'  Scale 1:300  Ben Line Ltd.
'ARCADIA'  Scale 1:144  John Brown
'EMPIRE VICEROY'  Scale 1:144  Pandelis Shipping Co.
'SAXONIA'  Scale 1:144  John Brown
'ORSOVA'  Scale 1:96  Orient Line
'OTAKI'  Scale 1:96  New Zealand Shipping Co.
'ARCADIA'  Scale 1:144  John Brown
'SAXONIA'  Scale 1:144  John Brown
Fishing Craft (5 types)  Scale 1:48  Department of Fisheries, Ottowa

1955

'SUNBRAYTON'  Scale 1:96  Saguenay Terminals
H.M.S. 'ALBION'  Scale 1:96  Swan Hunter
'CHUSAN'  Scale 1:144  P. & O. Co.
'JADOTVILLE'  Scale 1:50  Compagnie Maritime Belge

1956

'GENTIANA'  Scale 1:24  J. Thorneycroft
'HUBERT'  Scale 1:96  Blue Star
'ARGENTINA STAR'  Scale 1:96  Blue Star
'BRITISH VICTORY'  Scale 1:64  British Tanker Co.
'PRINCESS VICTORIA' Engine Room  Scale 1:48  National Gas & Oil Engine Co.
'WELLINGTON STAR'  Scale 1:96  Blue Star

1957

'BADOUINVILLE'  Scale 1:100  Cockerill Ougre
'ZENATIA'  Scale 1:64  Presented to Science Museum  Shell Tankers
'ATLAS' Floating Crane  Scale 1:48  Lobnitz
'CALISTO'  Scale 1:96  Vospers
'GWEN EAGLE' Motor cruiser radio controlled  Scale 1:20  Tec Ltd.
'CARNARVON CASTLE'  Scale 1:48  Union Castle Line
Motor Torpedo Boat  Scale 1:96  Vospers
'SCOTTISH PTARMIGAM'  Scale 1:96  John Brown
'BENMHOR'  Scale 1:96  Ben Line Steamers

1958

M.Y. 'GAVIOTA IV'  Scale 1:96  A. L. Willshaw
'NORTHUMBERLAND'  Scale 1:96  New Zealand Shipping Co.
'MERSEY 40' Dredger  Scale 1:48  Lobnitz
     do.    do.  Scale 1:48  Mersey Docks & Harbour Board
'LEIGHTON'  Scale 1:100  Leighton Shipping
Grab Hopper Dredger  Scale 1:48  Lobnitz
'FILLIEGH'  Scale 1:192  Bartram & Co.
'SOLFONN'  Scale 1:192  Sigval Bergesson
'TRESFONN'  Scale 1:96  Sigval Bergesson
'ALDERNEY'  Scale 1:100  Leighton Shipping

H.M.S. 'ARK ROYAL'  Scale 1:96  Cammell Laird
'SAN GERARDO'  Scale 1:64  Cammell Laird
U.S.S. 'CONSTITUTION'  Scale 1:48  Smithsonian Institution
'HELCION'  Scale 1:96  Singapore Harbour Board
Brave Class T.B.D.  Scale 1:48  Vospers
82' M.T.B.  Scale 1:48  Vospers

1959

'BRISTOL QUEEN'  Scale 1:192  A. Saunders
'MENELAUS'  Scale 1:96  Singapore Harbour Board
'LUCELLUM'  Scale 1:96  Cammell Laird
'WINDSOR CASTLE'  Scale 1:96  Cammell Laird
'MENELAUS'  Scale 1:96  Alfred Holt
42' dredger  Scale 1:48  Lobnitz
'BRITISH QUEEN'  Scale 1:192  John Brown

1960

'WINDSOR CASTLE'  Scale 1:385  British and Commonwealth Shipping
U.S.S. 'ALABAMA'  Scale 1:48  Smithsonian Institution
'TRESFONN'  Scale 1:96  Sigval Bergesson
'HELENUS'  Scale 1:96  Alfred Holt
Suction dredger  Scale 1:48  Lobnitz
'COYAHOGA' and Ore Handling Plant  Scale 1:48  National Museum of Norway
Pageant of shipping  Scale 1:64  Swan Hunter
'STORFONN'  Scale 1:96  Sigval Bergesson

1961

Corvette No. 66  Scale 1:48  Vospers
'NERIFS' Dragon Class Yacht  Scale 1:48  Emberius Ltd. for presentation to King of Hellenes
'TRANSVAAL CASTLE'  Scale 1:48  British & Commonwealth Shipping
'RETRIEVER'  Scale 1:96  Cammell Laird
'DE BROUWER' (ex H.M.S. Spanker)  Scale 1:96  Baron de Brouwer
103' Fast patrol boat  Scale 1:50  Vospers
92' Fast patrol boat  Scale 1:48  Vospers
Devenish Trophy (Half section Yacht on plaque)  Royal Dorset Yacht Club
'TRANSVAAL CASTLE'  Scale 1:192  John Brown

1962

U.S.S. 'HARFORD'  Scale 1:48  Smithsonian Institution
'KILLINEY' (Guinness Barge)  Scale 1:48  Guinness Ltd.
'CASTLEKNOCH' (Guinness Barge)  Scale 1:48  Guinness Ltd.
'BLACK KNIGHT'  Scale 1:48  Bowker & King
Motor Tanker No. 370  Scale 1:48  Bowker & King
'MERCURY'  Scale 1:96  Cammell Laird
Birkenhead ferry  Scale 1:48  Cammell Laird

1963

'CARMANIA'  Scale 1:144  Cunard Line
'CAPE HOWE'  Scale 1:96  Kuwait Port Authority
'TRANSVAAL CASTLE'  Scale 1:100  Kuwait Port Authority
103' Fast patrol boat  Scale 1:50  Vospers
177' Corvette Mk. 1a  Scale 1:50  Vospers
177' Corvette Mk. 2a  Scale 1:50  Vospers
Royal barge  Scale 1:32  Vospers
'TRAMONTANA II'  Scale 1:24  Vospers
'ROSS RENOWN'  Scale 1:96  Kuwait Port Authority
'CLAN MacGILLIVRAY'  Scale 1:96  Kuwait Port Authority

1964

'CLAN MacGOWAN'  Scale 1:192  British & Commonwealth Shipping. Presented to Mr. Marples
Libyan motor torpedo boat  Scale 1:64  Vospers
Peruvian minelayer  Scale 1:50  Vospers
Peruvian gun-boat  Scale 1:50  Vospers
Peruvian fast patrol boat  Scale 1:50  Vospers
Peruvian torpedo boat  Scale 1:50  Vospers
96' Danish fast torpedo boat  Scale 1:48  Vospers
Minesweeper  Scale 1:12  Admiralty

1965

'NIADA'  Scale 1:300  Northern Machine Works
K. N. M. 'STORD'  Scale 1:192  Royal Norwegian Embassy
'THUNDERFLASH' racing motor boat  Scale 1:16  T.O.M. Sopwith
9 Waterline models Cable ships  Scale 1:38.4  Swan Hunter
'PENDENNIS CASTLE' Deck scene  Scale 1:24  Union Castle
'Great Western'  Scale 1:64  Bristol Museum
Motor Rescue Ship (2 models) One each Silver and Gold plated  Scale 1:25  Vospers

'AUSTRALIA STAR'   Scale 1:96   Blue Star
    1966
'CARONIA'   Scale 1:96   John Brown
120' Support & rescue ship   Scale 1:48   Brooke Marine
'MARALA' motor yacht   Scale 1:48   Camper & Nicholson
'ORIANA'   Scale 1:300   Private client
    1967
Container Berth   Scale 1:48   Lloyd's Register
    1968
'MARGUERITE' pilot cutter   Scale 1:24   Bristol Museum
'NORRIS CASTLE' ferry   Scale 1:144   Vospers
'SAAM' 316' frigate   Scale 1:250   Vospers Gold plated for presentation to H.I.H. Princess Shahnaz Palari
    1969
'FAVELL' 3-masted Barque   Scale 1:64   Bristol Museum
'GREAT EASTERN' Scale 1:64   Pacific Bridge Co. U.S.A.
'GREAT BRITAIN' Machinery   Pacific Bridge Co. U.S.A.
    1970
'NORTHERN RANGER'   Scale 1:64   Canadian National Museum
    1971
'GREAT WESTERN'   Scale 1:64   Private Client
'SALISBURY'   Scale 1:64   Admiralty
    1972
'CARIBOU'   Scale 1:64   Canadian National Museum
    1973
'SCOTIA'   Scale 1:64   Canadian National Museum
'BRITANNIA'   Scale 1:64   Canadian National Museum
'RAVENSWOOD'   Scale 1:64   Bristol Museum
'BLAKE'   Scale 1:64   Admiralty
Type 42   Scale 1:48   Admiralty
Officer's Boat   Scale 1:48   Admiralty
Whaler   Scale 1:48   Admiralty
'CHALLENGER'   Scale 1:64   Nova Scotia Museum
'COURAGEOUS'   Scale 1:48   Harrods
    1974
'MARCO POLO'   Scale 1:64   Canadian National Museum
    1975
'CHALLENGER'   Scale 1:64   Canadian National Museum
'HERMES'   Scale 1:128   Admiralty
'UNOWAT'   Scale 1:48   Private Client
    1976
'WELLS CITY'   Scale 1:64   Bristol Museum
'PATRIARCH'   Scale 1:96   Financial Times
    1977
'ST. DAY'   Scale 1:64   Admiralty
'CUTTY SARK' (2 models)   Scale 1:64   Private Client
'TITANIC'   Scale 1:48   Private Client
    1978
'GLENCOE'   Scale 1:64   Canadian National Museum
'PRINCE HENRY' early English Ship   Scale 1:64   Canadian National Museum
    1979
'WINDSOR CASTLE'   Scale 1:38.5   Private Client
'RELIANT'   Scale 1:38.5   National Maritime Museum
'GREAT BRITAIN'   Scale 1:38.5   National Maritime Museum
    1980
'PERSIA'   Scale 1:64   Canadian National Museum
H.M.S. 'VANGUARD'   Scale 1:128   John Brown
'VIKING SEA'   Scale 1:144   Private Client
'RONSARD'   Scale 1:48   Private Client
'RONSARD'   Scale 1:200   Private Client
Standard Ship S.D. 14   Scale 1:200   Private Client
'BEN OCEAN LANCER'   Scale 1:100   Science Museum

# APPENDIX IV

# Miniature Railways of Great Britain Ltd.

*Established November 1904*

Managing Director –  W. J. Bassett-Lowke
Secretary       – Charles Battles
Engineer        – Henry Greenly

To build, install and operate miniature passenger carrying railways.

First project – purchase of 0–4–4 tank engine 10¼″ gauge with rolling stock and track from Fred Smithies of Brickett Wood. Laid on land adjoining Abington Park and commenced running Easter Saturday April 20, 1905

Second project – 15″ Gauge Railway on South Shore, Blackpool with a new design locomotive 'Little Giant' 4–4–2 tender type and passenger rolling stock opened on June 10, 1905 (Whit Monday).

Subsequent enterprises were located at Southport, Halifax, Sutton Coldfield, Imperial International Exhibition White City, Franco British Exhibition Earls Court, Exposition Internationale de L'est Nancy, France, Roubaix, France, Brussels, Cologne, Breslau and Rhyl, North Wales.

Company went into liquidation in 1911.

# Narrow Gauge Railways Ltd.

*Established 1911*

Managing Director  –  W. J. Bassett-Lowke
Director             – R. Proctor Mitchell
Secretary           – John Wills

Took over the Rhyl Miniature Railway in 1911 but sold it the following year to Rhyl Amusements Ltd.

Projects –

1912 Exhibition lines including 15″ gauge systems at Park des Eaux Vives, Geneva.

1914 '100 years Peace' Exhibition Oslo.

1915 Reconstruction of Ravenglass & Eskdale Railway to 15″ gauge.

1916 Reconstruction of Tramway to form Fairbourne Miniature Railway sold to Sir Aubrey Brocklebank 1924.

# 15″ Gauge 'Little Giant' Locomotives

Class 10   4–4–2 type
Length (with tender) 14 ft 1½ inches Width 2 ft 1 inch.
Weight (with tender) 1 ton 12 cwt.
Wheels. Bogie 9¼ inches. Driving 1 ft 6 inches
Trailing 11¼ inches. Cylinders (2). 3⅜ bore by 6 inch stroke.
Boiler. Steel 1 ft 3 inches diameter by 5 ft 5 inches long.
37 Tubes. Working Pressure 120 lbs per sq. inch.

No. 10 'Little Giant'. Built for Blackpool 1905. Transferred to Halifax 1910. Rebuilt 1923. In private ownership Dunn of Bishops Auckland 1948. Noble of South Shields 1957. Kerr of Arbroath 1960. Tate, Haswell, Co. Durham 1964. (Renamed 'Little Elephant' No. 14 when at Halifax.)

No. 11 'Mighty Atom'. Built 1908 for Sutton Coldfield. Used at Nancy Exhibition 1909. Sutton Coldfield 1910. In store at Oldbury since 1957. (Renamed 'Ville de Nancy' No. 13 for use at Nancy.)

No. 12 'Entente Cordiale'. Built 1909 for Nancy Exhibition. Used at Roubaix 1909. Brussells 1911.
No later information.

No. 15 'Red Dragon'. Built 1909 for White City. Transferred to Rhyl 1911 and renamed 'Prince Edward of Wales'. Used at Margate from 1920. In private ownership Milner & Butterell 1968.

No. 16 'Green Dragon'. Intended for White City 1909, but not used there. Roubaix 1909.
Brussels 1911. Exhibited at 'Model Engineer' Exhibition 1909 and awarded Gold Medal. No later information.

No. 17 'King Leopold'. Built 1910 for Brussels Exhibition. To run with it were 'Entente Cordiale' No. 12 and 'Green Dragon'. No. 16 renamed 'King Albert' and 'King Edward'. No later information.

No. 18 'George the fifth'. Built for Southport 1911. Transferred to Rhyl 1913. Used at Skegness by Bond in 1922 and at Southend 1930, Belle Vue 1938. In private ownership Milner and Butterell 1964.

No. 19 Hungaria. Built for Budapest 1912. (Photograph sent by Dr. Varga of Budapest in 1977 showed model with modified cab, etc. but still working.)

No. 15 'Prince Edward of Wales' and No. 18 'George the Fifth' were rebuilt as one locomotive. The locomotive chassis, with a new boiler was 'George the Fifth' and the tender was from 'Prince Edward of Wales'. The rebuild was carried out in the main by Roger Marsh and ran for a short time at Longleat. Then owned by Butterell and McAlpine. 'George the Fifth' is now owned solely by the Hon. W. McAlpine and runs at Steam Town, Carnforth.

It is possible other models were built but there is no existing record of any other locomotives or customers than those listed here. Nevertheless the practice of re-naming makes the picture very confusing and any other suggestions could only be supposition.

# 15″ Gauge 'Little Giant' Locomotives

*(Improved class)*

Class 20   4–4–2 type
Length (with tender) 14 ft. 9 inches
Width 2 ft 1 inch.
Weight (with tender) 1 ton 15 cwt.
Wheels. Bogie 9½″. Driving 1 ft 6 inches.
Trailing 11¼″.
Cylinders (2) 3⁹⁄₁₆″ bore by 6 inches stroke
Boiler 1 ft 6 inches by 5 ft 5 inches long
37 tubes. Working pressure. 125 lbs per sq. inch.

This was a heavier model than the No. 10 class and had forced lubrication for the cylinders and a grid superheater.

No. 20 unnamed. Built in 1912 for King Rama VI of Siam.

No. 21 'Prince Edward of Wales'. Built 1912 for Southport. Damaged in fire 1931. Rebuilt and offered for sale 1969. Now at Whorlton lido.

No. 22 'Prince Edward of Wales'. Built for Fairbourne Railway 1915. Used at Southport and damaged by fire 1931. Rebuilt and offered for sale 1969. Now at Carnforth (Steamtown).

# 15″ Gauge 'Little Giant' Locomotives

*('Sans Pareil' Class)*

Class 30   4–4–2 type
Length (with tender) 16 ft. 9 inches.
Width 2 ft 5 inches.
Weight (with tender) 2 tons 5 cwt.
Wheels Bogie 9½ inches. Driving 1 ft 8 inches.
Trailing 11¼ inches. Cylinders 4⅛ × 6¾.
Boiler 1 ft 7 inches by 6 ft 6 inches long
41 tubes. Working pressure 130 lbs per sq. inch.

No. 30 'Synolda'. Built 1912 for Sir Robert Walker's Sand Hutton Railway. In use at Southend 1930. In private ownership Dunn of Bishop Auckland 1938. Then used at Belle Vue, Manchester under name 'Prince Charles.' Now renamed 'Synolda' on R. & E.R.

No. 31 'Sans Pareil'. Built for Geneva 1913. Transferred to Oslo – under name 'Prince Olaf' 1914. Used on Ravenglass & Eskdale Railway until scrapped in 1926.

No. 32 'Count Louis'. Completed in 1923, from parts made in 1914 for Count Zborowski at Highams, Canterbury. Sold to Fairbourne Railway following the Count's fatal accident and is still in service.

# 15″ Gauge 'Colossus' Locomotive

Class 60   4–6–2 type
Length (with tender) 18 ft 2 inches.
Width 2 ft 5 inches.
Weight (with tender) 3 tons.
Wheels. Bogie 9½″ dia. Driving 1 ft 8 inches.
Trailing 10¼ inches
Cylinders (2) 4⅜″ bore by 6¾″ stroke.
Boiler 1 ft 7 inches by 8 feet. 41 tubes
Working Pressure. 150 lbs per sq. inch.

Only one was built, in 1913 for Captain Howey for his Staughton Manor Railway. It was named 'John Anthony' No. 60. In 1916 it was bought by Narrow Gauge Railways Ltd. for service on the re-gauged Ravenglass & Eskdale Railway when it was re-named 'Colossus'.

Dismantled and cannibalised in 1927 for the rebuilding of another R. & E.R. locomotive 'Riber Mite'. Bought by Barlow of Southport and offered for sale in 1969.

# Abington Park 1905

*The first venture*

Whynne was obsessed with the idea of operating public passenger carrying miniature railways, having seen several privately owned systems including that of Mr. Bartholomew at Blakesley Hall, Towcester.

An opportunity arose to test the possibilities when he was approached by Mr. Fred Smithies, a partner in a small firm at Brickett Wood near St. Albans, who had built a 10¼″ gauge locomotive and was wanting to sell it.

Whynne had founded Miniature Railways of Great Britain, Ltd., in 1904 and this company bought the locomotive 'Nipper', an 0–4–4 tank.

The Northampton Council refused an application to lay a railway in Abington Park, but arrangements were made to put it on adjoining land.

The straight track was elevated on a strong timber 'viaduct' which raised it on average about two feet above ground.

The railway opened on Easter Saturday April 20, 1905, the fare being twopence. Business was good and it influenced Whynne to proceed with the Blackpool scheme.

The locomotive could comfortably haul a train of 15 passengers.

# Blackpool – 1905

Negotiations with Blackpool Corporation in 1904 resulted in the granting of a franchise for the running of a Miniature Railway on the South Shore.

Henry Greenly designed the Locomotive, a 15″ gauge Atlantic tender type, which was the first successful engine made in true-to-scale proportions. It was given trials on the Duke of Westminster's Eaton Railway, which had a long track connecting the Manor with Balderton Station. Present were Whynne, Henry Lea M.I.C.E., A. G. Robins, M.I.Mech.E., James McKenzie, Henry Greenly, Fred Smithies and Harry Wilde (the driver). It gave a convincing performance, hauling 2½ tons for one mile at 22.5 m.p.h. and attaining a maximum speed of 26.4 m.p.h.

The Blackpool track was an irregular circular layout of 433 yards of flat bolted steel permanent way having a point leading to a siding on which there was an engine house and water tower. The station had a raised platform and booking office, decorated with enamelled metal advertisements and equipped with a slot machine for chocolate bars.

The train consisted of the locomotive – named 'Little Giant' No. 10 – hauling 4 twelve-seater bogie coaches. In the first week a total of 9,000 passengers were carried – fares 3d adults, 2d children.

An early and urgent need was for the open carriages to be fitted with roofs to protect passengers from cinders and soot.

Mechanical troubles were soon experienced as the fine sands of the South Shore penetrated the bearings of all parts.

On the busiest day the train made 120 circuits of the track – a distance of 30 miles. However, problems of maintenance became such that after five years the system was transferred to Halifax Zoo. 'Little Giant' had demonstrated its capacity for reliable service – given reasonable working conditions.

# Sutton Park, Birmingham 1907

Close to the main gate of Sutton Park an amusement centre was created by a local firm to provide entertainment for the large number of visitors from all over the Black Country. It was called Crystal Palace – in reference to a large glasshouse which was the central feature.

In the summer of 1907 the system used at Abington Park was

laid – the 10¼″ gauge tank locomotive being renamed 'Rover'. The event proved so successful that in 1908 it was replaced with a 15″ gauge track. The straight track was longer and at one end it formed a loop, giving the train a continuous run out and back to the terminus, where a turntable and short second track leading to a point enabled the locomotive to run round the train.

The locomotive of the 'Little Giant' class was named 'Mighty Atom' and numbered 11. The train of 4 twelve seater coaches was as in the case of Blackpool, provided with roofs.

In order to supply an urgently needed second locomotive at the Nancy Exhibition in 1909, 'Mighty Atom' was taken and an American loco. made by the Cagney Bros. was supplied on loan by Mr. Bartholomew of Blakesly Hall until another 'Little Giant' could be completed.

The third 'Little Giant' locomotive was 'Entente Cordiale' No. 12 which ran at the Nancy Exhibition in 1909, and would have returned to this country in November, although it was in service at an Exhibition in Brussels in April 1910. The track at Sutton Park was relaid with a heavier rail in 1910.

# White City, London 1909

The White City had been built for the 1908 Olympic Games. It was the venue in 1909 for an Industrial Exhibition following the successful Franco–British Exhibition which had been held alongside the Games.

An Amusements Company, Sideshow Railways Ltd. contracted Bassett-Lowke to supply and install a 15″ gauge system. The track was a peculiar shape which, starting from a terminus station, immediately took a left turn to continue in a long curving run to a 180′ tunnel in which it took a quarter circle, followed by a short straight to another quarter circle. From there it had a long 1,000 ft straight to a stop end from which it reversed and negotiated a large quarter circle to enter the station in readiness for the next run.

In anticipation of running two trains the points were signalled, but in the event, there was not sufficient traffic to justify this.

The locomotive used was a Little Giant 'Red Dragon' numbered 15, and the train comprised four 12 seater bogie vehicles with canopy roofs.

The second locomotive 'Green Dragon' numbered 16 was not used at White City but was shown on the Bassett-Lowke stand at the Model Engineer Exhibition where it was awarded a Gold Medal. There is an interesting photograph of the 'Red Dragon' standing on a horse drawn dray, having stopped outside the recently opened London Shop at 257, High Holborn, on its way to the White City.

# Nancy 1909

For the display at this Exhibition Bassett-Lowke were awarded a Diploma de l'Honeur and a Gold Medal.

For the Exposition Internationale de L'est de France Bassett-Lowke installed a 15″ gauge railway with a circular track of about one mile. There were two main stations, one at each of the exhibition gates and several small ones – the intention being to serve the exhibition by conveying visitors to various parts.

Two locomotives were put in service. The first was Little Giant class 'Entente Cordiale' No. 12, an improved version with bogie tender having greater water and fuel capacity. It was built in 36 days – and it was for this the Gold Medal was awarded. Fred Green, works foreman in charge of this remarkable effort, was awarded a silver medal.

The railway was so successful that the second engine was required urgently. As a temporary measure 'Mighty Atom' was taken from Sutton Park, overhauled, repainted and given the name 'Ville de Nancy' and renumbered 13. Both locomotives were used to 'double-head' passenger trains.

This was the first venture overseas with 15″ gauge and the appearance of 'Entente Cordiale' created considerable interest. A photograph of it taken alongside a Paris–Lyons express locomotive and a 3½″ gauge G.N.R. Atlantic loco. gave an impressive comparison of size. It was reproduced in the Journal d'Exposition (Nancy) and appears in December issue of *Model Railways and Locomotives* 1909.

The Lord Mayor of London, Sir George Truscott, together with

the Director of the Exhibition, M. Leon Laffette, took turns to run the first trains at the opening ceremony.

The remains of a 'Little Giant' locomotive were found after the 1914–1918 war and it is believed that it was used by the Germans.

# Roubaix, Cologne, Breslau and Budapest 1909–1912

There is very little record of these exhibition systems and it is most likely that 'Little Giant' locomotives and, in some cases, passenger cars, were bought and installed by local operators.

*Roubaix.* International Exhibition du Nord, 1911. It is not known which Little Giant locomotive was used, nor to what extent Bassett-Lowke were involved in the installation and running. The project was successful to the extent that Bassett-Lowke were awarded a Diploma de l'Honeur.

*Cologne.* 'Lilliputbahn'. Even the site of this layout is unknown, but it appears a 'Little Giant' class locomotive – possibly one originally supplied for the Brussels Exhibition – was used and all other equipment was made locally.

*Breslau.* 1909. Again no written record, but a photograph shows a 'Little Giant' locomotive hauling passenger vehicles very different from the usual Bassett-Lowke pattern. Most probably – as in Cologne – all other work was done by local contractors.

*Budapest.* Angol Park. 1912. Another instance of there being little record but a 'Little Giant' class, named 'Hungaria' and numbered 19 was supplied to the order of M. Meinhardt of Budapest. In 1974 a colour photo was sent by Professor Vargas showing the locomotive hideously re-styled as to the cab and chimney but otherwise as original and in regular working order. Latest reports indicate that the railway is still operating at the time of writing.

# Halifax Zoo, Cherin Edge 1910

Following the close-down of the Blackpool system, much of the equipment was transferred to Halifax for the construction of a new miniature railway in the Zoo grounds.

The track was an oval formation and it included a siding to an engine shed. The site was very sloping and required considerable civil engineering. On one side was a deep cutting and tunnel, opposite was a wooden viaduct some 14 ft high, while the other two sides were embankments. The length of track totalled about a mile. A double platform station was sited on the viaduct and was approached by stairs from a ground level booking office.

The locomotive was the original 'Little Giant' used at Blackpool, but completely overhauled, repainted in green and named 'Little Elephant', together with bogie tender.

The coaches were a new pattern 10 seater bogie type with canopies – a feature was the reversible seats.

In 1912 this railway, together with the Sutton Coldfield layout and two other locomotives, 8 passenger cars and 1,300 yards of track were offered for sale when Miniature Railways of Great Britain went into voluntary liquidation.

# Brussels Exhibition 1910

For this a quite interesting 15″ gauge system was created. A lengthy double road track connected two terminus stations. Locomotives detached from their trains could run through points to a stop end where they would then reverse along the second track and back over points to couple on to the train, this time to run tender first.

Points and signals were operated automatically by an ingenious arrangement of treadles operated by the trains. This enabled up to three trains to be in service at busy times. 'Single' and 'Return' tickets were issued, but there is no record that the suggestion of issuing 'season' tickets was put into effect.

The two main line tracks ran through separate 40 yard long tunnels, these having magnificent portals.

Three 'Little Giant' class locomotives were provided, named 'King Edward', 'King Albert' and 'King Leopold'. One was new and numbered 17. The other two were No. 12 'Entente Cordiale' and No. 16. 'Green Dragon', renovated and re-numbered after their previous service.

The railway was designed and supervised by Mr. L. Hervé of Brussels on behalf of Bassett-Lowke.

Passenger vehicles were the standard 12 seater coaches with canopy roofs – usually three to a train.

There was a serious fire at the Exhibition in August, but no mention was made of damage to the 15″ gauge railway. However, a 2″ gauge demonstration railway, supplied by Bassett-Lowke to the Great Northern Railway Co. who made it their principal exhibit, was completely destroyed.

## Llewellyn Miniature Railway, Southport 1911

This was built and equipped by M.R.G.B. – under contract to Mr. G. V. Llewellyn, with Henry Greenly as the engineer in charge.

The track was a straight run of about a half mile length with a tunnel at the mid-position. There were no loops or turntables, the trains being run back and forth from Lakeside Station, along the South Shore of Marine Lake to Pierhead Station.

Each rustic style station had a starting signal – hardly a necessity with one train on a single track.

The locomotive was a Little Giant class named 'George the Fifth' and numbered 18.

There were two types of passenger vehicles – some were open bogie coaches with reversible seats and others were twelve seater bogie coaches with seats facing in pairs, awnings and glass end screens. They may have been the first to be fitted with electric head and tail lamps.

There was another vehicle of massive proportions, totally enclosed and called the 'Royal Saloon'.

It was decided that a more powerful locomotive was needed and one of the new Class 20 Little Giants was ordered. It was named 'Prince of Wales' and numbered 21. The livery of this model was maroon with yellow and black lining.

'George the Fifth' was sold to the railway at Rhyl, and in 1921 they exchanged the Heywood locomotive 'Katie' for another Class 20 Little Giant named 'Prince Edward of Wales' and numbered 22, which came from Fairbourne.

## Rhyl Miniature Railway 1911

A very complete description of this is given in the June 1911 edition of *Model Railways and Locomotives*.

Created by Miniature Railways of Great Britain, Ltd.

The Marine Park and Lake had been developed on land at the mouth of the River Clwyd by Rhyl Council, which granted a lease for the installation of a miniature railway round the lake.

The site was surveyed by Henry Greenly, who designed the track layout and the various station and lineside buildings, and supervised the installation of the whole system. The first locomotive, 'Little Giant' class named 'Prince Edward of Wales' was built in the Bassett-Lowke works. Later a second, named 'George the Fifth' was added. The rolling stock was also made in the works, but all station buildings were constructed by a local firm, Messrs. E & E. Jones of Morley Road.

The six passenger cars had seating capacity for eight passengers each.

The track was made with Vignole section 12 lbs per yard rail secured in 15 ft lengths on to steel sleepers except, where rail joints occurred, wide wood sleepers were used. The layout was single road, roughly rectangular, with suitable sidings for locomotive and rolling stock. The length of run was just over a mile. When the second locomotive and train was put in service additional sidings were incorporated.

A vacuum brake system was designed and fitted to the trains, the first time this system was used on a miniature railway.

Fred Smithies (who had influenced design of small locomotive boilers a few years earlier) was principal driver.

Work on site commenced at the end of March and the first trains ran on May-day when 1,050 adults and 687 children were carried. On Whit Monday 3,630 passengers travelled in 99 journeys in 12 hours. Average train load – 36. Average speed 8.25 m.p.h.

Record business in the first year was on Bank Holiday August 7 when 5,003 passengers were carried over a period from 9.05 a.m. to 10.15 p.m.

Locomotives were painted Caledonian Railway blue and carriages finished in two colours – chocolate and cream.

## Luna Park, Geneva, 1912

Le Parc des Eaux Vives was originally laid out as a private estate for Louis Favre, the promoter and builder of St. Gotthard Tunnel. In the early years of this century it was developed as a pleasure park. It was planned to have an outstanding miniature railway as a feature for the year 1912, and Narrow Gauge Railways Ltd. secured the contract to design, supply and install this railway.

The site was alongside Lake Geneva and the terrain was such that it gave opportunity for attractive landscaping and the inclusion of railway features. Henry Greenly was engaged to design and supervise the whole system.

In an area 700 ft by 400 ft a pear shaped single road track with an internal oval loop was laid. Where it crossed part of an ornamental lake the track was laid on a viaduct, comprising a five span bridge. Elsewhere it was carried on embankments, through cuttings and a 150 ft long tunnel. A short spur led to a locomotive shed near the lake, and a large ornamental station was located conveniently near the Central Avenue. The whole system was correctly signalled and points and signals were operated from a signal box.

The first locomotive supplied was a standard Little Giant No. 10 class. It was not built specially for this railway and it is not known which of the various existing models it was, although it was possibly the loco used at Brussels in 1911. It was completely overhauled and fitted with cylinders having a slightly larger bore to increase power.

Later a second locomotive was provided. This was the second of the class 30 'Little Giants' and was named 'Sans Pareil'. It was a great improvement, being easier to run and having greater power.

The passenger trains consisted of standard Bassett-Lowke type but were made of teak, varnished and carrying gold plated brass lettering 'Luna Park Express'. They were fitted with gay canopy roofs.

## Norwegian Exhibition, Christiania (Oslo) 1914

There is no record of the miniature railway supplied for this Exhibition and it can only be assumed that the track layout would have been similar to those used elsewhere – probably an oval shape with a siding leading to an engine shed. There would, of necessity, have been a station and booking office.

The locomotive was one of the 'Little Giant' Class 30 previously used in 1913 at the Geneva Exhibition. There is a divergence of opinion as to whether it was named 'Prince Olaf' (which would have been in accordance with normal Bassett-Lowke practice) or 'Viking' as stated in *The Miniature world of Henry Greenly*. In any case it was numbered 31.

Seven passenger coaches, from Geneva, were used.

The railway opened in April, but the Exhibition was affected by the onset of the First World War on August 4. An employee, Wm. Vaughan, who had been sent to direct the railway and act as a co-driver, was stranded in Norway. In early 1915 he was instructed to pack the locomotive and coaches for their return to England for use on the Ravenglass & Eskdale Railway. The locomotive was then re-named 'Sans Pareil'.

## The Ravenglass & Eskdale Railways

In 1871 the Whitehaven Iron Mines, Ltd. was formed and in 1873 an Act of Parliament enabled them to construct a 3′ gauge railway from Ravenglass to Dalegarth, a run of about 7 miles.

The railway had a chequered career for although it carried passengers its main source of income was from the conveyance of minerals from the Nab Gill Mines. The railway closed down in 1913.

Whynne was looking for such a system with a view to converting to 15″ gauge and went with R. Procter Mitchell, Chairman of Narrow Gauge Railways Ltd. to survey the line in June 1915.

By August the 1¼ miles to Muncaster Mill had been converted and trains were running. Another 3 miles to Irton Road were in service by October and on to Eskdale Green the following year. The remaining 2¼ miles to Dalegarth Station at Boot were eventually completed but the gradient at the end was beyond the capacity of the 'Little Giant' locomotive.

The first locomotives put in service were the Bassett-Lowke 'Sans Pareil' class of the 'Little Giant' series of Atlantic type and the Pacific type which had been built for Capt. Howey in 1913 and bought back from him whilst he was P.O.W. in Germany.

The railway was enthusiastically supported by Sir Aubrey Brocklebank, who provided considerable mineral traffic from his Beckfoot Granite Quarry. In 1925 he and a friend Henry Lithgow took over the Railway to secure this investment and the Bassett-Lowke and Narrow Gauge Railways Ltd. interest was discontinued.

# APPENDIX V

50th Anniversary 1949
The main celebration was a spendid dinner at the Savoy Hotel when the following were present.

Guest of Honour – Lord Brabazon of Tara.

W. J. Bassett-Lowke

| | |
|---|---|
| C. Derry | Chairman |
| P. F. Claydon | Director (S.M.) Ltd. |
| R. H. Fuller | Director and General Manager |
| H. F. R. Franklin | Director |
| H. W. Franklin | Director |
| W. H. Rowe | Northampton Staff |
| V. S. King | ,, Bookkeeper |
| George Lewis | Shareholder Bassett-Lowke |
| H. M. Sell | London Manager |
| H. C. Foreman | ,, Staff |
| C. B. Cox | Manchester Manager |
| E. H. Clifton | Twining Models |
| R. Bindon Blood | Managing Director Precision Models |
| F. J. Prior | Precision Models |
| S. Kahn | Trix Ltd. |
| F. Bing | Trix Ltd. |
| H. Oppenheim | Trix Ltd. |
| J. Mackenzie | First Bassett-Lowke Works Manager 1901 |
| G. Dow | President Model Engine Trade Assn. |
| R. J. Raymond | Chairman Model Engine Trade Assn. |
| G. H. Lake | Secretary Model Engine Trade Assn. |
| H. Claude Palmer | A. C. Palmer & Co. |
| W. H. Shaw | ,, ,, |
| H. A. Bassett-Lowke | |
| C. E. Vivian Rowe | Town Clerk Northampton |
| H. Sanderson | Stuart Turner Ltd. |
| F. E. Courtney | Northampton School of Art |
| G. Holland | Author and Critic |
| H. A. Glenn | A. Glenn & Sons Ltd. |
| J. O. Crebbin | |
| V. B. Harrison | |
| B. W. C. Cooke | Editor *Locomotive Magazine* |
| J. R. Cox | Editor *Boy's Own Paper* |
| F. J. Camm | Editor *Practical Mechanics* |
| Representative of *Daily Telegraph* | |
| E. W. Stogdon | Manager 'M.E.' Exhibitions |
| J. D. Kiley | An ex M.P. |
| A. B. Storrer | Society of Model Engineers |
| A. Leach | Editor *English Mechanics* |
| J. R. Archer | Jarrold & Sons |
| A. J. White | Harraps Ltd. |
| W. E. Barley | Dixons West End Advertising |
| E. Courtice | Passport Office |
| W. Lines | Lines Bros. Ltd. |
| A. Robson | Union Castle Line |
| A. H. Redrup | Cunard White Star Line |
| R. A. Raulin | French Line |
| T. Aggett | Blue Star Line |
| D. Caird | Royal Mail Lines |
| R. T. Hingley | Holden Ltd. |
| J. H. Gallie | I.C.I. Ltd. |
| J. E. Timmins | David Harcourt Ltd. |

Guests not shown with a professional connection were H. A. Bassett-Lowke, brother of W. J.; J. O. Crebbin, an official in the Bank of England, who was a very keen model-maker and became a great friend of Whynne in the early years of the Company; V. B. Harrison, of the famous postage stamp printing company, an enthusiastic model railway owner whose experiments with small steam locomotives were most useful to Bassett-Lowke; J. D. Kiley, an M.P. in the period during and after the First World War when his position enabled him to help Bassett-Lowke in various ways as well as being a supporter to the toy trade.

The evening was a totally happy occasion, and, of course, the Savoy does give an added dimension to functions held there. At the reception Whynne received personal felicitations from nearly every guest and there was much joviality. Not that any was created by drinking for W.J. was very averse to any indulgence in this way. When he went to make arrangements for the evening he requested the waiting staff be instructed to keep the cocktails and table wine to the minimum!

There was the usual list of toasts for such an occasion – one to the Guests was proposed by H. M. Sell and one to the 'Gentlemen of the Press' by R. H. Fuller. They followed the main toasts, of course. Opening the proceedings George Holland made a eulogistic oration about the Company and its achievements – a rather over-long essay – this was followed by a toast to the Company by Lord Brabazon coupled with one to Whynne himself by his great admirer, Cyril Derry. Whynne replied in his usual stumbling way for he was no orator – preferring the pen to express his thoughts. However, the guests stood to give him a resounding applause and he must have been proud, in his 72nd year to feel that he was admired and respected by so many. At ten o'clock the guest departed – leaving a very happy band of Bassett-Lowke personnel to their thoughts.

A second celebration was for the London Staff. This was a dinner at the London Casino – a small private affair with Whynne, Cyril and Mrs. Derry, R.H. and Mrs. Fuller, Mr. and Mrs. Sell, H. C. Foreman and the London sales staff.

The Manchester manager could not be persuaded to arrange any kind of celebration in Manchester. The winter of 50th Anniversary celebrations ended with a dinner and entertainment for all Northampton personnel on February 3, 1950. This function was not staged in such elegant surroundings as those in London but the Whyte Melville Hall provided a very suitable setting for the 156 guests.

The meal was a simple one, since outside caterers supplied it but there was entertainment by six separate artists and music for dancing was provided by a trio. The chairman, Cyril Derry, gave the one toast of the evening to which Whynne again stumbled to reply, but the evening was a jolly occasion and a fitting end to the 50th year. It may be interesting to note that the charges were:

Hire of the Hall – £1 per hour, plus 10/- for piano and 10/- for a Microphone.

The meal comprised ham and salad, trifle, cheese and biscuits, cakes and biscuits, coffee – 4/6 per head (22½p)

For the reception – one glass of sherry per head at 1/9 (8½p).

Supplies of beer, cider and a full range of soft drinks to be provided free to guests all the evening 3/6 (17½p) per head.

One of the entertainers was Mr. Vaughan, who was a bench hand in the Bassett-Lowke works from 1900 to 1909. The total cost for the other five entertainers was £20. The function was made the occasion for the staff to give presents to Whynne and H. F. R. Franklin and for the Company to present watches to eighteen members with 25 years or more service. Auld Lang Syne at 11 o'clock was a sentimental moment.

## Distinguished customers of London Shop

Anglesey, Earl of
Ashfield Lord (L.P.T.B.)
Albert Prince
 later King George VI
Astor, Vincent

Baird, J. Logie
 (T.V. Inventor)
Birabongse, Prince
Brabazon, Lord

Campbell, Sir Malcolm
Chakrabongse, Prince Chula
Clemens, John
Cooch-Behar, Maharajah
Coogan, Jackie
Cowdray, Lord
Cuneo, Terence

Disney, Walter
Dmitri, Grand Duke
 (reputed murderer of
 Rasputin)
Douglas (Douglas Aircraft)
Downshire, Lord

Edward, Prince
 (later King Edward VII)

Galsworthy, John
Glenconner, Lord
Glentworth, Lord
Guinness, Alec

Halsey, Admiral
Harewood, Lord
Hearn, Richard (Mr. Pastry)
Hopkins Prince
Howey Capt (R. H. & D. R.)
Hulbert, Jack & Claude

Jodhpur, Maharajah

Kipling, Rudyard

Lascelles, Lord
Latham, Lord
Leverhulme, Lord
Lupino, Stanley

Mayerbangh, Maharajah
Moray, Earl of
Moss, Stirling
Mountbatten, Earl

Nichol, Sir Edward
Northesk, Lord

Patiala, Maharajah
Peter, King of Jugoslavia

Salmond, Air Marshall
Savage, Col.
 (Husband of Ethel M. Dell, Novelist)
Seagrave, Sir Henry
Seaman, 'Dick'
Selanger, Sultan of
Shaw, Sir George Bernard
Sheffield, Sir Berkeley
Shute, Neville
Sikorski, Count

Walden, Lord Howard de
Walker, Sir Robert
Wallace, Edgar
Westminster, Duke of
Zaragoza, Duke of
Zborowski, Count Louis

# APPENDIX VI

## Principal Museums

*In which Bassett-Lowke Models are exhibited*

Science Museum, London
National Maritime Museum, Greenwich
Bristol Museum
Royal Scottish Museum
The Queen's Dolls House, Windsor Castle.
The London Toy & Model Museum
Bombay Museum
Canadian National Museum
Smithsonian Institution, Washington U.S.A.
Museum of the Allied Landings, Arromanche, France.

This list does not include Museums which may be exhibiting Bassett-Lowke models which may have been donated or supplied on loan.

## The Carson Connection

James Carson was first noted as a model engineer being a member of The Model Engineers Co-operative Society founded in August 1904 at 57 Summer Road, Birmingham. The objects of the society included pooling model engineers buying requirements in order to achieve better discounts with suppliers.

In November 1905 Carson & Co. Engineers took over the society and in 1910 James Carson & Co. Ltd. appears to have been Incorporated (the same year as Bassett-Lowke Ltd.).

An extensive catalogue was issued in 1909 and in 1910 the company moved its principal place of business to Oaklands Road, Cricklewood in the north west of London. The tools, patterns and finished models of this company were acquired by Bassett-Lowke some time in 1913, although no reference is made to this transaction in the Directors Minutes of Bassett-Lowke for this period. Either the transaction was too small to merit mention or the acquisition was made by Winteringhams on Bassett-Lowke's behalf. Nonetheless in Bassett-Lowke's 1914 catalogue reference is made to the acquisition of Carsons business in London and Birmingham.

The locomotives listed by Carson and in some instances Bassett-Lowke, between 1905 and 1914 appear to be the following:

| Gauge 1 | LNWR | 'Experiment' |
|---|---|---|
| 2 | LNWR | Precursor Tank |
| | LNWR | 'Precursor' 4–4–0 |
| | NBR | Atlantic |
| | GWR | 'Great Bear' |
| 2½" | NBR | Atlantic |
| | GWR | 'Great Bear' (and 3½", 4¾", 5") |
| | LNWR | 'Experiment' (and 3½") |
| | LNWR | 'Precursor' 4–4–0 (and 3½", 4¾", 5") |
| | LNWR | Precursor Tank |
| | L & Y | 0–8–2 Tank |
| | LNWR | 0–8–0 Goods No. 1868 |
| 3½" | American | Mallet type |

All the above engines were available in steam. James Carson was profoundly disinterested in electric powered steam locos, nonetheless he would supply them to customers 'whose taste did not concur with his'.

Little mention is made of Carson production in the post First World War Bassett-Lowke programme.

# Bibliography

THE MODEL RAILWAY HANDBOOK
Edited by W. J. Bassett-Lowke/C. J. Allen.
Bassett-Lowke Ltd.    1906–1953

MODELS, RAILWAYS AND LOCOMOTIVES
Edited by Henry Greenly.
Percival Marshall    1909–1918

MODEL ELECTRIC LOCOMOTIVES AND RAILWAYS
Henry Greenly.
Cassell & Co. Ltd.    1922

DIE MODELLEISENBAHN (No English Edition)
Gustav Reder.
Union Deutsche Verlagsgesellschaft    1926

LILIPUTBAHNEN
Dr. Walter Strauss.
Buchdruckerei und Verlag Kichler    1938

FIFTY YEARS OF MODEL MAKING
G. Holland.
Bassett-Lowke Ltd.    1949

COLLECTING MODEL TRAINS
Louis H. Hertz.
Mark Haber & Co.    1956

MODEL RAILWAYS 1838–1939
Hamilton Ellis.
George Allen & Unwin Ltd.    1962

BASSETT-LOWKE RAILWAYS
A. L. Levy.
Bassett-Lowke (Railways) Ltd.    1968

MIT UHRWERK DAMPF & STROM
Gustav Reder.
Alba Buchverlag    1969

CLOCKWORK STEAM AND ELECTRIC
(English Edition).
Ian Allan Ltd.    1972

THE MINIATURE WORLD OF HENRY GREENLY
E. A. & E. H. Steel.
M.A.P.    1973

A CENTURY OF MODEL TRAINS
A. L. Levy.
New Cavendish Books    1974

MINIATURE RAILWAYS PAST & PRESENT
H. A. Lambert.
David & Charles    1982

THE TRAINS ON AVENUE DE RUMINE
Count Giansanti Coluzzi. Edited by A. L. Levy.
New Cavendish Books    1982

## PERIODICALS

The Model Engineer
(formerly 'Model Engineer & Amateur Electrician)
Ideal Home
Architectural Review
Model Railway News
Model Railway Constructor

# Index of named locos & ships

# Index

SEASON'S GREETINGS

FROM MR. & MRS. W. J. BASSETT-LOWKE

NEW WAYS NORTHAMPTON

A GOOD CROSSING 1931-2

GREETINGS FROM MR. & MRS. W. J. BASSETT-LOWKE NEW WAYS NORTHAMPTON CHRISTMAS 1947

WITH THE SEASONS GREETINGS FROM W. J. BASSETT-LOWKE NORTHAMPTON

BLACKED OUT

Listen to the ex...

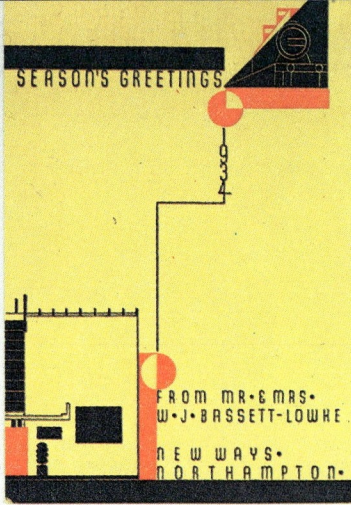

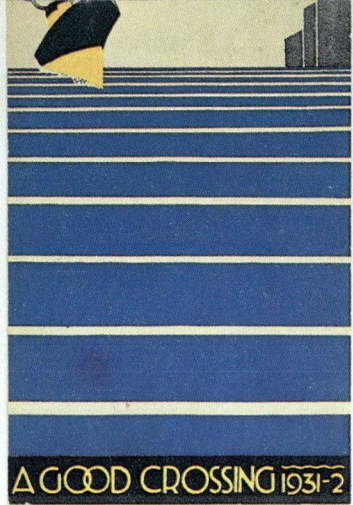

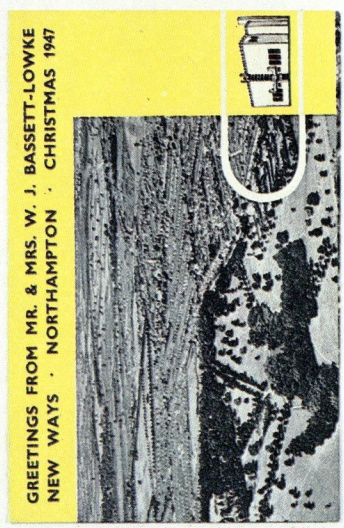

For yesterd...
And to-mor...
But to-...
Makes every yester...
And every to-m...
Look well, t...
Such is the sa...
From...

WITH SEASON...
MR. & MRS. W...
NEW WAYS...

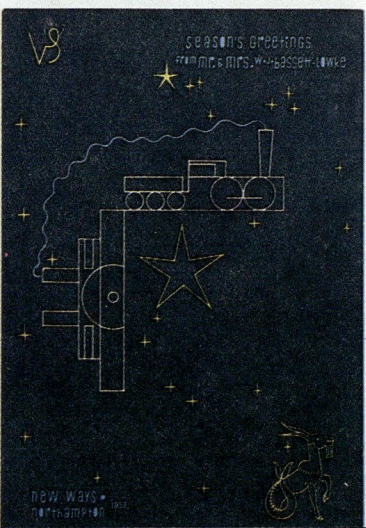

PEACE IN OUR TIME !!!

I AM ALWAYS PREPARED FOR PEACE

FREEDOM MARKS THE BEGINNING OF REAL PEACE FOR EVERYONE

FRANCE WILL RESPOND TO A MAN TO DEFEND THE PEACE

WE MUST DO OUR PART TO MAKE THE WORLD SAFE FOR PEACE AND DEMOCRACY

May they practice what they preach in the New Year

life's contrasts

peace & goodwill be with you and all mankind * christmas and New Year 1938 greetings from W.J.Bassett-Lowke Northampton

season's greetings from mr. & mrs. w. h. bassett-lowke

new ways northampton

THE SEASON'S GREETINGS FROM EVERY ANGLE AND NEW WAYS NORTHAMPTON

1936

1935

PEACE TO OF GOOD WILL

NEW WAYS FROM GREETINGS: